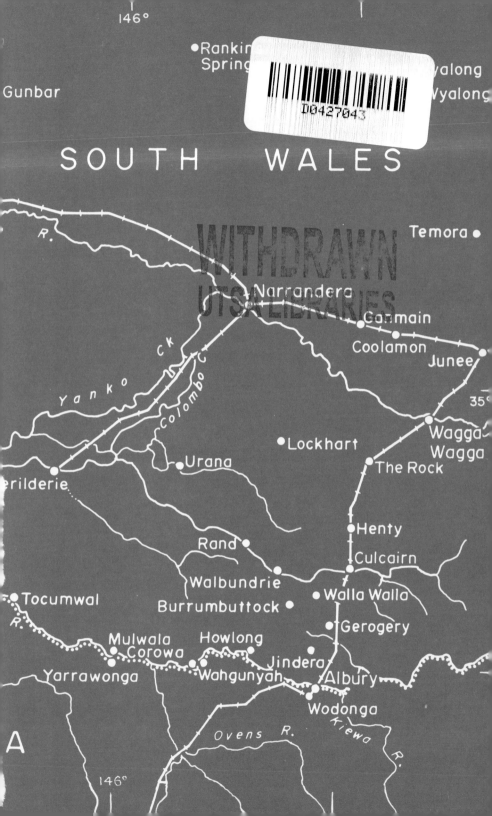

THE RIVERINA
1861–1891

THE RIVERINA
1861-1891

An Australian Regional Study

G. L. BUXTON

Lecturer in History
University of Adelaide

MELBOURNE UNIVERSITY PRESS

LONDON AND NEW YORK: CAMBRIDGE UNIVERSITY PRESS

First published 1967
Printed in Australia by
Melbourne University Press, Carlton, Victoria 3053
Registered in Australia for transmission
by post as a book

Dewey Decimal Classification Number 309.1944
Aus 67-2015

Text set in 10 point Caledonia type

ACKNOWLEDGMENTS

Most of the research for this book was carried out with the assistance of a research scholarship in the Institute of Advanced Studies at the Australian National University. In the preparation of the original doctoral thesis on which this book is based I was indebted to Mr L. F. Fitzhardinge and other members of the Department of History; to Professor O. H. K. Spate, Professor N. G. Butlin and members of the Departments of Economic History and Demography; and to Professor K. S. Inglis of the A.N.U. School of General Studies, for their suggestions, criticisms and encouragement.

I am also indebted to the librarians and staffs of the Mitchell Library, Sydney, the National Library of Australia, Canberra, the Menzies Library, Canberra and the State Library of Victoria; the staffs of the South Australian Archives and the Wagga Wagga Land Office; and the Crown Lands Agents and Clerks of Petty Sessions in the various Riverina towns mentioned, for the use of material in their custody. Acknowledgment is made to Angus and Robertson for permission to reproduce three verses of 'Saltbush Bill' from A. B. Paterson, *Collected Works*.

Thanks are also due to the proprietors and staffs of the Riverina newspapers listed, particularly of the *Pastoral Times*, Deniliquin; to members of the Gibson family of 'Keringal', Hay; to Mr W. Lamb of 'Willurah'; to the Historical Societies in the Riverina and to Mrs D. Smith and Miss M. Stoodley who typed the manuscript.

In the revision of the thesis for publication I have been most grateful to Professor A. W. Martin of La Trobe University, Melbourne, for his comments and suggestions, and at all times to my wife, Chloe.

CONTENTS

ILLUSTRATIONS

PLATES

ix

FIGURES

ABBREVIATIONS

In footnotes in the text, and in endnotes, the following abbreviations are used.

A.B.	*Albury Banner and Wodonga Express*
B.P.	*Border Post* (Albury)
C.F.P.	*Corowa Free Press*
D.C.	*Deniliquin Chronicle*
H.R.A.	*Historical Records of Australia*
H.S.	*Hay Standard*
J.R.A.H.S.	*Journal of the Royal Australian Historical Society*
N.A.	*Narrandera Argus*
N.S.W. G.G.	*New South Wales Government Gazette*
Parl. Deb. (L.A. N.S.W.)	*Parliamentary Debates* of the New South Wales Legislative Assembly
P.T.	*Pastoral Times* (Deniliquin)
R.G.	*Riverine Grazier* (Hay)
S.M.H.	*Sydney Morning Herald*
V.H.M.	*Victorian Historical Magazine*
V. & P. (L.A. N.S.W.)	*Votes and Proceedings* of the New South Wales Legislative Assembly
V. & P. (L.A. Vic.)	*Votes and Proceedings* of the Victorian Legislative Assembly
W.A.	*Wagga Wagga Advertiser*
W.E.	*Wagga Wagga Express and Murrumbidgee District Advertiser*

INTRODUCTION

The Riverina, 1861–1891 began as a research project in which the initial aim was to discover, as far as possible, exactly what happened in the process of implementing the New South Wales land legislation of 1861, embodying free selection before survey. The final study, while carrying out this aim for part of the colony, came inevitably to acquire an extended purpose by developing, in detail, a textured picture of Riverina society and its growth and mutation in the period 1861–91. Much of the work is exploratory rather than definitive. At times I have posed questions rather than supplied answers, and in particular have suggested uses which might be made of relatively untouched source material.

Having completed a smaller-scale analysis of South Australian land Acts I had hoped to study the effects of the New South Wales legislation, possibly making some intercolonial comparisons. It soon became obvious that there were important differences within the two colonies which made this course impractical. First, the areas settled in South Australia during the selection period were, geographically, relatively uniform when compared with the considerable climatic differences between the coastal strip, tablelands, western slopes and arid inland plains of New South Wales. At the same time South Australia's heavily indented coastline and easy gradients made transport arrangements simple. Such extreme environmental differences made nonsense of any attempt to compare the effects of different legislation. Even in South Australia the law makers finally admitted that it had been a mistake to have one land law for the whole colony. Second, South Australian statistics, as might be expected of that land of systematic colonizers, were compiled from the very beginning on the basis of counties and hundreds, invariably surveyed *before* settlement, so that statistical runs over long periods were possible. At no time was selection before survey ever countenanced. But in New South Wales all kinds of statistical divisions were used without any regard for uniformity. As Messrs Morris and Ranken, Royal Com-

missioners on the land laws, noted in 1883, echoing the complaint
of Registrar-General Rolleston twenty-five years before:

> the want of one fixed unit of division for the colony has
> greatly added to the difficulty of presenting many matters in
> an intelligible form. COUNTIES, LAND OFFICE DISTRICTS, SURVEY
> DISTRICTS, PASTORAL DISTRICTS, STOCK INSPECTORS' DISTRICTS,
> POLICE, CENSUS, ELECTORAL AND LICENSING DISTRICTS, have all
> been arranged without any attempt at harmony, and irrespec-
> tive of general practical results . . . The Registrar-General
> makes his statistics correspond with the Electoral Districts;
> the Lands Department uses Surveyors' and Lands Districts;
> other branches of the Public Service refer to Police or Live
> Stock Districts, but none have adopted Counties as the bases
> of their operations, although they alone never change their
> areas or boundaries. . . . The want of one fixed unit of division
> for the Colony has greatly added to the difficulty of present-
> ing many matters in an intelligible form. Counties, land office
> districts, survey districts, pastoral districts, stock inspectors'
> districts, police, census, electoral, and licensing districts,
> have all been arranged without any attempt at harmony, and
> irrespective of general practical results.[1]

And although the Registrar-General had chosen electoral districts
in 1883, before that date he had used pastoral, police and census
districts, even for the collection of agricultural statistics.

Furthermore, these units themselves changed from time to
time, with only the detailed descriptions published in the Government Gazettes to warn the historian. In fact the only boundary
which remained consistent throughout the period was the River
Murray and if the Victorians could have had their way even that
would have changed. Because police-district boundaries, for
example, changed so often, it was the practice in local police
stations simply to keep an outline marked on a rough map and to
alter this as new gazette notices appeared. I was able to locate
only one printed—but undated—map of N.S.W. police districts.
This showed boundaries corresponding to the 1859 gazette
notices. Thereafter it was necessary to trace boundary changes
from feature to feature on large-scale maps. Since the points of
reference were often no more precise than 'the northwest corner
of Mr. Tyson's back run' or 'a marked tree on the bank of the
creek running through the Bungambrawatha reserve', approximations often had to be made. Similar difficulties arose in the
attempt to trace boundary changes on pastoral runs before the
detailed surveys of the seventies and eighties. The map of runs

(Fig. 12) is a composite one derived from a number of sources and contains one example—'Willurah'—showing how parts of several original backblocks were later combined to make one new run. (The present 'Willurah' retains roughly the same boundaries.)

My decision to limit the study to one area of New South Wales was based in part on the foregoing considerations but also on the fact that other scholars were already working on other regions while the Riverina remained relatively untouched. To limit the field of study geographically had the advantage of permitting deeper analysis. It also allowed examination of a number of matters which were surrounded by controversy or obscurity in the writings of general historians—questions concerning not only land utilization and the operation of selection legislation, but also the growth of country urban centres and social structure and outlook of rural population and townsfolk. Equally, there were pitfalls in narrowing the scope of enquiry but if these could be avoided there remained the possibility of weaving together the social, political and economic strands to transcend parochialism and to suggest implications for historians writing in a broader colonial context.

The problems of statistical boundaries asserted themselves as soon as any attempt was made to define the area of study. For nineteenth-century writers like Furphy, Paterson and Lawson no such problem existed; everybody knew where the Riverina was. Indeed it was only the recurrent attempts of disgruntled squatters who felt themselves neglected by Sydney, and later of Riverina citizens generally, to form a separate colony, that inspired any attempt to define the Riverina. In 1857 J. D. Lang proposed an 'Inland and Riverine Colony' to include the western two-thirds of New South Wales, with a possible corridor across the high Monaro to a seaboard outlet near Boyd Town on Twofold Bay. Trollope and other writers of the seventies, moved less by propagandist purposes, spoke airily of the Riverina as that area 'drained by the Murray and its tributaries'. Twentieth-century statisticians, following T. A. Coghlan, have narrowed the limits of the Riverina considerably but generally speaking, in the nineteenth century, every man defined his own Riverina to suit his own purpose. For most of the present study I have taken the Riverina to be the area enclosed by the Murray and Murrumbidgee Rivers eastwards from their junction to a line joining Albury and Wagga, but those towns, stations or statistical divisions which straddle the Murrumbidgee are usually also included, particularly in the tables. Occasionally, for comparison or because the boundaries offer no realistic alternative, excursion is made as far north as the Lachlan River or east of the Albury-Wagga line.

There were good reasons for being dissatisfied with the existing literature on the history of selection in New South Wales. Most historians seemed to follow S. H. Roberts, who, having stated that the 1883 Morris and Ranken 'Report of Inquiry into the State of the Public Lands and the Operation of the Land Laws' was 'clearly biased [and] its recommendations useless', went on to quote it as his major source in demonstrating the 'failure of free selection in most of the colony'.[2] Certainly the report needs to be viewed with suspicion. No witnesses' names were printed and no minutes of evidence were published; instead the evidence was deliberately destroyed. No earlier enquiries on the land laws had required such steps to be taken but this commission had been appointed immediately after the fall of the Parkes-Robertson government. One of its aims was to discredit Robertson's Acts. The question was, what alternative evidence was available? Since Australian history had for the most part been written by people sitting in capital cities and none of them had cited other secondary sources, it seemed probable that there was little more available in the official records. In any case, there appeared to be slight hope of tracing the course of change without a detailed knowledge of the position in 1861 or at least in the decade leading up to that date, in which the passing of Robertson's Acts and the collection of a census were so conveniently combined. From secondary sources and official records, including statistics, I turned to the newspapers. Some early Riverina newspaper files are held in Melbourne and Sydney, but more complete records exist in newspaper offices in the Riverina, especially the *Pastoral Times* office in Deniliquin, where complete bound files from 1858 to the present are housed in the strongroom.

Generally, except where preliminary reading had given leads, I found that using newspaper items involved a large-scale collection of miscellaneous facts. These disparate pieces of evidence were sifted until patterns emerged into which most 'facts' fitted with some significance and a minimum of distortion. Quite early it became clear that in several cases these 'close-ups' were producing patterns somewhat different from those generally accepted by historians, either because the Riverina—like every region— was unique, or because some earlier historians were more concerned with testing a theory or putting a political point of view than with attempting to find out what actually happened (to reassert von Ranke's dictum). Either way it became increasingly obvious that I would have to paint my own picture of the Riverina in 1861, even though the method that had to be used would be tedious and would at times require much back-tracking to check results or trace the origins of new trends. Few diaries or personal papers could be located for this early period, though the diary of George Peppin Jr for 1859 and Mary Kennedy's 'Reminiscences' (both in the Mitchell Library, Sydney) provided useful details of the economic and social life of squatting families.

I began with the pastoral industry because the Riverina had been first settled by pastoralists, and the history of that industry appeared to have been fairly thoroughly examined, especially with the recent appearance of *The Simple Fleece*, edited by A. Barnard, and N. G. Butlin's *Investment in Australian Economic Development, 1861-1900*. But the correlation of official statistics —despite all their weaknesses—with both qualitative and quantatative material from newspapers, revealed that here again there were inadequacies in the existing works and at the risk of distorting the study as a whole I would need to discuss some aspects of the pastoral industry in considerable detail.

Part I, 'The Riverina in 1861', is therefore extensive and contains a large number of quotations, partly by way of justifying divergencies from received views and partly because the source material used is not easily obtainable and its inclusion may be useful to those engaged in teaching Australian history. This practice of including documentary evidence has been followed throughout.

Chapter 1, in which I discuss the Riverina pastoral industry up to 1861, is divided into two sections. The first outlines the settlement of the Riverina, the effects of the gold rushes and the rise and fall of the fat-stock market. Settlement resulted less from flock masters fanning out from the nineteen counties than from cattlemen following the rivers; the gold rushes did not produce decline or stagnation in the pastoral industry, and after the first year or so provided an invaluable source of casual labour. Nor did the gold rushes lead to fencing to cope with a shortage of shepherds. Rather, fencing was a response to the demands of the rising meat market and began on the *cattle* runs which predominated in the interior. The assumption of earlier writers that the 'pastoral industry' meant the 'sheep industry' has led to a

number of such errors. Nor have historians paid enough attention
to the effects of the need to feed a vastly increased Victorian
population; a need which influenced the whole of inland New
South Wales as well as Queensland and Victoria. Ignoring the
part played by cattle in satisfying the demands of this meat
market they have looked in the wrong places for early pastoral
investment. In this regard even more recent estimates of the
nature and level of pastoral investment in 1861 bear little resemblance to the actual state of affairs in the Riverina. The second
part of chapter 1 deals in detail with investment on pastoral
properties in the Riverina up to 1861, especially the two main
forms, fencing and water conservation, and offers some explanation of why, when investment on runs was first officially assessed
in 1870–1, half the total N.S.W. investment on pastoral leases
was to be found in the Murrumbidgee pastoral district and a
further quarter in the Lachlan pastoral district—that is to say,
75 per cent centred in the two south-western districts nearest the
Victorian diggings. A further trend I have sought to explain is the
swing from cattle to sheep around 1861 and the consequent
expansion of pastoral activity into the waterless backblocks.
Country newspapers, the *Pastoral Times* in particular, contain a
wealth of material in sale notices, reports of stock crossings and
court cases, and in stock market returns, which can be used to
answer such questions.

Chapter 2 describes the origin and growth of towns in the
Riverina; their functions as crossing-places where the stock routes
met the rivers and as rallying-places for a scattered pastoral
community; and makes passing reference to the growth of agriculture, especially round Albury, to satisfy the demand from
townsfolk and diggers—and their horses—for breadstuffs. There
is little existing literature on town growth and town life, though
a growing interest in urban studies promises to remedy this.
Much of the material presented is exploratory and descriptive,
ranging from the eating, drinking, sporting and religious habits of
the population to the incidence of scurvy and venereal disease.
Again most of the evidence came from newspaper sources. These
afford some opportunity for observing the life of the less literate
sections of the community, who can otherwise only be seen
through the eyes of their 'superiors' in birth, wealth or education.

The third chapter examines Riverina society of 1861 in some
detail, to show that it was largely a community of transplanted
Britons, of masters and servants, squatter-dominated except near

Albury with its beginnings of agricultural settlement and urban life. The chapter includes an analysis of the social and geographical origins of the squatters, 'a nice set of men of the true British type' according to one of their number,[3] revealing them, like the rest of the population, to be a very mixed bag. The composition of this essentially mobile population and its stratification and values are reflected in the elections of 1859 and 1860, in the latter of which four squatters were returned to the New South Wales Legislative Assembly. It is only from such a detailed examination of social and economic life in the Riverina that the operation of the selection legislation is explicable.

Having sketched this preliminary picture of the Riverina, I was faced with several choices. One was to attempt a chronological survey of the period 1861–91 from all available sources, a procedure which, on the face of it, seemed likely to be rather dull. Local historians frequently follow this course, concentrating on individuals in great detail at the pioneering stage and fading out later as the increase in numbers and growing mass of material swamps the clear lines of argument. I was determined that as far as possible individuals should not disappear from the scene by 1891. This increased the problem of selecting evidence, if only because the half-dozen four-page newspapers of 1861 had grown to twice that number by 1891, each with twenty or more pages published two or three times weekly. A further difficulty in the path of a strictly chronological approach was that the N.S.W. census material for 1881 had been destroyed in the Garden Palace fire soon after collection and before any but the most general analysis had been completed. No further census was taken until 1891 and hence no detailed official figures for 1881 are available.

An alternative course—the one which I chose—was to plunge straight into the years 1890–1 in detail and to seek to identify the main issues then agitating Riverina people, again using politics as a reflection of economic and social life. I could then, after examining the intervening period, link the two set pieces with broad strands or themes which seemed most relevant to the observed differences between the two terminal years of 1861 and 1891. Generally, the evidence led me to conclude that a major factor contributing to the changes over the period was the much criticized 'free selection before survey' clause in Robertson's Acts, the consequent struggle for land and the changing pattern of land ownership and land utilization.

Thus in part II, I discuss the aims and operation of Robertson's Acts. There was little in the state of agriculture in 1861—hindered by the strange environment, lack of transport and markets, and Survey Department difficulties—to arouse interest in these Acts. Nor did the expiry of Riverina pastoral leases in 1866* produce much selection, since these inhibiting conditions remained unchanged during the sixties. It was not until the seventies that selection activity began in earnest in the Riverina. Those historians who have noticed the booming New South Wales land sales of the seventies have done no more than suggest that they were related to the prevailing high wool prices at the beginning of the decade and to a government search for revenue. The precise nature of this relationship has not been explored. Previously-unused sources which threw light on this problem were the Lands Department records. The most useful of these were the Conditional Purchase Registers stored in the land offices or court-houses in Wagga, Albury, Hay, Deniliquin and, after 1876, also in Narrandera, Corowa and Urana. The survival of these invaluable documents is partly attributable to the whims of a number of landholders who still hold their land under one of the clauses of Robertson's Acts. Never having brought the land under the conditions of subsequent amendments or converted it to freehold, they or their successors continue to pay 5 per cent per annum interest on selections taken up at £1 per acre a century ago. For administrative purposes the registers were from time to time rewritten—at the usual rate of two or three selections per double page, a single year's applications often ran to several volumes—but many of the originals survive in basements and outhouses.† Even in the rewritten volumes which omit selections forfeited, disallowed or paid off, the original reference numbers are retained. Every selection applied for is recorded; the details include the name, age and address of the applicant for conditional purchase, the clause of the Act used, acreage, deposit paid, details of further payments and mortgage and, until 1876, whether the applicants were minors. Although a few early originals are missing, enough have survived for a comprehensive survey to be

*Leases under the 1847 Orders-in-Council were not granted until 1852; see p. 148.

†The Conditional Purchase Registers held in the Sydney Land Office record all these local applications but list them merely in order of receipt. To locate those for any one district is a mammoth task. Mr G. A. Price, a contemporary research scholar in the Australian National University, has attempted this task for his study of the Liverpool Plains and Lachlan areas.

drawn up. By supplementing this with newspaper items and parliamentary sources it was possible to find out just what happened on the land in the Riverina. Doubtless high wool prices played a part in reviving interest in land in the seventies, but the particular loophole which allowed selection in the names of minors, including infants, attracted many who sought economic opportunity. Victorians, wondering what to do with sons and daughters who had grown up in the twenty years since the gold rushes found the prospect irresistible and they flocked across the border into New South Wales in considerable numbers. As the Conditional Purchase Registers (and later the censuses) reveal, many of the selectors of the seventies were minors, a common entry consisting of the names of man, wife and any number of children. Here too can be seen the dummying squatter and the blackmailing swindler as well as the bona fide selector.

Both the passage and administration of Robertson's Acts indicate a very real lack of concern amongst New South Wales politicians for the fate of the lands entrusted to their care. In the seventies they sat tight, ignoring all pleas for reform, while loopholes in the Acts poured over £1,000,000 a year into the treasury and the basis was laid for those tales of perjury, immorality, corruption and violence which have become the standard version of events in the selection period. But despite all the difficulties, hundreds of families were settled on the land in the Riverina as a result of Robertson's Acts. By 1891 the population which had totalled less than ten thousand in 1861 had reached sixty thousand, sheep numbers had risen from one million to thirteen million and grain acreage had increased from eight thousand to nearly two hundred thousand acres. Analysis of the land administration which lay behind these changes, together with a proper criticism of the Morris and Ranken report of 1883 was made possible only by a combined use of Lands Department records, the evidence of the select committees of the seventies, local newspaper files and private papers. The study which resulted might be fairly claimed to embody a first step towards the rewriting of the history of selection in New South Wales, and demonstrates decisively that selection in the Riverina was far more successful than hitherto imagined.

As I asked in part I 'Who were the squatters?', so I ask in part II 'Who were the selectors?'. The answers indicate that the origins of both groups were equally diverse. The evidence of considerable social stratification and differentiation therefore calls into question those interpretations which uncritically lump the Australian population into masses, or even broad groups, labelled 'squatters', 'selectors' or 'the nomad tribe'.

In part III, I have described the Riverina in 1891, looking at the pastoral industry, agriculture, towns and finally the changed society as reflected in the elections of that year. The success of free selection led to the establishment of agricultural communities in which church, school and the farmers' union played important roles. Both in the small towns which served farming communities and in the larger, older towns there were some new features ranging from bicycle clubs and the Salvation Army to the Volunteer Rifle Corps and the Eurongilly Cavalry detachment. Throughout the period, the patterns of urban growth typical of Riverina towns are closely tied to the movement of the selector population, the availability of land and the prosperity of the agricultural and pastoral hinterland. Major changes in the pastoral industry were decreasing returns and increasing capital requirements, largely as a result of enforced freehold purchase; alterations in technique and environment; and the changing pattern of industrial relations typified by the 1890 shearing strike, a trial of strength organized by militant labour.

Important changes in population included the increased percentage of Chinese and the growth of 'Chinese camps', especially in some urban centres like Narrandera, where every second man in town was Chinese. In the farming districts north of Albury numbers of German farmers had settled after migrating from South Australia and to a lesser extent from Victoria. But apart from the existence of these ethnically distinct minority groups, there were more general changes in the structure of the population. By 1891 70 per cent of the total were Australian-born, and the numbers of women and children had risen considerably. Schools too had increased from some half-dozen in 1861 to several hundred in 1891. By 1882 thirteen thousand children attended Riverina schools.

Except for the brief burst of prosperity in the seventies, the thirty years between 1861 and 1891 constitute a period of declining economic opportunity. Men had first sought easy fortunes from gold; then less easily won prosperity on the land. Some had attained economic independence through radical land legislation and thereafter turned conservative. Many others, unskilled in tillage or grazing, or unwilling to try, rejected Samuel Smiles's gospel of work for that of Karl Marx, and swelled the ranks of the

unionists, breaking out openly against the established order in the
1890 strike. And although declining pastoral prosperity is reflected
in the decreasing liberality of station homesteads towards wanderers it was not only the economic position of the squatter that
had changed; there had been considerable changes in the structure of society. To borrow Asa Briggs's simile, it was now much
more like a cube than a pyramid. In 1860 political representation
seemed to be the virtually unchallenged prerogative of men of
birth, wealth, education or social standing, and Riverina electors
had returned four squatters. By 1891 only one squatter sympathizer
was elected amongst ten Members. The rest included a merchant,
a solicitor, a flour-miller, four selectors' representatives and
two Labor Electoral League candidates, one from the Wagga
Shearers' Union and the other from the Carriers' Union at Hay.
The unsuccessful candidates were equally heterogeneous, illus-
trating the extensive socio-economic changes that the Riverina
had undergone within one generation.

Thus *The Riverina, 1861–1891* clearly falls into three distinct
parts. At either end stands a picture of Riverina society. Between
these, since it explains most of the differences evident in 1891, is
a study of the changing pattern of land ownership. Some lines of
specialist enquiry had to be neglected to keep the study within
manageable bounds and a number of themes are not fully
explored. Pursuit of any one of them would have precluded the
possibility of taking an overall view. The frontier thesis, for
example, is nowhere applied seriously and the word 'frontier'
itself is only used—as in 'selector frontier' or 'ring-barking frontier'
—to indicate marginal areas for certain activities. The question
of the Sydney-Melbourne-Adelaide struggle for economic domination of the Riverina—the whole area is nearer Melbourne than
Sydney—and the related pattern of river and rail transport is
mentioned only briefly, as is 'the Victorian influence' and the New
State movement. Pastoral finance likewise has not been treated
in any depth. The most diligent enquiries unearthed few surviv-
ing early pastoral records. As the Conditional Purchase Registers
and other sources indicate, there were few foreclosures of mortgage before the nineties and the available records of those stations
which were taken over by companies have already been examined by Professor N. G. Butlin in his work on investment. The
study of urbanization is also limited, partly for reasons indicated
in the text* and partly because other scholars are currently

*See chapter 7.

working in a more detailed way on this question.* Political topics
are also dismissed briefly, and while a detailed study of changing
patterns in Riverina electorates would doubtless be rewarding,
the limited treatment offered here does no more than suggest
further lines of enquiry, for example on the early history of
selector organizations and Labor Electoral Leagues. All I have
attempted to do is to use the elections as reflections of change in
the social and economic structure.

One theme, the significance of which has grown during the
course of this study, is the importance of demographic factors in
south-eastern Australia in the post–1851 period, especially the
effects of gold-rush marriages, the greatly increased number of
women and children by the nineties and the resultant imbalance
between population and existing resources, including land. Related
to technological changes in the rural scene, a consideration of
these demographic factors contributes something to the understanding of Australia's rapid urbanization in the late nineteenth
and the twentieth centuries.

Finally it might be asked why I have not made more use of
other regional histories for comparative purposes. 'Every region
is unique.' For this reason, by their very nature regional studies
tend to concentrate on the points of uniqueness. In short, unless
other regional studies *ask the same questions* very little meaning-
ful comparison is possible. Indeed, one of the frequent criticisms
made of regional historians is that they fail, as Professor Sir Keith
Hancock once put it at an A.N.U. work-in-progress seminar, to
relate the parish pump to the cosmos. In the present study there
were frequent difficulties in reconciling the particulars of Riverina
economic, social and political life with generally-accepted traditional views of nineteenth-century Australia. Perhaps it is not too
much to suggest that a sufficient number of similar grass-roots
studies might result in a rewriting, or at least a change of
emphasis, in large sections of what currently passes for general
Australian history.

*E.g., M. Richmond's uncompleted research at the Australian National
University, which includes a study of Wagga.

Part I

THE RIVERINA IN 1861

1

THE PASTORAL INDUSTRY, 1851–1861

Settlement in the Riverina, as in so much of inland Australia, followed the watercourses. By 1832 pastoralists moving down-steam from the upper Murrumbidgee had taken up runs as far west as Wagga Wagga and by 1835–6 a further group had settled on the Murray around the present Albury, near where Hume and Hovell had crossed on their 1824 exploring trip. There seems to have been some hesitation at this stage about moving out on to the plains, the flat country that came to be known as the Riverina. This was due in part to the adverse reports of the early explorers. In December 1829, Charles Sturt, leading the first European expedition down the Murrumbidgee had written:

> We journeyed due west over plains of great extent. The soil upon them was soft and yielding, in some places being a kind of light earth covered with rhagodiae, in others a red tenacious clay, overrun by the misembrianthemum and salsolae.* Nothing could exceed the apparent barrenness of these plains, or the cheerlessness of the landscape. We had left all high lands behind us, and were now on an extensive plain, bounded in the distance by low trees or by dark lines of cypresses . . .[1]

and on the following day:

> Our route during the day, was over as melancholy a tract as ever was travelled. The plains to the N. and N.W. bounded the horizon; not a tree of any kind was visible upon them. It was equally open to the S. and it appeared as if the river was decoying us into a desert.

Many of the pastoralists of 1835 felt the same way. Peter Stuckey and Charles Barber followed Sturt's tracks as far down the Murrumbidgee as the Yanko Creek, decided against the country, retraced their steps and eventually took up stations near

*'Pigface' and saltbush—still common vegetation in the western Riverina.

Deniliquin, one on the Edward River and the other on the Murray.[2] Other parties probed down the Billabong Creek, but 'the burning plains of the Murrumbidgee' were uninviting in the summer heat and most were content wherever possible to squeeze in between existing runs on the larger rivers or to follow up the tributary creeks, so that the hilly country between Albury and Wagga and further east was rapidly filled in.

A further delaying factor in the settlement of the Riverina was introduced by Major Thomas Mitchell's 1836 report on his discovery of 'Australia Felix', the well-watered grazing lands of western Victoria.[3] Batman was already on the site of Melbourne and the Hentys at Portland, and indeed even as Mitchell's party returned they were met by Hepburn, Hawdon and Gardiner, the first overlanding party to the new district south of the Murray. But Mitchell's publicity stirred activity and within a year overlanding to Port Phillip along 'the Major's Line' was commonplace, mobs of up to five thousand sheep and hundreds of cattle crossing near Albury or Howlong. Within a few years the best of Victoria had been taken up as pastoral runs.

Meanwhile in 1836 the founding of a new colony at Adelaide in South Australia provided a ready market for the more enterprising travellers in stock. The version of the Wakefield system adopted in South Australia gave men of capital the right to purchase, at £1 per acre, Special Surveys of four thousand acres each. To these stock-hungry capitalists, anxiously waiting to exploit their newly acquired land, the overlanders now turned and in 1838 Adelaide welcomed within four months the parties of Hawdon, Eyre, and Sturt, each with three hundred to four hundred cattle. Commenting on the country they had passed through, Hawdon and Eyre stated that the route, though unfavourable, would be practicable for sheep. Sturt, however, though he too had kept to the banks of the Murray and had travelled this time in late winter, still wrote of the 'great sterile and sandy plain of the interior'.[4]

Despite the pessimists, stockholders had been edging westward along the Murrumbidgee, Billabong and Murray. Overlanding bred a familiarity with the two larger rivers and by the simple process of each newcomer squatting on the first available frontage to the west, runs had been taken up by 1839 to about half-way between the Albury-Wagga line and the Murray-Murrumbidgee junction.[5] To this movement downstream from the Sydney side was added, in the early 1840s, the movement northwards from the rapidly expanding Port Phillip district. Thus Phillips and Graves, travelling north with their sheep, crossed the Murray some miles upstream from its junction with the Edward River and followed the latter to the site of the present town of Deniliquin. Here on the sandhills on the north side of the Edward they found 'a small slab and bark hut and 4,000 sheep', the property of Ben Boyd and the Royal Bank. Boyd, as much as he was anything, was a Sydneysider, as was his resident overseer Augustus Morris who had travelled down the Billabong to the Edward country in 1842,[6] but the stock had been brought up by Morris from Port Phillip.[7] Boyd claimed an enormous area,* 'all the country North of the Murray River, all along the Edward or Kyalite River for over a hundred miles.'[8] Ignoring this grand claim, as many others were to do, Phillips crossed to the south side of the Edward, examined the country for fifty miles downstream, returned and stuck up a pole with an old sheet on it as his mark of occupation. Then while he watched the flocks, shot marauding wild dogs, slept in the wagons or argued with Boyd's overseer, Graves rode post-haste to Sydney, six hundred miles distant, for a £10 squatting licence.[9]

Further west, though still on the Victorian side, the Beveridges had reached Tyntynder near Mitchell's 'Swan Hill' in 1845,[10] by which time the converging streams of settlers moving down the Lachlan, Murrumbidgee, Billabong and Murray Rivers had met and had taken up frontage runs as far down as the Murrumbidgee-Murray junction.

So far pastoralists in the 'unsettled districts' had no security of tenure.[11] The most that their protracted struggles with Governors Bourke (1831-7) and Gipps (1838-46) had produced was a £10 annual licence to depasture stock on Crown lands. Under Bourke's 1836 Act this had been sufficient for any area and any number of stock, but by Gipps's 1839 Act an additional fee was levied in the form of an annual assessment on the number of stock. 'Parties originally taking up runs,' as Gipps pointed out,

> were limited only by their own moderation or by the pressure of other squatters on them . . . The occupiers of this vast wilderness, not having a property of any part in the soil they occupy, have no inducement to make permanent improvements on it. Some land indeed has been brought into cultiva-

*As late as 1850 the Deniliquin run, only one part of the original claim, still covered 700,000 acres. Three other remnants, Nyang, Neimur and Poon Boon, totalled 320,000 acres; *N.S.W. G.G.* 1848-50.

tion . . . and here and there a building has been erected which may deserve the name of a cottage, but the squatters generally live in huts made of the bark of trees.[12]

The attempts by Gipps on the one hand to avoid inequality and extensive alienation yet secure the licensee his improvements, and of the squatters on the other to pay as little as possible while extending their privilege for as long as possible culminated in the 1847 Orders-in-Council.[13] By these, squatters in the 'unsettled districts', which included the Riverina, were to be granted fourteen-year leases. Runs were to be large enough to carry at least four thousand sheep or the equivalent in cattle, Gipps reckoning 'one horse, ox or cow to be equal to eight sheep'.[14] For such leases the rental was £10 per annum, to which £2 10s was to be added for each additional thousand sheep (or equivalent). Provision to safeguard improvements was made in a clause which granted a pre-emptive right to purchase unlimited quantities of the run at a minimum price of £1 an acre.

Under these conditions the Riverina squatters of 1847 tendered for their runs and by 1852* were granted leases, promises of lease, or licences. By 1850 the pattern of settlement for the next decade was clear. Along the main rivers, frontages had been taken up for runs which extended several miles back. In the Albury-Wagga area the network of creeks and gullies had been cut up into a relatively closely settled patchwork of 10,000–50,000-acre runs, with 20,000–25,000 acres a common size. Further west the back country away from the main rivers was unoccupied through lack of water and runs were larger, particularly on the Murrumbidgee. In the Billabong and Edward River country, 50,000–100,000 acres was common and in the western Riverina, near the Murray-Murrumbidgee junction, Boyd and Wentworth had runs of 200,000 acres.

The position had barely been established when the gold discoveries in New South Wales, and more particularly in Victoria, brought about that colonial upheaval which was to have such a marked impact on the Riverina. Short-term effects on the pastoral industry included a dearth of station labour and disruption of the tenuous land-based transport system. Counteracting these, and of a more permanent nature, were the formation of a casual labour

---

*The delay in granting these leases pushed the expiry date forward to 1866. This preserved Riverina pastoral leaseholds from selection for five years after the passing of Robertson's Acts in 1861 (see p. 148).

force and the introduction of river transport. Most spectacular was the rise and fall of the fat-stock market.

The immediate effect of gold on the pastoral industry was the diversion of a large percentage of the *permanent* labour force. Of this period, one pioneer grazier wrote:

> It was now that . . . squatting . . . seemed to be most discouraging and at its lowest ebb. The country districts were entirely denuded of labour, provisions of all kinds had risen fifty per cent and more in price. Labour, such as shepherds and station hands were very difficult to procure, excepting at a very high price of wages: in fact the country seemed to be thoroughly disorganized . . . How all this was to end was difficult to predict and after undergoing ten years of peace and prosperity it seemed that the squatting interests were doomed. . .[15]

But one or two years experience showed that only a lucky few made fortunes and that the cost of provisions on the goldfields was higher than many diggers could afford. Furthermore, as the water in the creeks dried up with the onset of hot weather, no gold-washing could be done and many miners began to drift back to the stations and towns for the summer,[16] forming the nucleus of that *casual* labour force which was to be so useful to Riverina pastoralists for the next decade. It was fortunate for the sheep men that this annual migration coincided with shearing time.

Labour had always been a problem in a pastoral district where flocks and herds multiplied faster than population, and various remedies had been tried in the forties, when squatters used ex-convicts, 'Pentonvillains', 'ticket-of-leave men', and even Pacific islanders.*[17] Squatters were almost continuously dissatisfied with the quality of convict and ex-convict labour, but discovered to their cost, in the unsettled conditions of the fifties, that free labourers had the added disadvantage that they could walk off the job. Thus W. Howitt noted:

> At present the position of the squatters, especially near the roads to the diggings has its annoyances. They dare not speak

*Ben Boyd's remedy, in 1847, had been to send the schooner *Velocity* blackbirding to the New Hebrides. Sixty-five 'Kanakas', landed at Boyd Town, were overlanded to the 'Woolshed Station' at Deniliquin, where, for sixpence a week and three suits of clothes a year, they were to be employed as shepherds. But 'Boyd's Savages', despite their bows, arrows and clubs, were afraid of the 'other one country blackfellows'. They refused to work away from the head station except *en masse*, were ill-treated by the overseers, got out of hand and were eventually returned by a government order.

to any of their men, for they immediately march off saying *'do your work yourself'*. They shear the sheep very badly, they are in such a hurry to do a large number, and are by no means particular as to clipping large pieces out of them. I have seen sheep snipped occasionally in shearing in England but never saw such wholesale mangling as these fellows make. The other day one of the overseers had to stitch up the skin of two sheep's stomachs that they had actually cut right across.[18]

Throughout the fifties and even into the sixties, so long as occasional 'rushes' occurred, men left permanent station employment to seek elusive fortunes. The Victorian diggings attracted many early in the decade, but as late as 1861 the new finds on the Lachlan and the Snowy were still drawing men away, some for a short time, some for good. Five station hands left the employment of one Riverina squatter to go digging at Kiandra. They wrote back in April 1860 that two days of snow and four of rain had 'put the commissioners and the greater part of the miners in such a panic that they are making preparations for the road . . . two or three hundred miners are leaving every day at present.' The five in their own party were putting up a hut and preparing to stay. They had 'five months tucker' and 'plenty of wood and water at the door'. But as the *Pastoral Times* pointed out, 'these were all steady men, possessed of ample means to keep them for the winter.' One of them wrote 'we get on the average about 30s. per man each day . . . we prefer being our own masters . . . It is amusing to see the laughing faces as the little nuggets turn up. It is "will you ever go home?"'. Another of the party indicated that although they themselves were doing well, 'a great many have not done anything at all, and curse their unlucky star which coaxed them away from their homes.'[19] Thus the fortunes of the game, as well as seasonal fluctuations, eased the labour problems of the squatters and they suffered little on this account.

A second short-term effect was the disruption of the somewhat precarious transport system on which the pastoral industry had relied, a disruption intensified by the notorious 1852 flood. Floods like this, in a land of unmade roads and no bridges, as much as the shortage of reliable labour to work the station in their absence, made pastoralists hesitate before setting out to cart wool and supplies on their own bullock wagons. Phillips of War-breccan used to allow one month for his annual 170-mile trip to

Melbourne, leaving his partner on the station, while lower Murrumbidgee squatters took three months for a return trip to Sydney in the forties. At a particularly difficult time one Murrumbidgee squatter took nine months for the return trip to Sydney, driving one of the two wagons himself.[20] But no sooner had 'gold broken out' than teamsters and carters refused to go any further than the diggings. Full loads, quick turnover and inflated prices kept them there. 'No Melbourne teams would go beyond Bendigo nor Sydney teams beyond Bathurst.'[21] The result for the stations was that wool accumulated, supplies ran out and prices rose accordingly. One traveller in 1852 noted that nearly all the stations he passed were without flour. At the Edward River after three days without bread he met a teamster he knew who sold him 'three pounds of flour for nine shillings'.[22] In 1853, on Paika station at the Murray-Murrumbidgee junction (eight hundred miles from Sydney and three hundred from Melbourne), where twenty tons of flour were always kept against contingencies, 'no teams had been up or down for two years. There were two seasons wool stored in the sheds, the remainder of the flour was awfully musty; boots, saddles, tinware, "slops" and the like had long since given out in the store.'[23] Into this situation the South Australians cunningly thrust their river steamers, entering, as Pike has put it, by the 'back door'.[24] Spurred on by the offer of a £4,000 reward from the government, as much as by the possibility of landing goods within fifty miles of the Victorian diggings and thereby recouping their waning fortunes, the systematic colonizers sought compensation for their lack of gold and loss of population. By 1853 William Randell, son of a Gumeracha flour-miller, was afloat in his home-made *Mary Ann* and a few miles behind came Captain Francis Cadell, a man of substance, with his Sydney-built *Lady Augusta*. On board the latter was the Governor of South Australia, Sir Henry Young, whose favourite project was Murray River navigation. Accompanying him was his wife, the Lady Augusta herself. The effect of the steamers was immediate. In the forties, drays had brought 1½-ton loads 'smothered in dust and caked mud, bags worn with the impact of the dray wheels, all dirt and bad order at best.' By contrast the steamers arrived with 'clean white 50 lb. bags of flour, clean white boxes of loaf sugar and sperm candles; cases of brandy spick and span . . . everything clean and new; and a hundred tons of it too . . . The engorged wool sheds were quickly relieved of their contents and the price of Riverina station property went up.'[25]

Even before this pressing problem of transport had been solved, the pastoralists had turned to the diggings to see what could be made of them as markets. John Phillips of Warbreccan had been driving cattle to the Melbourne market but on reaching the vicinity of the diggings was told that the butchers, the salesmen and their customers had all left the city for the diggings and that he had better slaughter his cattle there and then.[26] Phillips rented a paddock from a neighbouring squatter for £100 and after repairing the yard and gallows drove in his two hundred stock. With his overseer, two station hands and two hired butchers —hired at the inflated rate of £3 per week—he set to work. Eight or ten beasts were shot daily, skinned, hung overnight, cut down between two and three in the morning, quartered, weighed, carted five miles to the diggings and sold to butchers for 2d a pound. Each day the carts were beset by poor and starving women whose husbands had not been fortunate in finding gold and who begged for meat.' 'Fever and dysentery' finally forced Phillips and his overseer to Melbourne. On their return they found the rest of the cattle had broken out and escaped—most to be slaughtered by the diggers. With this and the difficulty of extracting payment from some of the more mobile diggers and butchers the venture finished at a loss.

Within a few months, however, both the camp and stock selling 'became better regulated' and a very profitable market was established. The four Tyson brothers, following Phillips, erected a yard at the diggings. While one or two remained there the others brought fresh mobs from the stations, all four slaughtering the stock and selling it to the retail butchers. On one occasion James Tyson bought twenty thousand wethers at 6s per head on a station isolated by floods. Then, hiring a steamer and barges he crossed them to the Bendigo diggings where they sold for £1 8s per head. Tyson said that the deal was 'the best he had made in stock up to that time' and estimated his profit at £20,000.[27] From these beginnings developed the fat-stock market which with its emphasis on cattle was to dominate pastoral practice in the Riverina and beyond until at least 1861.

The relative advantages and profits from cattle raising simply underlined the disadvantages of the sheep men. In the forties many stations had been stocked first with cattle for the same reasons as the overlanders began with cattle; they could travel further and faster. Moreover, the keeping of sheep required more labour, both permanent and casual. As late as 1861, one hundred thousand sheep on Tyson's Deniliquin runs were being close-shepherded during the day and folded at night.[28] By contrast, until the mid-fifties cattle were allowed to wander over the runs until the yearly or half-yearly muster. They needed no shearers, there was no annual wool clip to be carted and if the meat market rose, cattle travelled faster and stayed fat longer. On the stations, because they could travel further from water at a time when frontage pastures had been eaten bare, they utilized more land. Until 1861 cattle diseases were no trouble, but sheep diseases had necessitated Acts of Parliament to control them. Whole districts had been ruined for sheep* by scab, catarrh, or Cumberland disease. As late as 1862 a flock of 3,780 scabby sheep were 'destroyed and burnt' to prevent them crossing the Murray into New South Wales.[29]

For the Riverina then, the result of the buoyant beef market was a growing emphasis, until the early sixties, on the production of fat cattle. Sheep were of secondary importance and where kept at all were for the local fat-stock market as much as for the world wool market. The position is reflected in Tables 1 and 2, which indicate that in 1850 the changeover from early stocking with cattle to the double security of sheep for meat and wool was proceeding as anticipated. During the fifties the trend to fat cattle had reduced sheep numbers while more than doubling the area utilized for cattle.† The magnitude of the trend can be

TABLE 1

Stock Numbers and Area Utilized, Murrumbidgee pastoral district, 1850-1859

	Cattle ('000)	Approx. area utilized (million acres)	Sheep ('000)	Approx. area utilized (million acres)*
1850	135	3·1	872	3·0
1859	323	7·4	614	2·1

*Based on sheep 3-4 acres, cattle 6-7 × area per sheep.
Source: *N.S.W. Statistical Register.*

*E.g., the Coolah district, north-east of Dubbo, the commencement of the 'great southern road, once promising, now in decay . . . runs held thousands of sheep . . . now not a single head . . . entirely attributable to Cumberland disease . . . swept off flocks, sold or disposed of the rest . . . now entirely cattle country'; *P.T.*, 7 September 1860.
†The swing back to sheep in the late fifties, evident in the figures for 1859 and 1861, is discussed on pp. 33-4.

TABLE 2

*Pastoral Labour Force, Murrumbidgee pastoral district,
1851–1861*

	Cattle (’000)	Workers[a]	Sheep (’000)	Workers[a]
1851	135	279	872	948
1856	225	444	475	528
1861	270[b]	720	873[b]	764

[a]Total of census figures for 'lessees' and 'persons employed in the management of . . .'
[b]Estimates—returns for 1861 not available.
Source: *N.S.W. Statistical Registers* and *N.S.W. Censuses.*

missed by the casual observer looking only at the gross numbers and ignoring the relative areas required for sheep and cattle. That there were twice as many 'head' of sheep as cattle in 1861 simply means that at the most moderate estimate of 6:1 for relative grazing areas per head, sheep were still only occupying one-quarter of the total area grazed. This may well have occupied the attentions of less than one-quarter of the hundred-odd pastoralists. A single squatter, James Tyson, who ran cattle as well as sheep, owned one-eighth of the total Riverina flocks in 1861, when 100,000 sheep were shorn on his Deniliquin runs.

In those areas within the Murrumbidgee pastoral district where the market response was quicker than in more remote parts, the bias towards cattle was even more marked. In the Albury (police) district the numbers of stock were:[30]

	Cattle (’000)	Sheep (’000)
1859	78	61
1860	47	36

indicating a ratio, in terms of area utilized, of over 8:1 in favour of cattle. This led to one curious result. On 29 August 1860 the *Albury Banner* recorded that, 'Mr. J. Smith of Chiltern (Victoria) crossed 300 sheep into Albury yesterday, to supply the demand for mutton amongst our townspeople.'

At first the new immigrants who flooded into Victoria in the fifties had been fed by the sheep and cattle men of that colony. But the Victorian suppliers of meat, geared for several years to feeding a slowly increasing population of less than eighty thousand, were suddenly faced, within six years, with at least a fivefold increase in the market.* The nature of the migration, predominantly adult male and thus greater meat eaters, further augmented the effect. Between 1852 and 1856 Victorian sheep numbers decreased by over two million, to which must be added the loss of the annual increase from lambing. If the growing Victorian demand for meat were to be satisfied from that colony alone, its remaining four million sheep would soon disappear. For the pastoralists of New South Wales, where population was growing much more slowly, this was a golden opportunity. Riverina squatters benefited particularly from the mushroom growth of populations measured in tens of thousands, first at Bendigo, fifty miles south of the Murray and one hundred miles from Denili-quin, and later at Beechworth and the Ovens diggings, less than thirty miles from Albury. In December 1861 populations on these two fields alone were:[31]

	Sandhurst (Bendigo)	Beechworth
Miners	11,000	16,000
Total goldfields population	41,000	23,000

To meet the demands of these markets the New South Wales fat-stock nexus developed. From the hazardous undertakings of enterprising individuals selling out their surplus stock, there evolved a complex and widely dispersed system in which Riverina squatters, for their part, operated on the margin between store stock and fat stock, for which operation Riverina vegetation proved admirably suited. Explorers, overlanders and later surveyors had voiced doubts about the value of the flat country seeing 'only the saltbush . . . its leaves covered with glittering saline particles'.[32] Even the pastoralists of the mid-forties, still preoccupied with English-type landscapes, expressed satisfaction that grass grew where stock ran and that the 'old and wild herbage had disappeared, giving rise to a better and more uniform description of grasses'.[33] But it was this once-despised salt-bush (and, until they were eaten out, the reed-beds which had so hindered the explorers) which proved the best fatteners of stock.

Once their initial surplus of beasts had gone, Riverina pastoralists began to draw on what became the breeding areas.

*Population of Victoria: 1851, 77,345; 1854, 236,798; 1857, 410,766; 1861, 540,322; *Census of Victoria*, 1861.

These included the pastoral districts upstream in the hilly country to the east from which the Murray, Murrumbidgee and Billabong descended and those to the north on the Lachlan and the upper Darling.[34] Areas as remote as New England and the Darling Downs were influenced and contributed, not because they could not fatten, but because Victoria was the market and stock would not stay fat over a thousand miles of denuded stock routes. Figure 1 indicates the strength of this trend away from sheep and towards cattle throughout the fifties. The effect was greatest in the Murrumbidgee pastoral district, the fattening area closest to the market, but it can also be seen in the more remote breeding areas, and in New South Wales as a whole.

Occasionally a late summer rain would start the northerners moving early* but it was generally the first of the autumn falls that heralded the beginning of the annual trek south. After three or four months of complaints about the dryness of the country and the lack of feed, local papers would suddenly announce the opening rains of the season.[35] Then on station after station mustering would start, and as the herds were cut out the drovers moved off down the long winding trails that followed the water to the south. In wetter seasons they travelled wide and to the west, down the Lachlan; in drier seasons they clung to the foothills, skirting the slopes until they reached the Murrumbidgee at Wagga or Narrandera.[36] Either way the bulk of the stock were destined for Deniliquin. By mid-winter the Deniliquin-Echuca road had become the neck of the funnel for the converging streams. As the mobs of two, five, ten, and even fifteen thousand lean store cattle reached the Riverina they were drafted on to the stations, while mobs averaging three hundred fat stock from the same runs were started for the diggings. Although there were fewer of the slower travelling store-sheep mobs they held larger numbers. Drovers from New England and the Darling Downs brought down flocks of twenty and forty thousand head.

Because store stock arrived in such enormous numbers within only a few months each year when travelling was possible, while the Victorian market was by comparison fairly steady throughout the year, the Riverina became a kind of holding centre, lightly stocked by the end of summer and overcrowded in the winter. By the mid-fifties almost all Riverina squatters had adopted the role

---

*The unusual figure for the Wellington pastoral district in 1864 is almost certainly related to this annual movement of cattle out of the district. The date of collection of stock statistics is of obvious significance in some years.

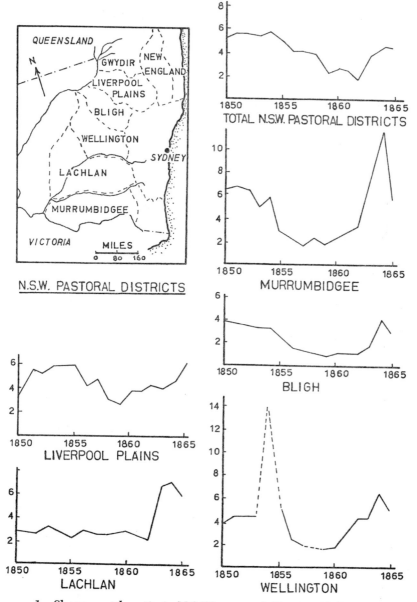

1   Sheep : cattle ratio in N.S.W. pastoral districts 1850–1865
Based on number of head of sheep/number of head of cattle
Source: *Statistical Registers of N.S.W.*

of dealers in stock. To maintain their new-found prosperity it was essential that interruptions to the traffic should be minimized. Characteristically, two major problems—shortage of feed and water on the well-travelled stock routes and lack of knowledge of the state of the market—were overcome by individual action.

The Tyson brothers, though holding their own runs for both breeding and fattening, bought others when Ben Boyd's stations were sold in 1855, and established a chain of runs all along their route from the Lachlan to the Murray. The Lang brothers similarly purchased six adjoining stations and could thus travel stock on their own land from their thirty-mile Murrumbidgee frontage to the Billabong Creek.[37] Between Hay and Deniliquin lay a fifty-mile waterless stretch, the Old Man Plain, notorious for the death of man and beast. In 1859 a subscription list was started at Hay and within a year a well had been dug between the two towns. While not an outstanding success—the water was brackish, though the promoters blamed the pine timber used for lining— the well did provide water suitable for stock.[38]

The second necessity, knowledge of the market, was provided by the extension of the Victorian telegraph line to Deniliquin. Originally squatters drove their own stock to Melbourne or the diggings and made their own bargains there. But in their eagerness, Melbourne agents, bypassing each other from town to town, soon reached the New South Wales border. Although the process was unduly prolonged and Melbourne dealers were even scouring New England at one stage, Deniliquin became the real end of the leap-frog movement.[39] Here a change took place in the method of disposal. At first, on conclusion of the agreement, stock were delivered to the agent at Deniliquin or Moama. He could either hold them there—and one agent held a flock of sheep for so long on the Deniliquin reserve that he had to shear them again[40]—or send them off on the well-worn route to Victoria. If they were not disposed of immediately there was no alternative but to travel them up and down the half-mile-wide stock road. To avoid this, dealers began to buy mobs on the station as they needed them, after which squatters no longer needed to take their own stock to market, though some, in the hope of greater profits, continued to do so even into the sixties. The final refinement was reached in 1857, when agents began to buy stock on the station at a fixed rate and contracted to have them off by a certain time: 'A thousand head, the pick of the herd' was a common arrangement.[41] While this may have cost the squatter a shilling or two a head at times, it saved him a good deal of trouble and the agent was able to choose his own market. But for the agent or the more independent squatter to do so with any degree of success, he must know precisely the state of the Victorian markets.

Like so many of the public works in a district 500-700 miles from the seat of government, the construction of the Deniliquin and Echuca Electric Telegraph Company's chief asset was 'completed by private enterprise'. The twenty-odd shareholders, of whom all but two were stock-owners or dealers, subscribed £3,500 and in May 1859 the line was declared open. As the pro-squatter *Pastoral Times* was delighted to point out, it was 'somewhat anomalous to see a company of squatters to whom ignorance assigned the character of "obstruction" leading the responsible Governments of New South Wales and Victoria.' The claim of 'public spirit' held water better than the later one for the 'thorough disinterestedness which characterised the proceedings of the company'. As the company's directors indicated in their official memorandum to the Postmaster-General of Victoria and to the New South Wales Premier, Cowper, to whom by June 1859, only one month later, they were already trying to sell out: 'The line pierces a pastoral country, from which the cattle dealers of Victoria draw the largest portion of their fat stock, it being estimated that one million pounds worth of stock passes annually through Deniliquin for the Victorian markets.'[42] The main object, they stated, was:

> chiefly to give better opportunity for the disposal of fat and lean stock through Deniliquin to the Victorian market . . . It enables the sellers and purchasers to know, in the interior, the prices in the principal Victorian markets . . . [and] prevents stock being driven backwards and forwards, (the driving entails a great waste of time and money; it deteriorates the fat stock very materially, the grass for a very long distance from Melbourne on this route being eaten up necessarily by reason of the passing and repassing over the same route of the same stock).[43]

Disinterested or not the squatters benefited. Because of the telegraph, speculation was less and the great losses and gains of former days no longer took place. But if the profits were not so spectacular, until mid-1859, they were at least steady.[44]

Following a dry summer, 1860 began with unusually favourable opening rains in the Riverina.[45] With the possibility of a good season ahead some apprehension was expressed. The *Pastoral Times* warned that 'unless population increases faster than it has during the last two or three years we shall have a super abundance of beef and mutton' and foresaw a return to 'boiling down'. By June 1860 it was obvious that Deniliquin prices, though not receding, would not rise above £8 for bullocks and £6 10s for cows. Some squatters turned to spayed cows when it was observed that they fattened faster, while others sought to acquire better quality stock; but it was noticed that large supplies of fat stock from Gippsland and the Western District were interfering with sales at Deniliquin[46]—the Victorian sheep and cattle men were at last catching up (see Figure 2). In August there was talk of depression in Melbourne and Sydney[47] and by October a Maitland editor was writing of the 'temporary interruption of the great inland traffic in fat stock'. Possible reasons suggested were that Victorian stockholders were now meeting the diggings demands or that less gold was being found and there was therefore less money to pay for dear meat. Temporary relief was felt by the middle of shearing, but when shorn sheep flooded the market cattle dropped almost to £5. By November Riverina newspapers were horrifying Victorians with editorials headed 'Shall we boil down our surplus stock?' and at local meetings anxious squatters were stating that so long as cattle kept above a £5 average in the Victorian markets this would not be necessary.[48]

> For the past two years the settlers have been bitterly complaining of the scarcity of fat cattle and ardently longing for a growing season. Now they have their desire and fat cattle are abundant, and what is the consequence? We hear nothing but complaints of cattle and sheep being worth nothing, a talk of boiling down, and long calculations as to the lowest possible price at which cattle might arrive.[49]

1861 was even worse. In January fat stock were growing lean on the roads between the Edward River and the markets, fat stock were wasting away unsold in bare paddocks around Melbourne, boiling-down tanks were advertised in country newspapers, and one boiling-down works was actually in operation.[50] These conditions intensified during the year, and by August the 'Deniliquin Stock Market' writer's only comment was that the overland trade was 'done' for the present.[51] Prices went down and stayed down.*

*Average [*sic*] prices of fat cattle in Melbourne: 1860, £8 10s–£9 10s; 1861, £6–£7 15s; 1862, £3–£10; 1863, £3–£10; 1864, £2–£10; *Statistical Registers of Victoria*.

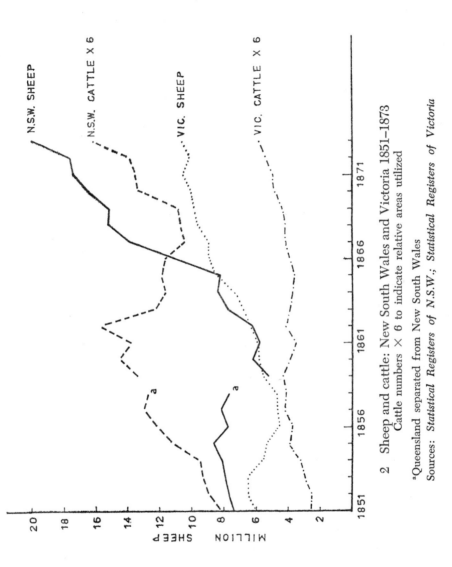

2 Sheep and cattle: New South Wales and Victoria 1851–1873
   Cattle numbers × 6 to indicate relative areas utilized

^aQueensland separated from New South Wales
Sources: *Statistical Registers of N.S.W.*; *Statistical Registers of Victoria*

One further blow was to be struck at the declining fat-cattle
market before the end of the year. In September 1859 the
Riverina press reported without comment that a disease which
had 'of late, prevailed to a most alarming extent in England' had
made its appearance in Victoria. Only one imported cow had
been infected, the disease had been noticed six weeks after the
animal's arrival, and the cow had died within a few days. Twenty-
three others in the herd had since been infected and all had died
except five which had only partly recovered. By order of a public
meeting the remaining fifty were 'destroyed and burnt' and subscriptions called to reimburse the unfortunate owner.[52]

A year later pleuro-pneumonia was common around Melbourne
saleyards. By April 1861 cases had occurred in a bullock team at
Beechworth. Riverina pastoralists, despite the extensive use of
horse teams, were justifiably alarmed and, with their usual faith
in legislation, petitioned the Hon. John Hay to introduce a
Bill to restrict 'the pleuro' to Victoria.* The Bill passed the House
but some time in the winter of 1861 'the pleuro' passed the
border. In August an anxious meeting was held at 'Ten Mile
Creek', forty-three miles north-east of Albury. There was 'pleuro'
at James McLaurin's Yarra Yarra station.† Other meetings quickly
followed since the McLaurins also held Cornalla station at the
Murray-Edward junction and another station in Victoria and had
travelled stock between them—but the saltbush squatters stated
that the disease would not affect their healthy district. The six
thousand cattle on the Yarra Yarra run were quarantined, but the
disease was already rife and by early summer the quarantine had
been extended to another nine stations and twenty-seven thousand
cattle. By December six more stations and the Albury municipality
had been quarantined.[53]

The task of destruction, 'wholesale slaughter', was described as
'perfectly sickening' as was the 'stench of the killing yards and
festering masses of burning flesh'. On two adjacent runs there
were eight thousand head of infected cattle to destroy.

The beasts are burnt in a deep gully, the bottom of which is
first covered with several layers of firewood. The dead cattle

---

*Like the earlier 'Scab Act' for sheep, which was re-enacted at the same
time, it could only recognize the existing state of affairs and authorize
inspectors and destruction. Until the mid-1870s when inoculation was introduced, quarantine was the only alternative.

†McLaurin, pastoralist and flour-miller, had bought the station only twelve
months before, stocking it heavily with fat cattle, to supply the Kiandra
diggings only two days travel distant.

are then hauled on to the logs, the carcases being cut open. It takes a long time to consume a large pile; the first herd of 900 being only just disposed of. The lot of 1600 mentioned above will have taken about a fortnight to destroy. For miles around the atmosphere is tainted with the odour of the roast beef of Yarra Yarra, and we may fancy the scent three miles off would be enough to turn the stomach.[54]

A few squatters may have been ruined—those with only one station and cattle on it—but the rest adapted themselves. Some, despite the relative disadvantages, had stuck to sheep all through. Others had run both sheep and cattle on different stations or on different parts of the same station. Others, perhaps wiser, had begun the change to sheep earlier.

Sheep farming conditions in 1861, however, were vastly different from those of the forties. To begin with, the 'double market' was even more certain. A greatly increased population for the meat market, the temporary embarrassment of beef as a serious competitor, and wool prices which had risen steadily from 16½d per pound in 1850, to 24⅛d per pound in 1860, all helped.[55] The quality and weight of fleeces had been improved by culling, selling inferior-woolled sheep for the meat market and introducing imported or improved rams into the stud flocks of pastoralists like the Peppins of Wanganella. Even flocks not considered as 'studs' were founded with rams overlanded from Macarthur's Camden flocks and ewes from Canowie station near Hallett in South Australia; the ewes being shipped by river steamer from Morgan to Hay.[56]

Nor was transport a serious problem. In 1859 the Riverina press had noticed a 'Revival of the Wool Trade'. Much of the wool came from further north, from the Lachlan and the Darling. 'Never since the time before the gold discovery', said an observer, 'have we seen so many heavily laden drays winding their way to Melbourne.' The increase seemed 'incredible' and what went overland was only part.[57] The rest went by river. By 1861 there were over thirty vessels on the river with an upstream and downstream traffic of four or five thousand tons a year.[58] Even live sheep were being shipped four thousand at a time.[59] Despite the difficulties at the Murray mouth and seasonal fluctuations of the river level, the steamers came through in most years and stations on the Murray, Murrumbidgee, Lachlan, Darling and Edward Rivers had access to markets.

Throughout 1860 the contemporary Press had noted 'the evident inclination to extend the sheep runs' and 'the desire to change stations from cattle to sheep'. By early 1861 'the transformation . . . [was] becoming almost epidemical.'[60] Typifying this optimistic swing was the advertisement for the Lang's Murrumbidgee cattle station, Eli Elwah, which stated, 'the whole tract, 24 square miles, is richly grassed, abounding in herbs. Every acre is available and *would make a beautiful sheep walk*.'[61] The stocking of Queensland was a further stimulus to sheep breeding and it was suggested that the Billabong country might profitably turn to the production of store sheep for the new areas.[62]

With the decline of the beef market and the advent of pleuropneumonia, cattle began to dwindle in importance, never again to dominate the Riverina pastoral scene. Despite shearers' demands for something better than tents to sleep in and a share of the same pie as the squatter was eating, despite hired hands refusing to get wet in the wash bin, despite native dogs, scab and catarrh, footrot in the wet seasons and impaction in the dry, from 1861 on, the Riverina, for the pastoralists, became increasingly sheep country.

Amongst the few station records to survive from this early period is George Peppin Jr's diary for 1859.[63] When, in 1858, W. A. Brodribb had subdivided his Wanganella run on the Billabong Creek north of Deniliquin, part was bought by George Peppin and his sons. Included in their first year's work was the erection of homestead buildings. Apart from this, the account is typical of the pastoral year on an unfenced sheep run.

For the squatters themselves, the work of the station had changed little since the forties. The year began with the return from a month or two in Melbourne or St Kilda[64] to the 'dreadfully hot' interior with 'life a misery'. Much time was spent hunting for straying horses and bullocks, engaging and paying-off labour, and in the supervision of building improvements—workmen plastering, papering and whitewashing walls, painting doors, pointing chimneys and laying brick floors and paths. Other workers felled pines for woolshed posts and rafters, stripped eucalypt bark for the roof and laid on 'jockeys and riders'. Some were employed clearing, fencing and ploughing the eleven-acre cultivation paddock. Tanks and dams were built, bullocks killed, loading collected from Deniliquin, supplies and water carried to backblock shepherds, flocks moved, and horses, cattle and sheep branded with the new PEP brand.

On 14 February George Peppin Jr started for Yass, travelling part of the way by horse and part in a most unsquatter-like manner, on the Gundagai stage, 'a Yankee dray filled with women and squalling children'. At Yass he bought a horse from the mailman's string. During his month in the Yass district he arranged the purchase of flocks and sent and received telegrams regarding prices, offers and dates of delivery. Then back to station routine; playing at gentleman farmer in the cultivation paddock or garden; inspecting the tank-diggers and fencers; attempting to arrange the purchase of adjacent property; but more often concerned with stock—counting flocks, rounding up sheep scattered by wild dogs and hunting off travelling stock, thus:

> *April 12 & 13* Blumer came in to say half his flock were away having been rushed in the night. Fred and self started in pursuit . . . Had in the ewe flock and counted them; found twenty missing. Took out 16 bitten to kill. At least thirty lost in this smash, the worst since we have been here.
> *July 23* Word came in at night that Dean had lost his sheep. Fred and self started immediately. I rode all night and passed within a gun shot without discovery.
> *June 15* chopped across a mob of nine thousand of O'Sullivans' sheep going across the run by Boyd's fence. Sent them to the right about in double quick time.
> *August 4* shepherded a lot of store cattle through the run.

Lambing and shearing were two of the busiest and most trying periods of the year when work for all hands began well before breakfast: '*June 26* Lambs dying like mice, stayed all day helping. Home after dark.' And after long hours of sheep washing:

> *September 30* Commenced shearing with only 5 men, three of them not much account. The sheep altho' only washed a week very dirty. All flocks in from back blocks, water having failed.
> *October 17* Ten shearers on the board, too good to last.
> *18* Sheared 616 sheep, a great tally.
> *19* The five fresh shearers knocked off saying tents were not a sufficient accommodation.
> *20* Being very disgusted with the shearing I went with Fred quondonging.
> *October 24* My court case with the shearers, they were all ordered to return to their work. My name was gazetted as a magistrate.
> *November 11* Finished shearing. O be joyful. Marking up books all day.

The year ended, as it had begun, with intense heat:

December 23 108°! Fearfully hot, real Billabong weather.
Could not summon up courage to go out all day.
December 24 Still fearfully hot. I never felt such weather
before. The hottest since we have been in the colony. 108°
nearly all day.

Life on a cattle run was at times more vigorous and dramatic, yet
on the whole more leisurely and less persistently demanding; but
for all, sheep and cattle men alike, there was ample time for
gentlemanly amusements. The presence of womenfolk eventually did much to ameliorate the crudities of early homestead
life, but the major aspects of the pastoral year remained; lambing
and shearing, summer and winter, and problems of pastures and
labour.

IMPROVEMENTS ON STATION PROPERTIES

Earlier writers have attempted with little success and with
less unanimity in their findings, to pinpoint and explain the
beginnings of large-scale fencing and other capital investment by
pastoralists. Part of their difficulty has been due to the method
of investigation. The later importance of wool in the Australian
economy has led them to concentrate on the sheep industry. Like
men looking through the wrong end of a telescope, they look
back along the sheep line and see that as late as the sixties
improvements and investment on sheep stations were minimal.
They then assume that what is true for sheep stations in 1861 is
true for the pastoral industry as a whole.* Until the early sixties,
as has been shown, in the pastoral districts of New South Wales,
cattle stations predominated. To look only at sheep is therefore
to miss much of the evidence. But to look only at one region
may equally lead to error, unless the uniqueness of that region
is clearly demonstrated. The position of the Riverina pastoral
industry in relation to the fat-stock market has already been
outlined. This position as a holding and fattening area on the

---

*E.g., Brian Fitzpatrick, *The British Empire in Australia*, discussing the
consequences of the gold discoveries, states (p. 123): 'Now during the
fifties . . . the pastoral industry had made small advances . . . at the beginning of the sixties there were fewer sheep in New South Wales and Victoria,
than at the beginning of the fifties.' He attributes this to labour shortages—
'shorthanded pastoralists' boiling down and slaughtering to meet the miners'
demands for fresh meat (apparently ignoring the separation of Queensland's
three million in 1859).
Cf. also N. G. Butlin, in A. Barnard (ed.), *The Simple Fleece*, and *Investment in Australian Economic Development, 1861-1900;* see also later footnotes in this chapter.

main stock routes to Victoria led to a greater degree of capital investment than elsewhere in New South Wales. The first detailed official appraisal of improvements on New South Wales pastoral leases was made in 1871-2. Of the total value for New South Wales, half was on runs in the Murrumbidgee pastoral district and a further quarter in the Lachlan district.[65] Over 75 per cent of the total pastoral investment on leaseholds in New South Wales was thus concentrated in this south-western corner. It is in the timing and degree of capital investment then, that the Riverina is unique.

Any quantitative analysis of capital investment on pastoral properties up to 1861 is hampered by a lack of early station records or information regarding pastoral borrowing. The generalizations made here are based on details, in varying degrees of completeness, for some forty stations scattered throughout the Riverina. This, at a time when the number of pastoral properties between the Murray and Murrumbidgee as far east as the Albury-Wagga line, was something over a hundred, is as adequate a basis as is likely to be obtained. The sources, except for a few diaries and station records, consist of local newspaper items: descriptions of properties, sale notices, tenders for work to be done, and court cases. This investment took three main forms: fencing, water conservation, and homestead buildings.

It is true that equipment on *sheep* stations was at a minimum. James Tyson, the largest sheep owner in the Riverina in 1861, held three stations near Deniliquin. A recognized leader among the pastoralists—they flocked to his properties to inspect new developments—his stations represented the height of achievement for the sheep men. But apart from Tyson's tanks for watering, and the buildings, mostly erected by Ben Boyd in the forties, and Robert Dun in the fifties, the only improvement on the Lower Deniliquin run was an uncompleted fence, and this had been erected by the Tysons in 1859 as a two-rail cattle fence. On converting to sheep in 1861 five wires had been added, and when the station was advertised for sale later in the year it was said that a 'small outlay would make it completely sheep proof'. Of Tyson's other two sheep runs, Upper Deniliquin had no fences—only nine shepherds' huts and the usual yards and hurdles—while South Deniliquin could boast only four shepherds' huts on an area of over 23,000 acres. Other large sheep stations, like Widgiewa on the Colombo Creek, with 26,000 sheep, remained unfenced.[66]

On Moira station where 7,600 cattle and 10,900 sheep were kept, the sheep run was unfenced while the cattle run of over 140,000 acres was completely enclosed with fifty miles of post and rail fencing. Similarly Perricoota and Tattaila cattle stations on the Murray were enclosed and *subdivided* with post and rail. Conargo station, on the Billabong, had fifty-four miles of post and *wire* fencing, while the sixty-five-square-mile Tumudgerie cattle station on the Edward River was enclosed with post and rail. These were typical of the cattle runs on the flat country.[67]

Until the mid-fifties fencing had been largely a matter of convenience. Early station plans and records show grass paddocks fenced to conserve feed for summer, small horse paddocks to facilitate the catching of horses and working bullocks, paddocks for entire stock to restrain bulls and stallions thereby eliminating promiscuous breeding, and cultivation paddocks. On the larger rivers and creeks the most economical fence was that which cut off one of the ubiquitous loops or meanders. Large areas could thus be enclosed by the erection of a single line of fence and scores of these were completed in the forties and early fifties, some of brush, but many of post and rail.[68] When in 1858 the Peppins took over the unimproved half of Wanganella station for sheep, one of the first tasks was to engage contract labour to fence a cultivation paddock.[69] Since there were no other fences the wanderings of his unpaddocked large stock moved George Peppin Jr to write in his diary: 'Horses cows and bullocks a regular nuisance to keep never to be found altho' there is lots of green feed everywhere.'[70] His horses wandered off to the Murray, fifty miles south.

Two reliable observers visiting the Albury district in 1853 had written, 'there is much of this country enclosed . . . principally for horse paddocks . . . with post and rail fences'.[71] But by 1859 fencing the boundaries of runs was becoming a major activity in the Riverina. At different times during that year the *Pastoral Times* commented:

> The chief part of this country lying between the Murray and Murrumbidgee will soon be a mass of gigantic paddocks enclosed by strong fences to prevent the escape of store stock placed therein for fattening . . . All are more or less trying to improve the runs by fencing them in . . . The whole of the country lying between the Murray and Murrumbidgee, or at least all the cattle runs, will soon be enclosed by strong post and rail fences.[72]

By 1861 the Hon. John Hay, in advocating the quarantining of the 'pleuro' area, suggested to the New South Wales Legislative Assembly that the government could effect this by completing the line of fences between the Murray and Murrumbidgee, since there was 'now a network in that district.'*[73] Travellers like the evangelist J. J. Westwood in 1863, were frequently 'balked by fences' or 'bewildered with fences and creeks'. On one occasion he 'made Mr. Lipscombe's fence, and ran it down for fifteen miles over an open plain, hoping to have reached his station on the Murrumbidgee' without success.[74] A hundred miles north on the Lachlan, as early as 1859, D. and S. O'Sullivan, whose Lake Cargelligo station was one of the largest suppliers of store stock to the southern stations, were calling for contracts for twenty-five miles of fencing.[75]

Fencing was usually carried out by contractors.† At first the length of the advertisements contrasted with the amount of fencing sought, thus:

> Wanted at Mr. Hennessy's Balobala, River Murray, parties to contract for the erection of a two-rail fence, 3 miles in length, the said work to be completed in a substantial and workman-like manner, price to be paid for the said work 4s.6d. per rod. Also a stock yard to consist of 4 rails and the cap rail for which the price of £1.5s. per rod will be paid. The whole to be completed in a reasonable time. Good rations will be supplied at fair prices. Balobala is distant from Albury 95 miles and from Deniliquin 35 miles and is on the main road between these two places. Apply to Mr. Hennessy at the station or to Evans Bros., Albury.[76]

Usually the dimensions of the fence were given as in the following, typical of scores of such advertisements between 1857 and 1861:

*Cf. N. G. Butlin, in *The Simple Fleece*, p. 330: 'Fencing had not been carried very far by 1870, at least outside the Western District of Victoria', and pp. 328-9: 'this was the position in 1870 . . . even in the more developed areas of New South Wales there was little fencing beyond that around small stockyards.' Identical statements occur in Butlin's *Investment in Australian Economic Development 1861-1900*, pp. 72-3.

†Cf. N. G. Butlin, in *The Simple Fleece*, p. 336: 'Almost total reliance on station resources [to improve assets] was the rule during the forties and fifties, and most stations continued to rely heavily on their own resources until well into the sixties.' This is certainly not true of the Riverina, as the following pages indicate. One of Butlin's main sources, Alfred Joyce, *A Homestead History* suffers from the severe disadvantage that the station named lay a mere seventy miles out, between Melbourne and the gold diggings, and can therefore in no way be taken as typical of New South Wales stations, or even of further-out Victorian runs.

TENDERS WANTED   31.1.57
Two rail fence, 21 miles in length, Wannock station, lower
Murray. Posts to be put 2 feet in the ground and 5 feet out
and to be 3 inches through the mortice holes; rail 7–9 inches
width and all met rails to be thrown out. Rations (if necessary) at Albury prices. Tenderers may undertake 3, 7 or 10
miles as may suit.

                                        C. H. Barber[77]

By 1859 the confidence of both squatters and contractors in the
latter's ability to carry out the task had grown and prices and
specifications as indicated above were so well known that adver-
tisers needed to state no more than the following:*

FENCERS
About 40 miles, 2 rail fence, strong pine rails and posts, plenty
of timber all along the lines desired to be fenced.

                                        Tyson Bros.[78]

When agreement had been reached, a written contract was
signed under the conditions of the Masters and Servants Act, an
Act consequently invoked in local courts when contractors
skimped work or left it uncompleted. Conversely, contractors
took squatters to court if there was no timber close to the line
of fence and in such cases the pastoralist called for further tenders for 'drawing and laying on the line' whatever timber was
available.[79] In the Riverina this was either the hardwood eucalypts,
box or River red gum, or the more easily worked—but equally
resistant to disease and termites—native Cypress pine.

Some degree of skill was required for post and rail fencing,
and 'splitters' and 'fencers' were usually accorded separate titles.[80]
Near Albury, farmers in off-seasons would contract to fence,
taking posts for their own blocks rather than cash payment.[81]
Generally in the western Riverina fences were longer, and
urgency required large numbers of workers efficient in the use of
maul and wedges, saw and axe, for splitting the tree trunks into
slabs, shaping the ends of rails, and mortising holes in the posts.
The Moulamein correspondent of the *Pastoral Times* wrote in
1859: 'The Chah Sing Station is giving employment to a greater

---

*Cf. N. G. Butlin, in *The Simple Fleece*, p. 337: 'the employment of non-
station contract labour organized as teams of unskilled labourers working
for contractors was common in Victoria in the sixties and spread to New
South Wales with the large-scale fencing programme of the seventies.' The
only reference given is 'In Victoria, the erection of wire fencing is a business
by itself and is contracted for by the mile', Australian Agricultural Co.
Papers, Merewether Despatch no. 87, 21 June 1867.

number of hands, and all who own drays and bullocks are fully engaged for some time in consequence of the proprietor fencing in the whole of his run',[82] and later in the year: 'the majority of cattle runs lying between the Murrumbidgee and Murray are about to be fenced . . . giving employment to hundreds of splitters and fencers.'[83]

One attempt was made to use steam power for fencing. Francis Cadell, the river steamer captain and entrepreneur, contracted to erect the thirteen-mile post and rail boundary fence between Moira and Mathoura stations with *sawn* timber. The finished product with its 6 inch × 3 inch posts, and 6 inch × 2 inch rails of 'sound red gum' was, by contrast with split timber fencing, remarkably uniform, 'without doubt the finest fence in Australia'. Even the mortise holes in the posts were cut by the steam engine. But though the contract was 'fulfilled—honestly fulfilled', it cost Cadell more than £100 per mile, and this was high compared with £72 per mile for fencing by manual labour. 'It was not that steam did not do its work in its usual style for the engine worked beautifully; but the expense of conveying the sawn slabs and posts was too great . . . bullock drays and waggons . . . swallowed up all the profits.'[84] Although it was suggested that a portable steam engine would overcome this, Cadell's prospect of 'fencing by steam' faded, and itinerant manual labour continued as the mainstay of fencing operations.

Post and rail fences were the most common, but some wire fencing had begun by 1861. In its column 'The Melbourne Labour Market', the *Albury Banner,* 24 August 1861, quoted 'fencers, 3-rails, 2s. to 2s.6d. per rod; wire fences, with rails, 1s.6d. to 2s. per rod'. As early as 1857 an 'experiment in fencing a cattle run' was attempted on the upper Lachlan 'using iron wire instead of wooden rails, the wire to be suspended to round wooden posts by means of iron staples.'[85] By early 1860 Melbourne firms were advertising wire in the Deniliquin newspapers,[86] and in July of that year, when the first river steamer navigated the Edward River to Deniliquin, its barge was left at Moulamein with 'several tons of fencing wire for Messrs. Ashcroft'.[87] By 1861 storekeepers at Albury and Jerilderie had wire for sale by the ton[88] and the forerunners of the change from cattle to sheep had converted post and rail to wire fencing,* and even begun to leave off the rails.†

*E.g., Lang's Eli Elwah, '24 miles post and rail and wire', Tyson's Lower Deniliquin, 92,560 acres 'nearly all fenced with 2 rail and 5 wire'.
†R. Dun's Conargo, 'whole station recently enclosed by very substantial post and wire fence 54 miles in length'.

As late as 1861, as has been shown, sheep equipment, including fencing, was slight, and though there were more hands employed on sheep stations than on cattle stations of the same area, shepherds had little time to spare for fencing. The simplest answer to the labour shortage of the early gold rush years had not been to fence, but to increase the number of sheep per shepherd. By 1859-60 individual shepherds were required to graze and fold flocks of 3,000-4,000. The sheep suffered little in good hands. It was said of one flock of 4,000 that 'they did great credit to the shepherd who had them in charge.'[89]

Any attempt to do more than shepherd with flocks of this size led to trouble. In 1858, as noted, W. A. Brodribb had subdivided his Wanganella run, taking the northern section and two back-blocks for himself and selling the remainder to G. Peppin and sons. Two years later, George Tingcombe, Brodribb's superintendent, charged John Harris, a shepherd, with having frequently lost sheep by allowing them to stray, and with having recently lost seventy sheep which had not since been recovered. The evidence showed that Harris had been given '3,478 sheep to shepherd and watch' and his young son '123 footrot sheep'. 'The yards were not good and some of the sheep, as they were wild, might jump over . . . The fence was broken down in three places and sheep could easily walk over it. The fence was made of brush.' Harris's plea was that while he mended the yard the sheep strayed—another shepherd saw six or seven hundred of them four and a half miles away—and he had no one to send to report. While his son was helping him the lame sheep also strayed, got on to Peppin's run and were taken by one of Peppin's shepherds. The shepherd's defence was ignored by the squatter magistrate, the agreement cancelled and all wages forfeited.[90] The case clearly underlines both the lack of sheep fencing at the time and good reasons for fencing as the land became more closely settled. Pastoralists may also to some extent have been influenced by reports from other areas that undisturbed sheep grew fatter and produced heavier fleeces, though exaggerated claims were questioned even by newspaper editors.[91] Whatever the reasons for fencing sheep—and a desire to utilize post and rail fences originally erected for cattle should not be overlooked —the reasons for cattle fencing were plain enough. The beef-growers fenced to keep their own cattle in and other people's out.

In the early fifties it had been the custom to hold half-yearly musters.[92] Cattle and horses being notorious wanderers, settlers

were obliged to attend every muster in their vicinity and it was
therefore usual to give neighbours a few days' notice. Later it
became common practice to advertise in local newspapers a
fortnight beforehand.[93] Unclaimed cattle, whether branded or
not, were sent to the nearest pound. But as the volume of travelling stock increased and the numbers held on Riverina runs grew,
trespass problems multiplied. Some of these would have arisen
in any case as the country was more fully stocked and became
more closely settled. Boundaries at first had been roughly defined
—a line of blazed trees or a single furrow plough mark—and in
the flat country this led to difficulties. 'Back Blocks'—those behind
the frontage runs—were so vaguely marked that when, later,
surveyors sought to fit in different claimants' A, B, C and D
blocks by working back from two parallel rivers or creeks, some
blocks simply disappeared. Nor were boundary disputes particularly neighbourly. Phillips and Graves lost £1,000 over one
trespass suit.[94] In another case, a fellow squatter seized and
impounded 1,645 sheep of Hon. John Hay's for trespass at a
waterhole, though no previous occupant had claimed this particular ground. At the standard rate of 1½d per sheep per mile for
the droving of trespassing sheep to the pound, Hay had to pay
costs of £205 12s 6d.[95]

The whole position was aggravated by the vast numbers of
travelling stock and the understandable attitude of the drovers.
Thus Paterson wrote:

> Now this is the law of the Overland that all in the West
>   obey—
> A man must cover with travelling sheep a six-mile stage a
>   day;
> But this is the law which the drovers make, right easily
>   understood,
> They travel their stage where the grass is bad, but they camp
>   where the grass is good;
> They camp, and they ravage the squatter's grass till never a
>   blade remains,
> Then they drift away as the white clouds drift on the edge of
>   the saltbush plains. . .[96]

Part of the difficulty lay in the inadequacy of half-mile-wide
stock routes established by law before the growth of the goldfields markets. Nor did it help when runs were fenced off right to
the river frontages leaving only a single gate at each end of the
run, a mile or two back from the water.[97] The *Pastoral Times* was

'besieged with letters respecting the difficulties experienced by drovers of cattle on the roads, caused by them being hunted off some stations'. Drovers were harried and 'dogged', while cattle risked impounding 'if a yard over the quarter mile on each side of the road'. Some herds suffered in consequence. One drover complained that he had been charged 12d a head for a mob of 320 trespassing. He paid with 'a fat cow and orders for £16, which would have bought a supply of hay for the mob.'[98] Of one herd of fifteen hundred from the Clarence, only five hundred reached the Murrumbidgee and difficulties were intensified as stock converged in Victoria.[99]

Reserves near the towns became overcrowded. At Deniliquin the 'pound herd'* consumed most of the feed on the north side reserve, while the 'town herd' ran south of the river. This left a limited amount of feed for travellers. Along the river frontages it was worse—first the overlanders, then the squatters, now the drovers. On lesser rivers and creeks some runs straddled the watercourses. Along the Murray few homesteads had been built right on the river, most were back on some large deep lagoon, where cattle could thrive in quietness.[1] But without fences no ground was safe. Even when the route was 'well known to all drovers from Melbourne to Carpentaria', there were plenty who would leave it in search of feed. In true *Such is Life*[2] style two drovers, charged with being illegally on the Warbreccan run, had camped for five nights with their cattle in the middle of the station. Some of their stock had wandered and mixed with the station herds.[3] A. B. Paterson paints a similar picture of the drovers in 'Saltbush Bill':

> From camp to camp and from run to run they battle it hand
>   to hand
> For a blade of grass and the right to pass on the track of the
>   Overland.
> For this is the law of the Great Stock Routes, 'tis written in
>   white and black—
> The man that goes with a travelling mob must keep to a half-
>   mile track;
> And the drovers keep to a half-mile track on the runs where
>   the grass is dead,
> But they spread their sheep on a well-grassed run till they go
>   with a two-mile spread.

*Poundkeepers often found it lucrative to run stock of their own on the reserve with the impounded strays, a 'privilege' to which some townsmen objected.

So the squatters hurry the drovers on from dawn till the fall
   of night.
And the squatters' dogs and the drovers' dogs get mixed in a
   deadly fight.

Later in the same poem, by a subtle manoeuvre the drover's
purpose is accomplished:

But the travelling sheep and the Wilga sheep were boxed on
   the Old Man Plain;
'Twas a full week's work ere they drafted out and hunted
   them off again;
A week's good grass in their wretched hides, with a curse and
   a stockwhip crack
They hunted them off on the road once more to starve on the
   half-mile track.[4]

So frequent and expensive were impounding and trespass claims
in 1860 that the bench of magistrates at Moulamein substituted a
special cheap droving rate for the original 1½d per head per
mile.[5] The trouble was far less in the Albury-Wagga district
where less than one-sixth of the total volume of stock crossed.
This smaller traffic and the more obvious and effective natural
boundaries had resulted in most stations in the hilly country
remaining unfenced.

Export of Livestock Overland (to Victoria)

	1859		1860		1861	
	Cattle (*'000*)	*Sheep* (*'000*)	*Cattle* (*'000*)	*Sheep* (*'000*)	*Cattle* (*'000*)	*Sheep* (*'000*)
via Albury	11.9	17.9	11.5	28.4	6.2	18.3
via Swan Hill, etc.	15.5	100.9	15.3	35.9	17.9	29.9
via Moama	88.8	247.4	70.6	249.4	80.9	160.6
via other places			14.4			

Source: *N.S.W. Statistical Register.*

The other major reason for fencing further west hinged on the
nature of the industry—'not losing their lean stock when they are
first turned adrift' and 'insuring large supplies of fat cattle at
short notice',[6] both of these leading quickly from boundary
fencing to subdivision into a system of paddocks. For a smaller
number of pastoralists, fencing had become essential when they
imported expensive stock for breeding. The Peppins had paid
high prices for the Napoleon and Negretti rams,[7] others had

imported Leicesters,[8] while cattlemen not only 'culled and bred with the greatest care' but imported Durham, Hereford and Ayrshire stock including Paris Exhibition prizewinners.

There were some activities to which fencing made little difference. Notwithstanding the efforts of 'The Society for the Suppression of Cattle Stealing' (Albury and Deniliquin branches),[9] George Hillas of Burroogo was moved to offer £20 reward, 'some evil disposed person or persons having taken down a portion of the dividing fence between [his] run and Mr. Hennessy's, for the purpose of removing cattle without [his] knowledge.'[10] Other pastoralists offered rewards of up to £300 in similar cases. Generally, however, fencing had the desired effect. So much so, that by December 1859 it was observed that the hedging-in of stock routes was prejudicing drivers against the Deniliquin route and that many mobs were being driven via Swan Hill or Albury where there was more chance to deviate.[11]

By 1861 one further advantage of fencing had been added. As the margin between store and fat stock dwindled, the greatest economy had to be observed. So useful was fencing proving in this regard that the *Pastoral Times* noticed that it was 'being tried on sheep stations . . . good secure post and rail fences are being made and sheep will be permitted to run unshepherded. There seems to be an opinion prevailing here, that the runs will carry more sheep, but whether or not the sheep will be safe from the native dog has yet to be tested.'[12] A further measure of economy, which also reflects the abundance of labour by 1861 was the proposal to cut shepherds' wages.

So far then from the truth lie the traditional tales that sheep runs were fenced during the gold rushes because of the shortage of labour. As Butlin has put it, after questioning Coghlan's acceptance of an earlier stock inspector's report on the virtues of fencing, 'it is doubtful if labour shortages in the 1850s played much part at all' but rather that 'station equipment was produced, in the early phases wherever labour was available.'[13]

The second major form of investment was water conservation. On frontage runs on the main streams there was little difficulty with water except in time of flood or in very dry seasons when even the Murray and Murrumbidgee could be crossed dryshod on stepping stones.[14] But frontage runs on the lesser intermittent streams posed problems for which pastoralists adopted various remedies, some co-operative, some individualistic and mutually exclusive.

The course of the Yanko Creek meandered from the Murrumbidgee to the Billabong and was filled only when the Murrumbidgee overflowed its banks. To ensure permanent water, in 1855, partly at Cadell's instigation, neighbouring squatters had assessed themselves at £29 per mile, and one hundred workmen removed 42,000 cubic yards of earth at a cost of over £5,000 from the Yanko offtake and 'the Yanko canal'. On 2 October 1856 just as the dry weather was setting in, local residents gathered, the barrier was removed, 'Mrs. Howell christened the stream "the Yanko River", and the water slowly descended the new artificial stream at the rate of three miles per hour.' But because of 'inaccuracy in the levels' water did not reach the Billabong that year, nor, despite £7,000 spent on attempts to pump, had it succeeded by 1861. Five years later, work was still proceeding.[15]

Less co-operation occurred on the Billabong itself. In December 1860, officers Breen and Fagan of the Deniliquin Constabulary had the inexpressible delight of 'bagging three squatters in one day'. Messrs Peter McGregor and Edward and James Ashcroft, three lower-Billabong squatters whose stock were perishing for thirst, had called on W. A. Brodribb and informed him that they were going to cut his dam across the Billabong. Brodribb 'received them with a great deal of urbanity' and told them to go ahead 'if they thought themselves legally justified'. They did so, most carefully. Shortly afterwards they found themselves immured in the Deniliquin lock-up, charged with wilful and malicious destruction of property. This and the counter charge of false imprisonment was, the *Pastoral Times* noted, 'only one out of several actions pending or about to be brought in regard to this unpleasant Dam business.'[16]

Dam-cutting as an act of reprisal had begun in 1858. Earlier, G. Desailly of Coree station had built a solid dam across the Billabong. As the flow stopped and waterholes dried up downstream, angry squatters marched upstream in a band and cut the dam. Water flowed for about ten hours, then Desailly stopped it with sandbags. Later he 'erected a log house on the summit of the dam with loopholes for musketry, with the avowed intention of shooting anyone who might attempt to open the dam', and as a petition claimed, 'the same party now openly threatens to shoot the first man who touches his dam'. His more legal action, to have Dun and Ricketson charged with wilful destruction, failed.[17]

Clearly, these were no real solutions. There were more than twenty runs on the 145 miles of the Billabong and if all were to have a share of water some kind of compromise was necessary. The first step was a petition to the Governor, setting out the position and asking for a meeting before the summer of 1859.[18] The petition of 'settlers . . . dealers in stock, and residents', showed that they had 'Invested large sums of money in stocking, fencing and improving their stations on the creek and that they [were] entirely dependent on the said Billabong creek for a supply of water without which their stations [were] perfectly useless', that the erection of large and numerous dams had stopped the flow of water for two years, and that on cutting one of these, 'although the water was lowered about three feet only, it ran indirectly a distance of sixty miles, supplying five stations with water sufficient for twelve months, three of which stations, but for such a supply, must have been abandoned.' After pointing out the disruption of the stock traffic occasioned by this drying up of established water resources, the petitioners concluded reasonably:

> That your petitioners, while believing that it is illegal, by the laws of England and of all other civilized nations, for any man to divert or entirely interrupt the waters of a running river to the injury of his neighbours, still admit that, in the peculiar condition of the Billabong River,* dams under certain arrangements are necessary and advisable, but they submit that those arrangements must be fair and equitable to all parties interested.

The alternative was:

> either that they must look on and see their property sacrificed and themselves ruined, or they must run the risk of asserting the right to a share of the water of the Billabong by removing and destroying the dams, which they are most reluctant and unwilling to do, believing that their property ought to be protected by the laws of their country.

The appeal to law and order resulted in a meeting of settlers with the Hon. John Hay, at which, despite lengthy and detailed discussions on dam heights, sluices, resident inspectors, flood gates and the relative permeability of different types of soil, nothing

---

*'That the Billabong only runs at a certain period of the year, in early summer, during the melting of the snow on the mountains among which the creek takes its rise, and that throughout the rest of the year it consists only of a chain of waterholes in the lowest part of its channel.' (Petition, *P.T.*, 26 April 1859.)

was settled. Each man had his own ideas. Further meetings were equally indecisive and it was left to Hay to work with the Legislature,[19] but when the heavy rains of March 1860 swept away every dam on the Billabong except Desailly's monster with its attendant fortress, the matter was shelved.[20] In 1866, after two years of drought, dam-cutting began again. Again it was George Desailly who was the chief target, this time on the Lachlan. Again men marched along the watercourses and again pistols were flourished:

> At the dam we soon arrived
> And went at it with a will.
> Our opponents they all stood there
> With firearms, but still
> They were not game to use them
> For they would have come off ill,
> For with the dam they'd have been swept away.

Finally the deed was done, and on the banks of the Lachlan at Booligal, stimulated by the flickering flames of a roaring fire and the contents of several bottles, the dam-cutters shouted their impromptu chorus:

> So now my dear Desailly
> You've put up your dam in vain.
> If you put up another
> Why we'll have to come again,
> Though you may defend it
> With all your might and main
> We will sweep you with your dam clear away.[21]

The most important aspect of water conservation in the Riverina at this period was the attempt to make the backblocks permanently usable. The original frontage runs taken up by 1850 extended no more than five or ten miles back from permanent water. This left enormous areas untouched, particularly between the Murrumbidgee and the Billabong. Gradually as stock numbers increased much of this was taken up as 'winter runs'. The constant rain and dew of winter meant damp pastures for stock, and casks of water could be carted to shepherds with their rations.[22] In the dry summer months sheep were returned to the frontages or sent to the mountainous 'summer runs' in the east.[23] With their usefulness limited to the winter months, backblocks were usually regarded as of little value and could change hands, as drought-stricken frontage runs had earlier, for as little as 'one pound of tobacco and two gallons of rum'.[24] As the *Sydney Morning Herald* observed on the opening of the Yanko Canal in 1856, 'this back country (or back blocks . . .) is now thoroughly waste, and can only be made practically useful by works like the Yanko cutting.'[25]

With the growth of the fat-stock market and overland traffic to Victoria, the fencing in of frontage runs and the progressive decline of over-grazed frontage pastures, covetous eyes were cast at the virgin saltbush and grassland lying virtually untouched in the backblocks. Water was the problem. The failure of the Yanko cutting and the strife with the Billabong dams were well known. Three solutions offered: expensive pumping machines could be purchased, wells could be dug—if satisfactory water was to be found—or dams and tanks could be excavated. By 1861 the Melbourne Pump Warehouse, B. H. Dods & Co., could list ten well-known Riverina squatters as referees for the effectiveness of their appliances. Pumping apparatus was worked by horse, steam or manual power and was installed at both natural and man-made water sources.[26]

Wells were occasionally dug by local labour[27] but the most successful contractor was John Benger of Emerald Hill, Melbourne. A man with a lifetime of experience in England and Ireland, where he had sunk wells up to 550 feet deep, Benger was widely employed in the Riverina. Because of his high charges —30s per day for himself, 14s per day for each of two men and 12s per day for another, all travelling expenses and carriage of all tools to place of work and back to Melbourne[28]—squatters sometimes combined to obtain his services. One well was sunk at the point of intersection of four runs, the four squatters sharing the expenses and the water without fear of trespassing.[29] Wells 140-200 feet deep were lined with zinc, brick or a combination of brick and timber, the water being raised by horse or bullock whim and emptied into long troughs.[30] With water being found up to eighteen miles back from the Billabong,[31] well-sinking became general and in September 1860 a 'powerful looking steam engine passed through Deniliquin for well sinking on Desailly's backblocks.'[32]

Other squatters attempted to utilize natural rainfall and run-off on a large scale. Late in 1859 James Tyson called for tenders for the excavation and removal of earth 200 feet long, 60 feet wide and 15 feet deep. The work, completed in four months, cost £1,400. A mile or so of 'races' twelve feet wide and six or seven

RXTSA 06/14/72

INV.NO. 681212809
67-030092
L.C.NO.

MELBOURNE MELBOURNE U P LONDON NEW YORK
CAMBRIDGE U P

THE RIVERINA, 1861-1891: AN AUSTRALIAN REGIONAL STUDY BY G. L. BUXTON.
BUXTON, GORDON LESLIE.
MELBOURNE MELBOURNE U. P.; LONDON; NEW YORK; CAMBRIDGE U. P. 1967, 1968.
XI, 338 P. 12 PLATES, ILLUS., MAPS, POR.

BOOK NO.

COPY 3

10.16
N

A = Richard Abel & Co., Nederland N.V., Van Hallstraat 167, Amsterdam, The Netherlands

B = 47 Athletic Field Rd., Waltham, Mass. 02154

C = 1312 27th Street, Zion, Illinois 60099

D = P. O. Box 10007, Denver, Colorado 80210

E = Richard Abel & Co. (England) Ltd., 6A Mill Trade Estate, Acton Lane, London N.W. 10, England

F = Richard Abel & Co., AG, Fischerweg 9, 3002 Berne, Switzerland

H = P. O. Box 241, Marion, Ohio 43302

J = P. O. Box 15469, Atlanta, Georgia 30333

K = Richard Abel & Co., Pty, Ltd. 1/33 Warraba Road, Narrabeen North, N.S.W. 2101 Australia

L = 1506 Gardena St., Glendale, California 91204

N = 1001 Fries Mill Rd., Blackwood, New Jersey 08012

P = P. O. Box 4245, Portland, Oregon 97208

S = Industrial Center Bldg., Gate 5 Road Marinship, Sausalito, California 94965

T = Richard Abel & Co. (Canada) Ltd., 128 Industrial Rd., Richmond Hill, Ontario, Canada

X = 3434 Dalworth St., Arlington, Texas 76010

feet deep had been cut leading to the tank, including one from a large swamp; and the sides of the tank, sloped to specification, had been slabbed to prevent them falling in.[33] So successful was the tank in watering 20,000 sheep that the following year a larger one, 240 feet × 200 feet was dug at the back of the run. Even with the first, the grazing capacity of the run had increased from less than 5,000 sheep to 20,000, making the backblock more valuable than the frontage.[34] Other pastoralists who flocked to see the completed work were quick to imitate and obtain the same results.[35]

Within a short time bidding at auction for waterless back-blocks had slowed considerably while those with watering facilities were bringing up to £800 without stock. At the same time the number of applications for new backblocks leases increased and the movement, swelled by Melbourne speculators, extended to the Lachlan and Darling country.[36] The *Pastoral Times* of 14 September 1860, pointing out that in the past they had been 'sold for an old song' and only two years before were considered as of no use, described the backblocks as 'pastoral gems' especially as 'for many years the "busy hum of men" cannot be expected to reach these secluded spots.'[37] A note of caution, however, was sounded by the *Sydney Morning Herald* on 5 August 1862:

> Everyone appears to think that many of the backblocks taken by tender will again be thrown open and only the pick of the blocks retained and an effort made to render them profitable, and even this will be more or less as an experiment than as a settled undertaking, as the proper working of the backblocks is as yet a thing to be learnt.

Nevertheless, even where well water was brackish, where tank-sinkers struck 'that confounded sand',[38] where flash floods along the incipient drainage lines destroyed dams and where wild dogs tore and harried the ewes,[39] the Murray and Murrumbidgee back-blocks were stocked. Much of the relatively enormous capital investment in the pastoral industry in the seventies and eighties as outlined by N. G. Butler[40] was the result of extending these established fencing and watering techniques to the backblocks of the Lachlan and Darling country.

The third form of investment on pastoral properties involved homestead structures. To generalize about the types of buildings and equipment on Riverina stations is difficult, but there were few homesteads remaining in the primitive bark hut stage by the late fifties. The nature and extent of improvements other than fencing and water conservation varied from station to station and depended on such factors as the interests, attitude and place of residence of the lessee—Sydney, Melbourne or the station itself, whether or not he was married, the number of previous owners and their interests and marital status, and whether the run was or had been used for cattle or sheep. Some indication of the whole range of improvements on Riverina stations in the late fifties can be gained from the following composite table:*

BUILDINGS:
1 Main living quarters—'gentleman's residence' and/or 'overseer's quarters'
2 Outbuildings
   (a) Related to accommodation:
   Kitchens, cellars, men's huts, laundry, shearers' huts, store (food and clothing)
   (b) Connected with the working of the station:
   Woolshed (sometimes with loft), wool store, blacksmith's shop, carpenter's shop, stable, cart shed, harness room, coach house, hayshed, milking yards or sheds, pigsty

OTHER IMPROVEMENTS:
Horse and cultivation paddocks, spaying, weaning and tailing paddocks; boiling-down paddock
Stockyards and hurdles
Gardens, orchards, vineyards

WORKING STOCK AND EQUIPMENT:
Team/s of working bullocks, saddle and draught horses, carts and drays
Sheep dip† or washing plant
Wool press

On some twenty stations for which such information is available little in the nature of a pattern is discernible. Homesteads, some of which are still occupied a century later, varied from slab or weatherboard to brick or stone with roofs of shingles or slate.

*As a result of his great leap from 1850 to 1890, N. G. Butlin, in *The Simple Fleece*, p. 324, and *Investment in Australian Economic Development*, p. 59, gives similar lists as typical of an established station in 1890. In the Riverina this degree of investment had been reached thirty years earlier.

†Dods & Co. of Melbourne, in addition to advertising well and pumping machinery, listed '1st class steam sheep dips, 2nd class revolving, 3rd class common'; *P.T.*, 6 September 1861. Station records simply state 'dip'.

A timber homestead sometimes stood beside a stone store or an enormous woolshed roofed with galvanized iron. Similar variations occur in Lachlan and Darling stations. The following sample inventories of two Riverina stations give some idea of the possibilities.

The unfenced Deniliquin run of 106,000 acres had seen a series of owners from Ben Boyd to James Tyson. Improvements, apart from the two large tanks already mentioned and nine shepherds' huts, most of which had smaller tanks nearby, consisted of an eight-roomed brick residence with a large cellar, detached kitchen with two bedrooms, large two-storeyed store 56 feet × 33 feet (all these of brick and slated), blacksmith's shop and residence (brick), large woolshed with first rate screw press, shearers' hut with four rooms, large hayshed and stable and two large grass and hay paddocks, all of which, 'with other improvements too numerous to mention' stood on 1,662 purchased acres.[41]

Moira station had remained in the hands of H. S. Lewes since his arrival in the early forties. In addition to fifty miles of post and rail fencing, a weaning paddock of five thousand acres, three cultivation paddocks, two other grass paddocks of ten acres and five hundred acres and a one-hundred-acre horse paddock, the homestead improvements consisted of:

> [an] excellent weatherboard and shingled cottage, lined and papered and nearly new, detached kitchen with pantry and servants' rooms, overseer's cottage and kitchen, three stores, one double and two single huts for men (two of stone), large stockyard, garden, orchard, stable and cart shed, large woolshed with loft above, and a weatherboard woolstore—five of these buildings roofed with iron.

The homestead and outbuildings, as well as an eight-roomed 'house of accommodation', a detached stone kitchen and three rooms, and a stable with twenty-four stalls, stood on 759 acres of purchased ground.[42]

In some cases the possibility of purchasing land under the pre-emptive right provisions of the 1847 Orders-in-Council had encouraged squatters to increase improvements and structures to form these village-like agglomerations. But homesteads, like dams, tanks and fences were more often erected on leased land, with only the Orders-in-Council and a 'promise of lease' to protect them.* Until 1861 this was evidently adequate. Stations were

*Section 15 of the Orders-in-Council provided that upon the expiration

bought, sold and changed hands, at times with bewildering rapidity. From time to time the squatters' catchcry of 'insecurity of tenure' was heard, as when radically minded surveyors chopped reserves out of the runs, often in response to local clamour. A few isolated instances of this had been enough to send some squatters to the more remote and therefore safer regions of the Upper Darling and Queensland. But it was the implied threat of free selection before survey which stirred the uneasy rest of the squatters most deeply.

The gold decade was thus an important formative period in Riverina pastoral history. The gold discoveries had occurred soon after the initial occupation of the last of the river frontages, bringing temporary depopulation and disruption of transport. There followed the rise of a casual labour force and an alternative transport system based on river steamers. The same few years saw the rise and fall of the fat-stock market. Post and rail fencing, begun to keep cattle in check and control the vast numbers of travelling stock, was rapidly extended to exploit the fattening qualities of the saltbush plains. Backblocks, previously only good for winter pasture, were fenced, subdivided and provided with watering facilities, the same techniques being applied to older frontage runs once their profitability was demonstrated. The gold discoveries which had led to mass migration and a vastly profitable meat market provided not only the capital but also the labour to carry out this pioneer pastoral investment. At the same time Riverina ties with Melbourne were strengthened.

The profitability of the meat market prolonged the emphasis on cattle, but with its decline and the advent of pleuro-pneumonia the double security of sheep for meat and wool asserted itself. Rising wool prices reinforced this trend. Subdivision was continued, watering facilities extended and post and rail fencing supplemented with wire. By 1861 the techniques for mastering the environment were established in the Riverina. By the end of the following decade, half the total New South Wales investment in pastoral leases was allocated to this corner of the colony. What followed in the seventies and eighties was merely an extension of these techniques to new areas. The drought of 1864-6 saw a temporary return to cattle* but thereafter sheep

---

of a lease, should the lease change hands or the land be sold, the amount of the improvements should be added to the upset price, and be paid over to the previous lessee.

*See Figure 1.

numbers rose continually, while cattle numbers remained relatively stable. Between 1861 and 1891, sheep numbers in the Riverina climbed from less than one million to over thirteen million, partly as a result of a changing pattern of land ownership, but largely in response to the extension of the investment techniques already listed.

In the Riverina in 1861 the initial phase in the struggle between European man and his new alien environment was ending. Yet to come, was the struggle between man and man for ownership of the land.

2

THE GROWTH AND FUNCTIONS OF TOWNS

CROSSING-PLACES

Town Growth to 1861

I have not met with any spot so central or so desirable as a site for a Town as the place in question for the capital of the Murrumbidgee district, it being at the best crossing place on the Edward River, a few miles above the spot where the Wakool bursts from the Edward, and having the advantage of high banks on both sides . . . The ground in the neighbourhood is generally a good sandy loam with a little alluvial deposit on the River banks.

Surveyor Townsend's report on the site of Deniliquin, 1848[1]

Just as early pastoral settlement of the Riverina had clung to the water frontages, so most towns began at crossing-places marked by explorers, overlanders, or settlers moving stock to new areas. A punt, store, grog shanty or inn, and blacksmith's shop followed. The need for protection of life and property against Aborigines and bushrangers led to the New South Wales government's somewhat reluctant erection of police posts and lock-ups.* With the establishment of mail services, village settlements already in existence acquired a further function. For continued progress, government action in the form of survey and land alienation was necessary. Then, as storekeepers, publicans and tradesmen purchased blocks and settled, court-houses, churches, coach services and racecourses appeared. Thereafter, growth depended on the volume and nature of traffic and the settlement of the town's economic hinterland, the latter tied closely to the fertility and rainfall of the area. As their census populations indicate,† Riverina towns reached these various stages of urban develop-

*One squatter complained that his station buildings had been burnt, his cattle dispersed, his stores destroyed and one of his men killed by blacks. The official answer was 'that as he had voluntarily chosen to settle beyond the boundaries of the police he must take the consequences'; see A. Andrews, *First Settlement of the Upper Murray*, p. 74.

†1851: Albury 442, Wagga 170; 1856: Albury 645, Wagga 336, Denili-

ment at different dates, while variations in environment, distance from larger settlements, traffic flow and population movements made for further differentiation.

All Riverina towns of the period began by straddling the watercourses. Then, for a variety of reasons, the south or north side assumed predominance. In some, as with Wagga, it was topography, the more easily inundated north side being less popular.[2] In the twin towns along the Murray the arbitrary drawing of a colonial boundary influenced the amount of revenue spent in a town; of all the towns in the Riverina, Moama alone favoured the border customs duties, hoping thereby to gain a government official and a government building.[3] Often the dominance of north or south in urban morphology was the result of chance, the energy of a founding father, or no more than a suveyor's prophetic view of the future.

Albury, although unique in its earlier beginning and position on the Melbourne-Sydney road, had up to 1851 developed along lines common to all Riverina towns of the pre-railway era.[4] By 1836 when pastoral runs had already been taken up around the original Hume and Hovell crossing-place on the Murray, Robert Brown was establishing Albury's first store and accommodation house—a slab hut with a tea chest of horse-feed nailed to a stump outside the door—and a hollowed-log punt service.[5] Two years later following the opening of the overland mail service to Port Phillip, news of a massacre by Aborigines just south of the Murray crossing reached Sydney. A party of police and military were accordingly despatched to 'establish posts at convenient distances along the road from Yass to Port Phillip, in order to keep open communication.' Camps were formed at river crossings —including Albury—and travellers accepted the security these represented.[6] By early 1839 Albury consisted of 'two inhabited dwellings and a smaller unfinished one'. The police station, which had taken seventeen days to knock up, was of split boards of stringybark, its roof covered with sheets of bark, the windows unglazed.[7] In October of the same year, following Townsend's survey, the first Albury land sales were held—in Sydney—by which time the town consisted of six or seven huts and two public houses.[8]

By 1845, 'its position had made the district known to all travellers between the two capitals and a large majority of the sheep

quin 155; 1861: Albury 981 (Municipality 1587), Wagga 627, Deniliquin 632, Hay 172, Moama 144, Moulamein 72.

and cattle with which Victoria was stocked had passed along its unmade but well marked roads. Its character for fertility was well established.'* Besides two hotels, Albury boasted two stores, a tailor, shoemaker, blacksmith, 'builder and undertaker', brickmaker and a mailman, while Richard Heaver was building the first steam flour-mill. Permanent residents numbered over fifty, with a considerable floating population about the crossings, including a number of fencers engaged in erecting 3-rail fences around cultivation and horse paddocks. Although there was as yet no place of religious worship, the annual Albury races had been established for five years, the Reverend J. D. Lang noting indignantly, 'Yearly at this fixture great excesses occurred, the hotel-keeper (Brown) having, even on the Sabbath, to serve out rum in buckets to those assembled at the racecourse close to his house.'[9] By 1846 (a New South Wales census year) the population had reached sixty-five and the following year a Court of Petty Sessions was gazetted for Albury; John Roper, recently returned wounded from Leichhardt's Northern Territory expedition, being appointed Clerk of Petty Sessions.[10] At the time of the 1851 census, Albury's population had grown to 442, with some eighty children enrolled at the National school.[11] The Royal Mail travelled from Sydney in four days (allowing passengers only six hours rest *en route*); Mate's store was concluding its flourishing first year of business and Victoria had recently been separated, making Albury a border town.

The only other town deemed worthy of recording in the 1851 census was Wagga, with a population of 170. This number included a doctor and four other 'educated persons', ten people engaged in trade and commerce, forty-seven mechanics and artificers, thirty-four other labourers and nine domestic servants. Because it was not on the Melbourne-Sydney highway, Wagga's development, though it paralleled Albury's, was slower. The future town of Hay was no more than 'Lang's Crossing Place' or 'Police Point', but although Deniliquin was only slightly larger, the boundaries of the town reserve had been surveyed and subdivision was shortly to be carried out.

No town could develop far without the services of a government surveyor. It was customary for surveyors, while carrying out their surveys of physical features and the approximate location

*From their first arrival in 1835, squatters had sown wheat on the alluvial flats near the crossing; other supplies travelled by dray from Yass or further east. A. Andrews, op. cit., pp. 22-3, 50.

of pastoral runs, to mark out reserves on suitable town sites. Sometimes, in answer to local petitions forwarded to the Surveyor-General's office, instructions came to surveyors in the field to mark out such reserves in a particular locality or to subdivide others for sale. When a Dr Coward sought permission to occupy a 'small spot of ground' at a 'place called Deniliquin' for the purpose of erecting a hospital, Surveyor Townsend, who was in the district, was asked to report on whether the place was likely to be on a leading thoroughfare, whether it possessed cultivable ground and permanent water, and whether its distance from other reserves and facility of communication with it recommended it for consideration as a town. His report and a plan showed that there were already in the neighbourhood Boyd's inn and station buildings, Bloxham's store, a private post office, a blacksmith's, a lock-up (government building), brick-kiln, punt, burial ground, and 'several mechanics of different classes . . . anxious to obtain land'. Townsend recommended the survey of a large town on the north side.[12] At Wagga, squatter John Peter entertained Townsend lavishly and succeeded in having the town surveyed on a neighbour's run—three miles further downstream than intended.[*13] But attempts by North Deniliquin residents Bloxham and Boyd to have surveys made advantageous to themselves cut no ice with Surveyor Parkinson whom Townsend sent there, and the major portion of Deniliquin was surveyed on the south side of the Edward River. In September 1851 Deniliquin's first land sale was held, seventy miles west at the earlier-established police town of Moulamein.[14] As a result of survey activity from 1847 on, several other sites were also bringing in land revenue by 1851. These included Moama (or Maiden's Punt), surveyed 1847; Mathoura, 1848; Moulamein—with a lock-up, court-house, post office, Clerk of Petty Sessions and licensed inn—and Balranald, the latter two surveyed in 1849. Purchasers at early land sales, as in Albury and Wagga, included publicans, storekeepers, squatters, artisans and doctors.[15]

Then came the gold rushes.

The immediate effect on the towns, as on the pastoral districts, was depopulation. Wagga's experience was fairly typical. 1850 and 1851 were seasons of distressing drought and settlers had no harvest for two years. Despite these local disadvantages a

---

[*]Dissuaded from surveying on high ground on John Peter's Gumly Gumly run, Townsend surveyed Wagga on J. H. Best's run, where the town, subject to inundation though it is, still stands.

National school was built by subscription and arrangements were made for regular church services. Then, during 1851-2,

> The accursed cry of 'gold' spread through the length and breadth of the land . . . and our artisans and labourers rushed after the flaunting banner of Mammon, our store-keepers and publicans also deserted their homes and busi-nesses for the golden illusion, and though in 1851 we mus-tered 120 children fit to attend the National school, we could not in August 1852 collect more than 27.

The flood of 1852 wrecked the school-house and the master left. The arrangements for church services fell through and building stopped. With the loss of a large part of the population and the ensuing depression, the writer concluded, 'in 1853 we stood just where we had in 1848.'[16] Such vicissitudes explain to some extent the dreary picture of country-town life painted by travellers like Howitt in 1851-2:

> Albury is like most of the towns up in the bush of this country. It is a village of one storied houses, scattered about on a wretchedly flat sheet of baked clay which at this time of the year grows only goose grass, chenopodium and the Bathurst Burr. The town consists of a number of inns, a shop or two, a bakehouse and a quantity of wooden huts. As usual there is scarcely a single garden, and what garden there is only growing weeds and cabbages in amicable disorder; but there is a large exhibition of backyards full of carts, heaps of wood and like lumber.'[17]

But by 1853 visitors noted that Albury, an established crossing-place only thirty miles from the Ovens diggings, was showing signs of recovery.[18] As the stream of fortune-seekers flowed south through the town, commercial interests revived. For a time the traffic was reversed by the discovery of gold in the Black Range, four miles north-west of Albury, but more enduring prosperity came from the settlement of a considerable agricultural popula-tion close to the town. 'Albury derives its chief importance' wrote the *Border Post* on 11 October 1856, 'from its agricultural resources and its proximity to the Ovens market.' Albury's nearest brewery was at Beechworth, but in 1856 the demands of public houses and adequate local grain supplies justified the erection of a local one.[19] By the end of 1856 Albury also boasted two flour-mills, a branch of the Bank of New South Wales, a newspaper (the *Border Post*), six hotels (with two more building), three wholesale and retail stores (with two more building), and an £11,000 Customs house. A steam saw-mill was being erected and demands for more brickmakers were constant.[20]

The making of quick fortunes at the goldfields led to increased Crown land sales around Albury, while prices were boosted by auction competition. From £1,013 in 1850, receipts had dropped to £366 in 1851 and £287 in 1852, but the return of successful diggers demanding land in 1853 had resulted in sales reaching £4,046 in April and £2,433 in December. Three further sales in January and February 1854 realised £6,300. Thereafter sales declined.*[21] Much of this land was brought under cultivation to supply the diggings markets, the same population which demanded meat also demanding breadstuffs, so that by 1861 there were five thousand acres under cultivation in the Albury police district, most of them close to the town. From a mere twenty-two in 1851, the total number of persons (male and female) engaged in agricultural pursuits had increased to 218 in 1856 and 489 in 1861. Some of this growth would have occurred, as it did around Wagga, simply to supply the demands of increasing local population and the corresponding number of horses,† but the proximity of the diggings markets encouraged greater expansion in the Albury district.

With unmade roads and unbridged creeks and rivers, supply and demand could not be matched, and the result, on which Albury farmers prospered, was such a marked variation in prices as indicated in Table 3.

It was not surprising that the South Australians took advantage of the high rivers which at the same time excluded their New

TABLE 3

Prices of Agricultural Produce, 4 April 1857

	Wheat (bushel)	Flour (ton)	Hay (ton)	Oats (bushel)	Potatoes (ton)
Goulburn	4s	£16	£3 10s	4s 6d	£5
Sydney	6s	£16 10s	£8	5s	£7
Ballarat	8s 6d	£22 10s	£14 10s	10s 6d	£11
Bendigo	n.a.	£27 10s	£19	12s	£16
Albury	9s 6d	£30	£23	10s	£20
Beechworth	n.a.	£37	£32	15s	£26

Source: *Border Post* (Albury), 4 April 1857.

*Of £25,000 revenue from Albury land sales in the ten years 1851-61, half was obtained in the ten months following April 1853.

†Between 1851 and 1861 the number of horses in the Murrumbidgee pastoral district increased from 5,000 to 15,000 (five-year averages, 1849-53 and 1859-63).

South Wales rivals and provided a broad highway for the Goolwa steamers laden with South Australian flour, nor that two South Australian Governors in turn,[22] to encourage this trade, 'performed the voyage up the Murray'. In 1856 alone, 10,000 bags of South Australian wheat came upstream, and a single steamer unloaded 1,800 bags of flour at Ford's station (Wahgunyah) for Beechworth.[23] The Albury Agricultural Society, incensed at this 'unnatural trade', protested that it was 'monstrous that wheat should be brought a distance of two thousand miles when a better article [could] be produced on the spot.'[24] Further competition came from the development of Victorian agriculture in the less extensive arable areas of the Ovens and Kiewa valleys.

In 1860-1 other markets opened for Albury farmers, the Kiandra goldfields upstream in the Snowy Mountains and the Corowa field in the low granite hills on the Murray banks downstream. By August 1860, with the snow-drifts ten feet deep at Kiandra, the price of provisions rose rapidly. Flour prices increased by £10 a day to reach £80 to £85 per ton. Albury merchants and carriers feverishly implored the municipal council to improve roads, and land values along Albury streets and roads leading to Kiandra rose rapidly. When fifty drays stuck on the way from Albury, a hundred pack-horses were used. Despite these measures the price of flour at the diggings remained at 10d to 1s per pound.[25] A more accessible but smaller temporary market existed at Corowa.*

Albury's population was increased and its reputation for fertility and prosperity further enhanced by the labours of a group of European migrants. In 1851 a party of two hundred Germans had reached Albury.[26] Some of these had arrived via Melbourne, but the leading families, including Frauenfelder, Schubach and Meyer, were members of the group of Rhinelanders imported by the Macarthurs and others to work as vintners. They appear to be 'forty-eighters' from their letters which revel in the absence of prying officials, gendarmes, tax-collectors and oppressive landlords, thus:

> Here is God's earth, the same as in Germany, but the soil is fertile and the climate healthy and God's blessing still lies in the earth. In Germany it has risen up in smoke, but here is

---

*Kiandra was entirely dependent on supplies brought in, but the opening of the Corowa field occasioned a small-scale boom in the already-established agricultural areas around Corowa—where there were private and government townships—and Wahgunyah (Vic.) on Ford's station, where farming had been encouraged; see *P.T.*, 16 June 1859; *A.B.*, 23 and 26 January 1861.

still an innocent earth. Here have not yet been committed so many sins, not so much innocent blood has been shed as in Germany, nor have our fellow-creatures been robbed of their goods and chattels.

There is no evidence that they went gold digging, but by 1857, of forty-four adult males amongst them, twenty-six were landholders and five vinedressers.[27] A few, like Christian Darkel, perruquier; Charles Schneider, hatter; Rudolph Winter, dyer; and Friedrich Keingendorf, blacksmith, with three shoemakers and three cabinetmakers, remained town-dwellers, but the majority lived in 'the remainder of the municipality', where every fourth male was German-born.[28] In addition to growing grain, fruit and vegetables, the Germans were particularly active in vine-growing.

By 1860 declining yields on the goldfields were leading to a dispersion of the diggers. Traffic through Albury had dwindled and was largely confined to the Chinese who operated after other diggers had left. In 1860-1 'several batches of the sons of Confucius'—their worldly goods suspended on swaying bamboo poles —passed through Albury on their way from Beechworth to Lambing Flat on the Lachlan. Though not as free-spending as the earlier European diggers, they created temporary shortages of some foods—especially rice—and it was suggested that 'sucking pigs and young puppies would rise to a premium'. They were mostly young men, more and more wearing European dress, and 'from long residence in the colony speaking English fluently'.[29] With the decline in traffic, storekeepers joined agriculturalists in chasing the vanishing goldfields markets not only west to Corowa and Wahgunyah and east to Kiandra, but further north, in competition with Wagga farmers and merchants, to the Lachlan diggings.

But while Albury had gained greatly from the gold decade, Deniliquin had grown even more rapidly. Its population, too small to be recorded in the 1851 census, had reached 155 in 1856, and by 1861, not as a result of agricultural expansion but largely because of the fat-stock trade,[30] totalled 632, an increase in five years which Wagga had taken ten to accomplish. Growth had been most rapid after 1856 as the fat-cattle market rose to its peak. In the early fifties magistrates held meetings in a hotel room, Sydney mail arrived once a fortnight, and clergymen appeared rarely. Bushrangers visited the town openly and freely, and unofficial justice, as when one unfortunate was saturated with turpentine and set alight, was violent and often spectacular. Even official justice was rough and ready, and the accused were chained before trial beneath burning sun or drenching rain in a calf pen behind the Highlander inn.[31] Any indications of potential town growth were slight. Despite the 1851 land sales, buildings were limited to two inns, one on each side of the river, and a few huts. No further land sales were held for four years, and with the discovery of gold and the rush southwards the town grew so quiet that 'the visit of even one stranger on horseback during the week was regarded as something rather extraordinary.'[32]

By February 1857, however, the boom was well under way, a local correspondent reporting 'we have more than doubled our population during the last twelve months and have disposed of every marriageable female. The butcher knocks at our door every morning; indeed Deniliquin is becoming a great cattle mart.' During the previous year over £600,000-worth of livestock had passed through the town for Victoria and large quantities of land had been sold, the price rising 500 per cent between sales. £200 had been paid for one town allotment and even suburban land had reached £10 per acre.[33] So satisfactory had the decade been that some Deniliquin storekeepers were in a position to retire, 'having realised a competence'.[34]

To a lesser extent, because only part of the travelling stock passed through it, Hay also prospered. This town owed its origin to the existence of a ford (Lang's Crossing Place), which southbound stock used when the river was low.[35] Despite local petitions and official instructions, however, the inadequacy and remoteness of the single surveyor stationed at Albury hindered the laying-out of Hay for several years.*[36] By 1858 the embryo town, situated in a deep bend of the Murrumbidgee, consisted of slabbed huts, weatherboard stores, inns, steamer landing-places, a sawpit, smithy and punt. But when Henry Leonard, American foreman shipbuilder of the River Murray Navigation Company, tired of waiting, began a punt and house, the squatter on whose lease this and other buildings stood hitched a team of bullocks to the structure and pulled it down. The resultant uproar led to the desired survey and sale in October 1859. Within the next three years a post office was opened, a Police-Magistrate appointed, a court-house, lock-up and pound erected, and funds raised for a National school.[37] Several land sales had been held, purchasers including the river-steamer traders, the usual storekeepers, publicans and blacksmiths, stock and station agents from Deniliquin, Wagga and Hay, and a number of squatters.[38]

*See pp. 133-4.

By the time of the 1861 New South Wales census, it was possible to assess some of the demographic effects of the dispersal of the diggers, many of whom migrated to these growing towns.[39] As might be expected from its more rapid growth and more remote location, in 1861 Deniliquin was still largely a 'man's town'. For the 372 adult males in Albury there were 259 females; in Deniliquin, for 323 adult males there were only 142 females. A similar surplus of males existed in other towns in the pastoral districts—Hay, Moulamein and Moama. But a more direct result of the dispersion is seen in the composition of the Riverina's male population by birthplace. Wagga, closer to the old settled districts of New South Wales and more remote from the Victorian gold-fields, was the most Australian town with 40 per cent of its male population Australian-born and all but six of these New-South-Wales-born. The male population of the surrounding district was likewise most Australian. In the township of Albury by contrast there was a higher proportion of English males, 29 per cent, compared with 33 per cent Australian-born. The surrounding pastoral district was even less Australian. Deniliquin, a boom town closer to the disintegrating Victorian gold population, was the least Australian town—20 per cent Australian-born—and contained the highest percentage of foreign-born. Its residents included Gustave Bruderlin ('John the Frenchman'), joiner and cabinet-maker; M. J. F. Dunsford, coach and buggy manufacturer from Broadway, New York; Thomas De Chong, Chinese baker, pastrycook and later boarding-house proprietor; Charles Jicknis, 'a Swede'; and two hawkers—'Russian Poles with unpronounceable names'.[40] In the surrounding pastoral district the non-Australian nature of the population was even more pronounced (see Table 4).

Much of this male population was engaged in the physical work of building the expanding towns. Scattered around each town was a cluster of sawpits, where red gum, box and 'Murray pine'* were sawn by the muscular topmen and pitmen, their heads masked in black crepe, while the larger towns boasted steam saw-mills employing up to a dozen men. Nearby were claypits and brick-kilns, so important where no stone existed locally, and advertisements for 50,000 to 500,000 bricks were common. Mortar for brickwork required lime and this was provided by local lime-kilns, decomposed shell beds on the river banks often being the only source of calcium carbonate. Plasterers too relied on this source. The most common form of roofing was shingling, for

Callitris spp. Known variously as Murray pine, Cypress pine, Native pine.

TABLE 4

Principal* Birthplaces of Male Population in the Riverina 1861

	N.S.W. and Vic.	England	Ireland	Scotland	Non-British	Total
Albury township	174	155	76	46	54	531
Rest of Municipality	123	71	46	15	97	360
Pastoral	412	506	288	138	121	1532
Deniliquin village	75	173	61	40	37	409
Pastoral	125	333	134	114	42	793
Wagga village	153	122	50	27	19	374
Pastoral	506	433	236	99	102	1420

*Totals do not tally because of omission of smaller groups.
Source: N.S.W. Census, 1861.

which hundreds of thousands of 18-inch box shingles were split. Laths for plaster walls and ceilings were also locally-made.[41] Even by 1856 the contrast between the transitory life of the goldfields and the relatively settled look of Albury was noticeable. Its buildings were of a 'very substantial description' and the town differed 'considerably in appearance from the neighbouring town of Beechworth. Nearly all the houses in the principal streets [were] of brick, some of stone.'[42] This settled air impressed and attracted storekeepers and artisans aware of the decline of the goldfields. George Mott, editor of the Ovens and Murray Advertiser, moved from Beechworth to found the Albury Border Post,[43] and storekeepers like A. B. Pritchard reversed the roles of their main and branch stores as Beechworth declined and Albury prospered.[44] This prosperity was reflected in a rise in marriage rates[45] and in the increased rate of building common to all Riverina towns between 1856 and 1861, as Table 5 indicates.

The number of buildings in Deniliquin grew most rapidly in the late fifties. The absence of stone of any kind on the deltaic plains of the western Riverina precluded building in that material* but local brickworks satisfied the demand for more substantial construction, so that while the twenty-one timber buildings of 1856 had increased to seventy-four by 1861, twenty brick buildings had also been erected[46] (see Table 5). One of the

*Even material for road making was produced by baking brick and crushing. Some footpaths in Deniliquin main streets are still (1965) composed of neatly laid bricks. Cf. the advertisement of a builder near Albury, for 'thirty stonemasons'.

TABLE 5
Riverina Urban Housing 1851-1861

		Stone or brick	Wood W/Board, Slab, Inferior	Roof		Total inhabited*	Rooms	Others including tents	Population
				Shingled	Bark or inferior				
Albury (township)	1851	25	54	26		81			442
	1856	34	70	54	50	104	714	7	645
	1861	99	90			189			981
Rest of Municipality	1861	12	83			95	378		606
Deniliquin (village)	1856		21	(4 metal) 2		21	498	8	155
	1861	20	74		15	94		28	632
Wagga village, (N. and S.)	1851	4	23	6		27			170
	1856	7	36	10		43	430		336
	1861	13	89		33	93		12	627
Hay (village)	1861	4	17			21	111	14	172
Moama (vill.)	1861	4	30			34	124	4	144
Moulamein (village)	1861		12			12	50		72

*This includes houses unfinished and not included in columns 1 and 2.
Source: *N.S.W. Census*, 1851, 1856, 1861.

more impressive of these was built by Bendigo contractors for the Bank of New South Wales at a cost of £3,700. It had freestone facings carted from Victoria, finely-chiselled marble fireplaces and elegantly-carved cedar mantelpieces.[47] Standing beside this were establishments like the shop and residence of 'Thomas Sullivan, fruiterer', consisting of 'strong calico, well lined inside with drug-getting and matting' and thirty tents dotted around the town. Older structures were being improved with glass windows, wooden floors and lined walls.[48]

Much of the building in Deniliquin fell into the hands of the ex-convict publican and speculator, John Taylor of the Royal Hotel, who illustrates well a contemporary assertion that 'two or three such men . . . are the making of every town in the interior.' Taylor's activities in 1859-60, though largely motivated by self-interest, contributed materially to the making of Deniliquin.[49] Unlike his contemporary speculator James Maiden of Moama (Maiden's Punt), who, in answer to all enquiries by would-be purchasers replied, 'I will never sell land', Taylor advertised 'one hundred allotments' regularly and sold whenever possible.[50] Besides erecting many of the public buildings in Deniliquin— visitors frequently noticed him supervising bricklayers and car-penters[51]—Taylor further relieved accommodation pressure with a row of seven 'working men's cottages' known as 'Taylor's Build-ings', neat weatherboard structures, each with a brick chimney and a shop front, all of which were speedily occupied.[52] In other public matters he was equally active, subscribing towards the building of churches, giving £100 for the free bridge and con-structing one bridge himself. When a joint stock company, floated for the purchase of a steam saw-mill, failed, Taylor purchased the mill privately, and when the *Southern Courier,* Deniliquin's second paper, started, its press was housed in the Royal. Local agriculture was encouraged by his extensive purchases of surplus livestock, grain and hay, and when floods cut communications Taylor himself struggled to Tocumwal and brought back a punt. Self-interest and town progress coincided, and complaints of irregular and inadequate transport were silenced by the founding of a new coach line based on the Royal.*

*Few issues of the *Pastoral Times* were published without some reference to Taylor's 'doings'. The samples listed here are from the 1859-60 files and Westwood's *Journal,* p. 343. The coaching troubles came to a climax in competition between Taylor and Wm McKenzie, the original proprietor, in 1859, with much 'smashing at speed'. His point made, Taylor sold out to Cobb & Co.'s Telegraph line of coaches (which still left from the Royal)

Stock moving south to Hay in winter: note drains leading to tank

'The line pierces a pastoral country . . .'

Post and rail

Winter in the backblocks: saltbush 12–18 inches high on the One Tree Plain between Hay and Booligal

Taylor's major architectural contribution, which cost over £10,000—including £3,000 for furniture—stood for a century* in Deniliquin's main street. Late in 1859 it was announced that the Royal was to be enlarged and rebuilt in brick. The old wooden building was demolished room by room—so as not to lose business—and in its place rose a handsome two-storeyed red brick slate-roofed mansion, complete with verandah and balcony. The building, one wing of which measured 180 feet × 32 feet and another 100 feet × 22 feet, was one of the most complete of its kind, catering for all classes of society and all tastes. It included a billiard room, bowling alley, shower-rooms and bathrooms and fourteen suites with sitting-rooms. Numerous outbuildings included solid stables for some fifty horses.†[53]

Similar buildings were more common in Albury, where elaborate homes stood side by side with equally substantial places of business. Typical of this better construction was the building later used by the Commercial Banking Company of Sydney. Besides the business chambers, the building contained three parlours, one drawing-room, one sitting-room, three bedrooms, a bathroom, pantry, cellar, kitchen and servants' rooms. From the hall, ten feet wide, circular stone stairs with cast-iron bannisters and a 'cedar-work' rail led to the second storey. A cistern on the roof, 10 feet × 24 feet × 3 feet deep, supplied water throughout the house. The whole premises were enclosed by a brick wall ten feet high. As a further refinement the drawing-room and sitting-room could be thrown into one, making a large and elegant ballroom.§[54]

Beside such elegance the crudities of 'colonial' town life were obvious, and the *Border Post* in editorials and published letters gave voice to an increasing sense of civic pride and public decency. The thirty-four goats 'playing up their innocent gambols and scenting the atmosphere opposite the Criterion' had given way to thirteen cows by 1860, but even this was considered

---

and a choice of cheaper regular daily services to Bendigo followed. (See *P.T.*, 7 July 1859.) By 1864 Taylor was employing over one hundred men. (*P.T.*, 24 December 1864.)

*The Royal was demolished in 1962. The present Coach House motel stands on the site, complete with Taylor's original bar-door keystone engraved 'J.T. 1861'.

†The opening (7 June 1861) was a grand affair at which a whole roasted bullock was given to local Aborigines, in town to collect their annual winter blankets from the Police-Magistrate.

§In 1965 the building was still in use as the Gloucester hotel on the corner of Smollett and Townsend Streets.

unsatisfactory, and the combined efforts of the *Border Post* and the *Albury Banner* finally resulted in four citizens being fined for allowing cows to stray in the streets.[55] But while wandering cows, offensive privies[56] and naked bathers might be considered subjects for police action, a number of other matters fitted conveniently into the framework of the newly-passed Municipalities Act of 1858. Consequently, with a minimum of difficulty, in June 1859 Albury became the Riverina's first municipality, the first half-year being notable only for the poor attendance of the elected councillors. 'As usual, no quorum', was a regular newspaper comment. Eventually, as it became obvious that councillors whose business was often fifty or a hundred miles away could not always be expected to attend, they were allowed to resign without penalty.[57]

Despite the unanimous displeasure of rate-payers at the assessments, rates collected in the first year amounted to £450, giving, with a £140 government grant for the repair of the Howlong road, receipts of £590. The major items of expenditure were salaries and contracts: town clerk £64, rate collector £13, town surveyor £87, assessors £60, thistle eradication £13 15s and clearing of streets £149.[58] The following year the council was again mainly concerned with thistles and roads. While the main street was being gravelled, others were being stumped and cleared and bog-holes drained. Frequent accidents to water carts going into the river were countered with the motion 'that council do take into their possession the public pump and put the same into repair', while a motion prohibiting the sale of butchers' meat on Sundays, which 'would greatly contribute to the better observance of the Lord's Day' was defeated.[59] In all such matters the town newspapers sought to lead the way with stirring articles headed 'Our Duty Towards Ourselves', in which it was deplored that colonial existence was a 'rough and ready substitute for civilised life and everything partakes of that greenhide and stringybark character for which we are becoming notorious.'[60] But newspaper complaints of the 'almost total absence of public spirit' in Albury were only relative. The most rabid harangues of Wagga's newspaper could achieve nothing with the inhabitants of that town, and ten years were to elapse before either Wagga or Deniliquin attained municipal status.*

---

*This was partly due to the suspension of the Municipalities Act. Similar developments of civic pride had begun in both of these towns by the late fifties.

As the frequent use of newspaper sources in this work indicates, the local Press forms a valuable source of information on social, economic and political issues, representing a unifying cultural feature in nineteenth-century rural Australia to which too little attention has as yet been devoted. One of the more important results of the publication of a country newspaper was the development of a sense of identity in a town or district; indeed, it is difficult to imagine any town developing beyond a certain stage in the latter half of the century without one, and in southern New South Wales none did. By 1861 the Riverina had five newspapers. In Albury there were the *Border Post* (founded 1856) and the *Albury Banner and Wodonga Express* (1860); in Deniliquin the short-lived *Southern Courier* (1861), which was incorporated in the earlier *Pastoral Times* (1859); and in Wagga the *Wagga Wagga Express and Murrumbidgee District Advertiser* (1858). The first four were published weekly and the last twice-weekly.

Newspapers provided some amusement to the literate, publishing serials like 'Hunted Down' by Charles Dickens, 'Captain Hind the Highwayman' and 'Arden of Feversham' (set in the reign of Henry IV), with—inevitable in an Anglo-Saxon dominated society—the usual comic Irishman tales. Some sensationalism is evident in the space-filler paragraphs—child murder in Staffordshire, a mad minister, suicide on a marriage morn, diabolical attempt at murder, tarring and feathering a reporter, a petrified spouse, and lynching at Los Angeles—but for the most part the Press seems to have been fairly responsible. Much space was devoted to local news and advertisement—mustering and impounding notices; the visit of a circus; political meetings; births, deaths and marriages; prices of stock or grain and numbers of stock crossings; the departure, progress and fatal end of the Burke and Wills expedition; and parliamentary debates and Bills of local interest. With the completion of telegraph lines by the late fifties prompter overseas reports were given—the Indian Mutiny, Garibaldi's progress, the Franco-Austrian War, the American Civil War, and the departure and doings of volunteers in the Maori wars in New Zealand. But local news, and particularly local advertisement, remained the main interest for readers. Just how much these publications meant to the literate can be gauged by the reaction of Nehemiah Bartley's roving party at the sight of a hut, typically lined with cuts from Australian papers. 'Like people off a sea voyage in having been shut out from the world for some weeks', they read avidly.[61]

The local Press saw itself as 'taking the place occupied by the forum and academy in older times, and in the middle ages by the pulpit and the bar' and quoted Bentham who 'considered the editor of a newspaper as the admitted president of a department of the public opinion tribunal—namely that portion of the public who support or are directed by the opinions of the newspaper.'[62] Despite their claims to 'foster all that is right and safe and liberal in politics', editors remained unashamedly conservative. Editorials, though of a high moral tone, were biased in favour of the established order, the squatters as landed gentry, and the respectable townsmen. This literate section of the community constituted the paper's main support. To the lower classes the Press offered only emancipation by industry.

A SORT OF RALLYING PLACE

Town and community in 1861

The spot is found to be very central, as a place of meeting for the neighbouring settlers, and this township on the Murrumbidgee will serve as a sort of rallying place to us in the same manner as Deniliquin does to the Edward river settlers.[*]

By 1861 the roles of Riverina towns, economic, administrative, political[†] and social, were fairly clearly defined. Albury and Deniliquin grew at different rates and for different reasons, as already indicated, while Wagga and Hay were pale shadows of each of these, with similar agricultural and pastoral hinterlands respectively. Although Albury's population (town 981, municipality 1,587) was greater than Deniliquin's (632) these towns supported almost equal labour forces (see Table 6). An examination of these labour forces on the basis of both census and local material gives some insight into the ecoonmic reasons for a town's existence.

The part played by professional men—legal, medical and clerical—in a developing community is obvious, as is that of surveyors, chemists, newspaper-men and teachers. The commercial interests of the town, apart from banks and agencies, were

---

[*]*S.M.H.*, 9 December 1858. Report on Lang's Crossing, the site of Hay township, cited in J. Jervis, 'The Western Riverina', *J.R.A.H.S.*, vol. 38 (1952), p. 146.

[†]Political activities in the towns are discussed elsewhere. See chapters 3 and 9 for N.S.W. Legislative Assembly elections; chapter 2 for local (municipal) government. In addition there was intermittent agitation for Riverina separation (see chapter 4) and perpetual demands for local improvements.

largely concerned with the supply of food, drink, clothing and household goods. As the towns grew, some specialization occurred but much of this trade was in the hands of 'general storekeepers' who carried a wide range of goods from the world's markets.* Simpler and more basic requirements—meat, flour, bread, cheese, fish, fruit and vegetables—were supplied locally, while beer, cider, lemonade and cordials emanated from local breweries and manufactories.[63] Kerosene, Congou and green tea, Mauritius and Java sugar, Liverpool salt, 'Patna currants', Chili beans, American sugar-cured hams, tinned sardines, salmon and oysters, and a whole range of brandy, whisky, port, sherry and champagne were imported, while colonial Negrohead tobacco competed with American (at one-third the price).

Local bootmakers, cabbage-tree hat manufacturers and makers of colonial tweeds supplied some needs, but most clothing and footwear was of British or European origin.[64] Although a few 'new improved family sewing machines' had arrived, much work was hand-sewn in homes or the establishments of tailors, dressmakers and mantle-makers and milliners, the existence of the latter representing a stage in the town's development, as did the presence of a maker of 'family, nursing and French stays'.[65] Some furniture was made locally or in Melbourne or Sydney, but imported American chairs (hundreds of cases of them), four-poster bedsteads—'bronze and ornamented'—'very elegant Morocco and spring seated sofas', looking-glasses with marble stands and chiffoniers were more common in country stores.[66]

Patent medicines like the famous Cockle's Pills, and Holloway's Pills and ointment, together with Epsom salts, bluestone, castor oil, rhubarb, senna leaves and Seidlitz powders were sold in both general stores and 'Apothecaries' Halls'. Jewellers, watchmakers from Geneva and London, and 'Professor Lane's Fancy Repository' sold ladies' gold guard-chains, gentlemen's Alberts, hair-work, best English lever watches, and 'spectacles to suit any sight'. Some jewellers combined photography with their trade, while other travelling photographers made a living from portraits and 'bird's-eye views'. In Albury, which supported a German

---

*Items listed are from advertisements in newspapers in Albury, Wagga and Deniliquin. Even an impecunious itinerant preacher could occasionally dine on bread and gooseberry jam, sardines or oysters—when he met with no shepherds, teamsters or drovers to share their mutton chops, beef, damper, suet pudding and tea with him. On occasion he shared his chocolate (cocoa) with them; see J. J. Westwood, *Journal*, pp. 303, 336, 352, 358, 363, 419.

TABLE 6

Male Occupations in Riverina 'Urban' Areas 1861

	Government and professional	Trade and commerce	Providers of food, drink and accommodation	Skilled workers and artificers	Primary production	Miscell., unskilled, etc.	Total stated occupations
Albury township	23	33	31	125	54	83*	349
Rest of Municipality	5	2	2	13	201	36	262
Deniliquin village	23	36	36	96	37	119*	338
Wagga village (N. and S.)	17	18	18	49	67	95	260
Hay village	6	8	8	28	3	33	91

*The variation between the numbers of skilled and unskilled in Deniliquin and Albury is due to census categories and the availability of building materials. Timber workers were 'unskilled', brick and stone workers skilled. (See notes to *N.S.W. Census*, 1861.)
For further details of occupations in Riverina towns, compiled from local newspaper sources, see appendix A.
Source: *N.S.W. Census*, 1861.

band, it was possible to buy from at least two shops a veritable orchestra, and Deniliquin for a time boasted a pianoforte manufacturer.

Booksellers and stationers, besides operating circulating libraries, stocked Bibles, prayer-books, Irish and other National school[67] books and a variety of periodicals including *Chambers' Journal*, the *Illustrated London News, Dublin University Magazine, Magazine of Fashion* and *All the Year Round*. Both they and the 'purveyors of fancy goods' sold chessmen, cribbage boards, draughts and playing cards. Growing demands for 'elegance' in the Deniliquin district encouraged James Barwick to open a 'Haircutting, Shaving and Shampooing Saloon, adjoining his Saddlers shop'.[68]

A further section of the workforce maintained vehicles and catered for travellers and their horses; coach lines, carriers and private means of transport providing much of their business. Smaller centres were coaching stops while the larger towns like Wagga could boast a 'carriage bazaar and coach manufactory' where omnibuses, phaetons, family sociables, dog-carts, gigs, and spring-carts were sold and made.[69] River transport played an increasing part for towns on the Murray and Murrumbidgee and a small boom in boatbuilding occurred with the clearing of the main streams, the development of the Murray River Fishing Company (which supplied fish to Bendigo),[70] and the popularity of regattas.* A large number of construction workers in wood, brick and iron were engaged in the construction of twelve bridges on the creeks between Yass and Albury in 1859-60, after seven mails had been lost in a few weeks,[71] and in building larger bridges at Albury (1861), Deniliquin (1861) and Wagga (1862). The section of the labour force engaged in building the towns has already been discussed; less skill was required to cut firewood for householders, breweries, river steamers, brickworks and lime-kilns.

Towns also operated as labour pools.[72] Squatters requiring extra labour for lambing, fencing, tank-sinking or homestead building had three choices. They could advertise in local newspapers, make arrangements through labour registries where these existed, or simply go into the town and state their needs at the various hotels. Domestic servants, particularly the Irish who pre-

---

*See p. 96 and *P.T.*, 10 August 1860. Other river-based 'industries' included punt building, leech gathering—120,000 were forwarded to London in 1862—and salt making at Lake Boga, near Swan Hill; *P.T.*, 11 April 1860.

dominated, were acquired in the first two ways, never very satisfactorily.[73] Thus much of the economic life of the community revolved around the towns, which served the needs of commerce and transport, supplied labour, supported small-scale industries and, as seen earlier, formed markets for agricultural produce. For the New South Wales government, towns served as centres for the administration of land and justice, and collection of revenue.

The local control of Crown lands was in the hands of the Crown Lands Agent (who was often also the Clerk of Petty Sessions) and the government surveyor. Through these officials land was surveyed and sold. Border customs, which operated intermittently through the fifties, required the presence of a uniformed government official, while post and telegraph offices were conducted under government contract. In the absence of a municipal council, the local bench disposed of government grants for road building and similar public works. The head of this local administrative hierarchy was the Police-Magistrate or in lesser towns the Clerk of Petty Sessions, either of whom appointed and controlled the police and gaoler. Squatters, and very occasionally other influential locals, sat as Justices of the Peace.

To contemporaries the administration of justice was in a number of ways unsatisfactory. To begin with there were the imperfections of the locally-recruited and untrained police force.[°] In Victoria the police were noted for their uniforms, trim appearance and 'almost military bearing'. All were responsible, through officers, to a recognized chief. In New South Wales 'a few non-descript characters of policemen equipped as deficiently as the worst company in a Mexican regiment' were responsible to a local Chief Constable and he to a Police-Magistrate or squatter J.P. who acted as judge and jury—an arrangement, according to local opinion, liable to abuse.[74] The lack of adequate dress, arms, pay and equipment was no inducement for the respectable or trustworthy to join the force which was regarded as 'a kind of refuge for the destitute'.[75] Moreover, police numbers were too few. The police district of Balranald, larger than the colony of Victoria, was the charge of a twenty-stone individual who could with difficulty

°In 1848 the Commissioner of Crown Lands, Bingham, had delivered two troop horses and four brace of pistols to the local squatter magistrates of Deniliquin, but 'much feared' that men would not be found to act as ordinary constables. A decade later the position was unchanged; J. Jervis, 'The Western Riverina'. *J.R.A.H.S.*, vol. 38 (1952), p. 135. Attempts were made to form native police and cavalry forces. For the result of an unsuccessful experiment, see illustration in J. Phillips, *Reminiscences of Australian Early Life*, p. 106.

ride twelve or fifteen miles a day. A Police-Magistrate visited Moulamein once a month. For an arrest warrant the constable had to travel twenty miles and even to do this he had to borrow a horse from the local publican, since none was provided.[76] Such an obligation could interfere with justice, as did the practice in Deniliquin of John Taylor lodging constables and magistrates in the Royal Hotel—free of charge according to contemporaries—to his own great advantage.*

The police force itself was continually broken up by dismissals for drunkenness and bad conduct. Constable Patrick Donnelly of Deniliquin, sent to Melbourne with £112, was found in the Bendigo lock-up, having 'gotten on the spree' and sold his horse, saddle and bridle into the bargain.[77] Constables Barrett and Kyle of Wagga were charged with drunkenness and grossly indecent conduct with female prisoners, one witness alleging, 'I heard skylarking and went to the window of the bedroom . . . the two females were undressed at the time.' The next day the constables and female prisoners were still 'beastly drunk', one young woman having downed twelve or fifteen nobblers before she left.†[78] As the *Pastoral Times* complained:

> We have done everything save taken to lynch law; thieves have escaped and the parties prosecuting have been scoffed at; witnesses have prevaricated on oath in the witness box, losers of property have in numbers of instances borne the loss quietly until the administration of the law has been looked upon as a mockery.[79]

*Once a squatter J.P. whom Taylor had annoyed refused to renew the Royal's licence until Taylor apologized; *P.T.*, 27 April 1860. But when, in the early sixties, a Police-Magistrate was appointed and lodged in the Royal, Taylor began to escape scot-free from his numerous appearances in court on charges of assaulting and robbing drunks, drovers and itinerant pastoral workers who came to Deniliquin with cheques to knock down. A rival publican and coach proprietor, the American-born Gustavus Whipple, closed down because of the 'constant persecutions of the police'; *P.T.*, 4 March 1862, 28 November, 12 December 1863, 27 February 1864. Earlier, when the Edward River was low, exposing a ford, the police stood by and watched Taylor fell two large trees across it, thus forcing traffic to use his own private (toll) bridge; *P.T.*, 2 June 1859.

†The incident compares unfavourably with the efforts of Peter Conway, acting gaoler at Albury. His one female prisoner ate separately from the men, and as the one airing yard was occupied by male prisoners, he allowed her out daily for a few hours in the guardroom, saying, 'I think it would be a cruel hardship to keep this girl locked up for months awaiting her trial.' He further stated, 'In order to guard against any false reports that might be circulated, I always take the precaution of handing over the keys of the cells to the Chief Constable, when the cells are visited and the prisoners locked up for the night at 10 o'clock p.m.' (*A.B.*, 15 August 1860.)

Dwelling houses, stables and hayricks were fired so frequently that in Wagga a subscription list was started to prevent arson; cattle stealing was common; tents and dwellings were repeatedly robbed.[80] In the centre of Deniliquin, within hail of the police depot, a tradesman was stuck up and robbed in his own store.[81] In October 1859 three Deniliquin sawyers walked a few hundred yards from their sawpit to the Bank of New South Wales which they robbed of £7,000, coolly telling the girl to untie the manager and his clerk as they walked off, scattering £3,000 around the town. The telegraph office was 'closed until Monday morning' and it was only the frequent visits to a hotel of one of the thieves, loaded with sovereigns, which led the police to the scene of a drunken debauch in the sawyers' tents.[82] With the superannuation (by petition) of Deniliquin's ageing Chief Constable in 1860,[*][83] some improvement was noticeable in that town, the new chief with the help of black-trackers actually pursuing three bush-rangers to the Black Range near Albury and effecting their capture.[84] As the result of another appointment a surprised bullocky yoking up his bullocks near a court-house—'perfectly sober'—found himself inside that building, charged with swearing in the streets. His defence, with which many agreed, was that bullocks require to be sworn at before they will do their work. The infliction of a 5s fine 'was stamped on his mind as an act of injustice and he could scarcely be restrained from attacking the constable.'[85]

A second complaint concerned the treatment of prisoners. A few years earlier 'the whole Australian press thundered' at the brutal system of chaining Englishmen—in a calf pen at that—for petty offences before trial. Until Quarter Sessions were established at Deniliquin, persons remanded for trial were sent to Goulburn, four hundred miles east via Albury, and until a gaol was built at Deniliquin even short-term sentences were served at Goulburn. By 1858 Albury served these purposes but meanwhile James Maiden of Moama, typical of many, had travelled two thousand miles and spent over £200 in one single horse-stealing case. Two or even three constables with prisoners or lunatics to escort could not prevent the former escaping or the latter jumping into the river during a walk which might last for several weeks

---

[*]After twenty-five years in the police—in addition to his service in the army—he was 'no longer fit for active service', knew 'no profession but that of arms', was unable to obtain a livelihood by 'ordinary labour', and had a wife and two children dependent on him.

across the 'burning plains of the Billabong and the Murrum-bidgee'. Not that Albury gaol, once reached, was much less punishment, particularly in over-century temperatures. Although the cell, 12 feet × 10 feet, had little ventilation, as many as thirteen unfortunates were herded together in it including an imbecile claiming divinity. When the number reached sixteen, including innocent prisoners awaiting trial, the local Press made allusions to the Black Hole of Calcutta and Judge Callaghan pronounced six months in Albury gaol 'fully equal to twelve months in any ordinary conducted prison elsewhere.'[86]

Whether it was the thundering of the Press and bench combined with Albury's newly-acquired municipal status, or whether, as politicians claimed, it was their efforts in the Legislature,[87] in 1860-1 a new two-storeyed gaol was built, including twelve cells, warders' rooms and guardrooms. At the same time an old slab and shingle building was replaced with what Judge Callaghan called 'the most commodious courthouse he had seen out of Sydney'.[88]

The most common kinds of cases in the courts included prosecutions under the Masters and Servants Act, vagrancy, horse and cattle stealing, robbery, assault, arson, sly-grog selling, drunkenness and obscene language, and the several varieties of indecency.[89] Penalties varied with the exact wording of the charge—the prerogative of the accuser—and the temper of the presiding squatter J.P. or Police-Magistrate. One squatter, bringing a charge against a seventeen-year-old who had ridden one of his horses to Melbourne with fat stock, showed leniency in preferring a charge of 'illegally riding a horse' rather than horse stealing, so that the sentence was a mere twelve months' hard labour in Goulburn gaol.[90] A less charitable squatter in a cattle-duffing case allowed more doubtful evidence to secure the condemnation of a young stockman to 'seven years on the roads' leaving a young Irish wife and a child to bemoan their loss.[91] In Albury a purely nominal fine was levied when an assault appeared to have resulted from 'great provocation'.* Further west, in Deniliquin, this mode of self-expression was so common and so lightly regarded that in 1860, on the results of two cases and after a little arithmetic, the *Pastoral Times* calculated that poundkeepers could be ' "whipped" at the rate of £60 per dozen' and 'medical men in their own houses at £36 per dozen'.[92]

*Wm A. Jacobs, tutor in Mr Heriot's family at Carabobala station, 'beat up' John McAlister—fined 5s with costs; A.B., 13 February 1861.

While in many ways the society, compared with that of later decades in the Riverina, seems to have been particularly violent and lawless, it may not have been more so than contemporary English, Irish or American society and in any case it is difficult to assess this quantitatively. The impression may simply be a reflection of the ready litigiousness of the population, while the particularly vocal Deniliquin Press may merely reflect the views of the large number of recently-arrived Englishmen, a group not backward in demanding their common law rights. The payment of 'hush money' lowers the number of cases that finally reached the courts, but whether by laying an information or by sueing for damages, wages, or recovery of costs and goods, Riverina dwellers —even neighbouring housewives—seemed to delight in hauling their fellows 'up before the beak' on the slightest pretext. Nor was this form of social action restricted to the 'lower orders'. On one occasion Elizabeth, wife of Alderman John Dornan, a respectable landed proprietor and a member of the Albury Municipal Council, was 'returning home with the meat on Friday evening', when Mrs Bridget Doubleday asked her in. Gin was drunk* and some time later violent assaults took place, in which the alderman himself was involved,† leading to a typical series of charges and counter-charges in court.[93]

Indeed much of the business of the courts could be traced to the drinking habits of the population. Information regarding the squatters in this respect is scanty, partly because of their comparative remoteness from town and partly because of their relative immunity from police action. George Peppin records occasionally opening a case of gin and once noted, 'Fred and self spent evening at Brodribb's and fell into the creek coming home.'[94] Nehemiah Bartley's droving party of gentlemen carried twelve bottles of rum 'for medical comforts'.[95] The preacher Westwood was once refused station hospitality by a squatter the worse for drink; once had a service deliberately and noisily interrupted by squatters and others who had been drinking—one dressed in women's clothes; and once, after retiring to bed in a hotel room, was alarmed to hear some squatters making £5 bets with one another that they wouldn't 'kick the parson's door in',

---

*'I just took a *leetle* drop . . . I might have taken a glass and a half . . . I was perfectly sober.'

†'Mrs. Dornan: My husband came in and asked me what brought me there . . . kicked and struck me . . . stupefied me . . . kicked or jumped upon me. Mrs. Doubleday: You did not knock her about, just knocked her down and gave her a black eye.'

which was duly done, 'and the gentlemen fled in all directions.'[96] Apart from such incidents, with the somewhat more civilized drinking habits of the squatters, alcohol may have acted as a social lubricant; but for the majority alcohol often exacerbated relationships and led to violence. The *Pastoral Times* thought it worth quoting the Melbourne *Temperance Times* which asserted that during 1858 Victorians had expended £4½ million on liquor, £700,000 on the suppression of crime and £248,300 on the erection of gaols, police and penal establishments. Nine-tenths of the crimes were allegedly traceable to strong drink, with murder, suicide and lunacy attributed to the same cause.* *Per capita* consumption figures may not readily be compiled, but certainly considerable quantities of liquor entered the Riverina via Victoria, forming one of the largest items of dutiable goods passing through border customs.†

Doctors, clergy and the bench alike testified to the incidence of excessive drinking.§ One senior government official considered that part of the trouble was lack of alternatives and in particular lack of encouragement to thrift, pointing out that of 113 towns and villages enumerated in the 1861 New South Wales census, there were 'Savings Banks in only sixteen'. 'How are we', he asked, 'to hold out to them inducements to a prudent forethought in providing for the wants of old age, or the claims of widows and children?'[97]

A few contemporary writers, like some later ones, took a somewhat romantic and lighthearted view of the bushworker's tradition of 'work and bust', but the more mundane details of the

---

*'Over four hundred cases of crime of which drink was reported to be the cause came before the Melbourne Police Court alone, 214 heinous crimes were reported by the Victorian papers as originating in strong drink, of which 74 were murder and manslaughter, 102 untimely deaths, 15 suicides and 30 aggravated assaults. Seventy per cent of lunacy was traced to the same cause.' (*P.T.*, 3 November 1859.)

†E.g., 1859 *Imports Overland* included (£'000): Beer, 4.0; Brandy, 13.4; Rum, 2.6; Gin, 1.1; Wine & Port, 3.7; Sherry, 2.3; additional *Imports via River Murray* included (gallons): Ale and beer, 2,964; Brandy, 1,196; Rum, 420; Whisky, 250; Geneva, 373; Gin, 360; Wine, 933; *N.S.W. Statistical Registers*. In 1861 alcoholic drinks accounted for half the total value of imports via Albury.

§When a case at Albury disclosed 'the great prevalence of drunkenness' there, Judge Callaghan stated that, 'On two occasions of his visiting Wagga Wagga, he saw men galloping out of town with bottles of gin or rum . . . flourishing them like stockwhips; and he had seen a father and mother quitting the place in a state of intoxication with a child toddling after them carrying a bottle.' (He had been told that the heat of the place induced drunkenness, 'but he never said that only pigs could live in Wagga Wagga'); *A.B.*, 22 September 1860.

process, from the participant's point of view, were revealed by one
Riverina teamster:

> I am a carrier on the roads. I came to Albury on Saturday
> morning from Tumbarumba. I had two drinks at Mr. Field's,
> The Horse and Jockey; another drink at Mr. Darby's, The
> Royal; another at Mr. Pritchard's, The Exchange, and two
> more at Mr. McGall's . . . one glass of rum and one of port
> wine. What drink I got at Mr. McGall's finished me.[98]

Drovers and stockmen, overcome by 'fatigue or some other cause',
went to sleep on hotel sofas while flocks and herds wandered
away;[99] a young man whose father had died, followed him soon
after from trying to 'knock down' the money left to him;[1] a
Deniliquin blacksmith, playing with young children on the banks
of the Edward, was suddenly seized with a fit of *delirium tremens*,
ran a short distance, jumped into the river and was drowned.[*]
The tales are legion but the theme is similar—the earnings of a
year swallowed up in a few days, or a life needlessly thrown
away. Part of the struggle against such frequently fatal influences
was carried on by hospitals, schools and churches.

Life expectancy at birth for New South Wales males in the
period 1861–71 was 46.75 years, and for females 50.64 years.[†]
Even the casual reader of newspapers for the period is struck by
the numbers who died in their thirties and forties. Whatever the
contrast in living standards, squatters were not exempt. John
Tyson died at thirty-seven, Peter Stuckey at forty. Nor did professional men, including doctors, live longer.[2] Much of the uncertainty of life itself in the pastoral districts can be attributed to
the vigorous outdoor existence led by the population. Sparseness
of settlement and the large number of wanderers accounted
for some of those who 'died in the bush',[3] but amongst the permanently employed, men were drowned crossing creeks or were
thrown from bolting horses and runaway vehicles, drunkenness
often being a preliminary to these forms of demise. Trees fell on
splitters and fencers, shepherds made mistakes with strychnine
intended for wild dogs, while others, despairing of life, took this
readily available way out. Sunstroke, leading to 'inflammation of
the brain' caused some deaths while pneumonia, 'inflammation of
the pleura' and 'consumption' accounted for others.[4]

Women died in childbirth, and high infant mortality was

---

[*]J. J. Westwood wrote in his *Journal*, p. 349: 'Alas! alas! This man has
had many warnings in his life; I have also preached opposite his shop.'
[†]See Life Table, appendix B.

matched by the scourges of 'scarlatina' and other 'fevers' and epidemics. In the last quarter of 1860, in Albury, there were ten marriages, twenty-two births and twenty-six deaths; twenty of the latter being attributed to scarlatina.[5] Earlier in the same year seven children, then their mother—'near the time of her confinement'—and presently their father, all died.[*] 'Of the whole family', wrote the *Albury Banner*, 'there now remains but one little boy.'[6] The sudden impact of sickness on families was often tragic. 'We were all very happy in those old days', wrote one settler's wife later:

> We knew nothing better and made our own pleasures . . . Then a severe form of whooping cough broke out and one of my little sisters died and I can yet see my pretty little sister gasping for breath, and as the sun rose one morning we saw her pass from this troubled world and we children crept about in silence.[7]

Doctors could visit the homes of squatters and townsmen; pastoral workers could go or be taken into towns, but because patients had to be housed somewhere it was generally agreed that hospitals based on the towns were desirable. In Albury where the hospital committee—apart from T. H. Mate as a storekeeper-squatter—consisted of townsmen, subscriptions were collected and in April 1861 the Albury hospital was opened.[†]

In Deniliquin, moves for a similar hospital had begun as early as 1856, 'purely from political motives' according to one source. When men came into Deniliquin sick or dying they could be accommodated either in the lock-up or by inn-keepers who were 'never known to close their doors against persons sick or destitute'. Until the Melbourne hospital refused to admit any more, they were sent there, giving Melbourne stump-orators the chance to declaim, 'See how these squatters treat their men; they grind them down almost to death; they put them in wretched hovels,

---

[*]The high mortality rates necessitated the services of an undertaker. In Albury, the following advertisement appeared regularly:
Thomas Allen, Contractor, Builder and Undertaker, begs to inform that he is prepared to conduct funerals, having just received a
SPLENDID HEARSE and PAIR OF BLACK HORSES
which, with his thorough knowledge of the business, enables him to conduct funerals on most reasonable terms (P.S. Iron palisades to enclose graves, On Sale. The trade supplied with coffin furniture).
[†]The Albury committee included a doctor, clergyman, government official, bank manager, newspaper proprietor and vineyard proprietor; *A.B.*, 21 July 1860, 16 January, 30 March, 18 December 1861. In Wagga, squatter John Peter was president; *W.E.*, 30 October 1858.

permit them to live like so many brutes, and when they have extracted all the work they can from them, they send them to Melbourne to die.'[8] The South Deniliquin Hospital and Benevolent Asylum, financed by squatters and townsmen and from impounding fees and fines from the district police courts, was not a success. The lack of a resident surgeon was a serious disadvantage but equally so was the method of admission, adopted to safeguard respectability.*

No non-subscriber could be admitted unless his application was endorsed by three subscribers. In October 1859 a station worker, seriously ill, was left at the hospital door in a spring-cart standing in the sun, while his mate trudged the town soliciting signatures, but three were not to be found. The sick man was finally discovered on the return of the medical officer, 'admitted *then*, given a little sherry, and in about three minutes after his being lifted from the cart was dead.' The £8 0s 6d found on the dead man was taken as a subscription to the hospital. Another old man suffering from 'inflammation of the lungs' hung around the town for four or five days seeking admission which was refused unless £5 was paid. He was finally admitted one afternoon and died that night.[9]

General dissatisfaction with such a state of affairs led to the founding of a second hospital on the north side of the Edward— the Deniliquin Working Men's Hospital and Benevolent Asylum. Peter Stuckey of Moira station gave £1,000, other squatters gave their hundreds or fifties, and within a short time £2,670 had been collected, 730 working men each having paid the £1 which entitled them to the benefits of the hospital. The *Pastoral Times*, preaching the 'greatest good to the greatest number', was delighted:

> The working man goes into the Asylum, not as a pauper—he need not knock at half a dozen doors, cap in hand, craving signatures to his order of admission, but walks up to the surgeon, produces his card, and is immediately welcomed. In fact he enters as of right, not of charity.[10]

Working men were equally satisfied. On one station twenty-three of twenty-four workers paid up when the collector called, and

---

*In some cases the respectable townsman, having subscribed for himself and his family, felt justified in his attitude. From Moulamein a worker in a 'plight too disgusting to relate . . . a living nuisance to himself and all around him . . . allowed to lie day after day and night after night on filthy rotten sheepskins' was finally brought in to the hospital to die; *P.T.*, 25 May 1860.

Constables entering Taylor's Royal Hotel, Deniliquin (top)

Deniliquin lock-up, with constabulary (centre)

Cart waiting outside South Deniliquin Hospital (below)

'A nice set of men of the true
British type' (Richmond Henty)

Augustus Morris: Ben Boyd's overseer,
Deniliquin, 1844; Royal Commissioner
on the Land Laws, 1883

James McLaurin: Albury flour-miller;
lessee of Yarra Yarra and Cornalla

George Peppin Jr, Wanganella: 'My
court case with the shearers, they were
all ordered to return to work. My name
was gazetted as a magistrate.'

requests for information came from Adelong miners and pastoral workers in other areas anxious to start such hospitals for themselves.[11]

Dr McGregor, a Scot with experience in the army and collieries, was installed in the new eight-roomed brick hospital* with its half-acre garden and patients began to arrive. There were a few early difficulties. Some gave their cards to unfinancial mates; others, sent in for treatment, spent 'two or three days at one of the public houses drinking, getting drunk, and aggravating their ailments.' One old man came to Deniliquin with £100, knocked down upwards of £80 in a fortnight and entered the hospital only to die. His will—a few lines—left half his money to the hospital and half to the Roman Catholic priest at Albury. Other patients, despite McGregor's discipline, escaped to hotel bars and were eventually found in court or the lock-up.[12]

Within the first six months sixty-seven patients had been admitted. These included:[13]

Syphilis cum Ulsuscula Venerea	27
Ophthalmia	9
Phthisis Pulmonalis	7
Catharrus gravis	7
Rheumatismus (aucutus and chronicus)	5
Midwifery†	2

Notwithstanding the vast quantities of painkiller, Holloway's Pills and sarsaparilla consumed,[14] rheumatism and chest complaints were common. This was largely due to the habits of bush life; swimming creeks, sleeping on damp ground, being out in all weathers and working in wet clothes.[15] Men suffering from the common 'sandy blight' or 'gravelly blight' made up the ophthalmic cases, and by the end of the first year five cases of scurvy had also been admitted.§ The prevalence of 'diseases of syphilitic origin' also contrasts curiously with travellers' tales of the healthy bush life. Even the more respectable South Deniliquin hospital had its share of such cases,‡ publication of statistics from both

*This building, with additions, is still in use (1965) as the Aratong homestead, North Deniliquin.

†One midwifery case was the widow of a patient who had died shortly before his wife's confinement.

§110 cases admitted January 1859 to January 1860 included syphilis, gonorrhoea, etc., 34; rheumatism, 15; accident (fracture, dislocation, etc.), 11; ophthalmia, 8; phthisis (pumonalis), 6; scorbutus, 5; skin, ulceration, abcesses, 6; *P.T.*, 27 January 1860.

‡Admissions July 1859 to 25 January 1860; total, 30; syphilitic, 5; rheumatic, 4; abdominal, 3; *P.T.*, 3 February 1860.

hospitals provoking a series of letters and editorials which generally affirmed that the bushman's weaknesses were 'drunkenness and this particular vice'—'THE sin of the bush, as it is the "sin of the great cities" '.[16] In the traditional manner of laying the blame elsewhere, syphilis was the 'black man's disease'. As late as 1861 miscreants were being given twelve months' hard labour for 'supplying blacks with liquor' and 'sleeping with gins'.[17] 'There was a time', stated a writer in 1859, 'when a colourable excuse could have been framed for tampering with a native woman, but that time has passed.'*[18] To some extent the place had been filled by characters like the 'vagrant woman', with a very large swag, who caused much annoyance to the various stations she visited and whose visit to Wagga coincided with the finding of the dead body of an infant in the lagoon; or by her urban counterparts and 'kept women' in the towns themselves.[19] In Deniliquin it was decided that as soon as funds permitted, separate wards would be provided for that 'considerable proportion' suffering from syphilis and scurvy.[20]

Those with the welfare of the working man at heart saw a danger in Deniliquin's 'two hospital position'. 'The grand aim of the British Statesman', said the *Pastoral Times* in 1860, 'is to elevate the masses. In forming our Medical Institutions we are try to effect this.' But the lessons of prudence and thrift were being undermined by the presence of *two* hospitals. Albury, a larger and older town, still had none. Not only did this place a double tax on the community, but, it was said, 'their existence teaches many of the labouring classes that we have two parties bidding for them. IT DESTROYS THEIR SELF RELIANCE. It encourages them to be unthankful.'[21] Despite much difficulty in compromising, by 1861 the two hospitals had been combined.[22]

An adequate system of education, it was believed, would avoid many of the pitfalls of intemperance and unchastity and inculcate the lessons of industry in those classes which most needed them. The *Albury Banner* considered the 'schoolmaster worth a dozen policemen any time' and looked forward to the day when the old offenders and 'old hands' would have died out.[23] Meanwhile, in Macaulayan paragraphs it stated, 'a solemn responsibility rests

---

*In the late forties the mother of one young squatter arriving at her son's station was 'somewhat shocked', 'when the sable handmaids selected for her service first appeared in the costume of our mother Eve before she was beguiled by the serpent'. (M. K. Beveridge, 'Pioneering on the Lower Murray', *V.H.M.*, vol. 1 (1911), p. 28.)

upon us to guard our rising population from their influence and contagion':*

> We cannot believe that any amount of wealth, or power or criminal jurisprudence can long preserve a country where so dreadful a blight hangs over its juvenile members, where our boys grow up in the gutters, and curse and swear and fight and steal; and our girls are early initiated into the vice of prostitution and the best sentiments of their being blasted with the miasma of a brothel . . . the great remedy . . . is not to be found so much in the clergyman, the magistrate or the police, as in the labour of the schoolmaster and the adoption of a sound, wise and judicious system of education.[24]

The children of squatters and some professional men and townsmen, when not taught by a tutor at home, were educated in Melbourne, Sydney or occasionally England. Some attended the King's School, Parramatta, or Goulburn Grammar school.[25] An Albury grammar school had opened in 1856 but had lapsed and later attempts to open a school 'for Gentlemen's sons' had been equally unsuccessful.[26] Most Albury children who went to school at all attended the National school which by 1860 had an enrolment of 127. This was rebuilt at a cost of over £2,000 in 1861 and had become a Model School for the district by 1863.[27] As in other towns, small private schools existed side by side with denominational and National schools. Vineyard House, Albury, an 'Academy for Young Ladies' was conducted by 'Mrs. Edwards, assisted by a competent governess'. The regular course of instruction included reading, writing, grammar, English literature, arithmetic, geography and plain and fancy needlework. The terms per quarter for day pupils were, under eight years £2 2s and over eight years £3 3s. For resident boarders the fees were £12 12s and £16 16s. The following were considered as extras: French £2 2s, piano £3 3s, singing £2 2s, painting and drawing £2 2s, harp £4 4s and washing £2 2s. Particular attention was paid to 'religious and moral training and to health, comfort and deportment'.[28] Other private schools promised Latin, Greek, Italian and German.†

*Cf. G. Nadel, *Australia's Colonial Culture*, ch. 14, 'Popular Education and Society', p. 161: 'The two basic assumptions made by the advocates of popular education were that society had witnessed a revolution, and that education made men moral.'

†Texts were available from local stationers for reading, spelling, poetry, grammar, Latin, arithmetic and geography, mostly at one shilling each (Irish National system and British & Foreign Schools Society); also 'a wide

Wagga Wagga Day and Boarding School (proprietor E. H. Tompson) had persisted from 1849 until the new National school was opened in 1861. Limited accommodation restricted the number of boarders, as did the cost: under ten years £25 per annum, over ten years £35 per annum, washing done at home, 'boarders bring stretcher bed and bedding'. Day scholars could acquire the 'principles of a sound mercantile education' for £1 6s per quarter or 2s per week.[29] But the uneducated state of most children was indicated by the reply of one mother to G. W. Rusden when he had visited Wagga to publicize the National system. 'We'd glory in a school like that,' she said. 'The children are fairly wild—just like the blacks.' Squatter John Peter of Gumly Gumly promised support in raising that one-third of the cost of building which was supplied locally, and Wagga's National school was reopened in 1861.[30]

West of Albury and Wagga the position had changed little since Rusden's gloomy reports of 1849.[31] Before the advent of National schools the position of teacher like that of constable was occupied by the unfit, the destitute or worse. 'Professor Vendré' of Albury, dancing master at Vineyard House, was presently unmasked as Alfred Walters alias Alfred Random alias E. A. Vendré and found guilty of obtaining goods by false pretences and stealing a gold watch at Beechworth.[32] Deniliquin's first school-house, built by private subscription in 1856, was successful until the teacher died at the end of the first year. During the next three years attempts were made by the Anglican clergyman to establish a denominational school, by a local doctor to arrange for a National school and by John Taylor of the Royal (who had eight daughters) to start a school on his own premises. During the same period four private schools were opened including those of Miss Parry, 'Late Kars old villa, Upper Hawthorn, with a long experience of education'—the most successful; Ricardo Floyd, itinerant and impecunious mender of pianos and teacher of music (and his wife of doubtful virtue)—both of whom returned to music and abandoned the school; the Misses Emmett of North Deniliquin—retired from want of support; and Alfred Key, whose enrolments dropped from thirty-five to nil in three months—closed for want of patronage.[33]

At a public meeting in 1861, despite support for religious

variety of children's story books including the time-honoured and thrilling narratives of Old Mother Hubbard, Cock Robin, The Butterfly's Ball, Puss-in-Boots, Robinson Crusoe, Bluebeard, etc.'; *B.P.*, 15 November 1856.

education, it was decided that there were not enough children for two schools and that the 'two hospital position' should be avoided. Although building was interrupted by the death of the contractor in a driving accident, by the end of the year Deniliquin education was under the National system too.[34] Thus the educational needs of most Riverina children in 1861 were catered for by no more than half a dozen schools of primary standard.[35]

Towns also provided a base for the work of the churches. The day was past when travelling clergymen visiting isolated stations preached to assigned servants cajoled into attendance with a promise of rum to follow,[36] but country clergy still travelled long distances. Sent to Albury in 1851 'to lay the foundation of several parishes, to build a church, a parsonage house and a school house',[37] the Riverina's first resident Anglican clergyman, the Reverend Henry Elliott,* rode thousands of miles over his 'parish', which extended from Albury to the limits of settlement and included north-eastern Victoria. Although church work was generally well supported by squatters—in Deniliquin L. Cockburn headed the list with one hundred guineas[38]—Elliott thought it necessary to commence the Albury subscriptions with £50 from his own pocket. Five years later, his church built, Elliott was looking forward to relief. His successor,† he decided, 'to be *efficient*, should have great powers of endurance, cheerfulness of disposition, and fondness of what is called "bush life" . . . clergymen, generally speaking, lose their health in a comparatively short time in all the Australian dioceses.'[39] In 1858 Elliott himself died.

A parson of quite a different persuasion was J. J. Westwood, Quaker turned Baptist, an itinerant preacher who travelled widely in Victoria and New South Wales in the early sixties, sometimes in a gig and pair, sometimes on horseback, sometimes on foot. Westwood commented voluminously on the frailties of Riverina society as he saw them. His journals throw light not only on the attitudes of several sections of the society towards a preacher not of the established church, but show interesting variations on the

---

*Elliott was chaplain on Norfolk Island until the reduction of the convict establishment there. He lived on friends in Hobart for a year, and was then offered a 'sphere of labour', £200 per annum and a house.

†Elliott at times expressed concern over the quality of replacements. When he conducted one newcomer 140 miles to Deniliquin his companion was 'quite surprised and somewhat terrified at the mode of crossing the river in curved sheets of bark stripped from trees . . . and I think his impression of these vast pastoral solitudes we rode over was anything but favourable'; E. Strickland, *The Australian Pastor*, p. 68.

traditional rules of hospitality, reinforce newspaper statements regarding morals and add colour to the picture of society generally.

Wherever he went Westwood had trouble with Roman Catholics. This was largely his own fault; telling them that their religion was a corrupt one was enough to make any 'real Irish Catholics' fly at him 'in a furious manner'. At Castlemaine in Victoria Irish navvies opposed his preaching with 'terrible yells and hooting' and threw road metal at him. At Gundagai, where the Roman Catholic church was the sole place of religious worship, he was only able to continue preaching from his gig in the main street on the intervention of 'a gentleman present'.[40]

In most towns he was appalled at the drunkenness, swearing, blasphemy, fighting and sabbath-breaking. At Deniliquin his 'soul was stirred . . . like one of old, at beholding the wickedness of this place.'* His usual reaction was to reprove the sinner; a puntman for swearing, Taylor and his workmen for sabbath-breaking, squatters and publicans for profanity and drunkenness, and a minister's son for smoking his pipe while Westwood was preaching.[41] Generally he was respectfully heard, though one squatter to whom he 'spoke seriously on the subject of the "New Birth", also of "Death" ', told him that if he did not leave off he would do something to astonish him, raising his arm at the same time.[42]

In towns along the road Westwood stayed at hotels. Sometimes on his first visit he would be told that no charge was made to ministers of religion; the rule, however, as he soon discovered, applied only to one-night stops.[43] Occasionally sympathetic clergy would introduce him into their churches as a 'bush missionary'[44] but such opportunities were rare and in the Riverina he preached wherever he could. From Echuca, where there was no resident minister and he had preached to a full court-house, he travelled to Deniliquin. After some difficulty with Taylor over the use of the Masonic hall,† Westwood, with a borrowed kerosene lamp, table and chair, began preaching to twenty or thirty persons 'collected in the open street, and several gentlemen listening from

---

*His impression was partly based on experience. E.g., Saturday 22 August 1863, 'Having in vain offered ten shillings for the recovery of my horse, increased the reward, when it was restored to me this morning.' (*Journal*, pp. 342-7.)

†'If you had been stopping at my hotel, you should have had the place for nothing, but as you choose to go to Irons', you must pay a pound', states Westwood's diary entry of Taylor's remarks; *Journal*, p. 309.

hotel windows and doors.'[45] The following day, Taylor having allowed him the hall free, Westwood distributed notices announcing an evening service. At seven o'clock 'the hall was lighted, seats arranged, and the bell tolled'; but although he waited nearly an hour 'not a single person came from all Deniliquin'.* After several more open-air evening services opposite Irons's hotel he was requested by Taylor to preach outside *his* hotel. Later Dr Synge, chaplain to the Bishop of Sydney, preached to a crowded Masonic hall but 'unaccountably' failed to read the notice Westwood had put in his hand.[46] In hotel parlours, court-houses, by creeks or the riverside on a Sunday afternoon, wherever men were found, Westwood preached his uncompromising gospel. A few were scoffers but most 'paid good attention'. Even a Commissioner of Crown Lands told him after one open-air service that he had 'pricked his conscience'. At Hay, where he noted 'an apathy and indifference to spiritual things', the preacher enjoyed the harmonium music and fellowship of South Australian Baptists, the Randall family, at their river-steamer depot.[47]

On the roads he met bullock drivers—up to a dozen gathered together at night—'camped under their waggons, and gladly shared their hospitality—a good log fire, meat, damper and tea' and 'had religious conversation and prayer before retiring for rest.' At lonely shepherds' huts on the Old Man Plain he was likewise welcomed, and after accepting a piece of quandong tart, read and prayed with the shepherds, his congregation sometimes including 'a blackfellow and his "gin"'. At Moira he visited the Fishing Company's huts and in a 'terrific hurricane of wind and thunderstorm', preached to the fishermen and the frightened wife of one of them, on 'the dreadful terror of the ungodly in the day of God's wrath'.[48] Later in the evening he was rowed in the fish-boat nine miles down the Murray, and from thence, about midnight, rode by a fish-cart to Echuca. Once when without a horse, he was refused accommodation by a Murrumbidgee squatter who had been drinking, and having 'reproved him for his sin' set off on the twelve-mile walk to the next homestead. Lost in the dark he stumbled on a splitter's tent where, he recorded, 'I was made welcome for the night; and being very cold, the woodsplitter tore his blanket in half to keep me warm.'[49]

---

*At Westwood's first service in the Wagga court-house only one person attended, he therefore preached in the street. Eventually up to forty attended his Deniliquin services. *Journal*, pp. 334, 387.

Traditional hospitality was the rule on Riverina stations, but when the squatter and his family were absent, the servants left in charge were less receptive and usually sent the preacher to the overseer's or men's huts. On some stations preaching was 'not acceptable', the reasons, when given at all, being that the family were Anglican, or Catholic, or no religion, or had colds. On others Westwood conducted prayers with the family or servants, or both, and formal services on Sundays. Where 'the men' were reluctant, he would persuade them to attend or, failing this, preach to them in their huts or in the kitchen, and distribute tracts. Often he had long evening conversations by the fire with squatters or superintendents.[50] At Tonganmain, where it was 'agreeable' for him to preach to the shearers, Westwood recorded that he 'preached to about forty or fifty men, after their day's toil in shearing; we also sang the praises of God. The men were very attentive; sold a few books and then returned to the station.' On Kerarbury one shearer stated, 'Give this gentleman, Sir, one pound on my account; I like the Baptists and was brought up amongst them.'[51] With donations like this from all classes, and sales of books (to the Kennedys he sold a family Bible for £9)[52] the evangelist lived his itinerating hand-to-mouth existence. His varied experiences in the Riverina reflect in part the different national and religious backgrounds of the inhabitants.

By 1861 a distinct pattern of religious adherence in the Riverina had emerged. Nearer to the old settled districts of New South Wales Roman Catholics were more numerous. With two exceptions—a few Northern Ireland Presbyterians[53] and the group of some two hundred German Catholics near Albury*—Irish were Roman Catholic and Roman Catholics Irish. Similarly, Scots were Presbyterian, the incidence of both of these churches corresponding roughly to the distribution of population by nationality. Of the ten thousand Riverina dwellers enumerated in the 1861 census, 51.6 per cent claimed to be Anglican, 28.9 per cent Roman Catholic and 12.1 per cent Presbyterian. The whole of the remainder made up a mere 7 per cent of the population.† In

---

*G. Schmidt, a German Lutheran Bible colporteur, travelled extensively in the early sixties visiting Germans. In 1860 he visited Albury and wrote, 'with but very few exceptions, all of them are genuine Roman Catholics, coming from Nassau'. His attempts to sell them Bibles and other literature failed; *Australischer Christenbote*, January 1861.

†*N.S.W. Census*, 1861. Within the census totals there were some significant variations. With minor exceptions, in both towns and pastoral districts, Anglican and Presbyterian males far outnumbered females, but

Albury, Wagga and Deniliquin, buildings for these three major churches had been or were being erected and clergy appointed or expected.[54]

Occasionally sectarian argument erupted; once a purist complained against the 'singing' or 'chaunting' of prayers,[55] and from time to time the role of the Church in education and the State-aid issue were discussed. Spurgeon's sermons were quoted in the Press, the Bible Society met in Albury each month, Albury Anglicans were informed that 'our reverend incumbent is about to commence a course of lectures on the Liturgy of the Church of England' and sabbath-breaking was condemned; but generally religion seems to have played an unobtrusive part in the lives of the people.

Besides hospitals, schools and churches, towns supported a number of other organizations including Mechanics' Institutes, Lodges and Friendly Societies, and dramatic, musical and debating societies. When the weather and the state of the streets permitted, public lectures were given in Mechanics' Institutes. These covered such subjects as 'The Electric Telegraph', 'The Zoology of Australia'—on this particular evening it was feared that the lecturer was lost in the marshes—travel talks, and politico-economic topics like free-trade.[56] At a half-yearly meeting at Albury a social and musical tea was provided for 2s 6d. 'Gentlemen of the town' gave improving addresses, 'gentlemen amateurs' and others provided vocal and instrumental music, and 130 men and women attended.[57] Literary taste was cultivated by an occasional evening of 'Readings from Shakespeare', though such activities soon devolved upon the 'School of Arts' or 'Debating Society' which appeared at about the same time and often used the same building. All of these institutions sought to provide a public library and reading room, the purpose of which was again the elevation of the masses—'a place where Mechanics might instruct themselves during their leisure hours' and where 'rational enjoyment' might 'do battle against the fatal attractions of the public house'.[58] If such organizations had been valuable in England, wrote the *Wagga Express* editor, 'where books are cheap and plentiful, how much more valuable here, where the common-

---

amongst Catholics there was approximate sexual parity, due in part to the ubiquitous Irish domestic, particularly in the towns and even in the pastoral districts contiguous to Albury and Wagga (i.e., those parts of the Murrum-bidgee and Lachlan pastoral districts included in the Albury and Wagga police districts).

est books rank among the luxuries of life and where too often education is limited to reading the brand on a bullock.'[59] In recognition of this value, squatters and prominent townsmen supported the Mechanics' Institutes with donations and gifts of books, a ladies' bazaar in Albury collected £302 in 1860 and the New South Wales government subsidized all funds raised.[60]

In the more settled Albury community, smaller societies could exist and serve charitable purposes. The Albury Amateur Dramatic Club raised £20 for the 'benefit of the orphan children of the late Mrs. Langley' with such programmes as:

> The Irish Tiger (farce)
> Musical Interlude
> Out on the Loose (laughable afterpiece)
> Front seats 4s., back 2s. 6d.[61]

The German Vocal Club and the Philharmonic Society combined with other groups to raise funds for the Albury hospital with 'Grand Concerts'. Admission fees to these were higher and programmes included such works as Handel's 'Hallelujah Chorus' and airs from *Lucia di Lammermoor.*[62]

Apart from such philanthropic gestures as these, there was a good deal of locally-based impromptu entertainment and social activity. Public dinners, at a price, were held in honour of politicians, Governors, magistrates or Commissioners of Crown Lands, and to mark the opening of bridges, telegraphs or buildings, the latter functions giving excuse for cavalcades of horsemen and vehicles in which bands and musical groups performed and the newly-formed Masonic and Oddfellows' Lodges paraded in regalia. While flags flew and trumpets blew, bullocks were roasted whole and vast amounts of liquor downed.[63]

On Christmas Day 1859 John Taylor's Royal Hotel was decorated with evergreens, and 'ornamental wreaths, with the letters VR in the middle, hung at every door'. Here 'the fine old English sports were revived'—climbing the greasy pole on which was hung a cabbage-tree hat, whip, spurs, etc., jumping in sacks and catching the pig with the greasy tail. In the evening sixty inhabitants enjoyed a free Christmas dinner, followed by dancing to a late hour.[64] Taylor's rival, Fred Burrows of the Highlander countered with similar entertainment on New Year's Day. At about 11 p.m. Taylor himself appeared 'as commander-in-chief over about thirty blackfellows and ten or twelve whites' with a variety of discordant instruments from violins to saucepan lids.

After much dancing and cheering, bottled porter and ale were distributed, the crowd sang and danced outside every house in town wishing the inhabitants a happy New Year and finally dispersed at daybreak.[65] Other publicans advertised more formal programmes of 'Old English Games and Sports'* to be held on Christmas, Boxing, New Year's or St Patrick's Day, with prizes of up to £3 10s for a single event.[66] Hotels also provided billiard rooms. Usually sports, horse races, regattas and any other excuses for gathering were followed by dances or balls, often held in a large hotel-room. Occasional prize fights were arranged between characters like 'Saul the brickmaker' and 'Flash Max of Wagga Wagga', the butcher's man,[67] but more regular functions were race meetings, cricket matches and regattas.

Small race meetings were held wherever men and horses gathered and on most public holidays, but each town had at least one major race meeting every year. The Wagga Wagga annual races, with squatters and townsmen as officials, offered the 'Town Plate' of one hundred sovereigns, the 'Publican's Purse' of seventy-five sovereigns and six other prizes down to £10.[68] In Albury, where to the Reverend J. D. Lang's freely-expressed disgust the racecourse had been completed five years before the first church was started,[69] the Albury Jockey Club arranged similar meetings. During race week the towns were full of visitors, accommodation was taxed, gambling and drinking were widespread and 'villainous frauds' made the most of their opportunities.[70] By contrast, a town like Deniliquin was deserted when the 'Grand Champion Sweepstake' was held in Melbourne,† only 160 miles distant, and the local Press ran articles headed, 'Dearth and Stagnation'.[71]

It is easy to overlook the importance of the horse in the nineteenth century. To contemporaries, horses and even bullocks were in some ways as important as people, and a good horse often meant the difference between life and death.§ Writers spoke in a

---

*These included quoits, foot races, putting the stone, running hop-step-jump and 'high leap'.

†Although the name has since changed to the 'Melbourne Cup' the effect on a town like Deniliquin remains the same.

§When news of the massacre of Faithfull's party by blacks reached Melbourne (1838), Irish squatter Frank Taaffe rode over two hundred miles through the bush to his Murrumbidgee station in four days on the one horse, which he afterwards turned out to grass for life; J. Gormly, *J.R.A.H.S.*, vol. 2 (1906-9), pp. 36-7. In 1849 a surveyor, by killing his exhausted horse and drinking the blood, gained just enough strength to stagger through the mallee to the Murray; A. S. Kenyon, *V.H.M.*, vol. 4 (1915), p. 37.

quite anthropomorphic fashion of their horses and bullocks. The reader of George Peppin's diary only realizes after the word 'mare' is used, that in the frequent references to 'The Governor and Mona', the former is his father, the latter a horse.[72] When John Taylor's decoy bullock was drowned, the *Pastoral Times* wrote, 'many of the cattle drovers who pass through Deniliquin will be sorry to hear of the death of Old Sparkes', and Taylor had the skin fixed to the wall of the Royal in memory.[73]

Each of the larger towns boasted at least one cricket team and matches were played between New South Wales and Victorian towns. Much interest was taken in intercolonial matches and when in 1861 the All England Eleven visited Australia, attempts were made to get them to play at Beechworth.[74] Regattas at Albury, Corowa and Wahgunyah on the Murray attracted even larger summer crowds. For three or four hours the dusty roads were thronged with spectators, 'squatters from the Billabong and Upper and Lower Murray shouldered huge diggers dressed in their go-to-meeting suits; and tradespeople of all kinds from every quarter within thirty or forty miles.' In front of the wharf at Corowa was moored 'a snug little schooner-rigged boat gaily decorated with flags and used as the starter's and winning post.' Crowds estimated at three to four thousand lined the banks on either side to watch two- and four-oared boats, many locally built, race for prizes of up to fifty guineas.*[75] At Wahgunyah the programme included a 'Grand Swimming Match' over a quarter of a mile, though there were persons who objected to such displays on the grounds of propriety. Indeed, Albury's swimmers found it difficult to practise at all. One pillar of respectability, signing himself 'Argus', pointed out that men and boys were in the habit of bathing 'in broad daylight', and that one evening, when he and his wife had walked towards the river 'with the intention of promenading the banks thereof', they were 'disagreeably surprised at finding the river full of bathers'. On New Year's morning at 10.30 a.m. he counted no fewer than 'fifteen men stark naked in the river opposite the town'. At Deniliquin, where young women bathing in the Edward had trouble with 'Peeping Toms', a ladies' bathing house was erected.[76]

Other entertainment was provided by visiting performers—

*The Albury Regatta, held on 17 March annually, included, besides the traditional athletics, men's and boys' hurdle races and 'FOOT-BALL'—entry five shillings, prize five guineas. Then, since this was St Patrick's Day, the bands played the national airs of 'Old Ireland' and three liquor booths supplemented the thirst-quenching trade of the town hotels; *A.B.*, 20 March 1861.

mostly circuses and musical entertainers—whose arrival often coincided with a race week or the exhibition of the Agricultural Society in Albury. One of the largest circuses was Ashton's Royal Marquee, from Sydney, capable of holding a thousand persons.* Its 'chaste, select and varied performances' included cavalcades, evolutions and trick riding, 'trampoline performances by the whole of the Male Artistes throwing summersaults over twelve horses in most rapid succession led by an Aboriginal of New South Wales pupil of Mr. Ashton', Mr and Mrs Ashton as the Grecian Nobles, daring leaps, fire balloons and dancing the silver globe in the air. Admission prices ranged down from five shillings.[77]

Amongst the more popular of the visiting concert troupes were Rainer's Ethiopian Serenaders.† According to advance publicity, their 'wonderful Ethiopian delineations' had 'astonished and delighted audiences in England, Ireland, Scotland and the United States' as well as Australian cities and goldfields. Following the overture and opening chorus came a series of songs and ballads; some sentimental, like 'Lilly Dear' and 'The Blighted Flower', some comic like 'Brudder Gum'; interspersed with the 'Ethiopian Dirge—as sung before Her Majesty Queen Victoria'—and the 'Phantom Chorus' from *La Sonnambula*. After the first interval came 'White, the champion dancer', with his celebrated 'Juba dance', 'open to dance any man in Australia for from £5 to £500'; duets and concertina solos; Aunt Sally's 'Lecture on Women's Rights' by Davis (one of the minstrels), which began 'Who am woman? Where do she come from? To whom does she belong? Where is she going to?'; with a further selection of items after a second interval. Admission, again, cost up to five shillings.[78] So far were the words of these performers incorporated into the common language of the people, that newspaper writers used them as freely as their more classical allusions, and a political candidate like Morris Asher could, with perfect comprehension by his Albury audience, begin an election speech regarding his

---

*Other circuses were Burton's, established in the colonies in 1851; The Australian Amphitheatre; and Worrell and Gardiner's North American Circus; *P.T.*, 4 May 1860; *A.B.*, 3 November 1860; 6 February 1861; *W.E.*, 19 February 1859.

†Other travelling troupes of the same kind included the well-known Thatcher, comic vocalist, author of *The Colonial Songster*, with Madame Vitelli and his musical Burletta 'The Colonial Servant'; the Buckingham family complete with operatic selections and the piccaninnies comicalities; several smaller minstrel shows, Tyrolean vocalists and bone-players; *A.B.*, 3 and 24 November 1860; *W.E.*, 26 February 1859.

Sydney opponent Badham, with the words, 'Who am Badham? Where do he come from?', etc.[79] Occasionally an entertainer over-free with local names in his parodies might be threatened with horse-whipping or cautioned by magistrates,* sometimes rotten eggs were thrown,[80] but generally audiences were large and well satisfied. Smaller troupes and individual performances included 'Madame Lee's Juvenile Troupe of Artistes' in which the proprietress herself performed Lola Montez's Spider dance, Irish comedians with comic sketches of Irish character, 'polynational mimics', conjuring exhibitions by Mons. Du Pree, and a whole bag of 'professors'—Professor Eagle, The Wizard, and his concert company, with a new song 'The Explorer's Farewell' or 'The Death of Burke', Professor Hansen and his 'biological performances' and Professor Bushell with his 'Electro-Biology'.[81]

While larger troupes performed in public halls, smaller groups tended to favour hotels, most of which had one large room used for balls, church services or as a music hall. Albury being larger and on the Melbourne-Sydney road was better served, but in 1860 competition between rival hotel-keepers in Deniliquin had resulted in an orgy of entertainment, with the importation of performers from Melbourne or the Victorian diggings as a nightly attraction. Despite the advertisement, 'nobblers down to 6d.' which accompanied the programme, the *Pastoral Times* thought this 'more intellectual repast' better than 'the old system of men drinking themselves to death or permanent ruin.'[82]

Thus by 1861 the little towns of the Riverina were well established as focal points for the varied activities of the community. From small beginnings as crossing-places or likely spots chosen by government surveyors, marked at first only by grog shanties or stores, towns had grown rapidly during the gold rushes. Albury's growth is attributable to land sales (and the presence of a resident surveyor), fertile soil, demands for agricultural produce at the gold diggings, and intercolonial traffic. Deniliquin rose with the meat market and the vast numbers of stock which funnelled through its streets. All towns, once recovered from their initial depopulation, benefited from the dispersal of the diggers and the perennial movements of the casual labour force engaged in building capital equipment on Riverina stations. The same decade saw the beginnings of the Chinese and German minorities. Despite the specific national and religious character of some parts of the

---

*Thatcher was threatened and cautioned in Albury; A.B., 24 November 1860.

Riverina, the area as a whole acted like a kind of melting pot for an essentially mobile population.

As this population settled down and men married, the building industry flourished and brick-kilns and saw-mills multiplied; town growth often being fostered by enterprising individuals. With solid buildings and the establishment of families a more settled air prevailed, while local government officials and district newspapers sought to set the seal of respectability over all. Although the towns originated as rallying places for a rural community, they developed in time a life of their own, eventually forming urban communities in which values, status and opportunities for investment differed from those of the countryside where land was still the ultimate status symbol.

Apart from the building trade, the economic activity of the towns was geared to the needs of commerce, finance, transport, the labour market and local agriculture. The New South Wales government used towns—indeed had often started them—to administer Crown lands and justice. But in a district so remote from Sydney, lock-ups were neglected, police were untrained and unreliable, and magistrates were not impartial. A general disregard for law and order, excessive drinking, promiscuity and violence added to the problems of the guardians of respectability. In hospitals, churches and schools, these self-appointed mentors, like their British counterparts, sought to 'elevate the masses'. But the masses were possessed of considerable inertia. Hospital admissions emphasized the prevalence of alcoholism; and the high incidence of venereal disease indicates that the Australian bushman was possibly rather more heterosexual than has generally been allowed. Despite assertions that the schoolmaster was worth a dozen policemen any time, the education of the masses was left to the unfit or destitute, at least until 1861 and the advent of the National schools. And although church buildings were erected, commitment, for the most part, seems only to have been nominal. Nor did 'improving' organizations like the 'Mechanics' Institute' achieve any greater apparent success.

Indeed, most of the population seem to have been more enthusiastic about impromptu or organized drinking, dancing, gambling, horse racing and sport. For Henley-on-Thames they substituted the Wahgunyah Regatta; for the Derby, the Melbourne Cup; and for Lords, the Albury Oval. No matter how unlike the village green and village duckpond the Wagga Wagga common and Wollundry lagoon may have been, the sight of men and boys chasing a pig with a greasy tail across this Australian backdrop in some way transported the watchers back to the land of their youth and lent continuity to their existence.

At circuses and musicals they laughed at Nigger minstrels and Irish comics or joined in the songs of Old England. It could hardly have been otherwise. Men who had spent their first twenty or thirty years in England were not entirely transformed by physical transplanting. Their values and vices remained European, and British in particular. Living together they formed a society too recently melted down to have developed any outstandingly unique characteristics.

3

MASTERS AND SERVANTS

Hospital for the Middle and Unrepresented classes
A number of Influential People of the above Class, finding
themselves unprovided for in either of the Asylums at present
existing in Deniliquin propose to raise Funds for an Hospital
to provide for their own wants. Owing to the collusion
evidently existing between the North and South sides of
Deniliquin it will be found necessary to erect the proposed
building on a punt to be moored *exactly* midway in the
stream.   *Pastoral Times*, 15 September 1859

Travers told me to go to Callaghan and get it the best way
I could. I mean by Callaghan his Honour Judge Callaghan.
(By the Bench) You ought to speak more respectfully of his
Honour, you might be talking of some bullock driver.
Albury Banner, 4 July 1860

You ask what I intend to do with my boys. My intention at
present is for the two elder to be squatters. It is by far the
best pursuit for youths who have any experience in these
countries.
The Reverend Henry Elliott, 1856, in E. Strickland,
The Australian Pastor, p. 69

In the minute of the New South Wales Cabinet of 1864 on a
petition for erecting the Riverina into a separate colony, it was
stated that there was, in the pastoral districts petitioning, 'no
middle class to any extent, the social relations of the community
being only that of master and servant.'[1] This polarization of
society was partly the result of the mode of settlement. When the
country was initially taken up for pastoral runs in the thirties and
forties, pastoralists had employed numbers of 'servants'; sometimes free Europeans, at other times Kanakas, and later Chinese,*
but to begin with, convicts and ex-convicts, the so-called dregs of

---

*The *Hay Standard*, 3 June 1891, stated that the sheep on Burrabogie in
the fifties 'were tended by Mongolians who lived in tents and were clothed
in their curious native attire, so that it was difficult for a Briton to guess
what sex they were of'.

British society. To these lower echelons were added, in time, free shepherds, bullockies and bush workers. For the most part both masters and servants were 'transplanted British'. Indoctrinated and nurtured in British notions of class, rank and station; the inheritors of British law and political institutions and an Old World social system; consciously and unconsciously as in their sports, amusements, language and literature, they carried over the values and attitudes of Anglo-Saxon society into the new environment. If a squatter's wife bore a son it was typically announced as follows:

> *Birth.* At Moira Station, Murray River, on 27th July the Lady of H. S. Lewes, Esq., of a son and heir.[2]

But lesser mortals were not 'Esquires', their wives were not 'ladies' and their sons 'heirs' to very little; hence the following equally typical notice:

> *Birth.* Sth. Deniliquin, on 12 inst., wife of Mr. Henry Smith, Chief Constable, a son.[3]

A similar distinction was made in reports of social functions. In short, in the pastoral districts the squatters were the masters, the apex of the social pyramid.

Geographically the pastoral lessees had originated from England and Scotland, or, very occasionally, Ireland, and by 1861 included a number of native-born, some from non-British stock. A few, men of capital, may have come straight to the inland districts, but most reached the Riverina as a result of a series of moves, often spread over two generations. Some, like the Lang, Henty and Learmonth families had come via Tasmania and Victoria. Others had migrated direct to Victoria, then crossed the Murray from Port Phillip to New South Wales. A further group was part of the gradual westward expansion from the old settled districts of New South Wales. Mary Kennedy (*née* Hume), a niece of Hamilton Hume the explorer, grew up near Appin and Campbelltown, close to Sydney, where her family associated with the Tyson, Kennedy, Warby, Vardy, Broughton, Dight and Keighran families. Later her family moved further inland. At Goulburn they knew the Barber, Read, Faithfull, Bradley, Thorne, Moore and Stuckey families and at Burrowa they counted as neighbours William McLeay and the Broughtons, O'Sullivans and Ryans. By the late 1850s all of these families had representatives in the Riverina scattered from the Murray to the Lachlan and beyond. Often it was the growing up of large families that prompted the moves. Mary Kennedy herself was one of a family of fourteen and knew two other families of twenty-two each.[4] Gradually the young men moved out but sooner or later some returned, seeking wives among their relatives or old acquaintances. Robert Kennedy was one of Mary's 'Billabong cousins'. From time to time they met, usually when the Billabong Kennedys were buying store stock. When they were married quietly at home in 1858, Mary Kennedy could list among her close relatives, besides numerous Kennedys and Humes, the Desailly, Carne, Barbour and Huon families; these, with others, forming a chain of related station families stretching across the Riverina. Within the Murrumbidgee pastoral district alone there were a score of stations on which she could claim ties of blood.[5]

Near Albury, the family of Gabriel Louis Marie Huon de Kerrilleau, a French emigré who enlisted in the New South Wales Corps, had married into the family of W. Mitchell, a retired officer of the Kent Militia. Other Mitchells had married into the Dight and Heriot families while A. A. Huon married the sister of Robert Brown, an Albury storekeeper turned squatter, whose family had also originated from the old settled districts. Near Deniliquin, Peter Stuckey, whose family also had runs near Wagga, had five daughters, all of whom married resident pastoralists, including one Huon. Relationships amongst the New-South-Wales-bred squatting families were thus widespread and complex.[6]

Some squatters had ranged widely before settling in the Riverina. George Desailly and Henry Gwynne had been to California,[7] Gideon Scott Lang had marched with Garibaldi,[*] Henry Ricketson had reached Australia via Nova Scotia,[8] and Thomas Robertson had fought in the Kaffir wars in Natal.[9]

The social origins of the squatters were equally diverse. Observers in 1853 enumerated 'doctors, lawyers, clergymen, military and naval officers, sons of wealthy merchants' and 'the son of a gentleman farmer in Devon'. T. H. Mate was a squatter turned Albury storekeeper, Robert Brown an Albury storekeeper turned squatter, James McLaurin a flour-miller and squatter simultaneously. Thomas Robertson, Scottish law student turned Mul-

---

[*]The poem, 'Garibaldi's March', in *P.T.*, 28 December 1860, 'written on reading that the hero was within one day's march of Naples; by the Murrumbidgee native' (tune, 'I loved ne'er a laddie but one') is almost certainly attributable to his pen.

wala poundkeeper, Kaffir war hero and former secretary of the
Australian Agricultural Co., later relinquished squatting, studied
more law in Sydney and practised at Hay. James Maiden, publican, of Moama, 'regarded as one of the best bushmen in the
country', held Perricoota and Tattaila; while Australian-born
stockmen and overseers like the Tysons eventually acquired their
own runs. 'College bred men', coach-line superintendents, circus
proprietors, drapers—it made little difference. A little luck, a
little capital, perhaps a little judicious duffing, and plenty of hard
work were the only requirements so long as land for runs was
available.[10]

It is difficult to be more specific regarding the origins of the
squatters. By 1861 most Riverina stations had changed hands at
least once, some having had six different 'owners'. Often these
'owners' were brothers, partnerships or families.[11] Government
lists are unsatisfactory in this regard. Sometimes the name appearing is that of the actual lessee, sometimes of the person sent to
pay the rent to the local Crown Lands Agent.[12] In one case a
station lease was purchased and later mortgaged to the original
lessee whose name alone appeared on the official list throughout.[13] By 1861 there were only two of the 'old or first settlers' left
in the Deniliquin district—Henry Gwynne and the McLaurins.[14]
Changes of such magnitude in two decades render precise quantitative analysis impossible.

There were a number of reasons for this twenty-year turnover.
Partly it was the result of the growing-up of families. The original
Kennedy run was Jerilderie, on the Billabong, with several backblocks attached. As the four boys grew to manhood each took a
backblock, and later the old frontage run was sold. Infant mortality blighted other squatters' hopes of founding a dynasty and
they sold out and retired to Melbourne, England or Scotland. The
increasing value of the backblocks under new methods of water
conservation led some squatters to sell part of their old run to
newcomers and spend the proceeds on fencing and watering the
better pastures further back. Some, like James Tyson, infected by
the spirit of speculation characteristic of the period, or fearful of
the anticipated results of radical land legislation, moved to the
Lachlan or Darling.

For squatters with families, education and sickness posed prob-
lems, sometimes precipitating a move to Melbourne. Mary
Kennedy recalled that in the fifties, despite the presence of a
Scottish doctor,

a virulent fever carried off a lovely child, daughter of Mrs.
Brodribb of Wanganella, also a little girl of Mrs. Brougham
of Hartwood died, then Mrs. Brougham of Currabunganung
was called upon to give up her four little girls. The same
fever carried them off in twelve days. So all the families fled
to Melbourne and our pleasant neighbourhood was desolate.

Later one of the Jerilderie Kennedys' children sickened and the
mother with the rest of the family left temporarily for Melbourne.
This particular child recovered, 'but the six little graves at Hartwood [bore] sad evidence of the terrible visitation.'[15] As early as
the mid-forties some squatters had taken their wives to the very
fringes of settlement, but some had returned to more settled
districts as their families grew.[16] Generally, the period up to 1861
saw increasing numbers of women and children settled in the
pastoral districts. They brought considerable changes to the
homestead and did much to alleviate the harshness and crudities
of early pastoral life.

Early homes had been primitive. One wife considered her 'little
house with its paper and hessian lining . . . a mansion compared
with some of the others.'[17] Frequently 'the table was a sheet of
bark nailed on the top of four posts that were driven into the
earthen floor.'[18] By the sixties, homesteads varied considerably.[19]
On newly-subdivided runs or backblocks being adapted for permanent residence, one-roomed slab huts still occurred,[20] but
wherever capital was available arrangements were more suited to
feminine tastes. In anticipation of his marriage in England, one
young squatter, Richmond Henty, had acquired Walla Walla
station on the Billabong, with three thousand head of cattle. In
March 1861, he sailed P & O for England, and 'what with the
morning tub, breakfast, cigars, sea-quoits and tiffin, cigars, sea-
quoits again, single stick, boxing, reading, dinner, whist, and
music etc . . . time passed merrily.' After his wedding at St
George's, Hanover Square, and honeymoon in Paris, he and his
wife travelled back to Melbourne, then via Deniliquin and
Conargo to Moonbria and Wallandool—other Henty stations—
and so to Walla Walla, 'for fifteen miles through our own
country'.[21] Here,

on the brow of the hill, with masses of granite rocks as a
background, [he] had built a pretty villa residence with
every comfort and convenience, and from this there was a
commanding view for several miles, over a wide sweep of
timbered country, and small open plains in the valley, with

glimpses of the Billabong Creek, which wound along the centre of the run for twelve miles.

But this was a dry year and the Billabong had stopped flowing. Water had to be carried thirty miles and as it was half mud, was cleared by throwing in salts and Boree ashes. They could 'scarcely afford water to wash with—nice experience for an English young lady.'[22]

The methods by which squatters acquired wives varied, but to judge from one newspaper advertisement it was a fairly matter-of-fact process for some.*[23] Many marriages took place at homesteads, giving occasion for celebrations and a short cavalcade when, as scattered settlers' homes were passed, 'the usual number of dogs would rush out barking . . . and strings of white haired children would prop themselves against the hut slabs to gaze on the strange sight';[24] then off the bride was carried to the flat country and the new home. To Mary Kennedy, Australian-born but raised on the coastal ranges, tablelands and western slopes, 'the salt and cotton bush looked strange and the myalls and pines beautiful.' Wonnamurra, her new home, was built on the edge of the forest leading to the Murray. 'At one point there was a small rise covered with pine trees [but] far away, on all sides, it was all flat and plain, and you could see the creek timber for miles.' She was surprised too at the 'black crumbly soil'.[25]

But though women brought some comfort and elegance to the homestead in the form of china and cut glass, silver spoons and linen, their environment was the same as for the men. Galvanized iron, for those who could afford it, was hot in summer; and in winter, when the creek was coming down, doors had to be taken off hinges, bed ticks emptied, and bags prepared for filling with sand. In drought years, gardens died, and if the wild dogs spared the lambs, it was only to ravage the chickens.[26] Adaptation was easier for the colonial-born. At fifteen Mary Kennedy could make butter, prepare and roast a turkey or sucking-pig, knead up a large batch of bread in a baking trough, wash, starch and iron clothes and make candles—with sewing to occupy the evenings.

> This was only when servants were almost unprocurable, [she wrote] and still, with all our work, we managed a good deal

*Two bachelors, aged forty-three and thirty-four, in good circumstances, tolerably good looking, residing in the interior of a pleasant part of the country, and desirous of marrying two respectable and well-educated young ladies, used the paper because their time was 'much occupied in pastoral pursuits'. The most inviolable secrecy would be observed in handling replies addressed to AA 43 and BB 34.

of reading, and I read many of Sir Walter Scott's works when
the rest of the household were asleep. How I revelled in
'Ivanhoe' and Grace Aguella's 'Days of Bruce' and Tupper's
Proverbial Philosophy.*[27]

The squatters had always been noted for their hospitality,
whether for travellers of lower degree in the men's huts or that
due 'from one gentleman to another' in the homestead proper,[28]
the latter including drinking parties, horse races and other mas-
culine entertainments. In keeping with their status as mounted
men, much of this consisted of hunting kangaroos, as they had
done for two decades, and at more formal hunts even the ladies
participated. Little excuse was needed to take out the kangaroo
dogs and hounds. George Peppin Jr's birthday occasioned the
Peppins' second meet, when two of the younger squatters, 'much
to the disgust of the field', 'laid on emus'.[29] A different kind of hunt
took place when the evidence indicated that a sly grog seller with
his 'bumboat' was supplying liquor to the men's huts. Armed with
a heavy hunting whip the squatter would start in pursuit and
despite the men's efforts with the bush-telegraph, 'it was "Give up
that grog!" No begging was of any use. "Smash!" "Smash!", until
every bottle was gone and bungs pulled out of the kegs until there
was generally a good stream.'[30]

With the greater number of women visiting, entertaining,
dances and more formal balls increased, parties travelling scores
of miles to demonstrate the latest skill acquired from some 'French
dancing master'. In the towns, the Deniliquin Terpsichorean
Club's Select Quadrille Assembly and similar organizations in
Albury, like the more exclusive subscription balls, limited attendance by charging one or two guineas for a non-transferable ticket,
with lady patronesses and stewards to ensure respectability.[31] All
such functions lasted at least until next morning, but festivities at
Wonnamurra homestead, to mark the anniversary of Robert
Kennedy's wedding, continued for a full week. Despite heavy
rains and deplorable roads—'one gentleman knocked up six
horses in sixteen miles'—'large numbers of the most respectable
settlers went to enjoy themselves.' Nearly all were there to hear
the band strike up for the opening quadrille in the ballroom, and
over seventy sat down for supper in a specially-erected pavilion
on the first night. The Billabong was famous for its horses, and as

*During his night watches on a long sheep-droving trip in 1853, Nehemiah
Bartley read *Martin Chuzzlewit, Uncle Tom's Cabin,* and *The Cruise of the
Midge* by the light of the log fire.

soon as the ground was dry enough, riders in 'proper jockey costume' raced 'on the sweepstake principle'. It was too wet 'to cart in stuff for fences', so the steeplechase was abandoned, but two teams contested a very satisfactory cricket match.[32]

Even though their ranks had been diluted with the colonial-born, the squatters were still the leaders of society. Politically they were the approved representatives of the district; in the administration of justice and the keeping of law and order they sat on the bench; while funds for hospitals, churches, schools, telegraphs and local improvemests came largely from their purses. When all other attempts to bridge the Edward River failed, it was decided to ask a local squatter to build it at his own expense and collect toll. Equally, despite the increased number of colonial-born squatters, they were 'Englishmen'. Not yet—in nationality or outlook—Australian, certainly not yet, by mere accident of colonial boundary, Victorian,[33] but 'a nice set of men of the true British type',[34] English in speech, loyalties, and social attitudes. Nor did they pre-empt this for themselves. Informed local opinion recorded that the 'squatters, as a class . . . regard their men, not as slaves, as is often alleged, but as *Englishmen,* entitled to all the kindness and consideration which, in the old country, are extended to the working class.'[35]

For many squatters the tie with 'the old country' was demonstrated in a trip 'home'.[36] During 1859-61 there were several fare-wells to Riverina squatters and squatting families: F. A. Gwynne; George McLeay; Robert Dun 'and his lady', home to Scotland; and Patrick Brougham, nephew of Lord Brougham, home to England after twenty-two years in Australia and fourteen in the district. Most retired there, few returning to the pastoral life, though Patrick and John Brougham, with their families, did so after two years in England and Scotland.[37] The attachment to the mother country was not limited to the squatters. The Reverend Henry Elliott expressed the views of many when he wrote home to a lady friend:

> I . . . freely confess to you, that a new country has greater charms for me than an old one. And the pure and healthy atmosphere, and the bright and sunny skies of Australia have quite wedded me to this part of the world, and I should scarcely wish to see England again, if it were not for the pleasure of seeing those whose disinterested friendship has made a much deeper impression on me than I can ever receive from external nature however beautiful.[38]

Similar sentiments, if less elegantly expressed, may have stirred the breasts of the less literate, but how far, if at all, the lower orders felt the pull of the mother country is difficult to assess. Mary Kennedy considered that 'many a man lives through drought, hardships, honeliness, everything, for has he not that "Beaconlight" ahead, that he will see the old country once more', but that the lack of facility for saving combined with the allurements of the wayside pub to frustrate this design.

In view of their diverse origins it might well be asked how the members of such a group as the squatters acquired and maintained their status. Place in society was accorded to the few professional men, but for the rest the basic criterion was wealth, whether of sheep or cattle or, ultimately, land. Some, gentlemen-born like the 'nephews of Lord Brougham' or well educated, would have held status in any British community and happened to have arrived in the days of cheap grazing and abundant land; or later, but with capital. Others, of more lowly birth, made up for this deficiency by industry and thrift. In 1853 Nehemiah Bartley wrote:

> At Towpruck we heard of three brothers named Tyson, who had sheep hard by, and who were remarkable for never smoking, nor drinking 'grog', nor sleeping in a house, nor marrying, but living a pastoral open air life of temperance and celibacy.[39]

Just how remarkable their non-smoking habits were is indicated by a paragraph from two other observers regarding the Australian bushmen:

> Although you rarely find them chewing the weed, yet they smoke the strongest Negrohead and Cavendish. Every man and boy in the bush smokes. Morning, noon, and night, you are sure to find the bushman with his pipe in his cheek after meals. He says, at breakfast it helps him to swallow his damper; at dinner it assists the digestion of the mutton; and at supper it acts as a soporific against the astringent properties of the tea; beside sundry pipefuls he smokes during the intervals, for which he has no other excuse than that it fills up the time.[40]

The *Pastoral Times* frequently praised station superintendents, describing them as superior men of liberal education condemned to the solitary confinement of the Australian bush and debarred from the social enjoyment of their masters. The best settlers—

foremost in wealth, in respectability and in worth—were those who had passed through all grades of bush life. They were 'not of the same genus as some of the squatters that fly like butterflies about the streets of the metropolis, dancing among the clubs, cafés, etc., of Sydney or Melbourne.'[41] On another occasion, in a typically Smilesian editorial it was stated:

> It is most pleasing to see that many have risen from the ranks in the Australian bush and have become squatters without the aid of any other capital than their health and labour. These are the men who mastered themselves, who did not disdain to reap, sow, plough, mow, fall a tree, split it for slabs, bark it or split shingles, make bricks, lay them, build a stockyard or erect a few miles of fencing, shear well, wash sheep, sort the wool, pack it, press it, load the dray for town, drive it thither, bring back the station's merchandise, catch an unbroken horse, tackle him, ride him, shoe him, yard wild bullocks, yoke them, drive them, make and bake a damper, take a turn at cooking, hutkeeping or shepherding, catch an opossum at times of emergency, cook and eat him, turn shoemaker or saddlemender or lend a hand at washing.[42]

But the stockman's road to squatterdom was long and hard, and few succeeded. Some made no effort, and drifted along as sundowners,* 'swaggies' or 'Murrumbidgee Whalers', living on station hospitality and avoiding work. Many settled for the smaller 40- to 640-acre lots surveyed near Albury and, to a lesser extent, Wagga. Further west, apart from a few town and suburban lots, there was no possibility of investing in land, and even near Albury, when demand outreached survey, rising auction prices reduced many a would-be squatter's dreams. Some of these were later to swell the ranks of the selectors, others were satisfied with alternative investment and status in the growing towns.

In Albury the overlapping of pastoral and commercial interests, the formation of the municipality and the growth of an urban middle class in the midst of a pastoral district, which had already done much to weaken the paramount position of the squatters, were posing some problems at social functions and in town organizations, and by 1859 had upset the squatting interest's election calculations. In Deniliquin, as yet, there was little evi-

---

*E.g., J. J. Westwood, *Journal*, p. 305. On one occasion Westwood noticed about a dozen men lying at ease. Upon his asking them whether they were camping for the night, they said: 'No, Sir! we are going on to the next station, only we are waiting till the sun is down.' (Cf. the opening words of *Such is Life*—'UNEMPLOYED at last'.)

dence of this. Major public functions occasionally included a
clergyman, Clerk of Petty Sessions, Police-Magistrate, or storekeeper, but were still largely squatter-dominated. The most an
ex-convict publican like John Taylor, however prosperous, could
hope for, was that his health might be drunk, with cheers, for the
able manner in which a dinner was served, particularly if he
managed to supply that rarity in inland Australia—real ice.

Though an obvious villain in some ways, Taylor was not more
so than many another opportunist and speculator in those times—
including some squatters—but he had been caught once, and
whatever may have happened to that particular myth in the
following century, in Taylor's lifetime 'the convict taint' was
damning. For a decade Taylor attended public meetings and
donated large sums without ever being elected to the squatter-
dominated public life of Deniliquin. Despite increasing lands,
wealth and respectability, a gentle ladylike wife and large family;
despite the public award of a silver trophy, donated and presented with speeches of commendation by squatters for his
bravery in capturing, singlehanded, four gaol-breakers; the taint
clung. At his most charitable, the editor of the *Pastoral Times*,
unable to ignore Taylor's public spirit and the large number of
buildings he had erected, could do no better than, 'There can
be no harm in wishing him success.'[43] But in Deniliquin's first
municipal election in 1869, Taylor had so far rehabilitated—or
ingratiated—himself with his fellow townsmen as to be elected
to the council, one of six returned from a field of eighteen. The
Pastoral Times was furious. The other five would make 'really
efficient aldermen':

> as for the sixth man (Taylor), he cannot prove either useful
> or ornamental in the Municipal council, and as he is unable
> to read or write in the common acceptations of these quali-
> fications it is difficult to see his recommendations for such an
> appointment. His return under any circumstances can only
> be regarded as a heavy misfortune for the town and imme-
> diate district. It would be unnecessary to refer to his con-
> nection with a town which has so offended the gods as to be
> inflicted [sic] by his presence.[44]

The vituperation continued for another half-column.

Taylor's rise, such as it was, is in many ways typical of the
effect of the new environment on immigrants noted by visitors to
nineteenth-century Australia. Some were struck by the 'smart and

robust appearance of the men' and stated that although the motley collection of

> shepherds, stockmen, bullock drivers and other members of the tribe of bushmen present a rough and somewhat uncouth aspect, they exhibit more manliness of deportment than you will find amongst the peasantry of the most favoured localities in Great Britain or Ireland. We seldom observed that loutishness which so strongly marks the English labourer, or that sullenness which stamps the Scottish farm servants, and certainly none of that whining servility which often disgraces the manners of the 'finest pisantry in the world'.[45]

Other writers attributed this evocation of manliness to the lack of comfort and conditions of life in the bush where 'each man who wants to succeed must think, plan and originate for himself.'[46] Until the late fifties at least there was adequate evidence of opportunity for advancement from the lower ranks of society, even if for some this reached a climax in the gold discoveries, when gold offered an easier road to affluence than the hard labour of taming the land. The waning of these opportunities—though still infinitely greater than in Europe—provides some explanation of the support for free-selection agitation and evidence of other social friction.

The squatters' economic relations with one another were appropriate to such arch-speculators. They cut one another's dams —albeit in a most gentlemanly fashion—trespassed on each other's grass wherever possible, and impounded each other's stock. Socially, their relations were those of one gentleman to another. Threats of horsewhipping were used against sly-grog sellers and upstart entertainers too free with local squatters' names in their parodies, but for more personal affronts—being 'insulted while out with a lady'—the whip was actually laid on in the public street.[47]

With their employees, their relations, like those of other employers, were those of master and servant. Newspaper offices, underlining and giving specific legal expression to this relationship, printed and sold 'forms of agreement under the Masters and Servants Act'. Under the clauses of the Act came cases like that of the Peppins' shearers considering tents an insufficient accommodation, shepherds losing sheep, ticket-of-leave holders absconding from their district or being illegally at large, and river steamer crews refusing to obey the master. A pastoral worker who preferred his old boss to the new station owner who had 'bought him with the station', was sentenced to a £9 fine or three months hard labour for absconding from his hired service.[48] Occasionally, as when one shepherd successfully sued squatter T. H. Mate for £30 wages, the position was reversed.[49] On the stations, the squatters' relations with their employees were, as befitted the master, mainly confined to superintending. Only occasionally, for diversion or in an emergency, as George Peppin Jr's diary entries indicate, did the master stoop to manual labour:

April 21 . . . I exerted myself to cut palings.
June 16 . . . I drove the bullocks at plough.
July 2 . . . All hands, that is all the swells, at work upon the dam stopping water with sand bags.

The rest of the society showed little tolerance of affectation or 'side', and uniforms as a badge of authority were particularly suspect. During the agitation for Riverina separation in the sixties there were suspicions that the esteemed president of the Riverine Council was aiming at becoming 'Duke of Mungadal'[50] and earlier, one Commissioner of Crown Lands had laid himself open to ridicule by always travelling in his district dressed in 'full regimentals with sword etc., and accompanied by any amount of frill':

Commissioner B., when you're out on the spree,
With your Border Mounted Police.
You think, by the Lord, you are loved and adored,
Like an Arabic Shiek, at the head of his horde;
You silly old 'Justice of Peace'.[51]

Disregard for the police was commonplace, and while a horseman galloping furiously around the streets of Wagga on Saturdays—a practice which the Police-Magistrate remarked was becoming very common—might tell a mounted trooper that 'it would take a better horse than he had to overtake him',[52] this and a more general anti-social attitude found its extreme form in bushranging. So frequent had this become by the end of the gold decade, with 'the facility with which lawless men can remove from one colony to another',[53] that the *Wagga Express* ran a regular column headed 'Bushranging for the Week', featuring the activities of the Gardiner Gang, Gilbert, Hall, O'Meally, Lowry, Dun and Dan Morgan.[54] J. J. Westwood visited one station on which, at shearing time, Morgan had ridden up to the woolshed, pointed a revolver at the squatter and 'made him sign cheques

for thirty pounds to each of his shearers; although afterwards, they were of no use, as the men returned them'.[55] Operating at the other end of the anti-social scale from these 'Knights of the Road', and occasioning less sympathy, were characters like 'John Baldwin, alias Black George' who at best was limited to assaulting two Chinamen; ethnic groups also had their place in the social scale. *
Apart from an occasional hold-up by bushrangers there was little direct evidence, in the Riverina, of the anti-squatter feeling which, it is alleged, led to land-reform legislation in the cities. More evidence is available to illustrate antipathy towards publicans; based sometimes on personal, sometimes on social and economic grounds.

Publicans were notorious for their facility in summing-up a customer's social status, and kept special rooms 'set aside for swells'. They were equally notorious for the facility with which they could fleece the shearer or bush-worker of his earnings. There was, therefore, little love lost between worker and publican. The old English custom of rick-burning, in its colonial counterpart, was directed not at rich land-owners but at publicans. A carpenter at Mulwala fired a publican's barn he had almost finished building, saying that he would 'see the b——y barn in flames before he put another nail in it'.[56] In Wagga, 'a gross and diabolical act of incendiarism was perpetrated on the premises of Mr. Patrick Fennel [also a publican] whereby property to the value of £300 was destroyed, viz., two stacks of Hay, one stack of Oats and one stack of Barley.'[57] At Deniliquin, John Taylor requested concessions for his customers from Joseph Simpson, the blacksmith. Unsuccessful, Taylor erected a smithy and an adjoining butcher shop on his own premises. Presently his hayshed went up in flames. This was the third time Taylor's property had been fired, twice successfully. Total damage amounted to £3,000, with one death.[58] Voluminous evidence was collected, and Simpson, the accused, made no attempt to deny that at the fire he had said, 'There's no b— mistake. I've got a down on Taylor and I wish he had been in the midst of the b— flames. What does a man want, to carry on a butcher's and blacksmith's shop? Let him stick to his public house.'[59]

To the inhabitants of the Riverina in 1861, the economic threat

*Xenophobic humour gave 'Niggers', Chinese and Irish a low rating, while eulogistic poems and prose raised the 'Anglo-Saxon' to the pinnacle. German settlers, falling into the latter category, represented thrift and industry, while the Irish stood for dirt, ignorance, slovenliness, dishonesty and vulgarity.

of the publican was obvious. The position of the squatter was at once more benevolent and more remote. It took the advent of free selection and the consequent struggle for land before the lower orders in rural districts identified the squatter as their chief enemy.

The extent to which the values of English society had been brought over in the 'cultural baggage' of migrants is underlined in their political institutions and attitudes. In the Riverina this was apparent both in the election results of 1859 and 1860, and in statements regarding the qualities desirable in members of the Legislative Assembly. It was three years since New South Wales had won the right of responsible government in 1856, and the election of 1859 was only the second held. In 1858, in response to popular clamour the so-called 'manhood suffrage' Act had been passed, giving limited voting rights to a large section of the male population. There were, as yet, no parties or platforms; even factions had barely begun to crystallize around leading members.[60] Elections were fought rather on the basis of preferences for individuals and their attitudes to contemporary issues. In the first Parliament, the Riverina had been represented by squatters only.

In 1861 the Riverina contained four single-member electorates, centred on the four largest towns; Albury (population 981), Deniliquin (632), Wagga (627) and Hay (172).* In 1859, these returned three squatters and one 'country entrepreneur', the latter defeating his squatter rival by three votes. In the 1860 elections four squatters were returned. The main issue in both elections was the land question. John Robertson's plan, embodying 'free selection before survey' and 'deferred payments', was the rock on which successive parliaments foundered. Following the dissolution of the second New South Wales Parliament in April 1859, Riverina members returned to their constituencies.

In Wagga, squatter George McLeay relinquished the Murrumbidgee seat in favour of his younger cousin, the forty-one-year-old William McLeay. The latter, who had represented the 'Lachlan and Lower Darling' in 1856-8, was the lessee of Kerarbury station, a hundred miles downstream from Wagga, and proprietor of the *Wagga Express*. A nephew of the Colonial Secretary of New South Wales (Alexander McLeay), William had been edu-

---

*All population figures cited are from *N.S.W. Censuses*. Albury's population is given as: Albury Township 981, Albury Municipality 1,587. It was the only municipality in the area in 1861.

cated at Edinburgh Academy and Edinburgh University.[61] In response to a petition signed by citizens of Wagga and resident squatters he attended a nomination meeting in Wagga. Cries of shame greeted his assertion that the government, after giving pastoralists fourteen-year leases with fixed rents, had quadrupled those rents during the period of tenure, without the consent of tenants. Concerning the Land Bill he favoured survey in advance and in excess of demand. State aid for religion he considered desirable. His speech was followed by questions regarding the Land Bill—'nobody is fonder of clap-trap than Mr. Robertson'; a railway to Wagga—he would give it to them in twelve months if he could;* free-trade versus protection—he now found himself doubting the former; the Chinese—'They are nasty fellows. But still they spend a good deal of money in the country, although they take a good deal out . . . Chinese immigration is a bad thing. It should not be stopped but money should be made of it'; the electric telegraph from Tarcutta to Wagga—'I find my name is down for a large sum'; a corporation for Wagga—if they petitioned for it they could have it; and artesian wells—'the Government ought to construct them'.[62] The electors were apparently satisfied with their man, who was accordingly elected without opposition in both 1859 and 1860.

Further downstream, at Hay, centre of the Balranald electorate, doubt existed as to whether the late squatter member, Augustus Morris, would stand and accordingly William A. Brodribb, lessee of Wanganella station on the Billabong Creek, was petitioned in the following manner: 'though a "squatter", your votes will always be recorded for the advancement of the colony, and not for a particular section of the community.'[63] Like McLeay, Brodribb was concerned with the land question and considered that a lack of courage lay behind the failure of Parliament, after four years of responsible government, to frame land regulations. The assessment on stock was too high, but as it raised revenue this should be used for road maintenance and the sinking of wells. 'The state of the roads he might tell them, had compelled all the sheep farmers west of Gundagai to sell their wool to Melbourne instead of Sydney.' Furthermore, although £18,000 was granted for improvements in Albury—a bridge, hospital, gaol and court-house —only £100 was allowed for a police paddock at Deniliquin and

---

*Twenty years were to pass before the railway reached the north bank of the Murrumbidgee. A further two years elapsed before it crossed to the main town on the south side.

'not a farthing' for Moulamein or Balranald.[64] Unfortunately for
Brodribb, Morris had intended to stand. The contested election
resulted in a victory for Morris, 119 votes to 27; Brodribb stating
publicly before polling day, that if Morris had made his intentions known earlier, he, Brodribb, would not have stood.[65]
Augustus Morris himself was well known in the district. Tasmanian born and educated he had joined in the exploration and
earliest settlement of the western Riverina, taking up runs for
both W. C. Wentworth and Ben Boyd and serving as the latter's
manager. From 1849 on, he was a pastoral lessee in his own right.[66]
In the election of the following year, 1860, there were no other
nominations and Morris was elected unopposed.

The hub of the Murray electorate, Deniliquin, straddling the
unbridged Edward River, was a town divided against itself. In
1859, utilizing the newly-completed and squatter-financed telegraph, Robert Dun, lessee of Conargo station on the north side
of the Edward, had telegraphed John Hay, former member for
the Murrumbidgee, 'Will you accept of a public dinner from your
constituency at the Wanderer Inn, North Deniliquin, on the evening of the nomination'. The squatters, storekeepers and publicans
on the south side of the river, who had not been consulted, were
so incensed at this that they arranged a luncheon in opposition.
As the *Pastoral Times* commented, 'Politics must indeed run high
at Deniliquin, when, to carry their point, the disaffected consent
to a cold luncheon in the room of partaking of a hot dinner.'
Despite a deluge of pamphlets and placards worded, 'Electors of
Murray! Do not pledge yourselves to Hay. Another candidate is
coming forward!', no candidate appeared,[67] and in the 1859
election, Hay was returned unopposed.

In his speeches the land question was again paramount. Concerning Robertson's Land Bills he stated, 'free grass means no
grass', and 'free selection before survey means no property'.

It would result in a tomahawk right. The lawless man would
throw down his tomahawk on the ground and say to the
tenant of the crown, 'Here are my 320 acres. Come! mark out
our provision and boundary'. No conceivable staff of surveyors could follow up such a mode of occupation as this.[68]

Hay himself favoured the 'South Australian system'—the establishment of Hundreds around existing centres of population, with
extension as required. Free selection would be 'ruinous to the
country':

If a modified free selection in pastoral tracts has resulted, as
it has, in so much and so mischievous confusion, how much
more would it be pernicious and inextricably confusing if
applied to the occupancy of innumerable small holdings. The
idea is sickening, all law, all order, would be subverted and in
the end, 'he would take who has the power and he would keep
who can'.[69]

The only other questions on which opinion was expressed were the
need for legislation to resolve the Billabong dams difficulty* and
the border customs dispute.

Despite their lack of a candidate in 1859, however, the south-
of-the-river men were not finished. They scorned statements that
'Mr. Hay was no ordinary man; he was not a member only', and
protested strongly that he 'neglected the local requirements of
Deniliquin, while looking after the general interests of the
colony.'[70] Such a man was not fit to represent them, and following
the dissolution of the third Parliament, in November 1860, they
sought a worthy opponent for the redoubtable Hay. They had
little success, but kept their opponents in doubt until nomination
day. Then their candidate was announced. To stand against the
man who had already been asked to form a government and who
was soon to became Speaker; the man who was for twenty years to
rule as President of the Legislative Council, they nominated
James Willoughby, Deniliquin's church sexton and grave-digger.[71]
Willoughby was a simple, earnest, hardworking man who lived
opposite the church, the scene of his labours, on a small block he
had purchased. Waifs and strays were given into his care by the
local magistrate.† The cruelty of the squatters' joke, for joke they
later claimed it to be, was apparent at his first and only public
meeting.[72] After a painful display of almost absolute unfamiliarity
with political procedure and current colonial issues, Willoughby
withdrew, and Hay was again elected unopposed. This, the
Pastoral Times considered, was just as it should be:

> The men who could trifle with such a constituency as ours,
> where, in a contested election, the shepherd would have to
> abandon his flocks, the hutkeeper his herds, the settler his
> homestead, and all these at one moment to exercise the fran-
> chise—the men who could thus sport with the constituency
> we say are not the friends of the district.[73]

*See pp. 47-9.
†E.g., a boy, Paddy, whose father was dead and whose mother was in a
lunatic asylum; 'the magistrate observing that he did not think the lad
could have been placed in better hands'; *P.T.*, 4 January 1861.

Thus in the three predominantly pastoral areas, the squatters, despite the much-vaunted Electoral Act of 1858 and fears of what the radicals might achieve by it, were in an unshakable position. Men of education, wealth and political and social experience were sent to Parliament by their peers in the interests of the dominant class, and, where these coincided, the interests of the district. In Albury alone were there signs of dissent from this established rule of the landed gentry. The Hume electorate, in 1859, had no less than four candidates for the single seat. These were Thomas Hodges Mate, squatter and local storekeeper;* Morris Asher, Jewish storekeeper, publican and entrepreneur; J. D. Badham, the Reverend J. D. Lang's† protégé from Sydney; and an Albury medical man, Dr Owen. With these four in the field, Albury's election campaigns were lively.

The main target for attacks was Morris Asher. Born in London in 1818, he had reached Adelaide in 1836 and Sydney in 1838, setting up as a country storekeeper in different New South Wales towns. Later, in New Zealand, he opened a store and two whaling stations. On his return to New South Wales he opened a store in Albury; then a boiling-down works, flour-mill and three hotels.[74] His political alignment was caricatured in a lengthy poem entitled, 'The Coming Men', in which Asher was seen as an illiterate, unthinking mouthpiece of an anti-squatter faction; but manhood suffrage would give him the victory, commonsense would triumph over Latin and Greek. In any case, it was said, money made the man and Asher had 'skill enough in penmanship to sign an alright cheque.' And there was precedent; did not John O'Shanassy, 'Victoria's great premier', 'deal once in nobblers' and 'wax fat on his beer'? Hence Asher's appeal was as an anti-squatter, self-made man.

> Here stand I, Morris Asher,
> Who have risen from the ranks
> With lands and houses all my own
> And cash in all the banks
> Earned by open honest means
> As ye who hear me know
> Although the so called 'better men'
> Sneer at a trade so low.[75]

*Mate's stores are still the largest in Albury.
†Lang's interest in the Riverina was long-standing. In 1857 he published in local papers a series of letters on country districts' grievances and Riverina Separation under the title 'An Inland and Riverine Colony on the Banks of the Murray'; *B.P.*, 21 February 1857.

The degree to which personalities were involved rather than party was further evident in the violent attacks of Dr Owen. Having accused Asher of illiteracy, using loaded dice, overcharging, watering brandy, kicking customers out of his house and being the most foul-mouthed in the town, he went on to discuss Asher's religion and Jews in general, bringing confusion and cries of 'shut up'. This 'liberal minded man', he persisted,

would take away human life by drowning the squatters in the Billabong Dams, and all to satisfy the passions of a Jew. His ancestors before him killed Moses in Egypt (sic!) and they afterwards crucified Our Saviour (cries of 'Shame!' 'Stop him!' 'Order!' etc.). On Good Friday . . .
The Returning Officer here requested that Dr. Owen would abstain from introducing religious subjects.

Of his other opponents Dr Owen was less critical, content to observe merely that, 'The whole three of them (Badham, Asher, Mate) had not as much learning between them as would qualify one man to offer himself for a seat in Parliament'.[76]

Badham's chief interest was as a quick-change political turn-coat. Although nominally a protégé of the radical Presbyterian J. D. Lang, before leaving Sydney for Albury, Badham had consulted Morris Asher as to the line he should take. Asher recommended radical leanings, reinforcing Lang's advice, and so it was as a radical that Badham reached Albury. As he met in turn Albury radicals, then moderate townsmen and finally hospitable squatters, the wheel turned full circle,[77] and his anti-squatter sentiments faded.

The most substantial showing in 1859 was that of T. H. Mate, the squatters' candidate. His meetings featured a large amount of good-natured heckling, particularly by one James Denison, better known as 'Jemmy the plasterer', an erudite artisan and a general favourite. Their dialogue covered the whole range of squatting and local interest: the land question, bridges, the Chinese, the Cowper Ministry, State aid and an elective Upper House, concluding with:

Chairman: Are there any more questions?
Denison: Come on Mate, what are you going to shout?
                                      (Laughter)[78]

On polling day, of the 925 registered electors, only 423 voted, and it was generally conceded that Mate, who was beaten by three votes, would have been at the head of the poll 'had not the swollen state of the creeks prevented many country electors from attending to vote.'*[79] In view of Asher's professedly anti-squatter sentiments the local pro-squatter poet was justifiably perturbed and sounded dire warnings:

> And are you sure the news is true
> That Asher's in for Hume
> Goodbye then squatters to your runs
> And tremble for your doom.

Here, too, doubts were cast on Asher's desirability as a representative:

> Bungs and Barrels! Room for Asher.
> Albury throw wide your gates
> Look up Pubs., a bottle washer
> Holds in trust our Federal Fates![80]

Less than eighteen months later, as noted, Parliament was again dissolved.[81]

The *Albury Banner* had been keeping a close watch on the Riverina representatives. After Hay's and Asher's activities in the house had been catalogued in detail, it was announced that the latter had 'neither been among the most industrious, nor the most idle or indifferent'.[82] Asher himself, in the 1860 campaign, indicated what he considered his achievements in a series of enormous advertisements like the following:

Working Men of Albury. Stand by the man who has fearlessly asserted your rights and privileges—That man is Morris Asher.
Electors of Hume, who got you the New Bridge now in course of erection. Morris Asher.
Hume Electorate—Who got you your Magnificent Court House and Telegraph Office. Morris Asher.
Mechanics of Albury. Who procured the endowment for our Mechanics' Institute. Morris Asher.
Brother Electors. Who has bridged your creeks and put your roads in order. Morris Asher.
Tradesmen of Albury. Who has advocated the extension of the Southern Line of Railway to Albury. Morris Asher.
Hume Electorate. Who is the poor man's Friend and the enemy of no man. Morris Asher.
Electors of Albury. Who opposed the establishment of Customs at Albury. Why, Morris Asher.

*The final results were: Asher 175, Mate 172, Badham 73 and Owen 3.

Electors of Albury. Shoulder to shoulder and Vote for Asher
who has always manfully stood foremost in your cause.[83]

These alleged achievements as a 'roads and bridges member'
constituted Asher's main plea to electors in 1860. Against his only
opponent, Mate, he brandished anti-squatter slogans of the type:

Who first availed himself of Free Selection?—
Why Mate the squatter.
Then don't vote for him.
Who now says Free Selection is bad? Why, Mate.
Then don't vote for him.[84]

To complete his campaign Asher unearthed an anti-squatter poet,
who, in six stirring stanzas, explained and extolled the virtues of
free selection.*
But circumstances contrived to rob Asher of further victory.
At a private meeting in Albury, five squatters, a newspaper proprietor, a storekeeper, and a goverment official formed a committee
to prevent the return of Asher.[85] And in December the scarlatina
epidemic, which had been raging in Melbourne, had spread to
the Albury district. Five of Asher's children suffered, and before
the election one had died.[86] This prevented much campaigning by
the late member and Mate, the squatters' man, was elected.
Even in this relatively urbanized electorate there was doubt
as to the qualities necessary or desirable in a member. As one
writer to the *Albury Banner* stated, echoing the tone of an earlier
editorial, every interest in the country ought to be represented,
'but is that any reason that a country storekeeper is to jump from
behind his counter into a seat in parliament?'[87] Later, in an
editorial, regrets were expressed that a large number of constituencies had sent to the house 'men of no standing or influence,
men of little education, and men whose experience and ideas fit
them only for the confined duties of the more limited spheres of
public life.'[88] It may have been the general acceptance of such
ideas that robbed the newly-enacted manhood suffrage of some of
its anticipated power, but more telling in country electorates was
the transport problem. It was difficult for Mate's squatter friends
to cross flooded creeks, but it was even harder for voters in more
remote parts to reach polling places at all, since there were no
more than half a dozen of these, widely scattered—some more
than fifty miles apart—in each electorate. It is hard to imagine a

*The poem is reproduced in full on p. 127.

squatter taking a wagon-load of his employees into town unless he had extracted promises that they would vote for his candidate, even if the problem of leaving flocks and herds untended had been solved.

Furthermore, the so-called 'manhood suffrage' Act of 1858 contained enough clauses relating to residence, freehold or leasehold qualifications, and board or salary, to exclude a good many rural workers.[89] Just how many it is not possible to assess, but the number of registered electors was no more than two-thirds of the adult male population; and even the act of registration was no guarantee of attendance at the poll. Of 449 (resident) registered electors in the town division of the Hume, only 266 voted in 1860, and of 713 country electors, only 208.[90]

In 1861, therefore, environmental factors and the nature and attitudes of the population prevented any real opposition to the squatting interest, except near Albury, with its beginnings of urban growth and symbiotic agricultural population. Although the geographical and social origins of the squatters themselves were varied, their control of large areas of land and the wealth associated with it helped them to maintain their position. Even the fact that the composition of this upper class might change completely during two decades made no difference to its dominance of society. As contemporaries quite clearly saw, Riverina society was polarized; a community of masters and servants. Men might still rise from the ranks and be accepted for their wealth, though declining economic opportunities towards the end of the fifties meant more support for radical movements and agitation for land reform. Still, even in Albury, 'Jemmy the plasterer' was content with no more than good-natured heckling. There was no suggestion that *he* should represent working men or the lower orders in Parliament, despite the 'improving' effect of the new environment. Wealth, education, and in some cases birth, set the squatter apart from the common herd. In the days before payment of members and universal education there was, between the 'Duke of Mungadal' and the village grave-digger, or ex-convict publican, a great gulf fixed. Most men of 1861 knew only too well their place in society—a society which reflected the values of 'Old England' more than any other.

Part II

FILLING IN THE GAPS

4

UNLOCK THE LANDS

Unlock! unlock! throw open wide, the portals of your land,
Let all enjoy those blessings given by an all bounteous hand,
Let all your voices clamorous rend Australia's sunny sky—
Selection, Free Selection let it ever be your cry.

Then shall the wilderness rejoice and blossom as the rose—
Then shall Australia's wilds bring forth each herb and fruit
    that grows
Then shall the sturdy sons of toil, each with a moistened brow,
The treasures of the earth unfold and cry 'God speed the
    plough!'

The burly Englishman and Scot, the son of Erin too,
Are waiting but the word to come and till the land with you.
Then welcome them—there's room for all, remove each sad
    restriction
And give your voice in favour of 'The Land and Free
    Selection'

Unlock the Lands, Unlock the Lands, and emigration's train
Shall quickly leave its native shore to cross the watery main.
Then German, English, Irish, Scotch, as brethren will hail you
And come in hosts to cultivate the soil of Australia.

Ye sons of industry who've been by poverty oppressed,
Would you not wish declining years to be with comfort
    blessed?
Remember then your little ones who look to you for bread;
O' spurn not such a tender call—give not a stone instead.

Then do your duty as should men, commit no dereliction,
But manfully lift up your voice for 'Land and Free Selection'
Then to the poll, your votes enrol, each tradesman, farmer,
    thrasher.
'Unlock the Lands', cry out all hands, and Vote for Morris
    Asher!

                              Albury Banner, 12 December 1860

127

As a brief study of the 1859 and 1860 elections shows, a good deal of political capital was made from the land question and free selection before survey. Before examining the state of agriculture in the Riverina in 1861 and events following the passing of Robertson's Land Acts, it is worthwhile considering briefly the views and opinions of the reformers in contrast with those of the local Press.[1]

Those supporting free selection included a number of Utopian idealists[2] as well as a large and quite blatant anti-squatter faction. Though apparently acting from different motives, these were allied and often indistinguishable. Both saw the squatters as 'monster monopolists', obstacles to the settlement of the country, the most useless section of the community, 'comparable only to the Persian Satraps of yore'. As locusts 'eating up the bowels of the land' or as a scourge converting a 'smiling province into a desolate wilderness', the squatters had usurped occupancy of the land. Free selection would remedy this. Every man, by nature, it was said, longed to possess a piece of land to call his own—not necessarily for agricultural purposes—and free selection would attract population into the interior, where, as men settled down and made homes, dissipation and the wandering habits which were 'so striking a characteristic of colonial life'[3] would be checked. Then would every man sit on his verandah or under his fig tree smoking his pipe in contentment, while the vine brought forth her fruit and the wilderness blossomed as the rose.[4] It is not intended here to explore the roots of this millennial vision beyond noting the biblical phraseology so frequently invoked and the projected image of the yeomen of old England.

But in the Riverina press the squatters were seen as the pioneers of civilization who by exploration, industry, investment and the production of a staple acceptable in world markets had done much for the colony. Any check on pastoral investment would hinder 'social progress' and prevent the growth of a great conservative element. The *Wagga Express* desired to see:

> a landed gentry springing up amongst us, with the influence to be derived from high mental culture and unimpeachable character, and whose extensive stake in the welfare of the country represented by large territorial possessions, would afford some guarantee for the stability of our institutions and the unsullied honour of our public administration.[5]

There was, furthermore, a principle of equity involved. The land was not an unoccupied waste, nor had the squatters occupied it feloniously or forcibly, but legitimately and profitably. They had therefore nothing to fear from argument but much to fear from a 'one sided and persevering agitation'.[6] Farming and squatting interests were not necessarily inimical or incompatible, but often identical, and, as in South Australia, there should be room for both. Free selection was thus seen as 'class legislation' in favour of the non-squatting section of the community. This anti-squatter agitation, it was said, promoted by a political riff-raff for pecuniary or party purposes and 'pandering to the base passions of the mob', *assumed* rather than *demonstrated* a public grievance:

> Disappointed demagogues, noisy litterateurs and the needy pariahs of every profession have poured in upon us like a locust swarm and Australia has become not only the Eldorado of the fortune seekers but the paradise and prey of pretentious political experimentalists.[7]

Although Riverina newspapers, pro-squatter or squatter-controlled, were conservative in tone, they displayed, like their contemporaries in other country districts, a good deal of commonsense in practical matters. Whatever the rights and wrongs of the land question there were a number of matters on which the Riverina Press was only too accurate and objective, and of these four are worth mention.

First was the assertion that many agitators in the city or on the coast needed to 'take a tour' to remedy their ignorance of the real state of affairs in the inland, and of country life and agriculture in particular. The Utopians' eclogues, idylls and pastoral poems were 'all very delightful in theory: but the man who sits "under his own vine and fig tree" would hardly "make the wilderness blossom like the rose".'[8] Land League orators nearly always omitted 'the knotty points', avoided reference to 'drought, murrain, blight, fire or other calamities', and substituted 'dashes of oratory'.

Second, it was seen clearly that any attempt to transfer an English or American land system to the Australian environment was unlikely to succeed. Vegetation, climate and water resources were all different from those of England. The case of America, so frequently cited by the Land League, was also considered inapplicable because of different physical characteristics; facilities for internal communication by water; proximity to European markets and sources of the choicest class of colonist; and the quantity of unoccupied land.[9] It was not denied that there might be a case for reform, but 'What we want in Australia' stated the *Albury Banner*, 'is men with the mind to conceive and the power to carry out such measures in all cases as are fitted for the circumstances and climate'.

Third, it was asserted that under the existing system of gradual expansion from town reserves, there was sufficient land surveyed and still unsold to meet demands.[10] Fourth was the question of transport and markets. 'We know we have grown and can grow wool' wrote the *Wagga Express* 'and we are TOLD to cultivate wheat': 'We have become prosperous by the mere occupation of the land, and we are called upon to appropriate it to the culture of an article for which no country within the scope of our commonwealth offers a single mart.'[11] Highways and markets, it was clearly seen, were at least as important as unlocking the lands.

Beyond such practical matters the squatter-ridden Press was as virulent as its opponents. Free selection, it was stated, could only create a class of settlers 'exceptional in character and miserable in condition'. Remote from markets, there could be no motive for cultivating beyond their own immediate needs, and in isolated clusters the 'active and thriving agricultural population about whom so much bombast has been uttered would sink into a state of sloth, ignorance and apathy for which we would have to look backwards to discover a parallel.'[12] Echoing this, the *Pastoral Times* in one of its most vitriolic outbursts gave its own version of the 'noble Australian yeoman'—'the depraved and dishonest "cockatoo" '. Having described the latter as the 'greatest cattle lifters in the colony'—'unwashed and cowardly', it continued:

> If we visit their residences we discover nothing there that is pleasing or inviting. Do we seek for religion, purity and intelligence? For religion we have the ribald and blasphemous jest; for purity poison and filth; and for intelligence, ignorance the most loathsome and repulsive. And instead of the neat farm house speaking of happiness and comfort, we have a miserable hut with the coarse spoken cockatoo presiding. This is the class for whose predatory convenience we are asked to revolutionise the colony by a new land bill.[13]

Whatever passions the issue may have aroused on both sides, the practical problems of agriculture as outlined by the local Press were clear enough and had persisted since the first settlement of the inland.

The earliest agriculturalists in inland New South Wales were the squatters. In 1844 Governor Gipps had noted that despite the squatters 'not having a property of any sort in the soil they occupy', they had brought some land into cultivation, 'in order to diminish the very heavy expense of obtaining supplies from the settled parts of the country.'[14] This expense and the uncertainty of supply had led the first squatters round Albury to grow their own wheat within a year of their arrival (1836), and prompted John Phillips, moving north from Victoria to Warbreccan, near Denili-quin, to have one of his drays 'loaded with about fifty bushels of wheat, put in loose, with sheets of bark on the sides of the dray forming a kind of box.'[15] When the 1847 Orders-in-Council were framed, legal recognition of this aspect of the squatters needs was given and they were permitted 'to cultivate so much of the land comprised in the said runs as may be necessary to provide such grain, hay, vegetables and fruit for the use of and supply of the family and establishment of such lessees, but not for the purpose of sale or barter.'[16]

Interest and success in pursuits not strictly pastoral varied with individual squatters. In the mid-forties, Henry Angel of Uardry station on the Lower Murrumbidgee had, like many others on the Murray, engaged in dairying, and from time to time set out for Sydney—four hundred miles distant—with a ton of cheese.[17] Others had fruit and vegetable gardens. J. J. Phelps, of Canally station near the Murrumbidgee-Lachlan junction, cultivated half an acre of 'potatoes, green peas, French beans and cabbages', which he irrigated by 'half an hour of hand pumping every morn-ing';[18] and George Peppin Jr noted with some pride, in his diary, those days when he 'cut the first *rock melon*' or 'the first *water melon*—a fine specimen of Billabong growth'.[19] There was nothing incompatible with the status of the 'landed gentry' in this kind of interest, indeed, it added to their sense of self-sufficiency, as is seen in the comments of visitors to one station in the early fifties, who wrote of their host:

> He grew as much wheat in his paddocks as supplied the station with flour, which was ground by hand in large steel mills. He reared an abundance of poultry upon maize, besides having sufficient for his horses and pigs. He cured hams and bacon, and made cheese and butter. In making the latter he had a commodious underground dairy to facilitate the operation of churning in the summer. Then he had a garden, where he grew fruit of many kinds, grapes, peaches,

oranges, apples and pears, besides kitchen-garden stuffs, from a potato to a pumpkin.[20]

Not all squatters were as independent of outside supplies (apart from the foreign articles of tea and sugar), nor, to judge from the incidence of scurvy amongst pastoral workers, did such benefits extend beyond the homestead to the out-stations.*[21] Early station records and plans,[22] however, indicate that most stations had fenced cultivation paddocks in which grain growing was attempted. On some stations these were small—ten to twenty acres—but where land had been purchased under pre-emptive rights, larger areas were cultivated. On Robert Brown's station, Collendina, fronting the Murray and close to the diggings markets, 150 acres were under crop. Across the river, Ford had seventy acres of wheat at Wahgunyah.[23] The success of crops depended on a number of physical factors, including soil type and the decreasing rainfall to the north and west. On some stations, in a dry year, the bed of a lagoon was ploughed up and sown; on others, sandhills, which retained moisture better in early summer, were cultivated.[24] Generally squatters near Albury and Wagga achieved some kind of harvest, while further west, heavier soils, lower rainfall and the hot winds of early summer sweeping across the plains made the results of sowing grain of English type more doubtful. One squatter on heavy soil, in an area which today marks the western edge of the wheat belt, had few successes over a twenty-year period from the early forties, and concluded that as he 'never got his money back' he had better 'give it up as a bad job'.[25] On Wanganella the Peppins chose eleven acres of light soil at the '2-mile Sandhill'. Despite all their preparations, the resulting harvest, in an area which is well beyond even today's marginal wheat areas, was hardly worth the effort.[26]

Innkeepers comprised a second group of pioneer agriculturalists. Like the squatters, they sought to avoid the high prices of horse-feed occasioned by transport costs,†[27] and except at the most blatant grog shanties, to provide a variety of foods for travellers. One such green spot in a dry and thirsty land was William Moore Carter's Red Bank Inn at Mathoura. As a result

*One newspaper suggested that milk thistle could be used as a substitute for cabbage; that the young leaves of saltbush, with a little vinegar, were 'not unpalatable'; and that the fruit of 'pigface' could be used for making jam.

†Even with the relatively low prices of 1861, cartage costs from Melbourne to Albury were £9 per ton by bullock team and £12 by horse team, and to Deniliquin £7 10s and £11.

of tremendous persistence on Carter's part in dealing with the government, in 1856 he was allowed to purchase first twelve and later forty acres on the Red Bank reserve. By 1859 he had three acres under cultivation. The soil, a typical western Riverina alluvium, was described as 'drift sand, minute gravel, interspersed with clay, at the side of the Gulpa creek, a tributary of the Edward'. It was 'land not worth a groat to the squatter, for it grows nothing but sickly looking gum trees and a few pines.' But as Carter found, it could grow enormous turnips and other vegetables, fruit trees, flowers and vines, so that 'the garden was the talk of travelling cattle men passing from the Lachlan, Murrumbidgee and Edward into Victoria . . . [who] strained a point to reach Red Bank to obtain a modicum of vegetables.'[28] George Kilminster of the Plough Inn, near Albury, typical of publicans where land was more easily obtained and conditions more favourable to grain growing, held 192 acres, which included twenty-five acres of wheat, twenty acres of oats, three-quarters of an acre of barley, and a garden, orchard and vineyard.[29]

Such oases, a direct response to the needs of travellers, were to be found at intervals all along the permanent watercourses and primitive dirt roads of the Riverina. Hopwood at Echuca, Maiden and Waltham at Moama, McKenzie at Conargo, McRae at Mulwala, Adams at Little Billabong[30]—wherever there were drovers with travelling stock, travellers on horseback or in gigs and buggies, mail contractors, coach drivers and passengers, station wagons piled high with wool or loaded with supplies—so long, in fact, as travelling men and beasts required feeding, small-scale agriculture and primitive irrigation were profitable. Even for this microscopic amount of cultivation to be legal—and by 1861 the total area under cultivation west of the Albury and Wagga police districts was less than a thousand acres—it was necessary for Crown land to be alienated.

Nominally, government policy was to survey land, not in advance of, but according to demand. What this meant, for most of the fifties, for both town and country lands, was that survey was well behind demand. Events at Lang's Crossing Place (Hay), worthy of a Dickensian Circumlocution office, were typical of the difficulties of that decade:

> When in the name of fate [it was asked], is a proposed township at this place to be laid out and sold? A surveyor comes down, looks at a place, nods his approval of the site of the town, goes away; comes back again perhaps in a year or so,

nods again, or even winks. By the end of the third year his eyes are again opened—the town is surveyed; off his plans go to Sydney where they lie on the shelf for another year. We now come to the fifth year and the land is up! Those who originally wanted the land have long since departed, and the land, when sold, falls into the hands of . . . speculators, who frighten away all newcomers by asking exorbitant prices for allotments bought at upset price . . . People want land and the Government want money. The remedy is obvious—more surveyors should be employed.[31]

For the whole of the Murrumbidgee pastoral district there was only one surveyor. As the *Pastoral Times* pointed out:

He lives at Albury 140 miles distant, and although Mr. Adams is a very active officer and means well still he cannot go over the ground. Were he a mammoth physical tripod— one foot in Albury, one at Lang's Corner and one in Deniliquin he would still only cover part of his territory.[32]

By mid-1859 this position had been eased, partly in answer to local petitions, by the appointment of a government surveyor to Deniliquin.

It was only by the use of petitions that the government or the Survey Department could be acquainted with local demands for land. In Deniliquin, would-be farmers approached a local doctor who drafted their petition for the survey and auction of a few small farms—'say of 50 acres'.[33] After a relatively slight delay four farms were offered in October 1859. The first, twenty-five acres of reasonable agricultural land with a river frontage, brought spirited bidding to reach £3 11s per acre; the second was withdrawn before sale; and the third and fourth, either because they were unsuitable for agriculture or because of a prior arrangement, sold at the upset price of £1 an acre to squatter John Tyson.[34] At later sales in 1860-1 country lands considered by locals to be unsuitable for agriculture simply remained unsold.[35] In other districts it had been stated that surveyors seemed to be in league with squatters in surveying dry stony spots, or that 'too much trust was reposed in inferior officers of the survey department who permitted themselves to be influenced' so that private interest retarded progress.[36]

Conversely, a radically-minded surveyor could mark out reserves quite damaging to a squatter's run. As has been seen, fencing created problems for travelling stock. To alleviate these, surveyors, on government instructions, began chopping reserves out of squatters' leases along the stock routes—'1½ sections from Mr. Peter Stuckey's Mathoura Run, 6¼ sections from part Brodribb's Wanganella and part Peppin's . . . 2½ sections from Lang Bros.' Mungadungadal'.[37] These travelling-stock reserves were accepted without demur by squatters, as being in their own interest, but other reserves—those made in response to petition— were less lightly regarded, particularly as in some hands they constituted a weapon of offence.

'Why Mr. Surveyor', said a gentleman in our hearing to Mr. District Surveyor Adams, 'the next thing Deniliquin will require will be some dairy farms on Warbreccan Run for supplying the town with milk, cheese, butter, etc.' 'Be it so', said the Surveyor. 'Bring me a document such as this requisition and so signed and I will take steps to get these dairy farms marked out'.[38]

Such a petition had been circulated by a mail contractor who wanted to erect a stable 'three miles in the forest between Hill Plain and Mr. Carter's'. The lessee of Mathoura run, Peter Stuckey, had objected—the spot chosen was in the centre of the run where cattle always came to drink—and offered to build free accommodation at his own expense on Hill Plain exactly midway between Deniliquin and Red Bank. The contractor ignored the offer and put up his own building, whereupon Stuckey pulled it down. Turning legalistic, the contractor circulated his petition for a reserve.*[39] The Deniliquin Press was horrified:

If a settler's run, by having a square mile in its centre sold, is to be destroyed because a mail contractor wishes to put up a stable in an objectionable spot, combined with the alleged suitableness of the locality 'for growing cabbages for the Deniliquin market', the settlers hold their stations by a very slender thread indeed. One victim had, and others must rapidly follow.[40]

The *Albury Banner*, similarly echoing the squatters' complaint of insecurity of tenure, stated: 'If a settler's runs are to be cut up on the authority of this or a like requisition, farewell to squatting in

---

*Unfortunately for squatter Stuckey the thirty-three signatories to the opposing petition included a number of his squatter J.P. friends. As some admitted later, on discovering their mistake, they had thought it was for something else, and in their defence it must be admitted that the stated location was vague; while one frankly confessed that he had not read the petition at all. The Surveyor-General, as a result, received at short intervals two contradictory petitions—Stuckey's and the contractor's—bearing the same signatures.

these parts. Between this principle and "free selection" the difference is small.'[41] In fact such situations rarely arose near Albury, because of its resident surveyor and greater survey activity, largely in response to the demands of affluent townsmen and lucky diggers who wanted to turn farmer.

By 1861 the cultivation and care of some eight thousand acres in the Riverina occupied just over seven hundred workers. Five thousand acres of this cultivated area was within the Albury police district and two thousand in the Wagga police district. Of this seven thousand acres, more than half was under wheat. In the other four police districts—Deniliquin, Moulamein, Moama and Balranald—a total of less than one square mile was cultivated* (see Table 7a). In the Albury police district 412 males or 23 per cent of the total male labour force were involved in agriculture, but within a five-mile radius on the New South Wales side of the town the proportion of male agricultural workers in the labour force was as high as 82 per cent.† Beyond Albury's immediate hinterland the area devoted to various crops and the proportion of the work force engaged was smaller as Tables 7a and 7b indicate.

The sizes of lots, when they were surveyed, were in accordance with contemporary ideas. Those surveyed and sold near Albury and the agricultural villages dotted around it in 1856-7 were of 40-100 acres.[42] 1860 surveys included thirty-three lots of 29-74 acres, twenty-one lots of 188-270 acres and twenty-eight lots of 41-353 acres.[43] Although the size was increasing, most farms were still less than 100 acres, with 30-40 acres a common size.

Even on the most developed farms, only a fraction of the total acreage was cultivated. The Albury municipality contained 17,760 acres and included some of the oldest farms in the district. Farm sizes within its boundaries varied from 21 to 590 acres (exclusive of one squatter's purchase of 3,717 acres, also within the municipality) and included the properties of capitalist farmers like S. A. Meyer (590 acres) and John Roper, Clerk of Petty Sessions (300 acres); German vine-growers like S. Schubach and P. and F. Frauenfelder (68 and 99 acres); and smaller farmers like J. and E. Kelly (54 and 66 acres). On one farm of ninety-two acres, forty-four acres or 48 per cent was under cultivation; on others the

---

*Five-year averages calculated from data in *N.S.W. Statistical Registers*, 1859-63.

†*N.S.W. Census*, 1861. Population of 'remainder of municipality', males aged 15-65, 235; engaged in agriculture, 192.

TABLE 7a

Acreages Under Cultivation in the Riverina 1861
(five-year averages)

Police district	Wheat	Oats	Other grain crops	Gardens, orchards, vineyards	Total under crop*
Albury	2,680	1,790	250	220	4,960
Wagga (N. and S.)	1,150	720	120	90	2,080
Deniliquin (including Moama and Moulamein)	70	430	100	40	580
Balranald	n.a.	n.a.	n.a.	n.a.	40

*Because of rounding, totals may not tally.
Source: N.S.W. Statistical Registers, 1859-63.

TABLE 7b

Male Labour Force Engaged in Agriculture in the Riverina 1861

Police district	Total males 15-65 yrs	Engaged in agriculture	Percentage of male labour force
Albury	1,813	412	23
Wagga	1,332	171	13
Deniliquin (including Moama and Moulamein)	1,469	46	3
Balranald	529	5	1

Source: N.S.W. Census, 1861.

percentage cultivated was considerably less. Even on the larger properties, purchased years before and let out to tenant farmers, as much as three-quarters was still uncleared.[44] Partly this was due to the need for a grazing area. Without livestock the farmer's land was useless; 'bullocks for his plough, horses for his dray and cows to supply him with milk and beef'.[45]

More intense cultivation took place in the market gardens near the towns—one optimist advertising 'Vegetables for the Million' at Deniliquin—and in the several vineyards near Albury where Germans were prominent, as the following list of leading growers for 1861 indicates:

Grower	Area of Vineyard (acres)	Quantity of Wine (gallons)
S. Schubach	4	2,230
E. Crisp	1½	1,080
Rau and Brownrigg	1½	1,068
J. P. Frauenfelder	1½	810
Johann Rau	1	800

At 7s 6d per gallon for new wine and 15s to 21s for wine one year old this represented a profitable investment in land.[46]

Of the total area under cultivation in the Murrumbidgee pastoral district 60 per cent was under wheat and 25 per cent under oats. Discussion of the state of agriculture is therefore chiefly concerned with the grain growers and their difficulties. These were fourfold: the nature of the physical environment, undercapitalization, primitive techniques and the state of markets and transport.

To begin with there was the alien environment. The opinions of explorers, surveyors and squatters had all agreed with that of a Crown Lands Commissioner who said in 1853: 'as for the Murray ever becoming an agricultural country, the idea is absurd.'[47] There was more truth to his qualification that 'the alluvial river flats constitute the sole land in any way suitable to agriculture and these are flooded during the spring',[48] but he spoke with the voice of one from a cooler, greener land. In good years, farmers near Albury reaped over twenty bushels to the acre; in bad years hot winds blasted their hopes and shrivelled their grain, or the locusts came in plagues. Near Deniliquin and Wagga, settlers turned to growing sorghum when oats failed, or experimented with Cape barley which withstood the hot winds better. Near Wagga, cotton growing was tried.[49] Riverina soils varied considerably in fertility. Near Albury and Wagga rich alluvial flats lay between the heavily-leached podsols on the hills, their tops crowned with granite outcrops; further north and west lay the as yet untouched red-brown earths of the western slopes, while on the plains round Deniliquin and Hay, apart from the prior stream levees marked by sand ridges covered in pine, the soil was heavy and cracked badly in summer.* Some lots, even near Albury, remained unsold because buyers doubted the quality of the soil.[50]

The second difficulty was the need for capital. Primarily, this was needed to purchase land. Despite extensive land sales in the mid-fifties, the number of independent farmers in the Albury police district was still small. As Table 8 indicates, tenant farming was more common.

This was, in part, the fault of the auction system and the lag of survey behind demand, which produced inflated prices for land— at times as high as £4 per acre for country lands.[51] Even if he acquired land the prospective farmer needed capital to develop it, as the methods of the larger proprietors indicate. First they

*See soil map, Figure 4.

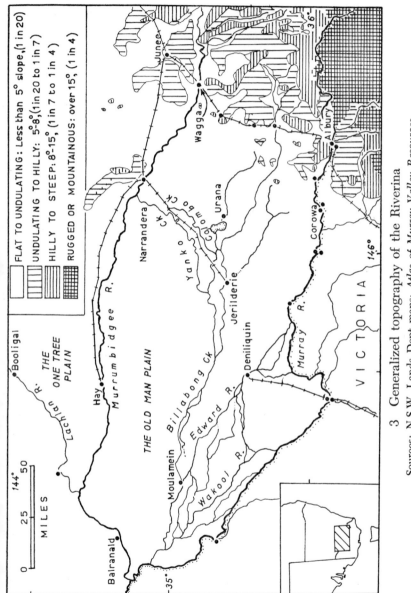

3 Generalized topography of the Riverina

Sources: N.S.W. Lands Dept maps; *Atlas of Murray Valley Resources*

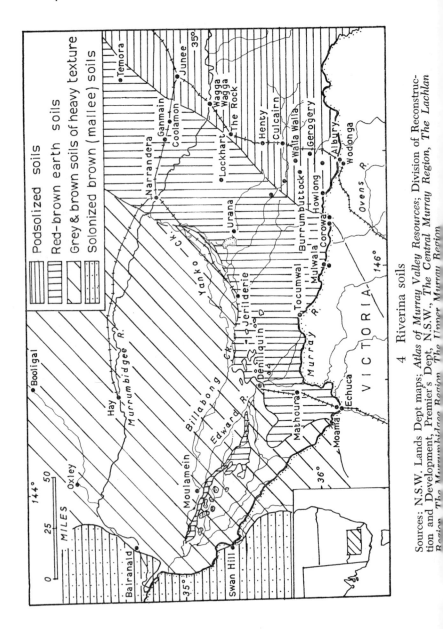

4 Riverina soils

Sources: N.S.W. Lands Dept maps; *Atlas of Murray Valley Resources*; Division of Reconstruction and Development, Premier's Dept, N.S.W., *The Central Murray Region*, *The Lachlan
Region*, *The Murrumbidgee Region*, *The Upper Murray Region*

TABLE 8

Persons Engaged in Agriculture, Albury Police District 1861

Albury police district	Proprietors employing		Tenant farmers employing	Hired farm servants	Totals
Albury township	M	4	14	13	31
	F	1	4	1	6
Rest of municipality	M	40	47	105	192
	F	16	8	20	44
S.E. part of Murrumbidgee pastoral district	M	18	46	125	189
	F	10	5	12	27
Totals	M	62	107	243	412
	F	27	17	33	77

Source: *N.S.W. Census,* 1861

acquired the choicest land at auction, in quantities adequate for cultivation and depasturing their own and their tenants' stock. Then, where the small man relied on family labour, the larger proprietors could call for tenders for clearing, stumping and ploughing, with the Masters and Servants Act to protect them from inefficiency.*[52] At harvest time machines reaped and winnowed their crops speedily and efficiently, and were then hired to others who were responsible for breakages; while their ability to secure the best transport enabled them to catch markets.[53] From their tenants they drew fixed rents, with the possibility of levy by distress in bad seasons. At the same time as one unfortunate debtor had to watch his standing crop of six acres of wheat and half an acre of barley being sold by auction, together with his furniture, cart, harness, etc., Messrs Meyer were offering thirty tons of hay for sale and Robert Brown, of Collendina, one thousand bushels of wheat.[54] Between the extremes of capitalist and hired labourer was a group of artisan investors who combined a regular skilled trade with farming. James Denison—the same 'Jemmy the plasterer' who heckled T. H. Mate at election time—had a thirty-two-acre farm of which eleven acres were cleared and fenced, including an acre of garden, vines and fruit trees. 'With a good and substantial cottage, large fowlyard and other conveniences',

*E.g., George Peppin Jr, after 'falling pines' with station labour, engaged a contract fencer and later a contract ploughman from Deniliquin. From January to June, hired hands were occupied in 'falling' and clearing, burning, fencing, filling holes, ploughing, sowing and harrowing. The paddock was mostly sown to oats with some wheat and barley.

the investment was worth £500. Nicholas Daniels the blacksmith had a similar property with twenty-five acres of wheat, patches of potatoes, maize, oats and barley, a plough, two cows and several calves.[55] Smaller farmers, even if they had acquired land—had cleared, fenced, ploughed and sown it—still had to wait months for their first harvest. During this slack period numbers took other employment. One worked for a surveyor, dragging the chain, another grubbed trees and cut posts, taking payment in posts for his own property, while many more acted as carriers. Near Wagga, with its restricted local market, landholders looked on farming as a secondary occupation, preferring to 'go to the bush for a load of slabs'. Others worked part of the year on stations, since seeding was followed by lambing, and shearing preceded harvest. After helping with shearing they carried the squatter's wool, alleging that 'in the best season they can earn enough money to make up the deficiency in their farming business during the year.'[56] The whole problem of undercapitalization was neatly summarized by the *Wagga Express*:

> No one can begin farming without capital and there is no man who has sufficient money to think about buying and cultivating a farm for himself, but is perfectly well able to give £1 an acre for land which he knows will remunerate him for the expense and labour of cultivation. It is a popular fallacy among those who have not a penny of their own to whine out that if they could only get a bit of land they would be able to live on it.[57]

Without a steady source of supplementary capital the small farmer had a limited number of alternatives.

> If he is poor, as he often is, his only resource is the hoe, by the use of which his utmost labour will hardly suffice to enable him to feed his children with the coarsest food . . . deprived of religion, without education . . . [his] markets at a distance with rough tracks over long lines of dreary wastes intervening, he becomes a discontented man.[58]

In the case of the Irishman, with the traditional prejudices of his race, revenge manifested itself 'in his beef cask, in his transactions in horseflesh, and such other stray stock as accident places in his path.'[59] That these were not merely the fulminations of an anti-Irish Anglo-Saxon was evident from the number of cattle-stealing cases involving Irish settlers. 'Let anyone in his right mind judge', insisted a Wagga writer, in a non-Irish case, 'if three or four miserable milch cows are likely, in five or six years, to produce 150 or 200 fat bullocks.'[60]

A third difficulty under which grain growers laboured was the rudimentary nature of agricultural techniques, though this too was in part a reflection of chronic undercapitalization. According to the *Statistical Register of New South Wales*, in 1861 there were thirteen reaping and threshing machines in the Albury police district. These were all in the hands of a few capitalist farmers. The bulk of cultivation was carried out by methods as old as they were primitive. Single-furrow ploughs were sometimes imported patent models but more often locally made, either of bush timber or with the local blacksmith's skill. Drawn by two horses or six to eight bullocks, they scratched the surface of the alluvial flats.[61] Despite the efforts of the Albury Agricultural Society in organizing ploughing matches at which a few 'crack ploughmen' showed their skill,[62] and much publicity given to the Victorian government's experimental farm,[63] Riverina farmers persisted with the 'slovenly colonial' methods deplored by English observers, who noted that bush farmers were

> not over-particular in ploughing mathematically straight furrows, or in having trim hedges to enclose their fields. A brushwood or log-fence serves the purpose . . . well enough; and frequently the furrows wind round the stump of a tree without offending the eye. Utility before elegance is the Australian ploughman's motto.[64]

Another noted that a ploughed-up field 'lay in huge lumps which farmers in England called "horses' heads" ', and was surprised to see a field near Albury with stubble standing a yard high 'as if the reapers had been too lazy to stoop and had only cut off the head of the corn.' The scene, complete with 'a couple of settler looking men in white linen coats and huge straw hats . . . on horseback, with dogs driving out bullocks' formed 'one of the most wretched attempts at tillage' that the observer had ever seen.[65] Harrowing was equally primitive,* and that done, apart from a few desultory attempts at weeding, the crops stood until harvest time. Whatever the preliminaries may have looked like to English eyes, a native-born Australian driving twenty miles into Albury along the Sydney road was 'constantly delighted with broad fields of waving corn ready for the harvest'.

*E.g., In the Peppins' cultivation paddock a horse-drawn harrow was used for half the area and a flock of wethers turned in to 'harrow' the other.

By December each year there was a heavy demand for reapers and mowers, the sickle and the scythe still being the chief implements of harvest. To complete the traditional English harvest scene, thirty-gallon quarter-casks of 'splendid beer' were supplied by local brewers and storekeepers.[66] In 1856 reaping had been hindered considerably by the dearth of labourers and machines, but by 1861, with abundant labour, the sickle was 'at work on all sides' and the number of machines increasing. One Melbourne-built side-delivery machine was considered excellent—'the machine travels all round the field, each time reaping a piece four feet in width; it is worked by two horses abreast and cuts down about one acre each hour.'[67] Other machines had been brought up by steamer from South Australia, where 70 per cent of the crop was reaped by machines.[68] Few of Albury's farmers were in a position to achieve the saving in costs and time effected by these innovations.*[69]

In the final harvest operations of threshing and winnowing, mechanization had also taken place. From 1856 on, hand threshing with flails was increasingly replaced by steam-powered or horse-powered machines.[70] Such machines were offered in Albury, either for hire or sale. In 1857 the relative costs of hand and machine threshing were 2½d and 1s, so that the hiring rate of 8d for each bushel machine-threshed still left a slight margin for the producer. By 1861 competition had forced hirers to reduce these charges considerably.[71] Most farmers, however, relied on hand threshing and winnowing, of varying efficiency compared with machine threshing, while the age-old system of having bullocks tread out the grain on earthen floors—as millers complained—did nothing to improve the cleanliness of the product.

Proportionate to the smaller acreage, mechanization was also increasing near Wagga, with patent ploughs, clod crushers, soil pulverisers, harrows, hayrakes, horse-powered threshing machines and chaff-cutters by a number of makers available for sale or hire.[72] In both Albury and Wagga, agricultural societies had been formed, the committees including squatters, capitalist farmers and townsmen. These arranged ploughing matches and, in Albury, an

---

*In a public demonstration at Albury, a machine cut ten acres in one day, with four men and two horses—costing less than £3. Cut by sickle this would have cost 30s per acre or £15. Apart from the saving of £12 on ten acres there was the saving of time so important in harvesting. Thus, according to a local writer, cheerfully ignoring the capital cost of machinery and depreciation, the mechanized farmer could sell at 10d a bushel cheaper than his neighbour.

annual show with prizes for pastoral, agricultural and horticultural products, together with an exhibition of agricultural
implements.[73]

The final difficulty for the farmer was the problem of transport
and markets. The rapid growth of agriculture round Albury, apart
from that geared to the needs of the town, was due entirely, as
has been noted, to the proximity of the Ovens diggings, thirty
miles away. Cartage of bulky commodities like flour, grain and
horsefeed to this market from near Melbourne or Goulburn was
expensive and, particularly in winter, unreliable. Fruit and vegetables were risky in summer heat or winter's delay. So bad were
the primitive dirt roads that one carrier wrote:

> We have taken a whole day to get our drays half a mile.
> Sometimes they were capsized and we had to drag our loads
> along on top of the mud. When you got off the track, down
> you would go with the dray, while the horses would sink up
> to their bellies, and then we had to dig both horses and drays
> out . . . frequently we lost our boots and had to dig them out
> . . . We have had as many as ten or twelve horses on one
> dray.[74]

Even the thirty miles from Albury to Beechworth were impassable
in wet seasons, the worst hazard being the Wodonga flats on the
Murray flood plain: a maze of intersecting creek beds, ana-
branches and mud banks. For four months in 1856 the only communication between New South Wales and Victoria was by boat.
Farmers and carriers with drays congregated until their means
were exhausted and then lost all in a ruinous sale. As late as
mid-November in the same year the *Border Post* recorded:

> What with swollen creeks, bad approaches, boggy ground,
> quicksand, lagoons and water holes, the flats are almost im-
> passable . . . The dangers are so many and so concealed that
> there are actually guides for the flats, who, we are told,
> realize £3 for the trip. At this moment there must be nearly
> one hundred drays occupied on the flats, many having been
> detained there for weeks.[75]

On the New South Wales side of the river, transport problems
akin to those noted in the pastoral districts arose from the general
fencing-in of roads by squatters and farmers. In one case the road
was eight or nine feet under water. A farmer taking his wheat a
few miles into Albury dismantled the slip-rail panel of his neighbour's fence which enclosed the road and was about to take his

horses and bullock team through, when the owner of the paddock, one of the district's numerous Kellys, armed with a thick stick and aided by his sons, drove him off bleeding.[76]

With such a chaotic transport system, supply and demand, as noted earlier, could not be matched.* At first, Albury growers had a monopoly of the Ovens market, but the advent of the South Australian steamers and the decline of the nearer diggings forced agriculturalists to chase markets over ever-increasing distances— first to Kiandra, then to Corowa. In 1861 the rush to the Lachlan attracted thousands of diggers northwards. Some Albury farmers, desperate for markets, attempted to cart hay and grain over two hundred miles to the new field; others took advantage of the temporary price rise to carry produce eighty miles over the new road through the hills to Wagga, seeking to undersell growers there, others again carted hay 140 miles across the plains to Deniliquin.[77] In 1856 the booming Beechworth market had inspired many small landholders to grow potatoes. When the market was glutted the *Border Post* commented: 'wheat can never be overcultivated because it is always available for export.' But by October 1861, with the growth of Victorian agriculture as diggers turned farmers, there were 1,950 tons of flour in the Ovens and Murray district, irrespective of wheat held by farmers, which brought the total to over 2,600 tons. With a weekly consumption of fifty-five tons this was reckoned enough to last for twelve months. By December, Albury farmers were cutting their unripe wheat for horse-feed; the price of 3s per bushel for wheat— compared with 11s a few years before—simply would not pay; while the *Albury Banner* unfeelingly talked of the 'delightful glut of flour in the district'.[78]

With generally depressed economic conditions in the colonies by 1861, the results of over-expansion near Albury became obvious in other ways than the perennial pursuit of markets. Land sales of 70- to 300-acre lots were held in Albury on three days in December 1861. On the first day squatter J. H. Mitchell bought, at the upset price, lots totalling 650 acres adjoining his own property. The rest of the lots were unsold. On the second day no business at all was done. On the third, squatter John Dight bought nine lots totalling 600 acres and squatter Ancrum Heriot 1,846 acres, all at the upset price, the balance of the lots again remaining unsold. To a 'gentleman' visitor who expressed surprise at the lack of bidding one local replied, 'There's no money, Sir.'[79]

*See Table 3.

Even in 1860 there had been some foreclosing of mortgages and
a few insolvencies amongst farmers further out from Albury. The
following year many were seeking employment as labourers.
With 'men offering themselves to farmers at lower rates than since
the discovery of the goldfields', wages receded fast.[80] The following notice, fixed to a tree near Albury's bridge in December 1861,
whatever its defects as literature, clearly indicates the parlous
state of the agricultural community:

> to all whom concerne Workeing
> Men of Albury reappers in Perticular
> Beware of the Cocktoo
> doging the ere holding on this
> yer the want to take a pint
> of the poor man this is to tell
> ye hould oute for yer price.
> Nothing under 30 shilling
> per acker we shant under
> this yer and we must hould
> out and get it.
> I hope now man will attempt
> to reap under 30 shilling per acker.
> A friend of the Working Class.*[81]

In short, with Riverina agriculture in this state in 1861, there
was little to excite the non-squatting population at the prospect
of the long-promised or long-threatened free selection before
survey. But thousands of words had been written and spoken on
the question of unlocking the lands, and in other parts of New
South Wales, particularly near Sydney, the fact that this had been
a deciding issue in the 1860 elections gave it greater importance,
especially in those areas closer to markets where there seemed to
be more chance of the small man succeeding. In these areas, men
had been sent to Parliament specifically to support free selection
before survey.

In 1860 disagreement on many points of John Robertson's two
Bills had led to deadlock and dissolution of the Assembly, but by
1861 so many members owed their seats to the cry of 'free selection' that, mindful of the 'threat of dissolution if on any clause of
a bill the exact idea of the minister is not adopted', the Assembly—
'a mere voting machine'—'tossed them both off on the same even-

---

*Presumably: Beware of the cockatoo (boss farmer) dodging. They are
holding on this year. They want to take a point (or pint) off the poor man.
This is to tell you, etc.

ing'.[82] Despite the gloomy prognostications of pastoral prophets, the serious opposition met in the Upper House,[83] and the obvious difficulties to be encountered by offering the same land to two different sets of people, the Crown Lands Occupation Bill and Crown Lands Alienation Bill (embodying free selection before survey in its 13th clause) became law in New South Wales in 1861.

In the Riverina, it mattered little for the first five years. Under the 1847 Orders-in-Council, leases were supposed to be granted for fourteen years to squatters in the unsettled districts (in which the Riverina was included). But so inadequate was the administration to deal with applications even at that stage that few actually obtained leases. Most were given a 'promise-of-lease' and even these were not granted immediately. To settle much confusion and for the sake of uniformity, finally all leases and promises were dated for fourteen years from 1 January 1852. In this way all pastoral runs in the unsettled districts were 'locked-up' until 1866 when the leases expired, not even John Robertson and his radical friends being prepared to upset this arrangement. Riverina squatters made good use of the breathing space. Many, as noted, had already invested in extensive improvements. Others now did so in order to take advantage of those clauses of the Act which allowed purchase by virtue of improvement, but the most active steps in protection of the squatting interests were taken in the declaration of reserves.

Provision had been made in the 1861 Acts for water reserves. Every fourth mile of water frontage could be reserved from selection, in a strip one mile wide stretching to the back of the runs, or alternatively, run-holders could have every fifth mile of frontage reserved on the same principle and take 'camping grounds' to the extent of 640 acres in every four thousand. These needed not necessarily to lie one within each four thousand acres of the run but could be amalgamated or taken on any other part of the run.[84] Most squatters did nothing about this until the runs were about to be thrown open. A minor panic had occurred in 1863 when some selection was made along the Murray frontage. But since these selectors, it was alleged, were taking up land merely to cut the timber which was then exported via Melbourne to India, the Survey Department acceded to the squatters' request and gazetted the Murray timber reserve, which extended for two miles back, all along the Murray from its junction with the Murrumbidgee as far upstream as Albury.[85] Little more was done until 1865. Then from January to December, and particularly in the latter month, the Lands Department was inundated with applications for the declaration of reserves.

It had been recognized that the Department would be unable to survey these, and indeed, was not even in a position to advise where they should be made. It was therefore decided to invite lessees to nominate reserves which could later be revoked if necessary. Besides those on individual runs, a number of larger reserves were made in special cases. Some Riverina squatters who had earlier assessed themselves at £29 per mile of frontage on the Yanko Creek and spent £15,000 on the Yanko cutting—rendering their properties workable in dry seasons—were successful in having the full length of the Yanko and Colombo Creeks for a distance of one mile back reserved from selection—an area of 173,000 acres. Similar vast reserves were made on the Willandra lagoon (two hundred square miles), which was fed by a squatter-financed cutting from the Lachlan; the Tuppal Creek, similarly fed from the Murray; and the lower Billabong. On individual runs the areas reserved from selection were considerable. On Moira station, besides several reserves of 320, 640, 1,280, 6,400 and 7,040 acres, a frontage reserve of 30,240 acres had been made, and this was typical of Riverina runs.[86] As the enormous lists of hundreds of reserves were published, the radical Press of Sydney waxed wroth, the *Empire* leading the way with articles headed 'Free Selection Strangled' and long lists of reserves. Even that conservative journal the *Pastoral Times*, anxious for population increase, but torn between its twin roles of champion of the squatters and leader of the opposition against the Sydney government finally decided that 'to have the pick of one-sixth of the run for camps after one-fifth has been reserved . . . besides choice sites purchased under the pre-emptive right and improvement, will not only take the cream of the land, but a good deal of the skim milk too'.[87] The result of the considerable publicity was the appointment of a select committee which, if nothing else, made it clear that when necessary these reserves could quite legally be revoked. Surveyor-General Adams, looking back five years later, stated that the object had merely been 'to enable the Government to avail themselves rapidly of the knowledge of the squatters and so save the public estate from having the most valuable portions picked up by conditional purchasers or by the squatters themselves.'[88]

As charges of corruption against squatter M.P.'s indicate,[89] there was a good deal of successful lobbying by Riverina squatters in the period 1861-6. Part of their success must be attributed to the threat of separation from New South Wales. The ingredients of this movement, as outlined by the original petition from a meeting of squatters in Deniliquin in 1858, were fear of what the 'manhood suffrage' Act—'the domineering influence of the people' —might do to their hard-won pastoral empires, and strong objections to the assessment on stock which was considered a violation of the 1847 Orders-in-Council, and was certainly additional to the rents stipulated therein. To this was added discontent at the perpetual neglect of the pastoral districts by the Sydney government.[90] Although the movement at first included and was partly financed by such diverse elements as the townsmen of Deniliquin and Wagga and the municipality of Albury, it was soon stripped to its essentials in personalities and tone as a pressure group working in the squatting interests. Its real nature became apparent when townspeople, suspicious of squatters who eventually conducted the Riverine Council meetings behind closed doors, began to consider annexation to Victoria as an alternative to separation; an easy-enough transition for them, since the original boundary of Victoria was to have been the Murrumbidgee and in any case their economic and social ties were largely with Melbourne.[91] The squatters viewed this move 'with extreme alarm', since in more democratic Victoria squatters had 'No security at all; they have broken faith from the beginning; they have never kept any faith at all.'[92] By 1865 with the extensive reserves already made and evidence of loopholes for evasion of the Act available in other districts, it became obvious to the squatters that their real aim—security—could be more successfully achieved under existing arrangements, so that agitation was abandoned before many of the demands of the petition were granted. By the time delegates were sent to England the cause had lost impetus and no great alarm was felt when the Imperial Council disallowed the request for the erection of a separate colony.[93] While the squatters had thus been safeguarding their interests, some selection had been attempted, as Table 9 indicates. But because of unexpired leases, the extensive reserves and a number of restrictive clauses in the Crown Lands Alienation Act, the areas in which clause 13 (free selection before survey, original selection) could operate before 1866 were limited. Nevertheless, even at this stage selections were being taken up by squatters in their own names or by others in the interest of the station.[94] Other

TABLE 9

Applications for Selections in the Riverina 1862-1866

Land district	1862	1863	1864	1865	1866
Albury	24	119	101	78	235
Wagga	4	19	10	34	171
Deniliquin	–	6	32	33	51

Source: Conditional Purchase Registers, Crown Lands Offices, Albury, Deniliquin and Wagga.

selections appear to have been genuine attempts to utilize the Act legitimately, particularly near Albury,* but these had little influence on stock numbers, population or the total area under cultivation by 1866. Whatever the motive for selecting, several factors mitigated against extensive selection or increased crop acreage in the area west of Albury and Wagga. Until 1866 it was easier to obtain land in Victoria.[95] And in 1864-6 the whole of the inland was gripped by the drought which in South Australia led to the drawing of Goyder's Line and in the Riverina ruined some squatters.† From 25.3 inches in 1863 Deniliquin's rainfall dropped to 13.02 inches in 1864, 0.84 inches in 1865 and 3.5 inches in 1866 —2.1 inches of the latter falling in January and evaporating immediately.[96] The day 'for which thousands were said to be waiting to rush the lands . . . the terrible day that was to ruin squatters and divide their domains among the masses',[97] and indeed the whole of the first year, passed quietly enough in the western Riverina. Near Albury and Wagga the number of selections increased slowly, but even in this more favoured locality the lack of markets and transport and the unexpired leases prevented extensive selection. Further west selection was more infrequent still.

In theory, free selection would populate the waste and make the wilderness blossom like the rose. In practice Riverina runs remained locked-up by law until 1866. By the time they were open for selection, not only had the squatters been able further to consolidate their position by improvement purchases and the declaration of reserves, but the prevailing drought served to

*This opinion is based on the evidence of Conditional Purchase Registers, which give the name of the selector and the location and size of his selection. Other local sources supplied information about individuals and the subsequent history of their selections.

†E.g., the Desaillys, who had amassed £80,000 on the Billabong, invested it in Lachlan and Darling runs. Before they were properly established, wool prices fell by 30 per cent. With two years of drought they were ruined; *P.T.*, 26 June 1869.

stress the inherent hostility of the flat country to big and small man alike. If sparse grazing was hazardous, what hope was there for the grain grower. In any case, without access to markets there was no motive for cultivation beyond subsistence level. Squatters and publicans could meet their own needs; artisans and other men of small capital might occasionally profit from investment in agriculture; but limited demands for agricultural produce made them, like their undercapitalized neighbours, only part-time farmers.

In short, although radical land legislation was passed in Sydney in 1861 in response to 'popular demand' and became operative in the Riverina five years later, the situation in an area so remote seemed hardly to demand it.* The Utopian idealists and anti-squatter faction in urban areas said their piece, but the small man in the country, like the big man beside him, knew better. It took a series of good seasons, the wool boom of the early seventies, a growth and influx of population, the discovery of major loopholes in the Acts and the extension of railways, to achieve any major changes in the extent of land alienation and the pattern of land utilization in the Riverina.

*That is, beyond the fringe benefit of providing a secure but fairly unproductive investment for the few with surplus capital.

5

SMASH THE CROOK AND SPEED THE PLOUGH

Free Selection in the Riverina 1866-1884

Peal the trumpet call to battle,
Echoing all the country round!
Till the cowering sheep and cattle
Quake with terror at the sound.

Fell not Abel at the altar
Martyr to his squatting creed?
And shall we bold Britons falter
To endorse a brother's deed?

As it was in young creation
Fate declares, so be it now!
Down with squatter, stock and station
Smash the crook and speed the plough.*

In 1924 S. H. Roberts stated that the 1883 Morris and Ranken 'Report of Inquiry into the State of the Public Lands and the Operation of the Land Laws' was 'clearly biased and [its] recommendations useless',[1] and then went on to quote it as his major source in demonstrating the 'failure of free selection in most of the colony'.[2] Since then it has been fashionable for writers on the period to denigrate Robertson's Acts and assume that the Morris and Ranken report is the last word on the matter and its 'conclusions' an adequate basis for explaining what happened to the Crown lands of New South Wales between 1861 and 1884.[3]

There is no denying much of what the report had to say. The Acts did result in fraud, blackmail, intimidation, perjury and wholesale alienation of land to the pastoral lessees. They were so loosely worded—in the interests of simplicity it was alleged—as to be liable to abuse, and even when used legitimately, were so subject to interpretation by Ministers and administrators as to be

*'Lay for the League', a twenty-four stanza work by Hugh K. Walker, in
W.E., 21 May 1859.

most elastic. But the fact that Morris and Ranken published no minutes of evidence and suppressed the names of witnesses—earlier enquiries had returned similar findings without the need for this[4]—and the very speed with which the Stuart Ministry appointed the commission immediately on the fall of the Robertson-Parkes government should have sounded a warning. The document is in fact little more than a political pamphlet. Like many another Royal Commission, this one returned the findings that were expected of it. It is in the selection of evidence and statistics, and the use to which these are put that the report is most misleading. In the Riverina, despite all the abuses and unintended uses to which the Crown Lands Alienation Act was put, much 'genuine settlement' did take place and the Act was influential in changing the pattern of land settlement, land utilization and social relationships. The Act was in fact as successful as it could have been under the circumstances. It remains to complete the discussion of what these circumstances were.

Because Robertson's Acts were passed merely in answer to political pressure, no steps were taken to prepare the departments of the Surveyor-General or the Chief Commissioner for Crown Lands for the anticipated business. By the mid-sixties the effects of even a moderate amount of free selection had rendered reorganization desirable and when the runs in the unsettled districts were opened in 1866 further stresses were placed on the already tottering structure. But the reorganization undertaken in 1867 still left the major faults of the system untouched.*

In 1865 acting deputy Surveyor-General Adams, formerly district surveyor at Albury, had presented an astonishing report to the Select Committee on Reserves.[5] Since his appointment to the Sydney office in 1862, he had been increasingly disturbed by the chaotic conditions in the department. Despite an annual increase in staff, arrears were increasing. Many of the delays and difficulties encountered in carrying out the provisons of the 1861 Crown Lands Alienation Act he considered were due to the unsatisfactory state of the maps. For this deficiency Adams advanced three reasons:[6] first, the use of the magnetic meridian with no know-

---

*In 1867 eight branches or sub-departments were created in the Survey Department (Roads, Charting, Compiling, Miscellaneous, Lease and Occupation, Deeds, Clerical, Auction Sale), and a separate administrative unit, the Lands Office, headed by the Under-Secretary for Lands, was divided into seven branches (Alienation and Lease; Ministerial and roads, bridges, ferries and goldfields; Miscellaneous; Records; Deeds; Auction and Statistical; Stock).

ledge of variation and no allowance for differences in it, and the use of different instruments by surveyors over a long period of time; second, the defective nature of old surveys which were mere sketches or rough approximations even in the original Nineteen Counties, a system dating from the days when the value of land was considered scarcely worth the cost of survey; and third, the practice of surveyors in the thirties and forties who, instead of making allowance for up-hill and down-hill, were content merely to give 'good measure'—an 'extra link or so in the chain'. These practices had given rise to serious errors which could only be corrected by resurvey.

> How it happens [he wrote] that after an experience of sixty years the surveys of this colony are found to be in such a state, or why, in all this time, they have never advanced a step beyond the method of measuring out land adopted by Jas. Meehan, the first Colonial Surveyor, at a period when neither the requirements of the Colony called for, nor its resources admitted of a better system, is not for me to enquire into; but it is sufficient to say, that every other British colony of one-fourth of the importance of New South Wales has adopted one or other of the great modern improvements in surveying —geodetic or trigonometric.[7]

In Victoria, which he had been allowed to visit in 1865 to report on the system of survey there, a combination of these was used. By triangulation the colony was divided into triangles with sides twenty to sixty miles in length and where surveys and alienation pressed, into smaller and smaller triangles, 'until a network of fixed points, sufficient in number to check the accuracy of the most detailed survey, is thrown over it.' Geodetic survey based on triangulation traced out on the ground the boundaries of the area to be subdivided. From the first preliminary clearing of hills and measuring of a base line this had cost Victoria, over a period of five or six years, some £35,000. On such a scientific and practical basis photolithography was feasible. In Victoria a single photographer and his assistant could, in six weeks, prepare 470 separate plans for printing off stone.

Adams suggested that a general triangulation of New South Wales be commenced—at an estimated cost of not less than £10,000 per annum for fifteen or twenty years—with the appointment of capable officers from England; or alternatively that in four of the counties in the worst confusion, base lines be measured, parish boundaries marked, and past and future measurements be referred to these. As matters stood in 1865 it was impossible to join 'maps' of adjacent counties and difficulties would increase enormously with the opening to selection of the pastoral runs in the unsettled districts in 1866. Despite his warnings, nothing was done, and six years later in 1872 he submitted the same report to the Select Committee on the Administration of the Land Laws.[8] In answer to the question put by the committee, 'Is the state of the maps such that a stranger landing here from California, or elsewhere, can walk up and ascertain where all the land open for sale can be obtained?' he replied, 'No, and never will be until we get some system of general survey into operation . . . I do not think any other British colony is in so backward a state.'[9] By this time, when the unsettled districts had been open to free selection for six years and the rest of the colony for ten years, delays and confusion in the Sydney office, hub of the centralized administrative system, were enormous. Similar conditions with additional complications prevailed in local land offices, making it even harder for individuals to obtain land by selection.

The first difficulty for the selector lay in discovering what land was actually available. Apart from the imperfect state of such maps as existed, there was delay in incorporating alterations in them, which resulted from all transactions having to pass through Sydney. The Hon. William Hay, describing what he obviously considered a model land office, stated that arrangements at Albury 'were very perfect and complete'. On a visit there, to his surprise, he found the maps almost plotted up to date—'up to within six months at any rate'—and Albury boasted a resident surveyor.[10]

Constituting a further hazard—as they had neither been surveyed, marked on the ground, nor even professionally described— were the six million acres of reserves scattered thickly over the land.[11] Persons paying deposits could not know whether the land they sought was on a reserve or not, nor could the land agent receiving the deposit always tell them, since these agents were for the most part mere clerks, holding the position of Crown Lands Agent along with other minor government offices. They could guess whether the land was really available or simply forward the application to Sydney, where frequently, such was the weakness of the principle of free selection before survey, the inability of the applicant to give a good description of his selection further confused the issue.[12] Concurrent with these transactions, intermittent revocations of reserves took place, notice of which was published in the *Government Gazette*. The *Gazette* often reached country offices on the actual day of revocation, allowing lessees to purchase immediately but preventing conditional purchasers from selecting until the following Thursday (the next land sale day). It was generally agreed that it was impossible for the public to keep abreast of such notices; indeed, even the land agents themselves had difficulty in finding time to read the lengthy and complicated descriptions, let alone mark them on their charts, had they been capable of this without specialized training.[13] The public, it was argued, could obtain the *Gazette* from the police, but as W. A. Brodribb pointed out, it was not the duty of the police to bring them before the public, who for the most part in his opinion knew little about the regulations. 'I never saw people', he stated, 'so ignorant of anything.'[14]

Charles McKeown, a Victorian, came to Moama to select in 1873 and approached Maunsell, the Police-Magistrate, who was also Crown Lands Agent. Because it was not a land office day— Thursday was sacred to that purpose throughout New South Wales—Maunsell could not handle the business. In any case he was unable to give McKeown the information he wanted; he had only old maps, and furthermore—being a personal friend of John O'Shanassy, lessee of Moira station—stated that he did not believe that any land was available on Moira. Far from being enlightened McKeown confessed himself in a 'greater mist than ever' and went to see for himself, whereupon O'Shanassy's men came riding furiously up to him and told him that he was trespassing. Later he was to discover that he had in fact been on the selection of another Victorian who had preceded him. Some Victorians were more successful, having hired a surveyor to assist them, but McKeown, after ten days, returned to his wife and family in Victoria. Others, with their cattle, milch cows, farming implements and household furniture, turned back with him from the promised land, unable to obtain information and 'afraid to risk their money'.[15]

There were other aspects of administration which contributed to the selectors' condemnation of proceedings in the local land offices. They objected to a Clerk of Petty Sessions, subservient to local squatter J.P.'s in the administration of justice, being also the Crown Lands Agent, since this had led to squatter magistrates being allowed access to selectors' application papers. On 'land days' the Deniliquin office was 'crowded with squatters and their spies' who kept 'patrolling through the room'. On receiving one selector's application, the agent turned to squatter A. Landale of Deniliquin station, J.P. and former M.L.A., who stood by with a sheaf of application forms filled in ready, and asked, 'Have you got an application to clash with this?' One being found to fit, the land agent allowed a ballot, putting in the papers and drawing them himself. Landale won.[16] Some Deniliquin selectors' applications were refused because the land was part of a temporary common and a population reserve. Soon after, despite vigorous local protests, two pastoral lessees, Robert and Alexander Landale, were allowed to purchase 2,800 acres of the same land at the upset price.[17] At Moama, selectors were told that the land they sought was part of a reserve. A short time later it was selected in the names of two Aborigines, both minors, the deposit being paid by John O'Shanassy, lessee of Moira. Another selector was persuaded by the Police-Magistrate to transfer his selection to Robertson and Wagner, proprietors of Cobb & Co., and lessees of Perricoota, on the offer of £25 and a position as coach driver.[18]

Quite reasonably, selectors suggested that there was too much business for a deposition clerk. They asked that surveyors or persons with some knowledge of land, maps and the law should be attached to all land offices, pointing out that 'men who intend to take up land would prefer to travel one hundred, two hundred or even three hundred miles to an office where they could get information that would not lead them astray'; and requested further that inspectors of conditional purchases be appointed. They, the selectors, were prepared to have the *police* inspect *their* selections.[19] All this preliminary skirmishing of the early seventies was merely a forerunner of the battle which was to ensue.

It was useless for John Robertson, author of the Acts, to protest that they were framed for 'honest men not rogues'. The plain fact was that they offered the same land to two different sets of people under different clauses. Amongst the squatters there were a few like W. A. Brodribb who kept themselves 'clean handed'. 'I never had a selection', he said, 'and I made up my mind I never would.' In his opinion the Alienation Act of 1861 was 'a very good Act if carried out in its integrity', but the fact that it was 'evaded in every possible way' had a 'demoralising tendency'. Because he saw a need for eventual closer settlement he was prepared to move further back. If one selector came on to his run and fenced his selection he would regard him as an eligible colonist, employ him to shear his sheep, and his team to take wool to market and bring supplies to the station. But if a hundred came, then, he said, 'I must recede as I have receded already.'[20]

More squatters took the view of P. A. Jennings, M.L.A., of Warbreccan station, who announced that 'there was no right or wrong in getting land and he would have it.'[21] Methods adopted to achieve this end varied. The most widely used of the legitimate methods in the western Riverina was the auction system,* whereby hundreds upon hundreds of neatly rectangular 320-acre blocks of level saltbush country were surveyed. Nominally, pastoral lessees should have shown to the satisfaction of the Minister that they were liable to suffer from encroachment. They could then call for land to be surveyed and auctioned. In practice, this became merely a matter of making formal application at the local land office. Despite the disadvantage that for thirty days after survey the land was open to selection, whole stations changed from leasehold to freehold almost entirely by this means, particularly in the mid-seventies. The price, except when speculators had to be beaten at auction or bought off, rarely rose above the upset price of £1 an acre.[22]

Purchases by virtue of improvements on pastoral leases were also widely used, some curiously-shaped 320-acre blocks resulting from attempts to utilize homesteads and the adjoining cluster of outbuildings in the most profitable manner. Elsewhere extensive improvements and even dummy improvements appeared; tanks excavated on the tops of rises, shallow wells which had never held anything but salt water, and a variety of movable huts and stockyards.†[23] There was nothing to stop a pastoral lessee selecting, in his own name, 320 acres with the attached 960 acres of pre-lease or 'grass right', and the evidence of Conditional Purchase Registers in local land offices shows that many availed themselves of this right. Of more doubtful legitimacy was the use of the names of employees and others as dummies.

Volunteer Land Orders were also permitted under the Acts. These cost £50 for the right to select fifty acres, which could later be extended to a normal 320-acre selection with 960 acres of pre-lease. The opportunity to acquire for £50 this transferable right to 1,280 acres for merely naming a 'Volunteer' was too good to miss. Although Volunteer Land Orders accounted for only a small

---

*See Figure 5.

†As late as 1878 the *Wagga Wagga Advertiser*'s 'travelling contributor' was protesting about dummy improvements in the Wagga district. He cites, for example, a dummy whim which he values at £10, but for which the lessee was allowed 640 acres; 30 January 1878.

proportion of the total land alienated, individual squatters made extensive use of the clause, the fact that the order named no particular portion of land—often only the county was stated—made it an especially useful weapon to squatters hard pressed by selectors or speculators.[24] In March and April 1874 Robert Rand, of Mahonga station on the Billabong, enlisted a small private army, taking out orders in the names of a captain, second-lieutenant, two colour-sergeants, an ensign, gunner, bugler, bombardier, three corporals, one lance-corporal and eleven privates, to which he added a further eleven of various ranks during the year.[25] Conditional purchases for mineral purposes provided another loophole and were utilized frequently on the alluvial plains where 'no minerals, not even pebbles the size of a hen's egg', had ever been found.*[26]

Selectors—if the term is taken to mean all those whose names appear in the Conditional Purchase Registers—included, besides the whole gamut of dummies employed over the period, bona fide agriculturalists and graziers, speculators, blackmailers, townsmen and investors, all of whom ranged themselves in opposition to the big men—the pastoral lessees. By the time the Select Committee on the Administration of the Land Laws met for its third sitting in 1873-4[27] the antagonisms engendered and the methods and weapons employed were already clearly defined in the Riverina.

The area posed a number of problems. From the time that New South Wales had ignored the instruction that the Murrumbidgee was to be the inter-colonial boundary and had fixed it at the Murray—and on the south bank at that—Victorian governments had cast covetous eyes at the Riverina. The whole of the area under study as far north-east as Wagga, lies nearer Melbourne than Sydney. Its economic ties were with Melbourne, and Victorian governments said that they would continue tapping the area and if possible annex it. In 1863 a Victorian Select Committee on the Riverine District had been appointed specifically 'to take evidence and report on the best method of securing to the Victorian Railways the Trade of the River in the district of the Murray, Murrumbidgee and Darling rivers.'[28] Partly on the basis of the report the Victorian railway had been extended in 1864 to Echuca, 120 miles from Melbourne and only forty-five from Deniliquin. Two years later petitioners were urging the New

---

*The complete absence of stone of any kind is a feature of the alluvial plains of the western Riverina.

South Wales government that the railway should be extended to Deniliquin. By 1870 the Deniliquin and Moama Railway Company had been formed and in 1876 the Victorian-gauge line was thus extended by private enterprise to Deniliquin.[29] The New South Wales government was here faced with a dilemma. Despite their objections to Victorians tapping the Riverina, they were anxious to obtain an enterprising, industrious population, and at the same time increase land revenue. Encouraging booklets were published eulogizing the mother colony and its liberal land laws[30] and disapproval was expressed at both the actions of Riverina squatters, and those administrative defects of the Act which led to disappointed Victorians returning home.[31] Victorian newspapers for their part compared the land laws of the two colonies and made public the opportunities in the Riverina, so that numbers of Victorians wrote to the *Deniliquin Chronicle* and the Sydney land office seeking information. With the reply from the latter they received government pamphlets urging them to come and select.[*][32]

Near Deniliquin, remote from Sydney, the squatters had been firmly entrenched for three decades and, unlike those near Albury, were unused to sharing the land with smaller landholders. By the investment of their own capital or by pressure-group tactics, such as the separation movement, they had obtained the public utilities and concessions they needed. Their ranks had been reinforced by men who had accumulated capital in Victoria in the two decades since the gold rushes, and who, anxious to invest in a booming industry, found the conditions of squatting tenure in New South Wales more secure than in their own colony. Lesser men in Victoria had also accumulated their share of capital and were anxious to invest in land, still *the* security in nineteenth-century Australia. Although they could not aspire to ownership of the large squattages, the greater quantities of land available, and the apparent ease of obtaining land by free selection attracted them northwards.[†]

By an accident of geography—a deep southward bend in the

---

[*]Even the *Pastoral Times,* in an article on 22 April 1866 which was criticized roundly by squatters, expressed regret that the opening of the runs had brought no influx of population, and pointed out how many hundreds of acres were available on the runs, all with 'splendid water' and 'magnificent soil'.

[†]For an example of the acquisition of a large run see the account of John Lamb and Willurah station in chapter 6. For an example of a smaller holding see the account of John Gibson in the same chapter.

Murray—the New South Wales county of Cadell was surrounded on three sides by Victorian territory. Hence it was the squatters in the Deniliquin district who, just as they had been the first to feel the impact of the Victorian meat market in the fifties, now first felt the pressures of the expanding, prosperous, land-hungry Victorian population; it was in the Deniliquin land office that they fought most desperately to retain their land; it was at Deniliquin that the weaknesses of the Acts and their administration were most clearly demonstrated; and it was from this southward-extending pocket of New South Wales that almost the entire panel of witnesses came to give evidence to the 1873-4 committee.

The enumeration of these witnesses illustrates the extent to which the divergent groups struggling for the land were clearly defined by 1873. They included four pastoral lessees; William Hay, P. A. Jennings, W. A. Brodribb and John O'Shanassy. The first three were, with M. Fitzpatrick, members or former members of the New South Wales Legislature, while O'Shanassy was a Victorian M.P. and former Premier of that colony. Supporting them was D. G. Jones, for fourteen years editor and proprietor of the pro-squatter *Pastoral Times*. Opposing them were A. Jameson, selector, and J. F. Mayger, selector, former employee of the *Pastoral Times* and editor and proprietor of the anti-squatter, pro-selector *Deniliquin Chronicle*. Both of these were delegates from the newly-formed Murray District Selectors' Association. This, the first such organization in New South Wales, had been formed in November 1873 to protect the interests of these new aspirants to a stake in the land. P. F. Adams appeared for the Survey Department, and later, in view of the evidence regarding proceedings in the Deniliquin land office, J. A. Broughton, Crown Lands Agent at Deniliquin, appeared to make his defence.[33] Between them this group gave a complete picture of the operation of the Crown Lands Alienation Act.

The first common grievance, which opened up a number of other issues, was the question of the pre-lease or 'grass right', whereby three times the area of a selection was to be available as a grazing area. Squatters and selectors, for different reasons, condemned this 'fiction'; the selectors because it was so rarely obtainable, the squatters because countering it involved them in extra purchases. A few selectors, despite insecure tenure, erected brush fences around their pre-lease; some compromised with squatters for part of the area, in return for immunity from molestation; but most were hemmed in by the squatter's use of any one of several different methods. Alternatively they competed for a grazing area with adjoining selectors. For a time the question of 'a pre-lease within a pre-lease' had fascinated bush and city lawyers alike, but even after it was decided that the pre-lease was indefeasible except by selection, squatters could still employ dummies to select on the selector's pre-lease.[34] Near Albury, where settlement was much closer, there was no possibility of obtaining a pre-lease at all. This raised the question of area. When P. A. Jennings of Warbreccan was asked whether 320 acres was 'a sufficient quantity to enable a sort of yeomanry to spring up', he suggested that 640 acres without a pre-lease would be more acceptable, and with this both squatters and selectors agreed.[35] Around Deniliquin, where land was required more for grazing than agriculture, selectors considered this to be particularly necessary.

Until the early seventies there had been few 'pastoral selectors', the few small selectors near Moama using their land solely for agriculture. But by 1873 great numbers of 'graziers' had appeared near Deniliquin, 'fencing, building, sinking wells and constructing dams'. Opinions varied as to their chances. W. A. Brodribb thought that 'the men who [were] now coming across the Border making a raid on the various runs in the neighbourhood of Deniliquin [would] all come to grief in the first dry season.' In 1865 he had lost twelve thousand sheep and all the lambs from sixteen thousand ewes. J. F. Mayger, however, knew a man and his son with 320 acres each and some part of the grazing right, who had sold a few cattle and spent £147 on purchasing sheep. Within one year they had cleared £290 from fleeces and lambs, and still had the ewes left.[36] Here the question of the intention of the Act was raised, thus:

> Q.1068 Do you think that in framing the Land Act the idea was to raise up a second class of graziers, or was it to establish a class of agriculturists, and to throw open the land of the colony for the spread of agriculture?
> I imagine [replied Mayger] that the idea was to enable the people to go upon the land and use it in the most profitable manner they could.
> Q.1069 To attract population in fact?
> Yes, and without dictating to them whether they should be agriculturists or whether they should be graziers.*[37]

*The term 'grazier' had been used by T. S. Mort when addressing the Select Committee on the Present State of the Colony in 1865-6 and had

On a number of other points selectors and squatters differed. P. A. Jennings alleged that the strong speculative feeling in Melbourne had led to the formation of a joint stock company of forty-seven persons who intended taking over whole runs by selecting land as soon as it was surveyed for auction. Although the committee had received a statement signed by thirty Riverina run-holders supporting this statement, the selectors' representatives denied ever having heard of such a thing. Jennings's further suggestion, that land surveyed for auction be not opened for selection, Mayger denounced as 'monstrous', and suggested that the lessees 'had better apply for the freehold of the runs as a gift'. His colleague Jameson added that, to confuse selectors, squatters went around reversing auction survey pegs after surveyors had left.[38]

The extensive reserves were also discussed. Squatters objected that some selectors had been allowed to retain selections they had improved, when eventually it was discovered that these were on reserves, while selectors protested against squatters being allowed to secure parts of reserves as improvement purchases.[39] One member of the committee expressed considerable surprise that the reserves made on Moira run, and ostensibly extending to the back of the run, were still enclosed by the Moira boundary fence, but this was common on all runs.[40] Reserves were in fact reserved for the use of the Crown lessee.

Much of the evidence concerned 'dummying 'or, as one squatter preferred to call it, 'vicarious selection'. Taking up selections in other men's names was not confined to squatters, but the method was used extensively by them, particularly in the more closely settled areas where more names were available. Jameson stated that between 7 October and 6 November 1873 there were 396 applications for land at Deniliquin under clause 13. Of these 216 were from squatters or their agents, the land taken up by them under free selection amounting to over 52,000 acres.[41]

The Landale brothers of Deniliquin, P. A. Jennings of Warbreccan and the Peppin brothers of Wanganella (and other properties), by the exercise of a little ingenuity and at little extra expense, found a way to avoid blackmail at the hands of dummies and at the same time protect land surveyed for auction. As soon as the

since been in common usage; *V. & P.* (L.A. N.S.W.), 1865-6, vol. 3, p. 614. ('You draw a distinction then between graziers and free selectors?') The term will be used hereafter to describe selectors who acquired or sought to acquire sufficient land to devote themselves mainly to pastoral pursuits.

land was cut up into 320-acre blocks, applications for selection were made, and 5s per acre deposit paid. Then, either in the Deniliquin land office or in Sydney, through M. Fitzpatrick M.L.A. or another of their associates, it would be represented that the selectors, because cut off from water or grass rights, wished to forfeit, whereupon the selection was purchased by the squatter at the upset price, making a total cost of 25s per acre.*[42] The method was particularly favoured by the Peppins who employed only a few permanent hands and on occasion applied for as many as twenty-six selections on one day.[43] One selector on the Forest Creek wrote in disgust to Mayger at the *Deniliquin Chronicle*:

> I see Mr. Peppin goes in heavy every land day, there are several men's names he has used three or four times within the twelve months as dummys [*sic*] . . . Mr. Peppin is about taking our grazing rights now, having them all surveyed in blocks for purchase, notwithstanding he had the use of them before.

Like others, the Peppins were seriously concerned about the quality of the sheep they were breeding and for this reason favoured the suggestion that fencing of selections be compulsory, though a Bill to enforce fencing had failed to pass the Assembly.[44]

Besides giving Aborigines on the stations enhanced value in the eyes of the squatters,[45] dummying found a new use—other than teaching or entering the constabulary—for the destitute. Thomas Glennon had originally been a policeman in the district under the old police system, 'but he left the Force when the new system was established and since then he had been an odd man or boundary rider or something of that kind to Mr. Jennings.'[46] In due course his name appeared as a selector. Jennings's attitude to him was the same as to the Murray family; man, wife and seven children making nine dummy selections on his run.[47] Said Jennings, 'I facilitated his selections as a friendly selector.' This indeed was the sole defence the squatters could offer for dummying. They simply defined two classes of selectors. One class included those who were 'never in conflict with the runholder' but 'useful to him', men 'who had been employed on the runs and who, knowing the country, prefer to settle down there. They are, as a rule, teamsters, contractors for fencing or bush hands who take contracts for improvements on stations, but who also desire

---

*P. A. Jennings had great difficulty in explaining his part in such a transaction.

to have a home.' These the squatters 'encouraged'.[48] The other class included blackmailers, speculators and residents of towns. The latter—drapers, grocers, storekeepers, hotelkeepers, professional and businessmen—had acquired capital which they wanted to invest in land and had to comply with the residence clause 'vicariously'. Tradesmen in Echuca (Victoria) had acquired New South Wales land in this way.[49]

In Deniliquin, squatter M.L.A. Patrick Jennings, and *Pastoral Times* editor, D. G. Jones, found John Taylor's dummying particularly objectionable. Using servants from the Royal Hotel, and eight or nine of his children, Taylor had purchased seventeen selections and boasted of it quite openly in a public meeting. With other selectors he completely hemmed in the Deniliquin-Echuca road, reducing it to a narrow fenced lane for miles. It had cost the government £1,000 to make an alternative road, but before this, travellers had been forced to pay for grass or night paddocking, and in winter, when the road was under water, coach operators had to pay a selector at the Yellow Water Holes for the right to cross his paddock.[*][50]

After discussing a number of other minor points and cursorily examining witnesses from other areas, who merely confirmed that much of what had been happening at Deniliquin was beginning elsewhere, the committee submitted its third progress report. Even while it had been sitting, however, a train of events was taking place on Moira station which was, for a few years, to have considerable effects on social relationships, land revenue and the pattern of land settlement.

In Victoria, selections could not be made by persons under eighteen years of age; but in the Supreme Court in Sydney it had been ruled in two cases that selection by minors was legal under the New South Wales Act, the whole question revolving on the legal interpretation of the term 'person'.[51] In February 1873, William Joachim, a Devon-born stock-dealer and butcher, who had moved from his Victorian property to Moama, 'goaded to the contest by the free and easy directors of and anonymous writers in the ultra-radical press of New South Wales and Victoria',[52] tested the limits of the law with regard to selection by minors.[53] Boldly entering a forty-two-square-mile fenced paddock on Moira

---

[*]Jones gave this as one reason for seeking a railway, and added, presumably because of the danger to drovers with travelling stock, that there were 'grog shops all along the road and a good deal of crime'; *V. & P.* (L.A. N.S.W.), 1873-4, vol. 3, p. 987.

station, he took up adjoining selections for eight of his children (all minors), paid to the astonished Deniliquin land agent a total of £640 deposit and began erecting huts and other improvements. The Hon. John O'Shanassy, once he had recovered from his initial shock, acted promptly, and M. Fitzpatrick M.L.A. approached the Minister of Lands on his behalf, alleging that to have 2,560 acres selected, 'practically by one man, was contrary to the clear intention of the law' and was indeed, 'a prostitution of the Land Law'. He stated further that seven of the eight minors were not residing on their selections, being all in the one tent. W. W. Stephen, Under-Secretary of Lands, sought an immediate report from Maunsell, the Moama land agent, who replied that Joachim intended to erect a junction house, covering several selections under one roof, and that when he had inspected the place there were two tents, part of a dwelling house, a bark kitchen and a covered dray for conveying the children to the selections at night. J. S. Farnell of the Sydney lands office ruled that this was a 'gross attempt to defeat the land law in its meaning, spirit and intention' and that junction houses were not to be allowed. He further recommended that six of the eight selections be forfeited. Joachim was accordingly informed of this and his probable loss of £480 deposit money.

In reply, he objected to the 'exceptionally urgent instructions issued by the Government to watch this family'; pointed out that the local land agent had found all selectors in residence, willing and ready to commence improvements; that junction residences were allowed in numerous other cases; and requested a thorough investigation. O'Shanassy now took matters into his own hands and in June ordered three thousand sheep to be driven on to the selections, whereupon Joachim successfully obtained an injunction restraining him. At the same time as he advised the Secretary of Lands of the trespass, Joachim forwarded a 'certificate' signed by neighbours, including the McLaurins of Cornalla, stating that the Joachim children were all bona fide resident selectors. This was promptly denied in a subsequent statutory declaration by O'Shanassy's overseer and station hands. With threat and counter-threat, argument and rebuttal, accusation and counter-accusation the dispute raged on, while squatters, selectors, and newspapers in both town and country took sides.[54] Selectors' arguments varied from the plaintive 'What are we to do with our sons?' and the view that it was 'a good thing that a father should be able to endow his children with land', to the more militant statements of

J. F. Mayger, who, writing of Morago run where there was more
reserved than leased land, stated 'however . . . I am happy to say
that only last month the first selection was made on this run by a
man with eleven children.'[55] The *Pastoral Times,* for its part,
pointed out the dangers of rushing between the fences of bellicose
squatters and praised the country available for lease in the
Lachlan backblocks, while one squatter boasted that Deniliquin
'would again be a sheepwalk as it had been before'.[56]

Meanwhile, on Moira, Joachim held the fort. Surveyor Finley
had been instructed to survey the eight selections to clarify
matters a little, and to report on residence and improvements.
Henry, twelve months of age, was resident. 'His mother, I believe,
lives with him', Finley wrote. On his selection a canvas tent had
been erected on a frame, with a chimney attached; value £8. On
James's selection stood a dwelling hut of two rooms built of sawn
timber with a 'zinc roof' (£40), a garden securely fenced and
planted with trees and vines (£40) and a tank and dam (£10),
making improvements worth £90. George had lived with his
brother Henry. 'On the supposition that the residence was on the
boundary line . . . he has resided in several different spots on the
land in consequence of not knowing where the boundary would
be.' His own house was worth £22. Selina's hut, tent and part of
another hut were worth £38; John Thomas's covered-in dray and
part of Sophia's hut were worth £25; William's hut was worth £20
and 'five acres of cultivation on excellent plain soil' was worth
£15. Annie, whose application form was returned from Sydney
because it did not state whether she was spinster or widow ('This
information is always required'), had a tent with a galvanized-
iron roof, worth £6, and Sophia had a tent and part of a hut worth
£22 10s.[57] To Surveyor Finley who, in July 1873, had been in the
neighbourhood for some time and had watched them closely, all
appeared to be bona fide selectors complying with the residence
and improvement clauses.

At first Joachim had driven the whole family around each
evening in a covered van, so that all were on each selection for a
time. Then, as the tents and huts were erected, children-in-arms
were carted around at night and one put to sleep in each. 'No
one in his senses' wrote one critic, 'will be found to maintain the
excellence of a system which necessitates young girls aged fourteen, twelve and ten years of age sleeping in separate tents on
separate allotments, in order to fulfil the residence condition,
especially with "bed rakers" prowling about.'[58] This latter soubri-

quet had been earned by John O'Shanassy Jr for his noctural inspections of the sleeping arrangements. At the same time O'Shanassy sought to hem in Joachim and twelve other selectors on Moira by the use of improvement purchases and dummies. The selectors checked the validity of residence on the latter by inspecting each morning thin strands of grass or string they had tied across the entrances to the dummies' huts or tents. Frequently O'Shanassy's men drove sheep right up to the doors of the huts and dared the children to come outside and startle the sheep.[59] In January 1874, twenty persons, led by O'Shanassy Jr, entered Joachim's selections and began erecting tents to take possession. Joachim protested and placed his foot over a post-hole, whereupon one Stephen Hagan was ordered to 'do his duty'. He rushed up and threatened to put a crowbar through Joachim's foot. Joachim retreated. The *Riverine Grazier* (Hay) and the Melbourne *Age* wrote that feeling was high and bloodshed expected.*[60]

In February 1874 O'Shanassy adopted new tactics and began fencing across the roads and tracks leading to Joachim's and other selections. When one selector, J. Rousch, returned home with a load of building materials, he found wires across the track and a boundary rider there watching. He cut the wires to reach his selection and was subsequently prosecuted and fined in the Moama court.[61] With interest widespread throughout New South Wales and Victoria, Joachim *v.* O'Shanassy was fast becoming an important test case. Events were expected to reach a climax in April 1874 when the trespass case was heard at Deniliquin. Accommodation in the town was taxed and the court-house crowded with selectors and squatters.†

Joachim, browbeaten and weary by this time, made no objection to the case being heard by Sir James Martin, who had set aside the injunction restraining O'Shanassy the year before. A jury of four squatters was sworn in, and the trial began. To many it was an anticlimax. O'Shanassy admitted trespass and was willing to pay half the damages claimed, on condition that he be granted

---

*The reason for the invasion was that Sir James Martin, Q.C., had reversed the restraining injunction decision against O'Shanassy on two grounds; the first, quite irrelevant, that the selections had been taken up inside a fenced paddock on which Moira sheep had grazed for years; the second, more valid, that the Joachims had not complied with the residence conditions *within one month* as required by clause 13 of the Act.

†O'Shanassy took a seat at one of the tables, 'on which he leant forward and rested in a manner reminding one of the posture and appearance of the claimant, as represented in English illustrated papers'; *Riverine Herald* [n.d.] quoted in A. Morris, *Rich River*, p. 89.

leave to apply to the Supreme Court in Sydney on the grounds that persons under the age of twenty-one years could not legally be selectors under the Act, either personally or by agent. Joachim cut his losses, pocketed the £150 and agreed.[62] It took until 1876 for the case to pass through the Supreme Court to the Privy Council in London to which it was eventually referred since it was obviously a matter affecting the general interest of the colony.[63]

Throughout the whole period the strife on Moira continued. For most of the time the New South Wales government had remained on the sidelines, but in April 1875 it voted financial assistance to Joachim to carry his case to the Privy Council, meanwhile blandly accepting the million or so a year accruing from selections in the names of minors.[*64] How far revenue from conditional purchases in the rest of New South Wales depended on selection by minors cannot be assessed, but in the Riverina, entries in the Conditional Purchase Registers at Moama and Deniliquin reveal that the bulk of the enormous increase in selections in 1873-6 was taken up as family selections based on a man, wife and any number of children. In the Deniliquin land office alone, from less than one hundred selections a year from 1862 to 1872, with an annual average of fifty-five in the years 1866 to 1872, the number rocketed to 686 in 1873, most of them in the months September to December, 1,052 in 1874 and 512 in 1875. Much of this, judging from the persistence of the families concerned, represented genuine attempts to settle on the land as graziers. Some no doubt was speculatory and some, where squatters could bribe or employ men with families, was dummying.[65]

Similar increases in conditional purchases took place in Albury and Wagga. The Wagga land office had handled an annual average of 166 selections from 1866 to 1872 with a maximum of 256 in any one year. The number rose to 997 in 1873, 728 in 1874 and 779 in 1875. Here too, much selection was in the names of minors, though, with a larger adult population and no land-hungry Victorian population just over the border, the proportion was lower. In Albury, from 1866 to 1872, selections had averaged three hundred a year. This rose to 984 in 1873, 1,328 in 1874 and 1,007 in 1875. Nearly 40 per cent of all the selections for two

*'And if the battle should look like a conflict of class with class, men of all but inexhaustible means with men of industry and limited means, and if it should bring out a great amount of bad feeling in the community, the Government cannot say they are clear of all the consequences, seeing that they have been silently encouraging the whole affair'; R.G., 11 March 1874.

decades in the Albury district were taken up within these three years, and again, many were in the names of minors.*

It is of course difficult to determine the motives of applicants for conditional purchase. What the hundreds of names in the Conditional Purchase Registers represent can only be determined from individual records, and the final fate of a selection need not indicate the original intention. Morris and Ranken, for all the assurance in their 1883 report, were undoubtedly mistaken in individual cases, as the *Pastoral Times*, despite its squatting sympathies, felt obliged to point out.† But whatever the original motive the result was clear. Vast numbers of selections passed into the hands of the pastoral lessees. In the meantime, pending the Privy Council's decision, and despite numerous petitions from selectors,[66] the 1875 amendment to the Act was passed, whereby selection by persons under the age of sixteen years was forbidden. There was therefore little interest in the final decision of the Privy Council,[67] which upheld the earlier Supreme Court finding, that selections by minors were valid, though they had no rights of transfer.

The 1875 amendment sought at the same time to remedy a number of abuses revealed by the select committees of 1872-4. Since selectors were deprived of a weapon with the stoppage of selection by minors, it was only right that 'vicarious selection', the squatter's weapon, should be made a criminal offence, or at least a misdemeanour. And although that 'fiction', the grass right, was not abolished, the maximum area of a conditional purchase was increased to 640 acres, leading, where land was available, to a wave of 'additional' conditional purchases.§ Although the revoca-

---

*In the Albury district a further factor must be considered. In 1873 Victoria's second line of railway to tap the Riverina had reached Wodonga, across the river from Albury. That this did not produce a rapid increase in wheat acreage may be attributed to the Victorian protective tariff, 1s per cwt on wheat from 1872 to 1881, and the relatively higher returns from wool, on which there was no Victorian tariff, during the early seventies.

†E.g., Portions 62 and 64, Parish of Yalama, County Townsend, coloured red in Morris and Ranken's map, indicating 'alienated in the interest of the station', had been transferred from one selector to another who was still, after the report had been published, an active independent grazier. Portion 88 of the same parish, marked in the same way, was 'nothing of the sort'. Half of it was a revoked reserve in the hands of a grazier, the other half remained reserved. These discoveries were the results of what the *Pastoral Times* called a 'superficial examination', having 'only cursorily examined one parish'; *P.T.*, 23 June 1883.

§Until 1869 in the four counties comprising the Wagga land district the number of clause 21 selections (Additional Conditional Purchase) had never

tion of reserves was stepped up, squatters were given a new loophole in that on the reserves, where they could still depasture stock under an annual lease, they were allowed improvement purchases merely by giving 'notice of intention to improve the waste lands of the colony'.[68] To improve administration, local land office staffs which had been increased to cope with the rush of business were further augmented, and in the Riverina, three new offices were established—at Narrandera, Urana and Corowa.

The location of these new offices confirms the impressions derived from Conditional Purchase Registers and local newspapers that the broad front of selection expansion and population movement up to the end of 1875 was travelling in a north-westerly direction. Six more years were to elapse before the first railways crossed south over the Murrumbidgee or north over the Murray,* but the continual agitation for the extension of the New South Wales southern line, the increased land revenue which could be used to finance this, and preliminary moves to extend the Melbourne-Echuca line to Deniliquin under the aegis of the Deniliquin-Moama Railway Company, all gave hope that if selectors acquired land they would eventually have access to metropolitan markets. Moving out north and west from the centres of population, represented locally by the towns of Echuca, Albury and Wagga, selection activity had gradually expanded into the Riverina as families moved out on to the lightly-undulating fringes of the western slopes and the dead-flat plains beyond. New counties and parishes, hastily contrived by surveyors, appeared almost overnight, but still not fast enough, as the frequent entry in the Conditional Purchase Registers—'320 acres, parish unknown'—indicates.

By 1876 the growing antipathy between the squatters and this ever-increasing selector population, fed by three years of intense strife, had reached sizeable proportions and had led to the formation of several selectors' associations. In that year the Jerilderie Show, established five years before by the Riverina Pastoral Association, was, according to the *Pastoral Times,* 'a complete

exceeded one-third of the total. By 1873 the number of clause 13 selections (Original Conditional Purchase) had dropped to half. During the wave of minors' selections O.C.P.'s rose again, but with the increase in area after 1875, many selectors sought to increase their holdings from 320 to 640 acres, so that the percentage of A.C.P.s rose again; Conditional Purchase Registers, Wagga land office.

*The New South Wales southern line was creeping south from Goulburn. Victorian railways, as already noted, were at Echuca (1864) and Wodonga (1873).

failure'. The reason given, apart from 1876 being the worst season for seven years, was the 'hostile political position' adopted by the selectors. In part, it was stated, this showed in a hostility to squatter M.L.A. William Hay. Confirmation of this changing attitude came in the following year, when the previously-undisputed rule of squatters in the Murray electorate ended and William Hay was deposed by selectors' representative Robert Barbour. Indeed, throughout the Riverina in the mid-seventies selectors combined to form associations to protect and forward their interests. By 1876 Albury, Wagga, and towns as small as Urana[69] and Jindera[70]—where selectors were advised in a public meeting to 'shoot the squatter' if he attempted to interfere—had selectors' associations. From 1877 a combined annual conference of selectors, largely concerned with the land laws, was held in Sydney.*[71] Besides lobbying and electing their own representatives to the Assembly, selector groups flooded Parliament with petitions. The Jerilderie Selectors' Association, which had sprung up following the earlier example of Deniliquin,[72] had forwarded six petitions concerned with the Yanko reserve alone. This enormous reserve, formed to protect the interests of squatters who had paid for the cuttings which ensured permanent water, stretched along the course of the Yanko Creek from the Murrumbidgee to the Billabong. Supported by similar petitions from Deniliquin and elsewhere, these six demanded the opening of the reserve to selection—a cry taken up throughout New South Wales and Victoria—and bore fruit towards the end of 1876.[73] The Deniliquin-based Murray District Selectors' Association pointed out that the term for which the pastoral lessees had been given the use of the reserve had expired; that much of it was suited for agriculture and the rest for pastoral purposes; that the Yanko Creek was the only permanent water in the area; that other land in the district was rapidly being purchased at auction or conditionally and that pastoral lessees were whittling away the reserve with improvement purchases.[74] The Jerilderie Farmers' and Traders' Association petition added that many of the members, 'men of moderate means', had travelled from Victoria and made

---

*The squatters, for their part, had formed the Pastoral Chamber of Riverina. At first this met at Deniliquin but one year was sufficient to show that most squatters were in Melbourne in mid-summer, after which meetings were held there. A further organization 'to fight against land sharks' was also formed, and within weeks boasted eighty lessees on its books; *R.G.*, 21 July 1874, *P.T.*, 5 February 1876; see also *Parl. Deb.* (L.A. N.S.W.), 1883, vol. 8, p. 508.

homes on selected land adjoining the reserve, on the understanding that they would eventually have access to water frontages.[75] A further petition presented by the Murray District Selectors' Association and the Central Land League (Sydney), and signed by twenty-nine selectors representing, with minors' holdings, 28,258 acres of land, implored the Minister of Lands to use his discretionary powers to stop the lessees securing the reserve by placing improvements on it.[*76] The *Pastoral Times* deplored such 'misrepresentation' and asked of the latter memorialists: 'if a thousand acres are not enough for any ordinary family to farm, what sort of soil is that of the Jerilderie district?' It suggested that the petitioners were speculators, and quoted the author of the Act, John Robertson, as saying that 'nearly all our troubles in land matters sprang from Victorian selectors.'[77] But land revenue had waned with the abolition of selection by minors; and a needy government, grateful for such an opportunity, ignored the protests of the squatters who had financed the Yanko cutting and subsequent works.[78]

There was much excitement at the government's decision to open the reserve and some remarkable estimates were made in both New South Wales and Victoria as to the quality of the soil— 'of the best in Australia'—and the tens of thousands of applicants to be attracted.[79] The soil question was easily decided by analysis, but the anticipated rush caused more concern in the Lands Department, slowly recovering from three overwhelming years.[†] Special preparations were therefore made. The land to be sold was surveyed, areas containing lessees' improvements were marked, small reserves were made at intervals along the water frontage—similar to water and travelling-stock reserves elsewhere —and reserves for towns were marked out.

Plans showing all this information in detail were prepared under the direction of the Surveyor General, lithographed

---

[*]The Minister of Lands said that he would give no right of purchase to the lessees by virtue of improvements on the parts of the reserve that they had leased. He could not open the improved lands to selection, but would send them to auction at an increased upset price. 'Movable fixtures' (iron huts, etc.) were not to be considered a bar to purchase.

[†]'If this measure were taken without proper precautions and arrangements, confusion, litigation, and difficulty of every kind would have been entailed upon the selectors, as well as irreparable damage and loss upon the possessors of the valuable pastoral properties of which the reserved lands were composed, and to whose enterprise and expenditure much of the present value of the lands is owing'; *V. & P.* (L.A. N.S.W.), 1875-6, vol. 3, p. 564.

and widely circulated, and maps of the various parishes were specially prepared on a very large scale and exhibited at the various district offices . . . some time previous to the actual opening of the land to selection.[80]

Careful consideration was given to the actual date of revocation, which followed thirty days after the date of the proclamation announcing it. Eventually a Saturday was chosen for the proclamation, so that revocation took effect from a Tuesday morning, giving the lessees two days—but only two—in which to do their worst (or best). On these days, individual lessees took up, quite legally, as many as thirty-six Volunteer Land Orders each, and utilized the improvement clause wherever possible.*[81] Two days later on Thursday, being 'land day', selectors were to have their chance.

It was also considered necessary to prevent crowding and subsequent confusion. A special regulation was hurried through, which permitted all applications received between certain hours to be regarded as simultaneous; additional staff were provided; and the land, depending on its location, was divided up and dealt with at four different offices—Wagga, Deniliquin, Hay or Urana. At Urana, centre of the land district in which most of the reserve was situated, large temporary sheds with several entrance and exit doors and adjoining separate yards, were erected. Over the doors were written the names of parishes; constables stood at the entrances, numbered tickets were given to applicants, and within two hours 215 applications had been received, 'without the slightest approach to disorder, crowding or inconvenience to the applicants or the officials engaged'.†[82] By the following morning examination of applications had been completed and the drawing of lots for contested selections took place, 'in many instances one lot being embraced by fifteen or sixteen separate applications.' After the drawing of sixty-five separate ballots it was found that 36,218 acres had been selected. The squatters could not give in without one last fling, however, and of this area 4,064 acres were taken up as conditional purchases for alleged mining purposes,

---

*122 Volunteer Land Orders were used to take up 6,100 acres and a further 3,890 acres were sold under clause 31, though some applications by lessees under this clause were rejected.

†Such proceedings were considered novel in New South Wales. In South Australia, where the concern with agriculture was from the beginning much more real and squatters less of a problem and less dominant politically, survey had always preceded selection and such more-orderly proceedings were usual; see G. L. Buxton, *South Australian Land Acts, 1869-1885*.

'and there could be no reasonable doubt that these selections were made purely in the interest of the pastoral lessee, and without any intention of working *minerals*.'[83] Altogether however there was a general feeling that something more nearly approaching justice had been done, and some sixty selectors signed a vote of thanks to the Lands Department officers concerned, for their 'courtesy and impartiality'.[84] Meanwhile, in the Hay land office sales to lessees in the western Riverina continued to rise, receipts for one week in November 1876 from auction and conditional purchases reaching £30,000 and two weeks later £27,000.[85]

One further provision of the 1875 amendment remains to be noted; the provision of Land Enquiry Courts. These provided a further skirmishing-ground for the squatter-selector struggle and further confirmed allegations regarding dummying.[86] By August 1876 over twenty selections had been forfeited for non-residence as a result of eight months' enquiries at Deniliquin. These included the selections of minors, members of such prominent selector families as that of Robert Barbour, who the following year would represent his fellow-selectors in the Legislative Assembly, and selections by or on behalf of squatting families including the Peppins.[87]

With more careful administration of the Acts during the seventies, squatter-selector antipathy took a more political and less personal form, though there were still legal actions of several kinds: Henry Ricketson, lessee of Barratta and other stations *v.* Robert Barbour in 'The Great Trespass Action' and other dramas;[88] the lessee of Brookong *v.* selector O'Connell, for mustering his sheep without giving the required notice;[89] the trespass of a squatter's sheep on a growing crop[90] and many another.

For the most part, like their British counterparts, New South Wales governments were content to amend legislation piecemeal —a specific remedy for a specific evil—but with overwhelming evidence of malfunction and maladministration, coupled with growing demands from selectors' associations and their Sydney conferences, attempts were made from time to time to overhaul the whole system. In 1878 Farnell's Land Bill,[91] which proposed considerable changes, was defeated, while in 1880 a minor amendment was made, further to that of 1875, clarifying the legal position of pre-leases and providing that applicants should not begin to use pre-leases for grazing purposes until their applications had been examined and approval given in the *Government Gazette*. Just how necessary this had become was indicated in the first year of operation alone, when of 1,971 applications, 497 were refused, and presumably as many cases of trespass avoided.[92]

In 1882 John Robertson introduced an amending Land Bill, making further minor changes but retaining the principle of free selection before survey. After a long debate the Parkes-Robertson government was defeated on the Bill, and in the subsequent election badly beaten, the 'Land Reform Cabinet' with Sir Alexander Stuart as Premier and J. S. Farnell as Minister of Lands taking over in 1883. Almost immediately Augustus Morris and George Ranken were appointed as a Commission of Enquiry to look into the state of the public lands and the land laws.[93] To the *Pastoral Times* the sight of these two gentlemen sitting down, and in six weeks examining a matter which for over twenty years had confounded the most eminent in the land, was ludicrous.[94] The commissioners themselves soon found the allotted time inadequate, but eventually issued their report.

There was little in the Morris and Ranken report[95] which was not common knowledge and which the earlier select committees had not discovered. But the commissioners had an added diffi-culty, having to show, at the same time, not only that the squatters had been victimized, but that the author of the Alienation Act and his supporters were unsatisfactory representatives of the people and that their policy had failed.

They showed first, with little difficulty, all the flaws in the Act and its administration; the ambiguity in its intent as well as expression and the delays and difficulties resulting from the centralized system.[96]

It would be a wonder [they wrote] if a law so framed showed any fixed principle and consistency in its administration. The history of its whole operation for years has been an unintel-ligible chaos, in which the rights of all have been the sport of accident, political interest and departmental disorder.[97]

They deplored the fact that the pastoralists' panic and the con-sequent enormous auction sales had converted their runs into 'little more than the assets of financing firms' as 'monied institu-tions . . . emptied their safes in buying up Crown Lands on Stations'. They suggested that pastoralists would have been better off with a smaller area under more secure tenure and that selectors, because of the 'phantom' grass right, needed a larger area, since 'the grass crop was the mainstay of the whole rural population.'[98] What they ignored was the vast improvement which had already taken place: the reorganization of the department in 1867; the tidying up which followed the committees of the early seventies, resulting in the 1875 amendment with the abolition of selection by minors, the increase from 320 to 640 acres for selection, the institution of Land Enquiry Courts and Conditional Purchase Inspectors; and the improved administration as illustrated in the opening of the Yanko reserve.

They showed, secondly, the inevitable strife resulting from offering the same land to two different classes* of people with 'no partition of the soil',[99] the fierce struggle between selector and squatter, particularly in what they called the 'Intermediate' territory, which included much of the area under study. What they did not show was that the case of Deniliquin, which they cited repeatedly and almost exclusively to show the nature and course of this struggle in the Intermediate territory and which 'always ended in the selector selling out to the squatter',[1] was in many ways unique—a biased sample. Carefully they avoided any attempt to show the results in the same detail in the areas nearer to Albury or Wagga; always it was Deniliquin which showed the 'uniform result of selection in Riverina'.[2] Deniliquin, most remote from Sydney, where survey had been most backward, staffing most inadequate and the squatter-land agent relationship most unsatisfactory. Deniliquin, closest to Melbourne and the Victorians, where the strife had first broken out, where selection by minors had been greatest, where Joachim had fought O'Shanassy, and where, because of the environment, a greater area was needed and the number of homesteads per dozen selections lower. This was Morris and Ranken's prize exhibit, and again and again they came back to it.

Thirdly, they showed that the land had not been a barbarous waste in 1861, but had been vastly improved by the pastoralists' labours of fourteen years. To protect the fruits of these labours the squatter, 'with his whole station liable to be confiscated'— not a word about reserves here—was urged to a 'desperate defence', 'had to fight for his life'.[3] Later Morris and Ranken listed the methods—auction, improvement purchase, reserve, Volunteer Land Order, and mining and mineral purchase—'freely used in defence of stations', and continued, 'it can hardly be said that these proceedings are considered as abuses, for it is argued that practices cannot be condemned as illegal and immoral in which

*The use of the word 'classes' by the commissioners, as in many of the sources cited, implies differentiation, not necessarily stratification.

persons of fortune, position and influence in the community have
been largely concerned.'[4]

Fourthly, the commissioners showed the great difficulties facing
any examiner of New South Wales statistics for comparative
purposes, showed that the number of selections was not equal to
the number of homesteads,*[5] and stated their unwillingness to
accept 'mere documentary statements'. But on the latter issue they
also wrote: 'Statements in the nature of mere opinion have not
been wholly excluded, because they have been given by men who
represent many . . . different classes, and show how they feel.'[6]
The opinions of surveyors, for example, used in drawing up the
maps in the report, that certain selections were taken up 'in the
interest of the station', are later classified as 'indisputable data . . .
verified by full departmental detail',[7] an assurance which even
the pro-squatter *Pastoral Times* questioned.† Some of the comparisons made are also of doubtful validity. Much is made of the
number of people settled in County Roxburgh, as compared with
an equal area in the Riverina,§[8] but no mention is made of rainfall
or other environmental factors, distance from markets or the
amount of capital needed to develop a maintenance-area in the
Riverina; nor of the fact that County Roxburgh lay only 140
miles from Sydney and contained or was bordered by the mining
towns of Bathurst, Sofala and Hill End. The growth of rural
population is contrasted with urban growth to show the failure
of the Act, but the figures apply to the whole colony and include
those for Sydney.[9] In an area like the Riverina the population in
both agri. ultural and pastoral areas had increased, as had that of
country towns. 'Rural stagnation'[10] which they suggest as a result
of Robertson's Acts had certainly not begun at the time of their
report.‡

Even less satisfactory is their treatment of the Albury-Wagga
area. The story in the western Riverina was relatively simple. The
squatters had been in control, the selectors came and took up
land on their runs. Some were speculators, others took the high

---

*Concerning the Upper Murray they were critical of the fact that for
5,328 selections there were only 1,034 homesteads. Considering the use
made of dummies and minors, this seems a relatively high percentage.

†See footnote, p. 171.

§'If the comparison is further extended to the three rich counties surrounding Deniliquin . . . it will appear that the poor patch of mountainous
country contains an amount of homestead settlement equal to that existing
on a tract of the richest district in Australia more than ten times the extent.'

‡For urban and rural growth rates in the Riverina, see chapter 7, Figure 8,
and Tables 14-18.

price offered and moved on to repeat the process. The genuine, by family selection and by buying out their fellows, gradually acquired a sufficient area to survive as graziers. By 1883 there were in the Deniliquin police district eighty-one owners of from five hundred to five thousand sheep, one with eight thousand, and beyond this the pastoral lessees with from ten thousand to eighty thousand sheep each.[11] In Morris and Ranken terms 'large estates were formed and selectors sell out as rapidly as possible . . . 1,424 selectors took up land, but . . . only 244 now remain . . . and wherever these have acquired over 2,000 acres they do well.'[12] Few had attempted grain-growing. Near Deniliquin, competition was too great from growers in the more suitable area near Moama, aided by the railway after 1876, and from Wahgunyah on the Murray, from whence grain and hay were carted overland.[13] Near Hay the lower and even more unreliable rainfall, coupled with competition from South Australian and Victorian farmers, who could ship grain and hay by river steamer, inhibited agriculture even more.[14] But in discussing the Albury-Wagga area the difficulty lies in disentangling the determinants. In this area, town and country population had increased, as had sheep numbers and the acreage under crop. With the advent of the railway to North Wagga in 1878, Albury and Hay by 1882 and Jerilderie by 1884, the area had already begun its tremendous expansion in primary production. Five years after Morris and Ranken, T. A. Coghlan was to write of the great changes that had taken place in the area since 1881:

> It is interesting to note that agriculture is gaining ground in those districts where the greater number of the huge freehold estates accumulated by the pastoralists under the auction sales and improvement clauses of the Land Act of 1861 are situated. It is in the valleys of the Murray and the Murrumbidgee that the struggle between the squatter and selector has been fiercest, and where the most remarkable increase of agricultural settlement as regards woolgrowing and agriculture generally has been exhibited.

Between 1882 and 1888, he showed, the area under crop in the Murray electorate had increased from 56,000 to 94,000 acres, and in the Murrumbidgee electorate from 13,000 to 59,000 acres. In the latter area the wheat acreage had increased ninefold in the same period.[15]

Certainly the railway had consummated this agricultural revo-

TABLE 10

Land Sold in New South Wales 1862-1885

('000 acres)

	Auction Country Lands	Unconditionally selected[a]	Improvement purchase	Pre-emptive right purchase	Conditional purchase
1862	29.7	22.3	3.4	30.6	357.3
1863	15.4	17.4	4.6	58.0	259.4
1864	31.4	12.4	9.7	13.1	165.6
1865	63.3	12.6	8.2	23.5	151.4
1866	65.8	16.4	8.5	25.6	358.7
1867	70.7	15.8	19.7	30.0	232.2
1868	50.6	18.6	29.0	52.2	239.5
1869	93.4	39.1	23.0	7.6	397.3
1870	51.7	23.4	14.2	3.7	329.3
1871	49.3	23.7	5.3	8.6	358.7
1872	61.1	83.7	17.3	3.3	749.6
1873	274.6	101.6	10.6	1.5	1391.8
1874	580.8	98.8	20.5	—	1586.3
1875	978.4	101.7	49.9	c	1756.7
1876	1685.6	95.7	86.1	189.6	1984.2
1877	1829.6	158.8	159.8	81.2	1699.8
1878	861.0	122.8	224.8	4.0	1588.0
1879	353.4	b	121.1	6.0	924.1
1880	346.7	39.4	237.6	6.9	1147.0
1881	523.7	328.2	474.1	7.5	2329.2
1882	503.5	353.1	165.0	5.2	2392.2
1883	25.8	31.4	103.8	2.3	1621.9
1884	38.2	—	252.1	—	1453.9
1885	1.6	—	292.3	—	1114.9

[a] Unconditionally sold by selection, after failure to sell by auction or forfeiture.
[b] From 1879 selected after auction.
[c] From 1876 provisional.
Source: *N.S.W. Statistical Registers*, 1862-85.

lution, but most of the land utilized had passed into the hands of small land-owners as a result of Robertson's Act. It needed only the railway, bringing access to larger markets, to produce the measurable change in cultivation. Such successes had no part in the Morris and Ranken story and they wisely avoided them, content merely to observe that in the Wagga district not above 12 per cent of the conditional purchases were held by the original selectors.

The methods by which they did so are worth noting. The purpose of the Alienation Act had been variously stated, usually with some vagueness. This indecisiveness the commissioners used. If the aim of the Act was the establishment of a yeoman population then the evidence from Deniliquin was used to show that settlement began but declined (pp. 91, 118).* In the areas where closer settlement had succeeded they fell back on the argument that the land had been recklessly alienated with no thought for posterity (p. 105) and that this 'waste of the lands for future use' (p. 92)—the source of a spurious 'flourishing land revenue' (p. 93) —had resulted, for example in counties Hume and Denison along the Murray, in leaving an 'area of unalienated land too small to offer a field for future settlement' (p. 117).

If the purpose of the Act had been to attract population, then the vast numbers of Victorians attracted, it was shown, were speculators and blackmailers (p. 122) who 'nearly all . . . sold to the lessee' (p. 118), or capitalists.

> Under a law which professed to part with the land only for Agricultural settlement, the cream of the Riverina has been mostly handed over to Capitalists in no way concerned with the welfare of New South Wales, who hold the soil without supporting a tax paying population, and carry away the wealth of our pastures without contribution towards the political or social well being of the Colony. (p. 119)

The German settlers who were attracted to travel overland from South Australia to the Albury district were not mentioned.†

When the report and the suggestions it contained were published, plans were made for an amending Act. Within the Assembly there was no unanimity over land reform, and the final product, torn and harried after long discussion, bore only slight resemblance to the original.[16] Few of the provisions made any

---

*Page numbers cited are those of the Morris and Ranken report, *V. & P.* (L.A. N.S.W.), 1883, vol. 2, pp. 77-248.
†See pp. 197-202.

TABLE 11

Number of Freeholders* in Riverina Electorates 1883

Acres	Electorate					
	Albury	Hume	Albury + Hume	Murrumbidgee	Murray	Balranald
40-300	110	302	412	272	122	38
301-600	43	212	255	167	138	15
601-1,500	22	231	253	294	189	52
1,501-3,000	9	39	48	72	59	11
3,001-5,000	—	19	19	26	31	1
5,001-10,000	—	13	13	29	9	7
10,001-40,000	3	20	23	37	20	6
40,001 and over	—	6	6	19	22	15
Total	187	842	1029	916	590	145

* Including conditional purchases.
Source: Compiled from *N.S.W. Legislative Assembly Votes and Proceedings*, 1883, II, pp. 118-19.

great difference to the Riverina where the greatest changes had already been accomplished.[17]

For the pastoralist the most important aspect of the 1884 Act was the clause which required him to surrender half of the *leased* portion of his run, to be known as the 'Resumed Area', with more secure tenure on the remaining leasehold. This resumed area was then, at the discretion of the government, to be surveyed and sold to selectors as 'Special Areas', in lots of up to 640 acres, at a minimum upset price of 30s per acre. The greatly-desired decentralization was furthered by the clause providing for Local Land Boards, while allowance was finally made for the great environmental differences encountered in New South Wales. The colony was divided into three major divisions: Eastern, Central and Western. In the Central division, which included the Riverina, the area of an individual conditional purchase was increased to 2,560 acres, with three times that area for pre-lease; but after five years residence, and on completion of other conditions, the pre-lease could be converted to additional conditional purchase.[18] But the plans for resumption came too late, and the effects of the 1884 Act were less than anticipated. 'In the Hume, at least', wrote the *Corowa Free Press,*

> Mr. Farnell's grand scheme of land resumption has been a farce. The small area of leasehold which reverted to the Crown has, in most cases, fallen again into the hands of its former occupants, and although a few bonafide selectors have been able to secure holdings, the increase in the settled population has been so small as to be scarcely appreciable.[19]

With the 'fatuitously abrupt stoppage'[20] of auction sales to lessees on Farnell's accession, land revenue had decreased. In the years following, charges were made that the 1884 Act was not paying its way and its defects were frequently cited.[21] In 1889 this Act was amended[22] and a further effort made to increase the revenue derived from Crown lands. Although there may have been less dissatisfaction with them, the amending Acts were in many ways no more satisfactory than the original Acts of 1861.

The achievements of almost twenty years of operation of Robertson's Acts in the Riverina were thus varied. Vast areas of Crown land had been alienated and pastoral lessees had been heavily committed to financial institutions. Large numbers of selectors had acquired land and were utilizing it in a manner dictated by environment and markets. Near Deniliquin and Hay

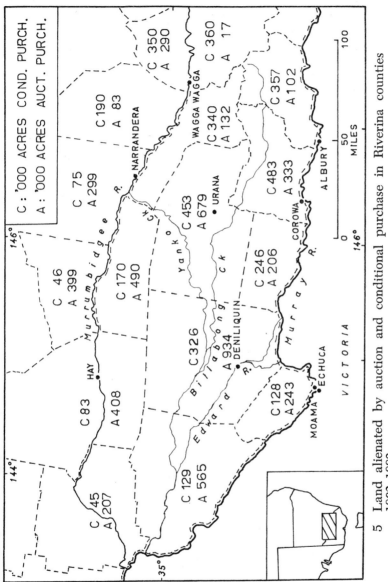

5 Land alienated by auction and conditional purchase in Riverina counties 1862–1883

Sources: *V. & P.* (L.A. N.S.W.), 1883, vol. 2, pp. 77–248, and supplementary volume; N.S.W. Lands Dept maps; Conditional Purchase Registers

this had led to the establishment of a new class of graziers, and progressively nearer Albury and Wagga, to the growth of a selector population who were able to turn increasingly from grazing to agriculture with the arrival of the railways. These new communities in turn promoted the development of the older towns and led to the growth of new towns, while the strife engendered between squatter and selector had led to the formation of new political groups which attained representation in the Legislative Assembly. The discussion in more detail of these effects will be undertaken in the following chapters under the general heading, 'The Riverina in 1891'.

Part III

THE RIVERINA IN 1891

6

THE YEOMAN FARMER

Agriculture in 1891

'Farmers are not to be made by an Act of Parliament.'
Riverine Grazier, 13 August 1881.

Between 1861 and 1891 the area cultivated in the Albury, Deniliquin and Wagga districts rose from less than 8,000 acres to nearly 200,000 acres. This overall rising trend was subject to annual variations common to agriculture. A year of low harvest caused by drought, floods, rust or locusts was followed by increased acreage, as farmers attempted to recoup their losses. Bountiful years, when grain prices fell and hay and horsefeed were adequate for two or more years, were followed by decreased acreage.

Besides these normal fluctuations, and sometimes acting contrary to them, a number of others occurred. Some related to the varying growth rates of Riverina towns[1] which comprised the local market, others reflected selector activity. Massive selection in the seventies had increased the acreage sown, but when some selectors sold out to squatters or fellow-selectors before moving further out, this acted as a brake. Further complexity was introduced in the border districts by the Victorian protective tariff. When good seasons lowered Victorian wheat prices in 1872 the tariff, which had stood at 9d per cwt. since 1868, rose to 1s per cental. In 1877 it rose to 2s per cental, and with further Victorian price falls from 1883 to 1889, it rose to 2s 11d in 1890.[2] The combination of low prices and high tariff nullified the advantage of the Victorian railhead at Wodonga for wheat growers in the Albury district.

The Deniliquin district had lower and less reliable rainfall, a limited area of soil suitable for agriculture and a smaller local population. Its markets beyond Deniliquin were subject to competition from South Australian and Victorian farmers, who had access via rail and steamer to the areas bordering the rivers. The

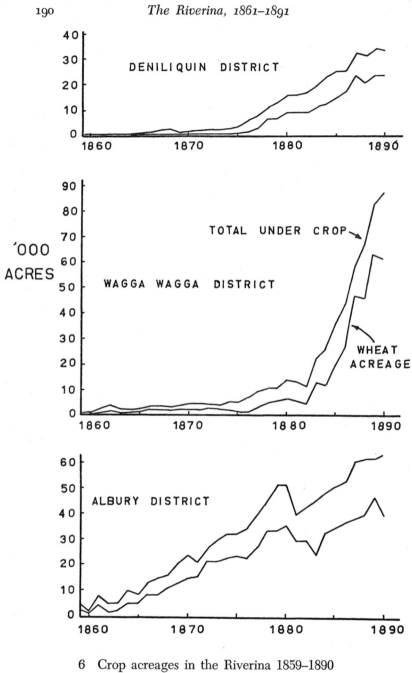

6 Crop acreages in the Riverina 1859–1890
Source: *Statistical Registers of N.S.W.*

red-brown earth soils in County Cadell,[3] close to the Deniliquin
and Moama Railway Company line to Melbourne, were suited to
wheat growing, but here the Victorian tariff and intercolonial
rivalry stifled expansion. (No rail link between Deniliquin and
Sydney has ever been completed.) The rise of a grazier class,
cultivating to supplement natural pasture, also accounted for
some of the increase near Deniliquin.

The simplest case is that of the Wagga district, and it was here
that the effect of the railway was most dramatic. In 1878 the
southern railway from Sydney had reached Bomen (North
Wagga), and in 1880, following the completion of the two-mile
viaduct across the Murrumbidgee, had continued on towards
Albury. By 1882 the Sydney-Wagga-Albury line was open, as well
as the Junee-Hay line. In 1884 the branch line from Narrandera to
Jerilderie was completed, running through the former Yanko
reserve. Within six years hundreds of selectors had gained access
to the Sydney market and, as a subsidiary bonus, could compete
with the South Australian and Victorian steamer traffic as far
downstream as the Hay railhead. The results are clearly seen in
Figure 6. Between 1861 and 1881 the total crop acreage in the
Wagga district, required only to supply local needs,* had rarely
risen above 10,000 acres, including 5,000 acres of wheat for grain.
In the next decade the total crop acreage rose to nearly 100,000
acres, including 60,000 acres of wheat for grain, while differential
rates increased the ability of Riverina farmers to sell competitively
on the Sydney market. These allowed a 10 per cent freight cost
reduction to places over 100 miles from Sydney, 20 per cent over
150 miles and 40 per cent over 200 miles, with a further reduction
for specified goods.[4] This lucrative link with the metropolis led to
keener competition for land, even for the annoyingly-small 160-
acre lots sold in the Special Areas after 1884. The increased
selection area of 2,560 acres, where sufficient unalienated land
existed for such a large area to be obtained, was additionally
attractive. Besides a growing land hunger, which became progressively more difficult to satisfy, the period is marked by a number
of changes in the economic and social life of the agricultural
communities.[5]

*Coghlan gives the annual consumption of wheat per head in N.S.W.
during the period as 6.4 bushels per annum. At an average yield of 13
bushels per acre, this required one half-acre of wheat per head of population. Before the railway reached Wagga this figure, on average, marked the
limits of wheat growing in the district. See T. A. Coghlan, *Wealth and
Progress of New South Wales 1888-89*, pp. 237-54.

TABLE 12

Crop Acreages in the Riverina 1859-1890

('000 acres)

Sowing Year	ALBURY[a] Total under crop	ALBURY[a] Wheat for grain	WAGGA[b] Total under crop	WAGGA[b] Wheat for grain	DENILIQUIN[c] Total under crop	DENILIQUIN[c] Wheat for grain
1859	4.7	2.7	1.3	0.6	0.2	0.02
1860	2.0	1.3	1.6	1.1	0.6	0.03
1861	8.0	4.6	n.a.	n.a.	0.5	0.02
1862	4.8	1.9	4.1	2.1	0.9	0.02
1863	5.3	2.6	2.8	1.4	0.7	0.03
1864	10.0	5.1	2.1	1.4	1.0	0.03
1865	8.4	5.2	2.8	1.6	1.2	0.03
1866	13.6	8.3	4.0	2.6	1.6	0.07
1867	12.7	8.3	4.0	2.3	2.1	0.08
1868	16.3	11.1	3.8	2.1	2.3	0.09
1869	21.5	12.8	4.3	2.4	1.3	0.2
1870[d]	24.1	15.0	5.0	2.3	1.7	0.2
1871	21.8	15.9	5.3	2.1	2.0	0.6
1872	27.6	22.0	5.5	3.1	2.1	0.7
1873	30.0	21.8	5.0	2.6	2.0	0.7
1874	32.7	23.0	5.6	2.2	2.6	0.6
1875	32.9	21.8	5.5	1.4	3.7	0.9
1876	35.0	23.1	7.1	1.3	5.9	1.6
1877	39.8	26.8	9.7	3.2	7.5	2.8
1878	46.1	34.3	10.8	5.2	10.9	6.3
1879	52.4	33.8	10.8	5.8	12.8	6.7
1880	51.9	36.3	14.0	6.4	15.9	9.0
1881	40.3	30.1	13.0	5.6	15.5	8.8
1882	43.4	29.7	11.2	4.4	16.4	9.1
1883	46.1	24.1	22.8	13.1	19.2	11.4
1884	49.2	33.3	26.6	11.8	23.2	12.5
1885	50.8	35.4	36.4	19.8	24.9	14.7
1886	53.2	37.3	43.9	26.2	25.6	16.9
1887	61.1	50.4	59.1	46.3	32.9	23.7
1888	62.1	39.1	66.7	45.3	31.7	20.5
1889	62.4	47.2	83.2	62.7	35.0	23.5
1890[e]	63.7	39.9	86.8	61.2	33.8	23.5

[a] Albury police district = Albury + Hume electorates.
[b] Wagga police district = Murrumbidgee electorate.
[c] Deniliquin + Moulamein + Moama police district = Murray electorate.
[d] Census districts.
[e] Different statistical boundaries after 1890 terminate the series at that date.
Source: *N.S.W. Statistical Registers.*

TABLE 13

Area Devoted to and Persons Engaged in Agriculture in Agriculture in Riverina Electorates, March 1891

Electorate	No. of holdings larger than 1 acre	Total area devoted to agriculture*	Average area agriculture per holding	Persons engaged in agricultural pursuits		
				Male	*Female*	*Total*
Hume	865	171,141	197.8	978	714	1,692
Albury	325	21,999	67.7	345	164	509
Murray	530	87,801	165.7	759	625	1,384
Murrumbidgee	1,589	212,923	134.0	1,897	941	2,838
Total	3,309	493,864	—	3,979	2,444	6,423

* Includes 'under crops, in fallow, laid down to permanent artificial grasses, cleared and prepared for cultivation'.
Source: *N.S.W. Statistical Register*, 1891.

In 1861 there had been a large number of tenant farmers and hired labourers, primitive techniques, a minimum of machinery, and a lack of transport to markets. By 1891 the selection legislation had made independence on the land possible for many. Some farmers still worked as contract ploughmen, went shearing in the off-season, or hired cultivation paddocks from townsmen landowners. Others, having invested in machinery, rented land from station owners or were share-farmers on station properties, their need for more profitable use of their time and machinery complementing the station owner's need for higher returns from purchased land.[6]

On farms of all sizes mechanization and capitalization had increased. On one farm of two thousand acres, typical of the larger selected properties,[7] one thousand were cleared for cultivation. Buildings included a substantial five-roomed weatherboard house with galvanized-iron roof, kitchen, chaff shed, blacksmith's shop, and stables for twelve horses. Subdivision into seven paddocks was by 6-wire or 7-wire fencing and the property was watered by three large tanks. Stock included twenty-five farm horses, ten saddle and harness horses, eight draught horses, twenty mixed cattle, eight young milkers, eight fat bullocks, sixteen working bullocks, nine hundred wethers and eight hundred ewes. Implements and vehicles included four strippers (three Nicholson and one Martin), a Robinson winnower, a Hornsby reaper and binder, a chaff-cutter and horseworks, a corncrusher, two three-furrow ploughs, two double-furrow ploughs, two paring ploughs, two rollers, four sets of zig-zag harrows, one set of disc harrows, two seed sowers, an eight-horse wagon, wagon and plough harness, and a complete set of blacksmith's tools. Others farms had steam chaff-cutters, damp-weather strippers, string binders, back-delivery reapers and drays, while outbuildings included buggy sheds, barns and machinery sheds. Homesteads were commonly of brick or sawn timber with galvanized-iron roofs. Although most paddocks were wire fenced, some horse and cattle paddocks and all drafting yards were still of post and rail.[8] Ringbarking and scrubbing, as on the pastoral properties, was sometimes carried out by Chinese.[9]

One of the most highly organized farms was Anthony Brunskill's Bon Accord at Sandy Creek, thirteen miles south of Wagga, with a five-and-a-half mile frontage to the railway line. In 1891 it was awarded the Department of Agriculture prize for the best managed farm in the south-western district.[10] Of the 2,300 acres, 1,070 were under crop in 1890 and 1,800 in 1891. The wheat and oat crops were all cut for hay and chaff for the Sydney market. In November 1890 the first of the crops, all of which were at different stages, stood seven feet high. Five reapers and binders were at work, 180 acres were already harvested, and men stooked the sheaves immediately they were cut. No time was lost in going to work at the far ends of the farm. Ploughing or reaping, each took a strip as he went. 'When we gang to our work', said one, 'and when we come hame frae it, we're aplowing the ground.'[11]

An avenue of ornamental trees led to the half-acre yard surrounded by weatherboard buildings with galvanized-iron roofs. Across the front stood Brunskill's private dwelling with a 'neat flower garden in front'. Along one side were the workshop, blacksmith's, and machinery sheds, the latter containing nine double-furrow Hudson ploughs and five McCormack reapers and binders. Next came the slaughter yard, cart shed—containing nine drays and one lorry— and the harness shed. Across the end of the yard were the living quarters of the engineer and bench-man, the engine shed, chaff-house and saw-mill. In the engine room stood a 6 h.p. Ransome and Sims engine used to drive the Buncle chaff-cutter and bag-filler, and the circular saw with which all timber for the buildings was cut. The fourth side of the square yard commenced with stables for forty horses. Of these, thirty-six were draught horses in matched teams of three, each team with its own driver, who looked after them. Stalls and loose-boxes were numbered, corresponding with the numbers on feed-boxes, lanterns, brushes, harness, ploughs, machines, men's bunks and lavatory basins. Beside the stables were the coach-house, buggy shed, grain shed, the men's room for the ten permanent hands, store, two dining-rooms, and a kitchen for the men's cook. Water was supplied by a small reservoir in the hills, three-quarters of a mile from the house, and conveyed by piping to horse and cattle troughs fitted with ball cocks, and to the house, engine, lavatories, garden and yards.

Besides the forty-three men employed during harvest, an 'expert' was engaged to service the machines, constantly patrolling the paddocks on horseback with a basket of tools, and oiling the machines while the men were at meals. The stack yards, one mile long and two chains wide, were fenced, like the rest of the property, with 7-wire fences and swinging gates—there were 'no slip-rails anywhere on the estate'—and ran parallel to the railway.

The New South Wales Railways Department, guaranteed 1,800 tons loading per year for four years, built a special siding— delayed slightly by the 1890 strike—and in that year carried 2,500 tons from Bon Accord.

Such organization marked a peak in agricultural efficiency. Below it stretched the whole range of large and small farms, all mechanized to some extent. Some machinery originated in Sydney, much came from Victoria following the selectors who moved north, while many of the German farmers who travelled overland from South Australia, in wagons, sent their strippers and winnowers by river steamer.[12] Some machinery was locally made. In their steam works and agricultural-implement factory in the little German town of Walla Walla, Gartner and Heppner manufactured horseworks, wagons, winnowers, ploughs and strippers.[13] Some of the changes in agricultural techniques in the Riverina thus resulted from the migration of Victorian and South Australian farmers. For years innovations had been tested, wheat-growing experiments conducted and machinery trials[14] sponsored by the local agricultural and horticultural societies, subsidized by New South Wales governments. With the formation of a government Department of Agriculture these efforts were co-ordinated.[15] Soils were analysed,[16] grain samples sent to farmers for testing, a Model Farm established at Wagga,[17] and an *Agricultural Gazette* published. But while mechanization had increased and greater horse-power was reducing man-power requirements, thistles, locusts and rabbits, drought, flood and fire, and diseases like rust and the dreaded 'take-all' constituted permanent natural threats to the farmers' prosperity.[18] To these were added transport and market difficulties.

From the seventies, flour-millers in the larger towns had been wheat-buyers, but the rising acreage and new towns developing at railway sidings had increased the number of buyers and agents.[19] Dissatisfaction with the business methods of some buyers[20] led to the formation of the Murrumbidgee Co-operative Milling Company in Wagga in 1890,[21] the experimental sale of wheat by tender in 1891[22] and sale by auction at Gerogery and Burrumbuttock in 1892.[23]

In 1891 the wheat yield near Albury was twelve bushels per acre, but 'beyond Howlong, towards the plain country', it was noted that twenty bushels were being harvested. Near Wagga between sixteen and twenty bushels were reaped, but further west, near Coolamon, eighteen to twenty-five were usual. All

Old Warbreccan homestead 1848

Shepherd's hut

In the tracks of the German farmers

Undulating country of the south-west slopes west of Henty (top)

Affluence and decay, Walbundrie

along the railway line the results were the same, the red-brown earths of the western slopes and plains gave higher yields.[24] In 1890-1 Railway Commissioners traversed much of this country, and all selectors interviewed agreed that if spur lines were laid wheat acreage would increase. On A. Matthews's property of 3,682 acres at Green's Gunyah (later Lockhart), thirty miles from the railway, only 120 acres were cultivated. Other Green's Gunyah farmers paid 6d a bushel to send grain to the railway. J. Herbert at 'the Galore' had 'travelled over a great part of Riverina inspecting farms and finally purchased a farm [there], as he considered it the best land seen.' Despite his years of farming experience in Victoria, the absence of rail transport prevented him cultivating more than one hundred of his 2,500 acres.[25] Other difficulties were cited, including the cost of bags and the lack of storage facilities at rail sidings, but for the most part Riverina farmers in 1891 were prosperous and reasonably content with their lot.

Amongst the more prosperous and contented were a group of farmers of German descent, mostly attracted from South Australia by Robertson's Acts. The Germans who had arrived in Albury in 1851 to begin vinegrowing or to practise their trades, were Catholic Rhinelanders. The groups who arrived from South Australia, and to a lesser extent from Victoria, in 1866-70, were North German Lutherans[26] from Brandenburg, other parts of Prussia, and Saxony[27] and included some Wendish families. Migrating to South Australia at the prompting of George Fife Angas, working as labourers or tenant farmers on his Klemzig or Barossa Valley properties, some had achieved independence and spread further north, forming small agricultural and spiritual communities cared for by the pastors of their church. But land was expensive and harder to obtain in South Australia, where selection legislation did not begin until 1869 and where free selection before survey at no time ever operated.[28] Between 1866 and 1870 several groups from South Australia and others from Victoria (where some South Australian Lutherans had formerly migrated), travelled overland to the Riverina. The best documented of these migrations is that of the party led by Elder J. G. Klemke. Eight families and two single men, fifty-six persons in all, travelled from Ebenezer (S.A.) to Blanchetown, then followed the Murray upstream in their fourteen covered wagons and two spring-carts, arriving at Albury in five-and-a-half weeks, and travelled on immediately to Jindera (Dight's Forest). Near the bushranger

Morgan's track they formed a camp. During the next ten weeks, leaving the women and children with the wagons from time to time, the men made a series of inspection trips, finally selecting on Stitt's Walla Walla station.[29] All who could took up the maximum of 320 acres.[30]

Other groups of Lutheran migrants settled in small communities within thirty miles north and north-west of Albury. Never out on the flat country, never back into the ranges, always on the gentle undulations of the western slopes, so like the country they had left in South Australia and in Germany before, settlement by Lutherans proceeded in a broad belt northwards from Albury to Temora.[31] No city dwellers, they had moved from farming communities in Germany to found similar communities in South Australia and the Riverina with equal facility; farm and church were their chief interests. Of the 1,850 Lutherans living in the Riverina in 1891—1,600 in the area bounded by Albury, Wagga, Narrandera and Corowa—only 124 lived in municipalities or boroughs, and most of these were farmers living within the Albury municipality.[32] The delight of newspaper editors—the *Albury Banner* regularly published a page in German—the lives they led were models of Anglo-Saxon industry and frugality, and their prudence and forethought are well illustrated by preparations made for the 1868 trek. Because of the lack of feed on the overland route, horse-feed was sent by steamer to Wentworth, machinery was loaded by steamer for Albury, and seed wheat was carried in the wagons.[33]

The first years on the selections were difficult. Baulked by the low rivers, their machinery travelled no further than Echuca in 1868, and in 1869 steamers only reached Corowa. Water was scarce and was carted from Gerogery Springs or the Billabong Creek, though small dams were dug with pick and shovel. Temporary huts were made with wooden uprights and bark walls and roofs, small trees were grubbed and larger ones ringbarked to clear a cultivation and garden patch, and brush fences were built to keep horses in and station sheep out. At the end of the first year a small harvest yielding between ten and twelve bushels per acre was reaped.[34] The record wet year which followed in 1870 made it difficult to cart grain to Albury and supplies back to the farms. Wheat was dragged to the wagons on sledges for two or three miles and several teams combined could hardly move the reduced wagon-load of two four-bushel bags per horse. Because of the wet season, many crops were affected by rust and much of the grain ruined. 'They had no money and no flour, but good old Mr. George Day [an Albury flour-miller] offered them enough flour to go on, and pay him back when they got a good harvest.'*[35] Better seasons followed, and in the seventies and eighties additional selections were made.[36] As sons grew, they moved further north and took up land for themselves. Sometimes the parents and younger children moved on. German farmers generally nurtured the soil, and on the death of older settlers it was not unusual for sons to return to the original holdings.

Although work on the farm was increasingly mechanized, it involved considerable use of family labour for those with little capital or taking up new land. Emilie Krause (*née* Klemke)[37] was eight when her mother died in 1889. Even at that age she could drive the horses and harrow, and when the cultivated area grew too large for broadcasting by hand from a tub hanging from one shoulder, the seats were taken off the buggy and the small girl sat in the front slowly driving, while her father rode in the back with a bag of wheat, casting it out with both hands. Later, broadcast machines,† with arms whirling like a fan, cast wheat out of a large dish and eventually drills were purchased. At harvest time, on the 600-acre Klemke farm, Gottfried Klemke, aged nine in 1891, and his two elder brothers helped with winnowing. The winnower stood in the paddock, and as the grain was brought in from the three-horse stripper and emptied on to sheets, the whole family helped. As Gottfried Klemke remembered, 'Gotthilf used to shovel it into the winnower. Mother turned the winnower and Willie and I used to bag it with the dish.'[38] Harvest was followed by carting and selling. Before the completion of the Sydney-Albury railway, some farmers carted to Albury. Others preferred Corowa, thirty miles distant, which involved a return trip of at least two days, but was mostly downhill when the wagon was loaded.[39]

With the arrival of the railway, transport was easier, but was still geared to the working day of the horses. For three weeks in January, six days a week, carting continued. At first the small German wagons, pulled by two horses, carried ten or twelve four-bushel bags. Later, larger wagons with five horses pulling fifty bags were used, but the pace and procedure were the same. Farmers rose at 4 or 5 a.m. to feed, groom and harness the horses,

---

*Day was later president of the Hume Farmers' Union, a member of the N.S.W. Legislative Assembly and of the Legislative Council.
†These cost £7–£8.

then drove the wagon, loaded the night before, in to the railway in the cool of the morning, trotting where possible, dust flying from beneath the steel-rimmed wheels, but usually averaging three or four miles each hour until at the railway station they joined the long line of teams standing in the summer sun. In the absence of sheds or wheat stacks, bags were loaded straight on to railway trucks, the buyer and agents supplying the lumpers. At midday the horses were fed again—another one- or two-hour wait —then driven home again to load for the next day. It was rare for farmers living further than ten miles from the railway to achieve more than one trip a day. Payment from buyers was made by cheque, often as a percentage or advance rather than at a fixed price, and some trying times resulted for farmers who sought to anticipate rising or falling prices. In Albury, T. H. Mate bought on a half cash half goods basis.[40]

Between seeding and harvest there was always work to be done on the farm. The small dams of the first year were enlarged and later contractors were employed to scoop bigger ones. Even so the sledge with its three casks—one for vegetables and the other two cleared with lime or Epsom salts for washing—had to be dragged home regularly until underground tanks were dug close to the house. Some post and rail fencing was erected but wire steadily replaced the brush fences which had grown during the first few years as land was cleared. After seeding and during harvest, flocks of white cockatoos and native companions had to be driven off, and while crops were growing, possums were a nuisance. Many evenings were spent in possum hunting, up to thirty being found on one tree. A never-ending chore for boys was chaff-cutting. Before school hay was carried in and damped down, after school it was cut, and after tea, bagged. When hand-powered chaff-cutters were replaced by horseworks, mischievous boys soon discovered that if the horse was whipped the belt flew off and work stopped. Every twenty minutes, in any case, work stopped and the cutting knives were sharpened with a flat file.

After the first year each farm had cows, which all the family joined in milking morning and evening. Pigs, poultry and sheep were added, while gardens, fruit trees and vineyards diversified the farm's economy and the family's tasks and diet. Breakfast, which varied from sago soup and bread soup to oatmeal porridge, rarely included meat, apart from the various pig-meat sausages. Fresh meat was available immediately after killing pigs, sheep or cattle, but the rest was salted; while fruit, vegetables, eggs, cheese and bread—sometimes made from rye grown on the farm—were regular items of diet.

The permanent homes of German farmers were 'pug' houses of upright pine saplings covered with mud inside and out. One still standing on G. Klemke's property after almost a century shows the stages of affluence which ensued. Whitewashed pug walls were covered with pine weatherboard on the outside or wallpaper on the inside. Pug ceilings were covered with calico, sagging between nails spaced two or three feet apart, then with pine matchboard, and finally, in some homes, papered. Pisé homes were later cemented, while outbuildings and dairies of 'pug' or pine, at first thatched, were later roofed with corrugated galvanized iron. Some small items of furniture had been brought from Germany, but most came from South Australia, Albury, or local clearing sales. Much clothing was made on the farm, material being supplied by storekeepers who travelled from Albury buying eggs and butter, or by Indian hawkers. The latter were regular monthly visitors to the farms and often several would arrive together, their baskets of drapery and working clothes on their heads or over one shoulder. Some travelled on foot, others with horses, and in return for horse-feed worked at moving chaff. They rarely bought food, but in exchange for potatoes, meat, milk and flour, offered safety pins, handkerchiefs, pipes, medicines, combs and brushes, or even mouth organs. At night they camped in the shed, lighting little fires outside.

Life seems to have been happy enough on such farms where work and pleasure coincided. Shearing, or pig-killing and sausage making, brought 'Uncle Christie' or 'Uncle Traugott', and when the grape harvest was gathered a small cask of wine was pressed; uncles, nieces and nephews all washing their feet to join in. 'They would laugh and joke all day long while they were there. It was fun for them.'[41] 'When all the foam and froth had gone', the wine would be run into bottles, and later, when visitors came, or at the midday meal, a small glass of wine would be poured. On some farms hop-beer and later horehound-beer were brewed. At Christmas time the whole house was whitewashed inside and out and families would return home. The Klemkes had brought a Christmas tree with them from Germany. The trunk, three feet high, had holes in it for dowels, which formed the branches. Each branch had 'a tack in the end for a candle, and little holes in it for pine twigs'. Decorations of biscuits, 'ring lollies' and cards were hung, and children were given presents of clothing, tea sets, work boxes, slates or books of fairy stories—'there was usually enough money to buy something.'[42] When Emilie Krause was ten, she took her mother's place and went with her father to the Christmas evening service for the first time.

Church was the chief bond amongst these people, and devotional exercises were part of their daily life. Within weeks of a migratory group settling, a church building would be started, and would soon be followed by a Lutheran school-house where lessons, like the church services, were in German. Where communities were more scattered, until a pastor was sent or a church built, lay preachers conducted services; travelling, like their congregations, from home to home. After lunch together, families would spend drowsy Sunday afternoons talking, or singing hymns, while children would go walking, sometimes eating the turnips sown amongst the crops.[43]

Each year families would attend the Albury show, the children being interested in the prizes for German handwriting. Some travelled by sulky and others boarded excursion trains which were run—at 1d per passenger mile return—from as far north as Junee, as well as from Victoria. Gottfried Klemke's brother, Gotthilf, made the Albury show his annual outing, saving £1 to spend. He paid one shilling entrance money, a shilling for each meal, and another for a bed in Menz's hotel in Albury. Families took this opportunity to buy, from Pütman the chemist, the traditional remedies imported from Nuriootpa, in the Barossa Valley in South Australia. After 1891 a trip to Wagga always included a visit to the Model Farm. Many German farmers had experimental plots in which they sowed seed provided by the New South Wales government for testing;[44] Purple Straw and Steinwedel wheats, as in South Australia, being amongst the more commonly grown.[45] Germans were also active in the farmers' unions and frequently held office in these organizations.[46] On the whole, however, they were only partially assimilated, and are still, a century later, a distinct ethnic group.

But while a characteristic of the Lutheran groups was their close connection with religious activities, the lives of many of the non-German farming communities revolved less around church and more around school, sport, farmers' unions and other secular activities.

It is in education that one of the greatest differences between 1861 and 1891 is seen. The two hundred schools which had replaced the half-dozen of 1861 reflect the growing involvement of the State in education[47] as well as the changed population structure* and declining infant mortality. At a meeting in Wagga, Alderman Hunter of the Municipal Council said that 'in the western states of America, where he had been, it was considered a fortunate family that was able to "raise", as they termed it, three out of six children that were born. Here they growled if they lost one out of a dozen.' He went on to cite several families of from nine to twelve children which had 'never lost one'.

Then there were the families of the Angels living here almost from time immemorial. Mr. A. Angel had 11 children, Mr. Wm. Angel 14, Mr. Richard Angel 13 and Mr. John Hurst, a son-in-law had 14 children also. They had here a family of 52 children reared in the neighbourhood and only three deaths.†[48]

The spread of the selector population over the Riverina in the seventies had increased the need for schools, and following the passage of the Public Instruction Act of 1880[49] the number of schools had grown further. Two years later, Mr Inspector Hookins of Albury, whose district extended from the head of the Murray to the Darling, reported his inability to inspect nine of his schools. His superior, Mr District Inspector Hicks of Wagga, the administrative centre, noted that the 'rate of increase in the number of schools was likely to be maintained', pointing out that although six schools had closed, owing to the removal of families from the older-settled hilly areas, twenty-eight had been opened further west.[50]

In 1882 nearly thirteen thousand children attended the 233 schools in the Wagga Wagga district.§[51] The largest Public schools were at Wagga, with 659 enrolments (and North Wagga, 287); Albury, 545; Hay, 385; Deniliquin, 369; and Narrandera, 265. The rest, only six of which boasted more than one hundred enrolments, included twenty-two provisional schools, three certified Denominational schools, seven half-time schools, three house-to-house schools and three evening schools. Provisional schools

*See Figure 7.
†These were descendants of Henry Angel. His wife, who died in 1890, had been born in Hawkesbury in 1812, brought up in Illawarra and accompanied her husband, when after his exploring trips with Hume, he settled on Uardry station on the Lower Murrumbidgee in 1845. In the sixties they moved to Lake Albert, south of Wagga. Her descendants in 1890 numbered thirteen children, ninety grandchildren and forty-nine great-grandchildren; W.A., 4 October 1890.
§This included 68 in the Wagga sub-district, 81 in the Albury sub-district and 91 in the Yass sub-district.

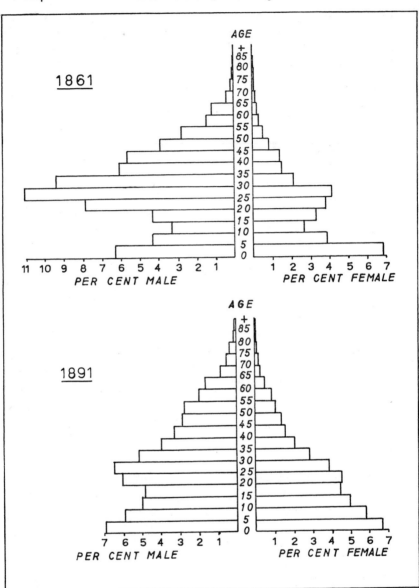

7 Age-sex pyramids for the total population in the electorates of Albury, Hume, Murray, Murrumbidgee and Balranald (boundaries adjusted) 1861–1891

Source: *N.S.W. Census*, 1861, 1891

were provided in response to local applications. After a period of adequate attendance they were converted to Public schools, the District Inspector noting that 'the proposal to substitute cheap weatherboard buildings for tents as temporary schoolrooms [was] likely to prove more generally acceptable to parents as well as to those who work in the schools.'[52] Boundary changes and sub-division of districts make comparisons difficult, but by 1890 the number of schools in the Wagga, Albury and Hay Districts were 69, 92 and 72 respectively; a total of 233.[53] Many school buildings were like that at The Rock, twenty miles south-west of Wagga; in 1882 a weatherboard structure, 18 feet × 15 feet with an iron roof, a chimney and two windows, but neither ceiling nor lining. Furniture consisted of four desks and forms for scholars, a table, chair and a large box. In 1888 when attendance rose above thirty, the room was enlarged, lined and ceiled with pine, and a new teacher, M. Walsh, arrived after a two-day ride from the Tumut district. Like other unmarried teachers he had difficulty obtaining board. In 1890 Mr Inspector O'Bryne reprimanded Walsh for 'improper conduct'; to which he replied:

> I have seen the residents (fettlers) and tried hard to get sleep-ing accommodation from them. In each case they expressed regret that their huts were so small, and that they had barely accommodation for their own families. It was only with a great compliment that I got a person to cook for me. Should you insist that I must not sleep in the school, I have no alter-native but lock the door and run away as my predecessor did or sleep under a gum tree. Perhaps the Department could see their way to erecting a residence, as this is a rising village.[54]

From the first year of the Act there had been trouble with the compulsory attendance clause and during seed-time and harvest, truant inspectors were kept busy,*[55] as attendance fell off dras-tically.[56] But increasing recognition of the importance of educa-tion and the changed structure of the population are indicated by advertisements which list amongst the advantages of farms for sale, the distance from the nearest school.[57]

Annual picnics at these schools, and to a lesser extent Arbor Day and Prize-giving, were occasions for gathering. At North Berry Jerry, eleven miles north of Coolamon, two hundred people

---

*The local Press was not impressed with early truant inspectors, the choice of which it regarded as 'pitchforking a number of superannuated nonentities into comfortable situations'.

attended the school picnic.[58] At Trickett, twenty miles north of Coolamon, three hundred people attended, and more would have been present if ploughing had not been delayed by the late season. Before dinner the Trickett children were drilled in the school yard by the teacher, Miss McKinnon, when 'they went through the movements so perfectly it would do credit to a Cadet corps.' Sports followed in the afternoon and in the evening a dance, which lasted until the following morning, was accompanied by a violin and concertina. At Kyeamba, twenty-five miles south-east of Wagga, where Miss Galvin, daughter of a local squatter, was the teacher, picnic and Prize-giving were combined. A local speaker 'pointed out the benefits derived from a primary education and that there was no royal road to learning; it was open to the poor as well as the wealthy. Those who worked hard and were attentive to their lessons generally succeeded in life.'[59] He then gave an illustration 'of self culture and perseverance in a brief history of George Stephenson and Abraham Lincoln'— Samuel Smiles was still suitable fare for children. The Mundawaddera school picnic, held at 'the Chinaman's tank',* twelve miles south-west of The Rock, attracted more than three hundred persons. 'Over thirty vehicles; buggies, covered conveyances and waggons lined the verge of the gentle slopes.' A ladies' committee supplied a 'sumptuous repast of choice viands' which included 'poultry, pastry, fruit and sweets'. In the morning a 'tilting match' for horsemen was held, and foot-races; at lunch the children 'sang sweetly, four songs and choruses' and after lunch the program included a ladies' race for 'maidens fifteen and upwards', an Old Buffers' race, a tug-of-war between married and single men—twenty men-a-side—and another between Mr Tugwell's mare and ten men. A local squatter who attended offered the use of his station shed and ground for future picnics and promised to obtain a brass band. At the end of the Mundawaddera school year, on Prize-giving day, two young women teachers—daughters of German selectors—attended from the neighbouring Pleasant Hills school. After the usual sports, high jumps, 'Siamese races' and lolly scrambles, Mr John Quirke, vice-president of the local farmers' union, distributed the prizes which had been presented by local squatters and selectors.†[60]

---

*So named 'because the labour had been performed by the celestials'; W.A., 26 March 1891.

†There is little resemblance between these selectors and the gloomy Lawson's heroine of 'Them Geraniums'.

On Arbor Day at Brucedale, eight miles north of Wagga, where Mary Cameron (later Dame Mary Gilmour) had been a pupil, twenty-one ornamental trees were planted around the Wesleyan church,[61] and at Hillston, blue gums, olives and Moreton Bay figs were planted in the school grounds. 'Strange to say . . . though the Government gave the trees, they did not make any provision for saving them from being trampled into dust by the pupils while at play', but the Hillston Amateur Minstrels came to the rescue and raised money for guards.[62]

Church services for these scattered agricultural communities were conducted by Anglican, Roman Catholic, Presbyterian and Wesleyan clergy stationed at Albury, Wagga and Deniliquin. In a typical arrangement, services were held twice every Sunday at Albury and Wagga, and each Sunday in rotation at the smaller churches. As with school there were special occasions for gathering, notably Harvest Thanksgiving and Sunday school picnics.[63] Services for the different denominations, like all other functions, were at first held in the one building on which the life of the community centred.*

Between 1881 and 1891, twenty new Riverina towns with populations of up to 500 appeared in the New South Wales census, and a further thirty 'localities'.† Some began as railway towns, others were simply rallying places as the towns of 1861 had been. Few had hotels at first. A school, church, hall, saleyards, and later a store, blacksmith's, police station and post office were more typical. Following the arrival of the railway in 1880, The Rock— a locality formerly marked only by a massive granite outcrop, a shanty, and a feed shed for the Urana coach line—began to develop as a town. The stationmaster acted as postmaster, Cobb & Co. enlarged their coaching depot, and a policeman was appointed—using Cobb & Co.'s feed room until a lock-up was built. The character of the police in remote areas was still doubtful. One early police officer, patrolling the Green's Gunyah races, 'gazed overlong on the wine', was secured to a post by locals with his own handcuffs, and after his release by a police inspector became a storekeeper at The Rock.[64] In 1886 the first Presby-

*Fifteen miles from Deniliquin stands an isolated grey weatherboard building. A battered but still legible notice wired to the gate states:
A.D. 1892
Berganbigil Literary Institute
Trespassers will be prosecuted.
†These 'localities', many with populations of over one hundred, are listed in the 1891 census. According to Coghlan they 'cannot strictly be designated Towns but are essentially agricultural, pastoral or mining centres.'

terian church service was held in a blacksmith's shop, and in 1887 local squatter John King gave land on which a weatherboard Presbyterian church was built and made available 'to ministers of all Protestant denominations'. Later he gave land for a Catholic church. Following his failure to have the town named Kingston, King sought immortality by building a hotel, the 'King's Own'.

Like those of 1861, these towns held races and sports meetings on public holidays, with concerts, balls and dances to follow, while some supported Progress Committees, brass bands, cricket teams, and a School of Arts, and served as bases for the ephemeral Railway Leagues[65] and the more permanent farmers' unions. The latter, a development from the selectors' associations of the seventies, were found 'useful in having grievances redressed.'[66] Many of their meetings and petitions were concerned with land. They objected to the resumed areas of runs and revoked reserves being sold as Special Areas at high prices, asking: 'What is 320 acres thirty miles from a railway or township for a family's support',[67] and kept up a running fight against the Lands Department administration.[68] In 1891 a local Land Board member severely cross-examined the seventeen-year-old daughter of a selector at Urana, reducing her to tears. He then disallowed her application for selection on the grounds that she was a dummy, her father having supplied the money, and declared the deposit forfeited. To resist this attack on the sacred principle of family selection and the right of a father to endow his children, farmers' unions all over the Riverina took up arms; funds were collected, motions passed, petitions signed and uproar created. 'The case', said the *Wagga Wagga Advertiser,* 'is perhaps the most important that has cropped up since the celebrated Joachim-O'Shanassy case', but the unanimous action of selectors brought quick results and the decision was reversed.*[69] They had similar success when they opposed the extension of scrub leases to some pastoral lessees,[70] raising the old cry, 'What shall we do with our sons?', but were less successful in their attempts to have roads improved and selectors' payments reduced.[71]

Problems of a different kind followed the rabbit invasion† of the eighties and government attempts to control the plague by legislation. Because rabbits were less of a problem in the more closely settled areas there was much indignation when government officials proclaimed districts infested.[72] Gottfried Scholz,

---

*O'Connell had nine other children; only the two eldest were selectors.
†The spread of rabbits in New South Wales is discussed in chapter 8.

president of the Jindera Farmers' Union, at an extraordinary meeting, expressed 'surprise that he stood a chance of having to put wire netting around his paddocks and would strongly object to having to do so'. Following a question from the secretary, W. A. Neal, 'why not a fence thirty feet high for grasshoppers?', a unanimous decision against rabbit-proof fencing was passed.[73] Beyond such practical issues, Riverina farmers had little interest in politics.

At the first conference of the Amalgamated Farmers' Union of New South Wales, held in Wagga in October 1890, a platform of six points, all relating to farmers' interests, was adopted. The first aim was the amendment of the Land Act. Objection was made to the extension of pastoral leases; Land Boards were to be elective; Land Appeal Courts were to be abolished and the Special Areas clauses were to be abolished or amended. An elective Upper House was sought—instead of 'as at present . . . nominees of necessitous Governments.' The Railway Commissioners were to be informed of the hardship under which farmers laboured under existing railway tariffs and the rates were to be revised; millers were to return bags to the producers of cereals, or reimburse them with two-thirds of the original cost; the government was to be urged so to have the statistics of farm produce collected as to form reliable records of the cereal products of the colony, and finally, the union advocated the advisability of farmers co-operating with the object of building grain sheds for the purpose of storing their grain. By so doing, the need to sell immediately after harvest, it was believed, would be obviated.[74] In their politics, as in their lives, farmers were practical men.

In considerable measure then, in those areas where soil and rainfall made it possible, the yeoman ideal had been attained by 1891. Robertson's Acts had given the selectors their land; railway extension and differential rates were giving them access to metropolitan markets, and co-operation was breaking the political and commercial monopolies of their opponents. Even though their very practical political aims were clearly stated and loudly demanded, these were mainly an extension of benefits already acquired. Considered radical in the seventies because they opposed pastoralists and the established order, selectors' demands by 1891 seem quite conservative, apart from their demand for protection, still a radical cry in a free-trade colony. But it was in fact the very land sales revenue which selectors had helped to boost which had saved New South Wales governments from having to resort to an extensive protective tariff system like Victoria.

Despite their complaints, Riverina farmers were relatively prosperous and bore little resemblance to the unfortunates depicted by writers like Henry Lawson and 'Steele Rudd'[75] who selected in less favourable environments. Certainly Riverina farmers worked hard, but the simple life and the comfortable homes seem to have been satisfying enough, and there was certainly less misery in 1891 than the incidence of drink, sickness and violence had brought to the 'lower orders' a generation earlier. Thus far, the influence of church, school and family life justified the optimists of 1861. Yet the very prosperity of the farmer, marked by rising living standards and swarms of children, precluded the possibility of all but a few of the next generation following father's footsteps. Growing capitalization and mechanization in farming gave each man control over an ever-increasing area of cleared land, so that as farming became less labour-intensive, demands for wresting ever more land from the pastoralist became more insistent. It was only the limits imposed by a horse-powered technology that postponed rural depopulation. Even though farmers may not have seen this clearly, their frequent cry, 'What shall we do with our boys?' explained at least in part their continued emphasis on land matters in their political activities.

The experience of twenty years had shown that the achievement of independence on the land and the attainment of the yeoman ideal, or at least its Australian counterpart, was possible, and had made for communities of increasing industry and respectability. The continuation of this possibility was the aim of the farmers of 1891.

TABLE 14

Population growth in Riverina towns (over 500 in 1901)

Town	1851	1856	1861	1871	1881	1891	1901
Albury	442	645	981[t]	2592	5715	5447	5823
Balranald			1587[m]	233	646	637[m]	741
Berrigan						254	523
Corowa			632	244	495	1171	2046
Deniliquin		155		1118[m]	2506	2273	2644
Germanton					462	393	560
Hay			172	664	2073	2741	3012
Howlong				107	422	425	479
Jerilderie				170	353	541	744
Moama			144	281	1204	716[m]	928
Narrandera				142	1142	1815	2255
Wagga Wagga	170	336	627	1858[m]	3975	4596	5108

[m] Municipality.
[t] Town.
Source: *N.S.W. Censuses, 1851-1901.*

TABLE 15

Population Growth in Riverina Towns (under 500 in 1901)

Town*	1861	1871	1881	1891	1901
Barooga					92
Bowna				122	268
Burrumbuttock					163
Carrathool				163	210
Coolamon				319	418
Culcairn				197	253
Finley					294
Gerogery			227	224	206
Henty				123	521
Jindera				130	425
Lockhart					329
Maude					92
Moulamein	72	81	120	131	121
Mulwala				206	417
The Rock					117
Tocumwal				325	417
Urana		113	398	397	301
Walbundrie				134	220
Wanganella					94
Yerong Creek				206	297

* Excluding 'localities' which Coghlan states 'cannot strictly be designated Towns, but are essentially agricultural, pastoral or mining centres'.
Source: *N.S.W. Census*, 1891, 1901.

River red gums, Edward River, Deniliquin

Forest of native pine *(Callitris* spp.), south of Narrandera

Deniliquin in the eighties

Court-house and Public School

TABLE 16

Riverina Town Population and Dwellings 1891

Town[a]	POPULATION			Dwellings
	Male	Female	Total	
Albury[b]	2704	2743	5447	1097
Wagga[b]	2361	2235	4596	921
Hay[b]	1459	1282	2741	501
Deniliquin[b]	1142	1131	2273	549
Narrandera[b]	1030	785	1815	370
Junee[b]	895	787	1682	349
Corowa	610	561	1171	225
Moama[b]	356	360	716	144
Balranald[b]	315	322	637	170
Jerilderie[b]	291	250	541	118
Howlong	229	196	425	79
Urana	223	174	397	94
Germanton	205	188	393	84
Tocumwal	195	130	325	68
Coolamon	199	120	319	68
Whitton	167	141	308	62
Gerogery	112	112	224	41
Mulwala	108	98	206	43
Culcairn	138	59	197	70
Oxley	118	72	190	45
Walla Walla	105	78	183	37
Mathoura	90	84	174	36
Carrathool	100	63	163	32
Booligal	70	76	146	30
Walbundrie	86	48	134	22
Moulamein	75	56	131	27
Jindera	64	66	130	31
Henty	71	52	123	19
Bowna	66	56	122	19
Illabo	58	37	95	20
Moira	41	49	90	17
Tuppal	54	13	67	18
Kyeamba	36	26	62	13
Grong Grong	28	30	58	27
Darlington Point	29	28	57	12
Conargo	33	17	50	10

[a] Exclusive of 'localities'.
[b] Incorporated.
Source: *N.S.W. Census*, 1891.

7

TOWN GROWTH AND TOWN LIFE, 1891

In 1891 the four largest towns in the Riverina were still Albury, Wagga, Hay and Deniliquin. Next, in order of size, came Narrandera and Corowa, the only other towns with populations of over 1,000. The overall pattern of population growth rates in the larger Riverina towns during the period 1851-1901 is one of rapid increase until 1881 followed by a considerable levelling off (see Figure 8). The major factors influencing this pattern were land utilization, job opportunities and the changing transport network. At first glance there appear to be two distinct patterns: one of steady growth for Murrumbidgee towns—Wagga, Narrandera, Hay; and another of absolute decline in the eighties followed by recovery in the nineties for towns further south—Albury, Deniliquin, Moama and Jerilderie. There is some distortion in the 1881 figures for Albury, Hay and Narrandera, all of which had experienced a large temporary influx of railway construction workers, numbers of whom were accompanied by their families. Advertisements when railway works were in progress sought splitters (for post and rail fencing along the line), brickmakers (for drains and viaduct construction), bushmen and timber squarers (for bridge-building and sleepers), bullock teams and tip drays (for cartage of rails, timber and ballast), carpenters (for railway station buildings, store sheds and refreshment rooms) and tank sinkers (for building engine watering facilities).

But it is true that the southern Riverina declined earlier as a result of the general movement of population in a north-westerly direction. Selectors selling out to squatters or their fellows and the accompanying rationalization of holdings caused depopulation of the southern towns;* as did the progressive outward movement of casual workers and contractors, including Chinese, engaged in fencing, dam sinking and ringbarking; while teamsters and those

*Some consideration should possibly also be given to the ageing of the selector population of the seventies, particularly the passing of women beyond the age of child bearing.

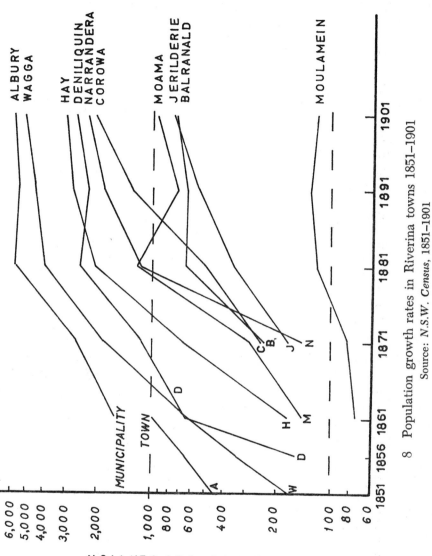

8 Population growth rates in Riverina towns 1851–1901

Source: *N.S.W. Census*, 1851–1901

employed in coaching and the river-steamer traffic continually retreated before the advancing railways.

Beyond these general influences, the patterns of growth and economic functions require examination on the basis of individual towns, but there are a number of difficulties involved in such a detailed investigation. The first is caused by the destruction of the 1881 census details in the Garden Palace fire, while they were being prepared for publication. Apart from total 'town' populations no other information is available. The 1891 census contains no breakdown of town or municipal populations into occupations; these are only covered on a county basis (see appendix A (ii)). The attempt to supplement both of these censuses from local newspaper sources, working on advertisements, reports of meetings, subscription lists, court cases, etc., as had been done for 1861, proved unsatisfactory, as did the attempt to use 'Directories' published on a subscription basis, the same names appearing in both directories and newspapers and rarely covering more than half the number known to be engaged in various occupations. Rate books and business records—rarely obtained—suffer similar limitations. Where newspapers have survived, a study of the three years around a census date might be attempted; but where towns supported two papers of over twenty pages, published two or three times weekly, an independent study is indicated. This is beyond the scope of the present enquiry and a broad outline only has been attempted here.

If the several hundred temporary residents engaged in building railways and associated works at Albury are excluded, and some allowance made for Wagga having become a municipality with consequent extended boundaries between 1861 and 1871, the growth rates of Albury and Wagga are parallel. Both grew rapidly in the seventies but were required to share with other towns which developed as rural service centres the prosperity resulting from closer settlement. Deniliquin grew rapidly with the fat-stock market of the late fifties, declining as that traffic did in the sixties. Growth recovered during the seventies, with rising prosperity from family selection and a further boost from the private railway link with Melbourne. The extension of the New South Wales government railways to the area in the early eighties, partly in answer to Victorian economic aggression, effectively reduced Deniliquin's economic hinterland, while movement of selectors out of the district further decreased the need for services. A combined flour-mill and brewery, a wool scour, soap factory and the railway marked the limits of local industrial enterprise. The seasonal wool traffic to the railhead provided Deniliquin's major annual economic activity, with livestock movements of less importance as the Victorian protective tariff increased.[1] Brick-works and saw-mills, as in other towns, operated according to the demands of the building trade. In the southern Riverina, building activity generally declined during the period. Between 1881 and 1891 the number of houses in Narrandera increased from 248 to 370 and in Wagga from 594 to 921. By contrast, the number of houses in Albury rose only from 1,051 to 1,097 and in Deniliquin from 546 to 549. In Moama the number decreased from 356 to 144 (see Table 17).

The railways to Hay and Jerilderie ended the domination of Deniliquin in the western Riverina, both of these towns growing at Deniliquin's expense. Within a year of the railway reaching Jerilderie a flour-mill had been built. During the seventies Hay had grown in importance as a transport centre for teamsters, Cobb & Co.'s coaches, and river steamers loaded with wool or station supplies, including fencing wire. Thousands of tons of copper ore brought by teams from Mount Hope, 160 miles north, and the Araunah mine at Nymagee, 220 miles north, were loaded on to steamers at Hay for smelting in Adelaide, and machinery passed back along the same route.[2] Until the railway reached Hay in 1882 the bridge was opened for as many as six steamers a day, but in the whole of the following year only six passed through. Some squatters, accustomed to dealing with Melbourne, continued to send wool by steamer to Echuca when the river was high, but differential rates netted an increasing amount of this traffic for Sydney, while the existence of the railhead enabled Hay's pros-perity as the centre of the outback transport system to be maintained.

Narrandera and Corowa both grew as a result of selection activity, the need for services increasing as the district was more closely settled. Corowa's agricultural and pastoral hinterland gave rise to flour-mills and a wool scour; saw-mills cut red gum and pine; and in 1892 the completion of the Culcairn-Corowa railway link to Sydney assured further growth. By 1891, Narrandera, on a population basis, was the most highly industrialized town in the Riverina.* Besides being a railway junction for the Hay and Jerilderie lines, and before that a steamer port, Narrandera was

*See population of County Cooper, which included Narrandera and only one other town, Coolamon (pop. 319) in appendix A (ii).

TABLE 17

Building Materials Used in Riverina Urban Dwellings 1891

Boroughs and Municipalities	Stone	Brick	Concrete, Adobe, Pisé	Iron	Wood, Slabs	Lath and plaster, Wattle and dab, Mud, Bark	Canvas, Calico, Tents	Indefinite, not stated	Total
Albury	17	612	4	6	403	6	19	30	1097
Balranald	—	38	—	2	126	—	4	—	170
Deniliquin	—	219	1	3	325	1	—	—	549
Hay	—	172	—	3	398	1	13	4	591
Jerilderie	—	34	—	1	67	—	7	9	118
Junee	—	65	2	5	265	3	7	2	349
Moama	—	25	—	—	116	—	3	—	144
Narrandera	—	62	—	3	283	—	12	10	370
Wagga	2	599	2	2	306	5	2	3	921

Source: *N.S.W. Census*, 1891.

the centre of an extensive timber trade which drew on the surrounding natural pine forests. Timber from its several saw-mills was sent all over the Riverina and as far as the upper Darling. A coach factory, brewery and cordial factory, flour-mill (1884), wool scour (1886), and meat freezing works (1890)—in which rabbits increasingly replaced sheep—all contributed to the town's stability; while earlier gold had been mined.[3] Narrandera's most rapid growth had been from 1871 to 1881, from a population of 142 to 1,142. The 1871 census return included only twenty-two 'householders'; the rest were recorded as 'persons sleeping on premises', thus:

> 1 resident engineer (2 persons sleeping on premises), 1 constable (5), 4 hotelkeepers (45), 1 storekeeper (6), 2 butchers (8), 1 baker (5), 2 gardeners—1 Chinese—(9), 1 bootmaker (9), 1 contractor (8), 2 carpenters (4), 1 blacksmith (7), 2 domestics (15), 1 labourer (4), 2 'no occupation' (10).

Of the one thousand additional inhabitants recorded in 1881, a large number were railway workers and another group were tradesmen thriving on the growth of selector population, while by 1883 the Narrandera Chinese camp was the largest in the Riverina, with 303 Chinese, nine European women married to Chinese, ten children, and eighteen prostitutes.[*4] By 1891 many Chinese formerly living in Riverina towns had followed the 'ring-barking frontier' further north.

Detailed explanation of the rise and fall of Moama is hindered by scanty evidence. In general terms, Moama suffered from the decline of the fat-stock market, the movement northwards of Victorian selectors, the decline of steamer traffic and river-boat building, the removal of its sole industrial enterprise, the 'Boileau' boiling-down works, and the competition of the larger Victorian town, Echuca, across the river.[5] The town of Moulamein is included in Figure 8 to illustrate the persistence of a town in a purely pastoral environment. Untouched by agriculture, railways, steamers or industry, Moulamein, gazetted as a police town and furnished with a lock-up in 1849, reached a population of 120 in 1881, rose to 131 in 1891, and with the removal of ten people (possibly a single family), declined to 121 in 1901. Urana, made the centre of a land administration district in 1876 like Corowa

---

*Sub-Inspector Brennan, who inspected the camps with Sydney merchant Quong Tart, noted that 'at some periods the population is much larger, when the Chinese employed by squatters and surrounding land proprietors return after having performed some ringbarking or other contract.'

and Narrandera, and enjoying similar rainfall, soil and selector activity, never matched the two latter towns. The water requirements of a large urban population could not be satisfied from low natural rainfall on flat country. While small towns could cling to the railway, large towns developed and survived only on the major permanent rivers, where they had first begun.

The close relation between rural activity and town growth and prosperity in the Riverina is seen in Table 18, which indicates that the six-fold increase in population in three decades was distributed evenly between the urban and rural sections of the population.*

TABLE 18

Urban and Rural Population, South-West Slopes,[1] *1861-91*

	Urban ('000)	Rural ('000)	Total ('000)	Urban percentage of total
1861	2.8	6.0	8.8	32
1871	5.5	13.8	19.4	28
1881	15.8	26.5	42.3	37
1891	18.2	32.7	51.0	36

[1] Electorates of Albury, Hume, Murray, Murrumbidgee, (Balranald n.a.). Source: *N.S.W. Census 1891, Statistician's Report.*

More pronounced changes in the population had occurred on the basis of nationality or birthplace (see Table 19). By 1891 New-South-Wales-born and Victorian-born had risen to 69.9 per cent of the population, while those born in England, Scotland and Ireland had declined to 19.3 per cent. German-born accounted for 1.5 per cent† and Chinese-born 2.7 per cent. Victorian infiltration was limited to the southern and western Riverina (see Figure 10),§ expansion westward from the older-settled districts of New South Wales accounting for much of the closer settlement along the Murrumbidgee. The excess of males over females, except in the more remote pastoral areas beyond Hay and Deniliquin, had steadily declined. In the towns the male to female ratio of 3:2 in

*The urban-rural classification is Coghlan's. Because of the difficulty of definition, the terms have generally been avoided in this study. Where the size of a municipality is reckoned in tens of square miles there is doubtful value in calling the municipal population 'urban'.

†The percentage represents only German-born members of the Lutheran community and a small number of German Catholics; see p. 234.

§Census covers only Victorian-born. It excludes immigrants who were born overseas but resided in Victoria for two decades (from the gold rush years), before moving into New South Wales to select.

TABLE 19

Principal Birthplaces of Population in Riverina Counties 1891[a]

Counties	N.S.W.	Victoria	England	Scotland	Ireland	German Empire	Chinese Empire[b]
Bourke	2,012	561	278	109	190	34	94
Boyd	323	211	118	56	62	3	52
Cadell	623	656	247	70	90	13	3
Caira	505	386	168	60	90	7	45
Clarendon	4,548	429	575	140	414	48	91
Cooper	1,707	644	387	117	220	24	212
Denison	588	712	178	104	142	10	17
Goulburn	4,902	1,739	812	269	557	313	115
Hume	2,173	1,155	465	164	371	198	77
Mitchell	1,394	362	188	90	183	85	27
Sturt	315	137	95	44	33	7	85
Townsend	1,420	1,164	474	169	252	33	108
Urana	1,255	757	341	202	259	47	83
Wakool	242	373	121	56	57	5	50
Waradgery	1,849	1,014	548	160	317	23	148
Wynyard	8,761	736	1,069	211	735	87	487
Total	32,617	11,036	6,064	2,021	3,972	937	1,694
Percentage of total counties' population	52.2	17.7	9.7	3.2	6.4	1.5	2.7

[a] Figures listed total 93.4 per cent of total population in sixteen counties.
[b] The total number of Chinese was slightly higher (1,818).
Source: *N.S.W. Census*, 1891.

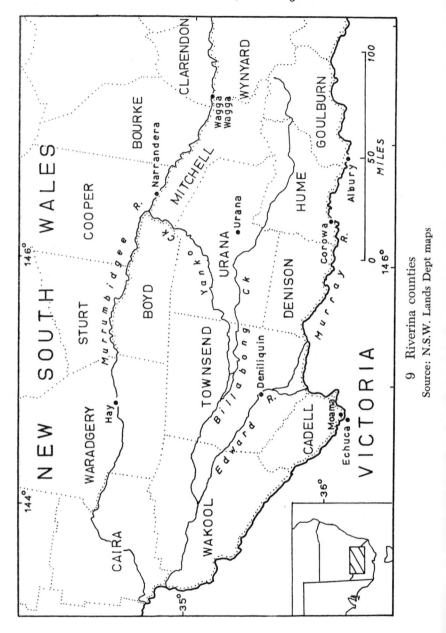

9 Riverina counties

Source: N.S.W. Lands Dept maps

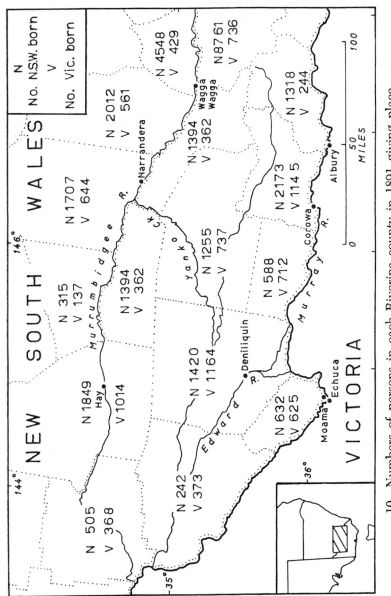

10 Numbers of persons in each Riverina county in 1891 giving place of birth as New South Wales or Victoria

Source: *N.S.W. Census*, 1891

1861 had been replaced by approximate sexual parity, while amongst the rural population the ratio had moved from 3:1 to 3:2 (see Table 20).

TABLE 20

Male : Female Ratio in Urban and Rural Population, South-West Slopes, 1861-91*

	Urban		Rural		Total	
	Males (%)	Females (%)	Males (%)	Females (%)	Males (%)	Females (%)
1861	58.82	41.18	71.87	28.13	67.65	32.35
1871	55.62	44.38	63.76	36.24	61.42	38.58
1881	55.21	44.79	62.92	37.08	60.04	39.96
1891	51.47	48.53	61.23	38.77	57.74	42.26

* Electorates of Albury, Hume, Murray, Murrumbidgee (Balranald n.a.).
Source: *N.S.W. Census 1891, Statistician's Report.*

Although the Chinese were, numerically, a minority group, the presence of three hundred adult Chinese males in a town like Narrandera, where the total population in the early eighties was 1,400, meant that every second man in town was Chinese. Given also their distinctive appearance and habits, their presence could hardly be ignored. The population of Riverina Chinese camps in 1883 is indicated in Table 21. The largest camp, that at Narrandera, had streets and lanes and contained 'stores, joss-house, a very large cookshop, two lottery houses and several fan-tan rooms.' Most of the land was held under eight-year lease from Europeans by two Chinese and sublet to others. The Chinese— as became a nation with traditional reverence for scholars— showed great interest in the education of their children, most of whom attended Riverina Public schools or Catholic schools, though one boy—'cleanly and intelligent' according to a sympathetic report—was excluded from Albury Public school 'because the child was wearing his hair in the queue.'[6]

Towns in 1891 served the same administrative purposes as in 1861: land, customs, local government and justice. Although the main wave of selection had passed and no new land offices were established after 1876, land revenue was still extensive even in districts where most of the land had been alienated. In 1891, £44,000 was collected in the Albury land office, the main items being: interest and balance on conditional purchases, £27,380; auction deposits and balance, £6,820; deposits on conditional purchases, £4,976; and conditional lease rent, £1,828.[7]

TABLE 21

Population of Riverina Chinese Camps, October 1883

Name of Chinese camp	No. of European women married to Chinese	No. of Chinese	No. of Chinese women	Children		No. of prostitutes in each camp	Total population of each camp
				Male	Female		
Narrandera	9	303	—	6	4	18	340
Wagga Wagga	6	194	1	9	7	6	223
Deniliquin	11	113	—	11	6	4	145
Hay	5	100	—	8	6	5	124
Albury	5	90	—	6	5	4	110
Total	36	800	1	40	28	37	942

Source: *V. & P.* (L.A. N.S.W.), 1883-4, xi, p. 664.

Customs revenue was smaller, amounting in Albury to just over £32,000. Despite the assurance of politicians that 'taxation through the back and stomach was preferable to land taxation',[8] local opinion saw this amount as being 'the increased cost of living which the people of Albury district have had to pay for the luxury of protection.'[9] As previously, the largest single import was alcohol. Of the £3,332 collected in customs duties in December 1891, the largest amounts were: spirits, wine and beer, £1,300; 10 per cent *ad valorem* duties, £692; tobacco and cigars, £490; and sugar, £250.[10] To escape the Victorian tariff on wheat, growers in the Corowa district forwarded New South Wales wheat, in bond, over the Victorian lines from Wahgunyah to Albury, and thence to Sydney.[*11]

As towns grew in size the duties of local government increased and varied. Expenditure in 1891 related to: road and street making and the cost, carriage and carting of metal, sand, loam, and drain pipes; the salaries of office staff, librarian,[†] collector, and inspector of nuisances; the maintenance of parks, gardens and recreation reserves; weed eradication; the lighting of streets —by kerosene at first but by gas in 1891; the administration of saleyards and town common, including herdsman's fees and the cost of mustering goats and exterminating rabbits; the water supply—engineer's salary, firewood for steam engines which drove the pumps, blacksmith's work, and pipes; and sanitary arrangements like night-soil contracts and the emptying of Public school cesspits. The largest receipts came from: general and water rates and to a lesser extent commons fees and park grazing fees; a series of licences—cab, cab-drivers', cart and plumbers'; some government endowment towards park maintenance; the removal of rubbish; night-soil fees; and large overdrafts. When the gasworks were owned by the municipality this provided revenue from gas, coke and tar—but where they were privately owned, the cost of street lighting and asphalt were added to the council's expenditure list.[12] Waterworks were a profitable investment, rapidly repaying the original outlay and providing reliable income, while complaints about the tarry taste from new pipes, or

*This traffic ceased with the completion of the Culcairn-Corowa railway in 1892. Its existence necessitates some qualification in the use of border statistics of imports and exports. The 1890 wheat imports via Albury totalled £4,692 of which £4,656 was New South Wales wheat from Corowa. What percentage of the £53,783-worth was thus 'imported' in 1889 went unrecorded.

†Part of the librarian's task was to care for the books and newspapers in the School of Arts.

the quality of Murrumbidgee water in the summer[13]—'when the fluid (if it can be so called) approaches the consistency of pea soup with a resemblance in colour to a much darker liquid'[14]—led to further improvements and filtering. In Albury £50,000 was spent on completing the water supply in 1891 and the new 75,000-gallon iron tank above ground level, filled and 'holding well', was claimed to be 'the largest of its character in the colonies'.[15] Stimulated by town water supplies, parks and gardens flourished. As early as 1883 Deniliquin was claiming that the scenery in its park—featuring two rustic bridges and a willow-fringed lagoon—'was almost equal to that of the Yarra near the Botanical Gardens or the Parramatta River in the vicinity of the orange groves.'[16] In Wagga in 1891 the public were cautioned against plucking flowers or leaves or in any way damaging the trees, shrubs or plants in the streets or public gardens within the municipality.[17]

Some aspects of town life were less attractive. Before the appointment of an inspector of nuisances in Hay it was possible for complaints to be made that for nearly a week a dead cat had been 'lying putrefying in the gutter alongside the most frequented portion of our main thoroughfare'. With kitchen stuff habitually thrown out at the rear of hotels and private houses, sewage exposed in long open gutters, and pigs kept in filthy sties in the town, it was not surprising that offensive smells met the inhabitants wherever they went and that fears of cholera were widespread.[18] By the nineties earth-closets or the bucket system of sewage disposal were more common, but drainage of household water caused concern. The editor of the *Wagga Wagga Advertiser* saw no justification for the 'barbarous expedient of compelling householders to create permanent receptacles on their premises for the storage of all the foul water accumulated from domestic use.' Others objected to such water being allowed to run into the street gutters, where it was 'likely to become offensive through becoming impregnated with soap'. To these the editor replied: 'Surely it is better to have this nastiness exposed to view where means can be taken to deal with it, than to bury it in backyards to impregnate the soil with the germs of death dealing disease', and suggested daily flooding of the street channels, a system used in the greater number of Sydney suburbs and which 'might be supposed to have better results in Wagga'[19] with its abundant water supply.

In each town the Chinese camp, situated on flat land next to the river, was one of the most noisome localities, since, where there was neither natural nor artificial drainage, stagnant water and putrid substances accumulated. In addition, two inspectors noted, 'the water closets are allowed to become neglected, and as a consequence in hot weather the effluvium which these places give forth is sickening.'*[20] In Albury in 1890-1 uproar and a libel suit followed the *Border Post* report of the 'Chinese disinterment cases'. Filial piety required that the bones of dead Chinese should be returned to their native land. In the eighties, one steamer had called at Sydney carrying '286 boxes of defunct Chinamen supposed to be bones only.' According to the *Pastoral Times* they had not been delivered in good order and condition, several being 'too high'.[21] To avoid a repetition of this, Albury Chinese were particularly careful about scraping bones. Unfortunately for them, the Bungambrawatha Creek, in which they scraped and washed the disinterred bones, provided the water supply for a number of Albury residents. Within a week every newspaper in the Riverina was bursting with indignation at a proceeding so 'repugnant to the European sense of cleanliness' and opposed to the first law of sanitation—'we are not cannibals'. Nor did it help when the bones were packed in the same truck as a consignment of fruit for Sydney.†[22]

It was with the Chinese camps too that much of the work of the courts was concerned, though less with the Chinese themselves than with the women and hangers-on. To contemporaries the sight of a Chinaman taking oath in court was ridiculous. Nominal Christians swore on the Bible, the occasional Indian hawker swore on the Koran,[23] but the Chinese swore by blowing out a match. The formula varied but one used at Deniliquin was typical. While the lighted match burnt down towards Ah Tie's fingers, 'Constable Anderson slowly recited:

> So sure you blow that match out
> So sure you tell a lie
> So sure you go to Hell

"S'welp 'im Bob", added the Chinaman with a groan as he blew out the match, and then the magistrates, police, lawyers and the

*The sewage service in Hay was not extended into the town block formerly occupied by the Chinese camp until after 1960. Although sewers were all around the area, the former Chinese residents could not or would not pay.

†It should be noted, however, that wool scours and fellmongers polluted the Murray upstream from Albury, and dead stock were commonly allowed to lie in gullies and creek beds; *P.T.*, 22 March 1890.

public giggled at the grotesque exhibition.'[24] Chinese were charged with gambling at *mipon chong* or fan-tan, but the charges were dismissed when it was shown that the Act did not provide a penalty for playing those games. They were charged occasionally with robbery and sly-grog selling, and more often with evading the £10 poll tax,[25] imposed under the New South Wales Influx of Chinese Restriction Act of 1881.[26]

In the five camps inspected in 1883 there were thirty-six European women married to Chinese. Some appeared respectable and kept aloof from the 'bad characters who made the camps hideous by their vile conduct', but others made the lives of their unfortunate Chinese husbands miserable.

> They conduct themselves [reported an Inspector of Police], regardless of consequences, and set their husbands at defiance as far as conducting themselves improperly with Europeans is concerned. When not at war with their husbands they fight with one another, seek redress in the Police Courts, and the Chinese husbands have to pay the penalties incurred by their European wives, and consider themselves fortunate that they too have not been included in the litigation; most of these women have been prostitutes for years before they get married to the Chinese . . .[27]

Besides these the camps contained another thirty-seven unmarried prostitutes and on occasion double that number. There was no suggestion that the Chinese were the seducers. Most of the women had been prostitutes for years and 'many found pleasure in recounting a history of criminal experience and of their youthful precociousness.' All preferred 'the nomadic life of the camp with its licentiousness to the quiet repose of settled habitation.' Many were addicted to opium. In their rooms they were visited by Chinese and European 'men *and sometimes boys*, for immoral purposes', the police having 'on some occasions hunted as many as ten young men from off a Chinese bed, where the central figure would be one of the females already mentioned, and as soon as the police left the camp those fellows returned again.'[28] All except four of the women—the four including one from London and one from Mauritius—were natives of Victoria. They had money, dressed expensively in velvet, silks and jewellery and when in the streets conducted themselves for the most part with propriety. But when, on occasion, their behaviour in the camp was violent and bloody, police action could be taken.

During the shearing season, the camps, particularly those at

Wagga and Narrandera, were 'thronged with shearers and others', who indulged in drink and contributed 'largely to the disquieting elements observable at that period', while the recklessness of the women, anxious to reap a harvest while they could, increased the incidence of sly grog selling, prostitution, gambling and robbery.[29] Although objections to the Chinese finally resulted in discriminatory legislation, the law usually provided the same protection for them as for other citizens. Two Corowa boys who threw stones at Chinese were charged with inflicting grievous bodily harm.[30] Even in the Riverina, there were those who appealed to the notion of 'fair play'. After the 1881 Act the *Riverine Grazier* commented, in a series of tolerant editorials, that it was unreasonable to prosecute and ill-use Chinese on the grounds that they were 'immoral idle gamblers given to intemperance or evil propensities'. They were not more so than others, it stated, and 'no more immoral than our men in similar circumstances'.[31] In connection with 321 offences committed by persons residing in Riverina Chinese camps ('or who habitually frequented them'), during 1881-3, 198 European females were prosecuted, 49 European males and 74 Chinese. One leading Chinese blamed all vice, immorality and corruption on opium, and after referring to the Opium War and its unhappy results in China, implored the New South Wales government to restrict or prohibit opium imports, obtaining a large number of Chinese signatories to his petition. The New South Wales government, however, allowed imports of over 25,000 lb. of opium per year, levied duty of 10s per lb. and accepted the revenue.[32]

Whatever the causes of crime in the Chinese camps, lawbreaking by the rest of the population showed little variation from the pattern of 1861. Court records list larceny, manslaughter, assault and robbery, theft of a saddle, horse stealing, breaking and entering, and outdoor incendiarism, with perhaps a little more forging and uttering—as literacy increased—and some diminution of drunkenness and associated crimes. Although in 1891 there were fewer hotels, on a population basis, in both old towns and new, what this means in terms of consumption and whether it represents a more sober population is difficult to tell. Some of the decrease in hotel numbers is due to the change from horse transport to steam and the resultant decline in the need for stopping places. It may also reflect a growth in the size of individual hotels. The composition of the population had also changed in some areas and farmers with families undoubtedly tended more to sobriety than nomadic bush-workers. Sly-grog selling was still prosecuted, drunken rows in navvies' camps led to bloodshed and men still died in the bush from alcoholism.[33] A Bacchanalian orgy took place at Coolamon one Saturday night, when 'an army of shearers, farm labourers and sundowners' visited the small town and formed two camps.[34] Until late in the evening they frequented the two hotels, but when morning dawned the hotel-keepers found their cellars broken into, and at the camps, men and bottles lay scattered in all directions. Nor was gambling exclusively the prerogative of the Chinese. Admittedly there were twelve Chinese fan-tan tables at Albury, and Narrandera Chinese hawked lottery tickets for money prizes* in the streets and from house to house and even sold them to children.[35] But Australians could invest in the Riverina Art Union or Tattersalls Monster Consultation, and gambling took place every Sunday on the Wagga racecourse, in a large excavation known as 'the sand hole'. 'Lads of respectable parentage', said the *Wagga Wagga Advertiser* in reporting the matter, 'are known to frequent this *hell* and we may therefore hope that the intimation here given may be the means of breaking up the school.' As in 1861, the guardians of respectability waged unceasing war against all such unwholesome influences. Their main instruments of reform were still hospitals, churches and schools.

Local finance for hospitals in 1891 still came from subscriptions. Collectors travelled from station to station, Chinese storekeepers collected from their fellow-countrymen, and local committees, no longer squatter-dominated but controlled rather by townsmen, arranged race-meetings or other entertainment to raise funds. In more closely settled districts, finance from subscriptions was adequate and in Wagga in 1891 no special function was necessary. Further west the greater number of migratory workers increased demands on hospitals. Patients treated at the Hay hospital in 1890 came from places as widely separated as Howlong, Hillston and Balranald. Of 184 treated only forty-four were Hay residents, leading to complaints that other districts were sending their sick to Hay.†[36]

Following complaints about the management of the Deniliquin hospital in 1890, Dr F. Noyes, resident medical officer for over

---

*The use of *money* prizes for *pak ah pu* or *pow chong* evaded the Lotteries Act, 16 Vic., no. 2, which specified only *goods, wares* and *merchandise*.

†Cf. the similar complaint from the Melbourne hospital in 1860 (see pp. 83-4).

thirty years, said that the fault lay with the patients, who were 'not of a desirable class of people' and were unaccustomed to control. 'A great many', he continued, 'were the outcasts of society. These men always grumbled, no matter what was done for them . . . the fact was that country hospitals were partly benevolent societies . . . You can manage the patients when they are in bed, but as soon as they get up they want to go into town.'[37] The latter trait had been characteristic of patients a generation earlier. How true his other allegations were is more difficult to judge, particularly as one of the complaints concerned treatment of a five-year-old girl patient. In defence of his action in this case, Noyes stated that the female ward was empty and he had put the girl in a ward with a male patient, so that she would be properly attended to. When complaint was made, he had removed her, protesting that only the most prurient minded could have taken offence.[38]

Of 139 males and 17 females admitted at Deniliquin in 1889—apart from 275 outdoor patients—16 had been relieved, 6 forwarded to Sydney and 104 cured, while 13 remained in the hospital and 17 had died. Deaths had resulted from typhoid, abscess of the liver, *morbus cordis* and disease of the heart (4), cancer, senile bronchitis, extravasation of urine, phthisis (2), injury followed by gangrene, decay of nature, diphtheria, alcoholic poisoning, pleurisy and rupture of the liver. The greater diversity evident in death and disease is partly the result of increased skill or changing fashions in diagnosis. Noyes had returned to England several times during his thirty years in Deniliquin.[39] Of eighteen patients who died at Hay in 1890, at least one-third had arrived at the hospital in an advanced state of hopelessly incurable disease. Because this raised the death rate, discredited the hospital and added to expense, the committee agreed that such admissions should be discouraged.[40] As might be expected, towns with such primitive sanitary arrangements suffered spasmodic outbreaks of 'an intensified kind of English cholera known by medical men as "gastro-enteritis" ', while in 1888, fifty-two cases of typhoid had been admitted to the Wagga hospital, seven proving fatal.[41] In the younger age-groups recurrent epidemics still caused deaths, and when diphtheria cases were admitted to hospital, the disease spread to other patients, causing dissatisfaction and alarm.[42] Of the cases admitted to the Wagga hospital in 1890, the highest numbers were for alcoholism—men still drank themselves to death or the D.T.s, or suicided in despair.[43] At Wagga even the superintendent and nurse were asked to resign because of their intemperance.[44]

Some patients were undoubtedly outcasts. At Narrandera a Chinese leper camped in a tent by himself, one-and-a-half miles from the town and three-quarters of a mile from the nearest habitation, but Deniliquin residents complained that a Chinese leper was not only admitted to their hospital after being excluded from the Chinese camp, but was actually housed in an old weatherboard building only one hundred yards from the female ward. They suggested that the practice that obtained elsewhere of erecting a tent on a quarantined patch of ground and leaving meals at the edge of it was more desirable. Twelve cases of leprosy were recorded in New South Wales in 1891, including nine Chinese and one Javanese. That the other two cases were native-born Australian youths who had been living with Chinese, and who were now separated from their families never to see them again—'isolated to die'—explains some of the concern of Deniliquin residents.[45]

'Diseases of syphilitic origin', so prevalent in 1861, had either declined, or, in the more respectable society of 1891, gone underground.[*] For lesser ills chemists and stores still offered miracles of healing with patent medicines like the redoubtable Holloway's Pills,[†] as did herbalists who claimed to have cured with their nostrums 'more cases of chronic disease than any ten men in Australia'.[46] More insidious were the advertisements of quacks who preyed on the fears of the intemperate or unchaste. American 'Vital Pills' for nervous debility, lost vitality, sexual weakness and error, and American 'Private Pills' for discharges, contagious sores and blood diseases, were offered to readers who had 'unhappily fallen into objectionable habits and are suffering in consequence and are unwilling to hand on an enfeebled constitution to their offspring.'[§][47]

The churches may have been to some extent responsible for increased respectability and the feeling of guilt associated with unchastity; they were more positive in their approach to intemperance. The Band of Hope, under the guidance of which children signed the pledge of abstinence, operated in the larger towns, particularly amongst the Methodists. The nominal religious adher-

[*]Details of admissions to Riverina hospitals in 1890-2 have not survived and were not printed in the Press.
[†]Newspaper advertisements also list Beecham's Pills, Scott's Emulsion, Ayer's Pills, Cherry Pectoral and eucalyptus oil, amongst others.
[§]'Female Pills' were also offered.

ence of Riverina residents in 1891 is indicated in Tables 22 and 23. Of the 62,000 inhabitants in the sixteen counties listed, 44.9 per cent were Anglican; 29.7 per cent Roman Catholics—still more numerous near Wagga and Albury; 13.3 per cent Presbyterian—proportionately stronger near Deniliquin; 6.6 per cent Methodist; and 3.2 per cent Lutheran, the latter clustered in the three farming counties north of Albury. Although lightly represented in the rural areas, the Salvation Army, Congregationalists, Baptists, the Church of Christ and smaller evangelical groups were active in the towns. There was little that was new to the Australian scene in the three older churches. Anglicans and Roman Catholics still opposed secular education and established their own church schools in the towns, as Lutherans did in the farming areas. In 1878 a Jesuit mission in Wagga had marked the opening of St Michael's School[48] and in 1883 a convent had been established in Hay.[49] Occasional musical evenings were held to raise funds for these.[50] More variety was provided by the newer churches, which also generally required greater personal commitment of their members.[51] The Wesleyans emphasized Sunday schools—at Wagga 135 children attended—and Sunday school anniversaries were functions of some importance. They also organized Sunday school teachers' conferences, concerts, cantatas and conversaziones. Other activities included song services like 'The Boy Martyr', on Good Friday, and an Annual Fruit Soirée, featuring the town band, anthems, solos and duets, followed by a rock-melon and water-melon supper. At Deniliquin, seventeen boys and thirty-four girls, aged from seven to fourteen years, enrolled in the Band of Hope at a fee of 1d per month.[52] The Salvation Army, active in the streets and outside hotels, was occasionally the target for rotten eggs and fireworks, their sufferings attracting the sympathy of the respectable. Less enthusiasm was felt for General Booth's scheme to export part of the 'submerged tenth' from England. When he visited Australia, the *Border Post*, quoting his *Darkest England*, said that it would not be received with much cordiality and that there was a 'decided objection to the colonies being made a penitentiary or even a receptacle of pauper immigration.'[53]

In Hay in 1879 there had been forty hotels and two churches.*

---

*'This,' said one writer, 'gives one a good idea of the tendencies of the inhabitants', while another considered that, 'the thirst for drink in this hot climate of ours is wonderful'; J. Jervis, 'The Western Riverina', *J.R.A.H.S.*, vol. 38 (1952), p. 181; *R.G.*, 7 March 1874.

TABLE 22

Principal Religions in Riverina Municipalities 1891

Municipality or Borough	Church of England	Roman Catholic	Presby- terian	Methodist	Baptist	Congre- gational	Lutheran	Church of Christ	Salvation Army
Albury	2,251	1,927	484	327	23	101	56	8	83
Balranald	306	200	77	4	6	1	6	–	3
Deniliquin	882	564	404	263	11	6	8	–	52
Hay	1,157	689	308	271	24	12	13	–	53
Jerilderie	218	160	99	18	4	1	2	–	–
Junee	731	471	205	198	2	8	3	–	20
Moama	356	146	81	73	16	1	5	–	20
Narrandera	933	413	182	74	3	6	5	–	31
Wagga	1,796	1,584	435	411	9	24	26	17	75
Total	8,630	6,154	2,275	1,639	98	160	124	25	337
Percentage	44.4	31.7	11.7	8.4	0.5	0.8	0.6	0.1	1.7

Source: N.S.W. Census, 1891.

TABLE 23

*Principal Religions in Riverina Counties 1891**

Counties	Church of England	Roman Catholic	Presby-terian	Methodist	Baptist	Congre-gational	Lutheran	Church of Christ	Salvation Army
Bourke	1,504	940	452	252	43	11	57	9	17
Boyd	336	210	193	45	3	2	13	—	2
Cadell	849	356	254	197	22	2	19	6	32
Caira	654	362	229	14	12	2	11	—	3
Clarendon	2,949	2,010	624	583	13	19	24	20	44
Cooper	1,663	863	427	157	6	14	18	1	35
Denison	663	618	425	67	15	10	6	4	6
Goulburn	3,807	2,887	985	443	33	120	530	—	105
Hume	1,909	1,256	625	229	77	42	650	40	11
Mitchell	965	873	289	91	14	6	282	—	5
Sturt	314	163	146	22	2	9	6	—	—
Townsend	1,598	871	739	357	17	11	21	—	61
Urana	1,233	855	579	98	23	2	137	1	12
Wakool	423	162	258	55	11	1	6	—	3
Waradgery	1,888	1,112	552	318	26	13	24	—	57
Wynyard	5,643	3,893	1,056	940	31	62	46	26	174
Total	26,398	17,431	7,833	3,868	348	326	1,850	107	567
Percentage of total counties' population	44.9	29.7	13.3	6.6	0.6	0.6	3.2	0.2	1.0

* Because of rounding, figures in the percentages listed do not add to the recorded total.
Source: *N.S.W. Census*, 1891.

In 1891, following a visit from a member of the Evangelisation Society of Victoria, a local Evangelistic Association was formed, drawing support from all Protestant denominations. In Wagga, a united prayer meeting was held regularly in the Y.W.C.A. building, while the Church of Christ met each week in the Temperance Hall, conducting worship services at 11 a.m. and gospel services at 7 p.m.[54] When one of its young women adherents sought baptism (by immersion), an open-air service was arranged on the banks of the Murrumbidgee. Such an unusual event attracted several hundred spectators, and although the majority were respectable citizens, 'other more youthful members of the male sex kept pressing forward to obtain a closer view of the proceedings. In the end they crowded around so much the girl fainted.'[55]

Just as the growth of Sunday schools indicated increased numbers of children, so did the number and size of Public schools in the larger towns, where enrolments fluctuated, as they did in the smaller schools, with population movements. Wagga Public school enrolments increased from 171 to 340 between 1871 and 1873, then rose to 628 primary enrolments in 1880, besides some 200 infants, so that a tent seventy-three feet long had to be erected while the school was enlarged. So overcrowded were the narrow rooms in 1882, with the added influx of railway workers' children, that fire guards were ordered. The voluminous clothes of one teacher who had been forced too close to the fireplace caught alight, necessitating six months' sick leave. By 1890 there were three Public schools open in Wagga, one on the north side of the river and two on the south; the Grammar school having finally closed the year before.[56] Town schools were less affected by seed-time and harvest, but did feel the impact of extreme seasons. In 1882, a drought year, the well in the Wagga school-yard began to dry up and required deepening; and when, in the flood of 1891, with thirty families sheltering in the school, the headmaster rang the bell at 9 a.m., 9.15 and 9.25, only three children attended. In any case, as he pointed out, the school floors were in a filthy state, 'consequent on the cooking and other domestic work which had been freely carried on', and he decided to close the school until it was clean.[57]

In the Wagga Superior Primary School in 1891, five boys obtained the Junior University certificate and two girls the Civil Service certificate. In the Albury High School in 1890, where the object was 'to prepare pupils for all examinations (Melbourne and Sydney Universities) and for commercial pursuits', eight boys had matriculated, five for Melbourne and three for Sydney, and nine had passed the Civil Service examination.[58] University education was highly valued by leading townsmen, and considerable resentment was caused amongst them by the appointment of a teacher with a degree to one Wagga school when the other had no graduates. So far had standards of literacy increased that North Wagga primary school boys could write to newspapers when they felt that South Wagga pupils were getting an unfair share of prizes.[59]

A further feature of school life in 1891, and an indication of growing nationalism, was the military cadet training scheme. Protests might follow the arrangement by an 'irresponsible Drill Instructor' of a 'sham fight' at Junee, without first consulting headmasters, but the cadet force generally was regarded with approval. A Wagga teacher who volunteered and served in the Sudan, returning in 1885, was something of a hero.* In the field of adult education, the technical education branch of the Department of Education offered evening drawing classes at the Wagga School of Arts. A special course in 'sheep and wool' included class teaching, practical demonstration and instruction, and popular lectures on wool sorting, wool classing and other branches of the industry.[60]

Some changes had also taken place in sport, entertainment and the nature of town organizations. The most widespread organized sport in the Riverina in 1891 was cricket, and the number of teams had grown with the population. Most small towns and localities supported one team, and the larger towns had several: Banks *v.* Land and Survey, Federals *v.* Fire Brigade, and Mechanics *v.* Carltons. Football too, with from fifteen to nineteen men in each team, was played regularly during winter, Wagga town teams including Mechanics, Federals and Commercials.[61] In the larger towns on the main rivers, rowing clubs and regattas remained popular, with single sculls and fours entering Australian championships. Swimming had likewise become more organized. W. J. Gormly, swimming in the Wagga 'Natorium', claimed a world record for two hundred yards from a Kensington Baths (London) swimmer.[62] Roller-skating, a winter activity, had reached a peak in the early eighties and larger towns still had rinks, but with the world-wide bicycle boom, cycling clubs had

*Alfred Bennett. In World War I he joined the A.I.F., was awarded the D.S.O. and rose to the rank of Colonel. After the war he was a headmaster of metropolitan schools ('Wagga Wagga Public School').

outgrown them in popularity. Regular bicycle races were held and annual sports meetings attracted nearly one hundred cyclists. From time to time intrepid sixteen-year-olds, despite the state of the roads and summer dust, would ride the thirty-six miles from Albury to Corowa in four hours, returning the following day. Two older cyclists, undeterred by the nature of the country, ventured on an eighty-mile trip up the Murray into the hills east of Albury.[63] Boxing matches and 'instruction in the art of self defence' catered for the more belligerent.[64]

Although some squatters and their sons joined cricket teams, polo clubs held more attraction for the status-conscious, including wealthy townsmen. Other townsmen joined in pigeon shooting—their answer to the squatters' 'Gun Club'—using galahs when the supply of pigeons failed. Further evidence of class distinction in sport may be seen in the two carefully stratified horse-racing clubs that existed in Deniliquin.[65] The newer sections of the community provided their own amusement. The Wagga Cabmen's Picnic was followed by the Cabmen's Ball, and railway employees held an annual picnic and sports. Race meetings and sports carnivals still attracted large crowds. Liquor booths produced the same scenes as earlier, and at the inevitable dance which followed, town bands and Quadrille Assemblies continued to give the lead.[66]

Circuses, with elephants and hippopotami, Wirth's Wild West show, 'direct from America with Redskins and Mexican cowboys', variety companies and touring artists, balloon enthusiasts and Edison phonograph demonstrators, all provided entertainment, often arriving in the larger towns to coincide with the annual show. More classical tastes were catered for with *H.M.S. Pinafore*, philharmonic concerts, visiting baritones from the Paris Opera singing excerpts from Gounod and Meyerbeer, and Melbourne and Sydney actors playing Ibsen's *A Doll's House*.[67] At Hay, the annual hospital fête opened with an enormous procession, which included mounted police, marshals, the fire brigade band, the Dark Town Fire Brigade—with three donkeys pulling the engine—the Dark Town Koarsing Club, the fire engine, the Sons and Daughters of Temperance, the Foresters, dressmakers, Monkey Soap squad, carts of business firms, Chinese and Hibernian costumes, the ambulance wagons, Indians, Zulus and cavaliers; following which fifteen hundred people gathered in the park for sports and a concert.[68] Later in the year a Moonlight Serenade was held on the Park Oval. Gas was specially laid on to 'three hundred fairy lights', hop beer and cordials were sold and a gypsies' tent set up. Another procession was formed, rockets were fired, and songs, cornet and violin solos, maypole dances and highland flings entertained the fourteen hundred present.[69] Generally, compared with the roaring years of the gold rushes, entertainment had, like the towns themselves, become more respectable, reflecting the vastly increased percentages of women and children in the community.

Town organizations, as those already mentioned indicate, were much more diversified in 1891, reflecting not only the increased size of town populations but a number of changes in Australia and overseas. Besides groups already noted, Lodges maintained strong membership; horticultural, pigeon and poultry societies held festivals, and semi-political groups like the Railway Leagues and Federal Capital meetings operated intermittently. Mechanics' Institutes and Schools of Art still held dramatic and musical performances and 'Musical Melanges', and provided reading rooms.[70] Reading material included country and city newspapers (which were frequently stolen), 'reference' libraries of several hundred volumes, including such works as: *Monograph of the Horny Sponges, Catalogue of the N.S.W. Court at the Melbourne International Exhibition,* Coghlan's *Wealth and Progress of New South Wales in 1889,* and the *Water Commission's Report and Maps.*[71] In the same building, groups like the Murrumbidgee Tax Reform Association[72] would gather to debate 'The Single Tax *v.* Socialism'[73] (Henry George *v.* Karl Marx), or hear lectures on 'Irish evicted tenant farmers', 'Kissing', 'Archimedes', 'Cremation' and 'Land Monopoly'.[74]

Increasing concern with the concept of nationhood, federation and national defence found expression not only in editorials and detailed reports regarding 'The Australian squadron', 'The Defence of Australia' (report of the Conference of Military Commandants), and 'New Australian Cruisers', but in the active steps taken, as amongst the school cadets, to instil at least the rudiments of military knowledge. Volunteer forces had existed in New South Wales in the fifties, and the usefulness of Volunteer Land Orders already noted had added to their popularity. But in 1874 when the system, under this influence, had attained its maximum strength, recruiting was stopped in order to avoid further liability in regard to the issue of land orders. In 1878 the 'Volunteer Militia' or 'partial payment' principle was adopted. Recruits were required to drill for four nights a week for three months before being passed into the ranks. Only then did they receive pay and clothing. Pay for a private amounted to 10s per day while in camp, or 5s per day for attendance at detached drill on Saturday afternoons, with bonuses for efficiency. In the Riverina, Volunteer Infantry Companies, Rifle Reserve Companies and Reserve Rifle Corps met regularly for shooting matches, combined mounted parades were held, and the Junee and Eurongilly detachment of cavalry met and were exercised in lance drill. Besides short week-end camps, a large Easter encampment of the field force was approved by the government.[75]

While the economic, adminstrative and social functions of the larger towns thus underwent a number of changes during the thirty years from 1861, these were in many cases connected with changes in the pattern of urban population growth itself. This changing pattern was, in turn, related partly to changes affecting eastern Australia as a whole and partly to factors more particularly affecting individual towns.

Amongst the more general changes were the westward and northward movement of the 'selection frontier' and the 'ringbarking and fencing frontier'. The first followed available land, the second the spread of improvement techniques to an ever-increasing area. Both led to a movement of land seekers and casual labour to areas progressively 'further out'. Similarly, as the railway fan opened out, a further outward migration followed; that of the teamsters and those engaged in coaching and river traffic. All too often the programme of railway development in eastern Australia was directed by intercolonial rivalry, as the use of different gauges and differential rates indicates. The line to Hay effectively cut off Deniliquin's northern hinterland; that to Jerilderie severed it from the east. This was the New South Wales government's eventual answer to the Victorian policy of tapping the Riverina at a series of points along the Murray. Thereafter Deniliquin's link with the Victorian railway system strengthened its economic ties with Melbourne rather than Sydney, though on a more limited scale than formerly because of its reduced hinterland. Socially it made less difference. Even in the eighties it was said of the residents of Hay that they wore Melbourne clothes, read Melbourne newspapers and drank Melbourne beer; and in the four southern Riverina counties, half the population were Victorian-born. At the same time the extension of railways contributed to the growth of a number of small service centres, particularly in the wheat belt nearer Albury and Wagga. These railway towns, scattered at regular intervals along the line, formed focal points for the activities of farming communities. Often the extension of the railway was the result of sucessful closer settlement in the more favoured areas of the Riverina. It is this closer settlement which most influenced the growth of Narrandera, Corowa and Urana. The rise of these towns during the seventies is directly attributable to selection under Robertson's Acts, while the slowing of their population growth rates resulted from a decline in available land, rationalization of holdings, and depopulation of the surrounding area as selectors sold out to squatters or fellow-selectors. But Urana was never able to match the growth of Corowa and Narrandera. Indeed even in this century the largest towns in the Riverina remain those on the major permanent rivers.

Other significant changes took place in the structure of the population—particularly of the urban population which had increased at the same rate as the rural section. In Narrandera in 1891 every second man in town might be Chinese, but in the Riverina as a whole the percentage of Australian-born had steadily increased to reach 70 per cent. In the four southern counties, as noted, as a result of Victorian infiltration half the population were Victorian-born. In religious adherence, the period saw an increase in those denominations requiring greater personal commitment of their members, particularly the Nonconformist and Lutheran groups. Amongst the rural population the proportions of females to males had increased from 1:3 to 2:3, but in the towns sexual parity had been reached. As might be expected, the increased percentage of females meant increased marriages and increased numbers of children. As the population pyramids indicate (Figure 7), this was a major change in the structure of the population between 1861 and 1891 and posed problems for the future. The sudden increase of young adult population during the gold-rush years and the marriages which followed, brought its own population explosion in the seventies, with resultant increased pressure on land resources and job opportunities. By the nineties the third generation had arrived. But by this time little good land was available in the Riverina and town growth had already begun to stagnate, partly because the surrounding area had already passed the period of maximum demand for labour and services under the existing technology. Self-supporting industries in the towns were on a very small scale; most, indeed, depended on the primary industries of the surrounding area. Timber milling continued to flourish and supplied pine and red gum to a wide area, though within Riverina towns themselves the building trade had declined and railways progressively replaced coaches. Brick-kilns likewise suffered from the reduced building activity. Breweries, cordial manufactories, flour-mills and wool scours maintained their place, while new industries and services, repre-sented by railways, water, gas and freezing works, brought some changes in the composition of the labour force and increased its skilled component.

While many of these changes are fairly easily quantifiable they produced others which are less easily measured. The thoughts and moods of men, reacting to economic change or the impact of new ideas, may often only be assessed in an impressionistic way, but this in no way lessens their importance. While the farming population, with its greater proportion of women and children was apparently as respectable as its champions desired, some bush-workers and townsmen displayed the same weaknesses as their fellows a generation before. Yet there seems to have been a more serious approach to life in 1891, and for many this found expression in the 1890 strike. To judge from the reception of one doctrinaire republican, most Australians still regarded themselves as British.* At the same time, the period 1861-91 was marked by gropings toward a national image or national consciousness, as the existence of embryonic military forces indicates. Paradoxically, at the same time, for many Riverina dwellers, particularly those aware of declining opportunity and unequal rewards, there was a growing interest in that form of internationalism which called on workers of the world to unite. As always, such ferments were most clearly focused in the towns. The Mechanics' Institute of 1891, unlike its counterpart a generation earlier, was far less concerned with respectability and self-help than with political ideas and action. For many residents of the Riverina in 1891 the Smilesian soporific had been replaced by a militant Marxism.

*See p. 282.

8

THE CHANGING PASTORAL SCENE

'Eh! What, you won't? Why you *adjectival substantive*, you *adverbially adjectival substantive*, you're too *adverbially* flash to drink with such as me, I suppose.'[*]

For the banks are all broken they say,
And the merchants are all up a tree.
When the big folks are brought to the bankruptcy court
What chance for a squatter like me?
No more shall we muster the river for 'fats'
Or 'speel' o'er the fifteen mile plain;
Or rip through the scrub by the light of the moon
Or see the old stockyard again.
Leave the slip-rail down, it don't matter much now
There's naught but the crows left to see,
Perching gaunt on yon pine, as though longing to dine
On a broken down squatter like me.[†]

In 1861 Riverina flocks totalled less than one million sheep. These were the property of just over one hundred pastoral lessees. By 1891 the sheep population had risen to over thirteen million,[§] while the number of sheep owners had also grown considerably. In some cases the increased number of owners resulted from subdividing the large original leases, but more often it derived from the growth of the grazier or large-selector class and the rationalization of family selections or other small holdings. It was relatively easy for selectors to acquire enough land to graze up to five thousand sheep (see Table 24). Fewer could depasture 10,000-20,000, and flocks beyond 20,000 were all on the old established stations; so that despite the greater total number of owners,

[*]Bushworker to squatter in an outback pub; Percy Clarke, *The 'New Chum' in Australia*, p. 154.
[†]*B.P.*, 3 July 1891, reprinted from *Sydney Mail*.
[§]Precise comparison is difficult. Sheep statistics were collected on the basis of police districts, pastoral districts, electorates and sheep districts (amongst others) and some of these boundaries changed quite radically during the period. The figures here cited are on the basis of the electorates of Balranald, the Hume, the Murrumbidgee, the Murray and Albury (see note to Table 24). Fluctuations in cattle numbers were slight by comparison.

TABLE 24

Riverina Sheep Owners 1891

No. of sheep owned	District*			Cf. Deniliquin 1883
	Wagga	Hay	Deniliquin	
Less than 500	203	n.a.	n.a.	n.a.
501- 1,000	94	17	40	40
1,001- 2,000	78	45	23	23
2,001- 5,000	71	46	18	18
5,001- 10,000	22	11	2	2
10,001- 20,000	17	9	9	9
20,001- 50,000	26	17	11	11
50,001-100,000	5	8	4	4
over 100,000	1	2	–	–

* Sheep district, corresponding roughly to the electorates of the Murrumbidgee (Wagga), Balranald (Hay) and the Murray (Deniliquin). Original stock returns for Albury not available.
Source: Compiled from detailed lists of individual stock-owners in *Wagga Wagga Advertiser*, 31 January 1891; *Hay Standard*, 24 January 1891; *Pastoral Times*, 10 February 1883, 14 February 1891.

the bulk of the sheep population was still concentrated in relatively few hands. In 1883 in the Deniliquin district, 80 per cent of the sheep belonged to the large established stations which had been pastoral leases in 1861; in 1891 the percentage was slightly lower. In the Wagga district there were over four hundred owners with up to 5,000 sheep, thirty-nine with 5,001-20,000 and thirty-two with over 20,000. Further west, in the Hay and Deniliquin districts, there were nearly two hundred owners with up to 5,000 sheep, thirty-one with 5,001 to 20,00 and forty-two owners of over 20,000. The three largest owners in the Riverina in 1891 held over 100,000 each.

Apart from the numerical increase in sheep and sheep owners, a comparison of the pastoral scene of 1891 with that of 1861 reveals major differences in three important aspects; environment and techniques, capital requirements and labour relations.

The extensive freehold purchases of the squatters had committed them to rising interest payments in a period during which, overall, wool prices were declining. Strenuous efforts were therefore made to extract the maximum yield from the land. The large selectors or graziers attempting to make far smaller holdings economically viable, faced a similar task. It was suggested that the increased yield obtained by some small men was the result of flogging the ground, and that when they finally sold out to the station it took years to recover.[1] This was undoubtedly true in some cases, but the same could be said of some squatters. Other graziers survived by developing their properties more highly. To the north of Deniliquin, several holdings as small as 640 acres were fenced and subdivided into numerous paddocks with watering facilities in each.[2] On holdings of 2,000-3,000 acres, where some irrigation was practised, the number of stock that could be run was increased fourfold. One homestead lessee* with one thousand acres of irrigated land ran 1,000 sheep, 80 cattle and 450 horses. The remaining 1,500 acres of his holding was 'as bare as a camping ground'.[3] Some small men combined agriculture with grazing, hand-feeding their flocks during summer.[4]

Similar methods were adopted on the stations. The change from post and rail fencing for cattle to wire fencing for sheep, noted in the early sixties, had continued and intensified during the seventies and eighties with the erection of hundreds of miles of wire fencing† and a comparable increase in watering facilities. In 1891 Mathoura station on the Murray contained 104,000 acres, of which 81,900 were freehold and 15,000 Crown lands (6,600 leased); and ran 80,000 sheep besides horses and cattle. To achieve this it had been subdivided into paddocks of from 40 acres to 5,000 acres. 140 excavated tanks, averaging 5,000 yards or 850,000 gallons each, as well as a number of wells, watered the paddocks.[5] Coree station straddled the Billabong, to which it had a twelve-mile frontage on both sides with the Yanko Creek running for nine miles through the northern half. 150,000 acres of freehold were included in the 168,000-acre run, which had been divided into eighty paddocks with 6-wire and 7-wire fences. Besides the two hundred tanks of 1,000 to 6,000 yards, artificial lakes were created by portable engines and centrifugal pumps as required, and these irrigated large areas. Willurah station was similarly subdivided and watered and on Warbreccan station three hundred acres were under irrigation.[6]

Besides private irrigation schemes there was some government activity. A series of Royal Commissions on water conservation[7] had led to preliminary government surveys of canals stretching north and west from the Murray and from the Murrumbidgee to the Lachlan; while works like the Yanko cutting, because of

*A newcomer to the selector-squatter complex, under the Act of 1889.
†As yet little use was made of barbed wire, the American cattleman's innovation of the seventies; see W. P. Webb, *The Great Plains*, pp. 295-318. Where barbed wire was used, considerable objection was raised. Windmills of similar pattern to those in America, where they appeared at the same time, were common in the late seventies.

silting, were still being extended in 1890 to divert 1/139 of the total Murrumbidgee flow. Interstate arguments over riparian rights were in full swing during the same year.[8]

With the disappearance of much of the saltbush and softer native grasses,[9] some attempts were made to improve pastures or promote grass growth. As early as 1876, Rye grass and clover had been sown on the 18,000-acre freehold estate, Hawskview, near Albury. Near Wagga, lucerne grew admirably on the rich, low-lying flats and trefoil on the creek banks was often three feet high. North of the Murrumbidgee, one property of 4,660 acres was divided into seventeen paddocks of which one, of forty acres, was sown to couch grass 'from Hindoostan', while a visitor to Barooga station on the Murray, in mid-summer 1891, noted that 'instead of the white line of sandhills stretching away down the river . . . the rolling banks were everywhere covered with a luxuriant growth of lucerne.'[10]

The attempt to promote natural grass growth had led to the technique of ringbarking, whereby trees were killed by cutting a continuous ring of chips out round the trunk. While this avoided the labour of chopping down trees and grubbing stumps afterwards, it was most effective in improving grass growth. In 1876, a reader of the *Sydney Morning Herald* expressed concern at reports of 'seventy Chinamen . . . ringbarking on a single run near Albury',[11] and by 1881 ringbarking of trees upon pastoral leases had increased 'to an alarming extent' as 'perfect armies of Chinamen were going about ringbarking every tree at the rate of 9d. per acre.'[12] In 1883 Ranger Manton of the Forest Branch, Department of Mines, reported from County Townsend, of which 83 per cent had been alienated, that, except on the reserves, 'all the timber . . . has been ringbarked'.[13] There was ample scope for this work in the Riverina: heavily-timbered hilly country to the east, belts of box, pine and boree on the plains of the western Riverina, and the red-gum forests on the network of creeks between the Edward and the Murray; besides vast areas of box forest extending from the Billabong to the Murray between Corowa and Deniliquin, and pine scrub from the Billabong to the Murrumbidgee near Narrandera. Their existence is recorded in the names of runs, and later of surveyor-named parishes: 'Piney Ridge', 'Piney Range', 'Boree Creek', 'Mahonga Forest', 'Dry Forest' and 'Billabong Forest'. It was into such a forest that Ned Kelly rode after his daring raid on Jerilderie in 1879 when he took over the whole town, including the police station.[14]

Throughout the eighties newspapers advertised thousands of acres of 'ringing and suckering'. Much of this work was carried out by Chinese, partly because of their willingness to work long hours at lower rates and without accommodation, partly because of the dreary monotony of the task.* By the eighties, each of the larger Riverina towns had its 'Chinese Camp'.[15] Usually these were on low-lying ground near the river, where many Chinese had gardens, and consisted of wood and iron homes, shops, joss-houses and gambling and opium dens. Some of the two or three hundred Chinese males in each camp engaged in commerce, but most were casual pastoral workers. In 1883, in the condescendingly humorous style of contemporary newspapers, the *Pastoral Times* described a typical 'Chinese Exodus', at which 'local houris shed tears like rain at their temporary abandonment by the much loved yellow boys'. With an 'occasional brick-bat heaved by small boys', the Cobb & Co's coach hired by the 'Boss Celestial' hurried its 'rose-odoured occupants' to the 'artistic occupation of scrub-cutting at Coree'.[16] Both 'scrub-cutting' and 'suckering' were sequels to ringbarking and were considered the most expensive item, as for five or six years suckers had to be cut annually.[17] Some blamed the rapid spread of pine scrub north of the Murrumbidgee on ringbarking, which led to seed-dropping.[18] Others attributed this to increased stocking, as hardening of the ground led to greater run-off and seeds were carried to gullies and flats (as in long-stocked country).[19] Generally, however, where ringbarking was practised, up to double the number of stock could be carried.

There was additional incentive to improve grazing potential after the rabbit invasion of the early eighties.[20] By 1880, rabbits spreading north from Victoria had crossed the Murray into the western Riverina and by 1886 had reached southern Queensland. In the western Riverina the annual lease of those parts of the runs resumed under the 1884 Act was inadequate tenure to justify rabbit fencing or control, and these areas were the worst infested. On Benerembah station the resumed area was abandoned to the rabbits.[21] In the drier country beyond the Murrumbidgee, the combination of rabbits, drought and pine scrub, had led to the leasehold as well as the resumed areas of some runs being deserted —a favourable year for sheep was also a favourable year for rabbits.

*Of all the complaints made by white workers against Chinese labour, none ever contained the suggestion that Australians were being deprived of the opportunity of ringbarking, scrubbing or suckering.

At Balranald in 1891 thousands of rabbits on the edge of the swamp were extending into the town, while in Hay, on the green river-frontages they could be 'knocked over as one walks along'. In scores they over-ran the towns, infested the streets and vacant lots, were chased by boys and dogs, and caused havoc in the gardens. One Hay resident, finding forty or fifty on his house verandah every morning, was driven from home. At Hillston, rabbits were so thick that even the 'dogs were disgusted and refused to kill'.[22] In drought the rodents died of thirst by thousands; ten thousand a week on one station and sixty thousand in two months on another. In floods they swarmed in hundreds on stumps, fences and the branches of trees.[23] In the more closely settled districts, especially where there were fewer sandhills, they were less of a problem. It was worth noting in the Press when in 1891 a full-grown rabbit was killed on the North Wagga Common, though one sceptical Wagga writer considered that 'the number of rodents was being multiplied by the fears of the settlers.' But by 1892 at Germanton (Holbrook) the rabbits were 'coming like a wave from the westward and were crossing the upper Murray in hundreds from Victoria.'[24]

Control, such as it was, was based on the 'landholder onus' principle. Under the 1883 Rabbit Nuisance Act, bonuses of thousands of pounds were paid for destruction. A further Rabbit Bill on the same principle—'the Government no more contracted to save him [the lessee] from the rabbits, than it did to save him from the consequence of bad seasons'—followed the Royal Commission on Rabbits and became law in 1891.[25] Methods of control varied. Poisoning water with arsenic, strychnine or acetic acid; poisoning bran, chaff, jam, or sticks of sandalwood; spreading phosphorized grain; trapping or yarding—one enthusiast invented a 'yarding machine'; organized rabbit drives and the erection of netting fences were all tried.[26] The latter was the most favoured and the 1891 Act defined as rabbit-proof, a 'substantial fence hung with galvanized-iron netting of maximum mesh of 1⅝ inches, minimum width 36 inches, with wire minimum gauge of 17 . . . furnished with suitable gates'. On Willurah, such netting cost £23 per mile, and with erection, £45 per mile, adding considerably to the cost and value of fencing improvements.[27] But where rabbits were so thick that almost a million could be killed on a single station in one year, and four men could yard 9,827 in one day, pastures were devastated and stock-carrying capacity greatly reduced.[28]

Considerable changes had also taken place in the carriage of wool. Stations with a frontage to navigable rivers preferred to load wool direct on to steamers or barges,[29] by which it travelled to Echuca and thence by rail to Melbourne. From other stations it was carted by dray to the nearest railway. With the advent of Victorian railways to Echuca (1864), Wodonga (1873) and Deniliquin (1876); New South Wales railways to NorthWagga (1878), Albury and Narrandera (1881), Hay (1882) and Jerilderie (1884) and the introduction of differential rates, river traffic declined. The changing transport pattern was, as noted earlier, partly the result of intercolonial rivalry and economic competition between Adelaide, Sydney and Melbourne.[30] Inevitably, wool-growers sold to the highest bidder—in this case, the colony offering the cheapest access to the seaports. Except in 1890, when the shearing strike blocked ten thousand bales of Melbourne-bound wool at Wodonga alone,[31] there were no serious difficulties in transporting wool, the quality of which had been continually improved, as had the yield per animal.

The movement of livestock was another matter. Victorian protection, ministering to the commercial interests of Melbourne, had avoided a tariff on wool. But protection for Victorian meat-producers led to ever-increasing duties on livestock imports. In the late seventies, despite the 1s per head tax on sheep, as many as twelve thousand a week were railed to Melbourne via Moama.[32] Until 1891 it was reckoned that 75 per cent of the cattle sold in the Melbourne market came from Queensland and New South Wales,[33] but by 1892, with protection an election issue, tariffs became prohibitive—rising from 5s to £1 per head on cattle—and smuggling was rife.[34] The problems that fencing had created on travelling-stock routes were intensified by the eighties, so that despite increased government expenditure on public watering facilities,[35] it did frequently pay owners to forward stock by rail, and this led in turn to arguments over trucking conditions and shunting.[36] Nor were the drovers of 1891 any more careful over rights of grass ownership.[37] Some of these problems of moving livestock cheaply and efficiently were avoided by the introduction of meat freezing and chilling works at Narrandera.[38] By 1891 meetings had been held in other towns to encourage the building of freezing works there.[39]

Following expansion back from the water frontages it had become more difficult to wash sheep on the station before shearing. Gradually the percentage of greasy wool increased while that of washed wool declined. Town-based wool scouring establishments catered for those who still preferred to avoid paying freight on dust and grit; whose clip was burry or full of grass seeds; or whose bales had sunk when a steamer or barge leaked or was holed and sank.[40]

The only other major technical innovation in the pastoral industry by 1891 was the substitution of shearing machines for hand shearing. The most widely used machines were those developed by F. Y. Wolseley, formerly lessee of Cobran station. Shearers at first objected to the 'new-fangled implement', remembeing their two-year apprenticeship with blade shears, but with the Wolseley machine, by the end of one season, complete novices were shearing eighty or ninety sheep per day and experienced shearers were reaching 140. It was only a matter of time before machine shearing became universal.[41]

While these considerable changes had taken place in the pastoral scene, other aspects remained unchanged. Despite the development of vaccines, inoculation, dips and other treatment, disease broke out intermittently.[42] Droughts, alternating with floods, still drove men from the land and flocks and herds to the mountains. And if bush-fires appeared more frequently and caused more damage, this was as much due to closer settlement as to deliberate incendiarism[43] which at times marked a growing antipathy towards the squatter as the rural representative of the capitalist class. Damage to fencing caused by bush-fires and grassfires in 1890-2 gave employment to scores of fencing contractors and workers, and the economic opportunity the replacement of burnt fencing offered may well have accounted for a number of the 'accidental' fires so frequent in those depressed years. It was noticed in particular that rabbit-proof fencing 'burnt like string'.

But while the number of deliberate acts of arson proved against casual workers and wanderers indicate changing political and social relationships, the sheepmen themselves found a growing difficulty in maintaining anything like the profitability that wool growing had promised in the early seventies. In part their changed economic status stemmed from the increased capital requirements of the industry. There is little in contemporary writing—except for that done by pastoralists themselves—sympathetic to the position of the squatter, but in 1891 the *Border Post* reprinted from the *Sydney Mail* the following lines, which indicate that at least in some quarters there was an awareness that all was not well in the pastoral industry:

When the country was cursed by the drought at its worst,
And the cattle were dying in scores
Though down on my luck I kept up my pluck,
Thinking justice might temper the laws;
But the farce has been played, and the Government aid
Ain't extended to squatters old son.
When my dollars were spent they trebled my rent
And resumed the best half of my run
It was done without reason, for, barring the season,
No squatter could stand such a rub;
And its no use to squat while the rents are so hot
That you can't save the price of your grub;
And there's nothing to choose 'twixt the bank and the Jews
When a fellow gets put up a tree.
So, no odds what I feel, there's no court of appeal
For a broken down squatter like me.[44]

It is this changed economic position of the pastoralist which must now be considered.

When John Phillips arrived in Port Phillip in the early forties he had £40. This he handed, in his innocence, to an ex-convict overseer of flocks, to learn the trade of a squatter. Later he superintended the flocks of a Scottish barrister until his charges all died of catarrh. A remittance of £500 put him on his feet again; he purchased five hundred old ewes at £1 per head, borrowed grazing for them in thickly timbered country on the Goulburn, and at the end of one year's breeding and shearing was beginning to prosper. A year later he entered partnership with P. G. Graves who also subscribed £500. With their combined flocks they swam the Murray and travelled down the Edward, crossing it where Deniliquin now stands. A £10 licence fee was adequate to legalize their wresting of a fifty-thousand-acre portion of the public estate from the vast claims of Ben Boyd, and Warbreccan station was formed.[45] During the ensuing thirty years the speculative fringe of the pastoral industry moved beyond the Lachlan and Darling country and northwards far into Queensland. By the mid-seventies, the purchase of even back-blocks leaseholds in the Riverina required tens of thousands of pounds, with the added expense of improvements to be carried out, and freehold purchases to cope with real or imagined threats from selectors.

In 1861 John Lamb, whose Kentish family had always been in the wool trade, had arrived in Australia following the failure of his father's business. After several years of employment in

Clough's wool warehouse and in agencies, he commenced the Atlas Wool Scour on the banks of the Yarra in Melbourne in 1869. With his own increasing prosperity from fellmongering and the good seasons and high wool prices of the early seventies, he was encouraged to invest in pastoral property. In March 1874 with one of his customers, William Kiddle (a Geelong butcher) as partner, he bought Steam Plains station, situated on the saltbush backblocks between the Billabong and the Murrumbidgee, together with 25,000 sheep and the station plant, for £31,875.*

After purchasing shearing supplies—four dozen shears, 1½ dozen knives and forks, a dozen tin pints, a dozen tin plates, nails, needles, brooms, Turkey stones, linseed and castor oil, a drum of tar, three cakes of branding paste and a bale of wool-packs—they were ready to begin. Profitable sales of sheep and wool made a satisfactory first year. One lot of 208 bales— 107,374 lb. at 13d—brought over £5,000. By 1876 a further partnership, Lamb, Kiddle and Dale, was formed to purchase the adjoining 139,000-acre Willurah run from the Hon. William Campbell, Victorian parliamentarian and investor.[46]

Like Steam Plains and other backblocks, Willurah was still almost entirely leasehold, and lacked permanent natural water. The run, which comprised parts of Conargo A, B, C and E blocks, included forty acres of freehold land and one hundred acres selected under Volunteer Land Orders. Its leasehold value, as was usual, was calculated mainly as price per head of sheep, thus:

65,000 sheep	at 27s	⎫	
5,000 sheep	at 11s	⎪	
200 cattle	at £6 10s	⎬ = £92,537 0s	
59 horses	at £8	⎪	
40 acres land	at 20s	⎪	
100 acres land	at 45s	⎭	

The capital was payable as £8,000 cash, £22,845 13s 4d in seven days and the balance in four promissory notes of £15,422 16s 8d each, in 12, 24, 36 and 48 months. Interest, adjusted annually, was payable every six months, making the total commitment £103,332 19s 7d.

---

*This was payable as follows:

Half cash			£15,937	10s
⅓ Balance,	12 months		5,312	10s
⅓	,,	24 ,,	5,312	10s
⅓	,,	36 ,,	5,312	10s

(Willurah station papers.)

Within the first year extensive auction and improvement purchases had been made and these were added to during the next decade; finance for these freehold purchases all coming by way of mortgage from Campbell. In 1879 Kiddle withdrew from the partnership, and in 1882 Dale followed him, leaving John Lamb alone. By 1881 mortgages of freehold to Campbell amounted to £76,000 and by 1886, mortgages and overdue bills to £115,000. By 1891 this had been reduced to £107,000. The growing freehold area reduced the Crown rent on the remaining leasehold area, but this was a drop in the bucket compared with the mortgage interest payments.

The underlying cause of Lamb having to 'buy the station twice', as well as the means, was John Robertson's Act. Little use was made of conditional purchase. A few selections were taken up by adult male members of the Lamb and Dale families, and several by men like Hugh McIntyre, who had been 'bought with the station'. Other employees were also used. A journal entry for 15 October 1878 states: 'Alexander Tolmie, Bonus for throwing up his selection upon Willurah, as arranged by Wm. Kiddle.— £12.10s.0d.' and a similar prize is awarded to another employee the following day. More use was made of improvement purchases, since real improvements, particularly wells, whims, dams and tanks were needed to utilize the run fully. But typical of western Riverina runs, the bulk of the purchases were uncontested auction sales. Once, in 1881, after a large block of 320-acre lots had been surveyed, alternate lots only were bought, in the hope that these would protect the remainder. The plan misfired and the very real threat from selectors was realized as the following letter to John Lamb, who was in Melbourne at the time, from H. E. Best, manager of the Hay branch of the Bank of New South Wales, indicates:

Dear Sir,　　　　　　　　　　　　　　　　　　　19 Oct. 1881

Alexander Ross[47] of Argoon, Jerilderie, who is a large selector on Kerarbury, attended at the Crown Lands sale this morning and ran Mr. McCaughey's agent for every lot on Goolgumbla Run, which was put up, except three small ones, making him pay 28/- to 30/6 per acre. He would not be remonstrated with but persevered up to what he said he considered the value of each lot. Finding himself baulked in this attempt he went into the office subsequently and took up, as selections after Auction, every one of the lots which were passed in at that sale on 14th Sept. last; paying cash down.

The letter followed a telegram, to which Lamb had replied promptly. Next morning Best attended the Land Office and took up the remaining 2,731¼ acres available on Willurah, paying £3,198 on behalf of Lamb. Two days later he wrote:

> Ross was hanging about the Land Office yesterday and appeared to be well informed as to what land in the District was open for selection after Auction . . . He particularly wanted to get a look at the plan showing the Powheep Lots *but it couldn't be found!!!* . . . I am inclined to think from what I have heard, that, though Ross is a man of some little property, he has merely gone into this affair on Willurah, in order to levy 'black mail' upon you. Lavender appears to have had a conversation with him in which he said 'Mr. Lamb had better square it by letting me have the land he bought on 14th Sept. I'll give him what he paid for it'. This may be only 'bluff' and probably, if you . . . give him to understand that you will make him fence, he will cave in.[48]

Four days later a fellow-pastoralist, the lessee of Burrabogie, wrote:

> My Dear Lamb,
>   I heard from Hay that you had been victimised for some 4 to 5,000 acres. We are not safe now when cash is so plentiful. This Mr. Ross says he has another £16,000 ready to pay for 8,000 acres in a compact block . . .

Early in May 1882, Lamb began fencing and presently billed Ross for:

> 1,600 posts, battens, 7¼ tons of No. 8 wire at 22s. and labour: total £261.0.0.

On 22 May, Ross did cave in, selling to Lamb his eighteen lots, totalling 4,719 acres, for £7,078 10s, a profit of 10s per acre. With this kind of competition it was not surprising that squatters well beyond Wagga, Albury and Deniliquin resorted to increasing land purchases, nor that from 1875 on, returns from auction and improvement purchases were 'the principal item in Treasury receipts'.[49]

When in 1884, following the Morris and Ranken report and the subsequent Act, pastoralists were invited to surrender half the leasehold area of their runs, the only leased land left on Willurah, apart from a few selection pre-leases, was on the reserves running through the run. This amounted to less than 40,000 acres. The bulk of the run, nearly 100,000 acres, had been converted to free-hold. Similar transactions had taken place on most runs in the Hay and Deniliquin districts.[50] Closer to Albury and Wagga, where reserves had been revoked and pre-leases rarely sought or obtained, leasehold areas had often disappeared altogether. The Hawksview Estate, formerly Thurgona run near Albury, had, as early as 1876, been converted to 10,712 acres of freehold and 6,888 acres of conditional purchase, still retaining eighteen miles of frontage to the Murray.[51]

The prosperity of the seventies, which had made it easy to borrow large sums for loans and mortgages to finance pastoral land purchases, had also made the pastoral industry singularly attractive to investors. As a result of the succession of very favourable seasons: 'Nearly all moderately stocked country looked remarkably well and squatters were surprised to find that selectors would take up country that they (the lessees) considered quite safe [from selection]. Then a panic set in amongst the squatters'.[52] The case of Alexander Ross, seeking a compact block for grazing, was in fact not an isolated one. The activities of the border-hoppers and family selectors has already been noted. Others who had accumulated capital travelled further.

In 1854 John Gibson, aged twenty-seven, a native of Ayr-shire,[53] had arrived in Victoria with his savings of £50, following the advice of his brother David who had migrated before him.* Temporarily he decided against his trade of bootmaking and broke stones at Geelong for 8s a yard, saving £20 in two months. Six months later he began his own bootmaking business. In 1856, with £100 in the bank, he moved to Colac, eventually employing two men and an apprentice. By the sixties he owned a four-roomed weatherboard house and a seven-roomed brick house. In 1874, seeking 'better opportunities for [his] boys, and the improve-ment of [his] health', he planned to migrate north to New South Wales, 'encouraged a good deal by an answer given by Mr. Howetson, Mr. John Calvert's nephew, to [his] question whether a man's success in sheep farming in Riverina depended on a knowledge of sheep or in good seasons. His answer was, "In good

---

*Letter dated 'Ballaratt, 2th August, 1852', lists wages for different trades and continues: 'A shoomaker can make frome £1 to £1.10 per day. English made watter Tights sell at £2.5. Blutchers at £2. All others in Proportion. This is the Best Tread in the Collony. Tell my brother John and Matthew Gilmour and the old Bossen and William Gilmour not to lose a day in coming hear. As for you sell all your materials and come hear. In a few years, whither diging gold or not a man will make [a] fortune.'

seasons decidedly".' 'With a wagonette', he wrote, 'William McKinnon, Mr. Ackland and I, took a tour of inspection into N.S.W.' They travelled via Echuca to the Deniliquin land office. Not meeting a very cordial reception they pushed on through Jerilderie and Bundure station—where McKinnon selected the next year—to Narrandera and Wagga, returning via Albury; nine hundred miles in eight weeks.

'I had about £500 worth of boots to dispose of', he wrote, as well as a shop (£400), house (£450), furniture (£70) and three lots of land, 'and it took about a year before we were able to get ready.' Travelling by coach to Melbourne and by train to Albury, he bought a horse for £7—'having my saddle with me'—and rode via Walbundrie and Urana to William McKinnon's on the Yanko Creek; thence to Hay, from where he telegraphed to his two eldest children 'to start at once so as to reach Hay before Thursday week in order to select land on Kerarbury that was to be sold by auction.' But because Cobb's coaches were already overcrowded, the youngsters were stranded at Deniliquin, only reaching Hay after the sale. Gibson now rode fifty miles north with the son of the licensee of the Gunbar hotel, then west towards Booligal. Here, on the sparsely settled Lachlan backblocks, nine miles from Gunbar near a sandhill dotted with pine he decided to settle. The following Thursday he selected 640 acres with 1,920 acres Conditional Lease for himself, and similar lots for Robert and Marion, making '2,560 acres each, 7,560 acres in all' [*sic*]. He then rode back to Colac to collect the rest of the family and two buggies, and a week later travelled by train to Echuca and by steamer to Hay. On Narringa, as they called the new property, the Gibsons erected a 'canvas house of three rooms on a wooden frame and a fly above it, also an iron kitchen with a clay floor. Fenced in a horse paddock of about 80 acres, and sank a well, getting water about 15 feet.'

In April of the following year, 1876, Gibson bought six hundred wethers which were travelling for sale from the Monaro country. He had shorn these and got £500-worth of wool before 'the season turned dry'. Because he had as yet no tanks, the shallow well, which ran ever more slowly, had to be emptied every few hours day and night with the windlass and two buckets.[54] Before the next shearing they had 'lost a good many of these sheep on account of drought' and fluke. It was eighteen months before the land was surveyed, and during this time the sheep were shepherded seven nights a week. After survey the family complied with the residence and improvement clauses of the Act; fencing, building huts, and providing watering facilities, though Gibson himself had a low opinion of the policing of the Act, thus:

> The residence conditions were in reality a sham. The inspectors themselves were not a bad lot and in their dealings with us showed only fairness, and we generally managed to hear of their coming to inspect the residence conditions beforehand and tidy the tents up and make a fire and clean the few cooking utensils and managed to get the Inspectors to put the highest value on all improvements.

But even under these conditions the selector's life could be made difficult: 'Our aim in coming on the land was to make a permanent home, but no sooner were we on the land than we were made to feel as if we were illegally there.' Forty-five years later, however, they were still there, and so were scores of other such persistent men in the western Riverina.* Nearer to Wagga and Albury their numbers rose to hundreds, and Victorians were reinforced by New South Wales families and Germans from South Australia.

Recently N. G. Butlin has criticized the over-dramatization of the selector-squatter conflict, largely by writers who have made unqualified use of the Morris and Ranken report. He continues: 'The failure of selection policy seems less interesting than the modesty of the outlays by pastoralists during the 'sixties on land purchase.'[55] But this very modesty of outlay in the sixties was largely the result of a *lack* of selector-squatter competition. As the preceding chapters indicate, runs in the unsettled districts were not open to selection until the expiry of the leases in 1866, which opening coincided with one of the worst droughts of the century. By this time six million acres of reserves protected many of the squatters' improvements. Even in the Riverina, where improvements were much more scattered and more highly developed,[56] this was adequate protection. Butlin states further:

> The selection legislation represented two risks to pastoralists: either desirable sections of leasehold area might be selected by small farmers; or those sections of the runs on which improvements had been erected might be occupied by selectors. This legislation did in fact directly stimulate a brief burst of investment to enclose small specific pieces of land on pastoral stations.[57]

*Later the Gibsons moved to the present family property Keringal on the south bank of the Murrumbidgee a few miles east of Hay.

Such statements have little application in the Riverina, nor, one suspects, in much of inland New South Wales. For western Riverina lessees the real danger came not from 'small farmers' and 'small farming'—Butlin uses the expressions three times in nine lines—but from would-be graziers. It was precisely this competition between the pastoral lessees and men of smaller capital—not a desire to protect scattered improvements—that lay behind the extensive purchases of the seventies and eighties.

Nor is there any basis for the assertion that 'pastoralists had a strong incentive to buy key areas, since freehold title implied complete legal title to improvements, not merely rights of compensation.'[58] Some improvements were on the reserves or 'camping grounds' chosen by squatters; improved lands were not liable to selection*[59] but could be bought by lessees as improvement purchases; and after 1875, 'notice of intention to improve' gave rights of purchase to lessees. Far from land being purchased to protect improvements, the reverse was true; improvements, real and dummy, were carried out to facilitate land purchase. It was not improvements that the squatter was protecting, but land, and it was this that led to his rising indebtedness.

In cases like Willurah, where individuals acted as mortgagees, the survival of records is a matter of chance and in any event these are less typical cases. But the Conditional Purchase Registers, covering a wide range of pastoral properties, indicate that during the seventies there was a growing reliance on mortgage finance for land purchases. There is however no suggestion of foreclosures in the eighties or at least up to 1891. These, like the widespread use of resident station managers by banks and finance companies were a feature of the nineties. Butlin has shown that in 1870-1 on a number of Riverina stations financed by the Australian Mortgage Land and Finance Company, interest payments were less than half the gross wool proceeds of these boom years, but that by 1889-91, 'despite very much higher total debts, wool proceeds had not nearly kept pace', and that by the end of the eighties or beginning of the nineties, 'many of the pastoral clients of finance companies were in critical financial straits.'[60] With poor seasons, low prices and generally depressed conditions later in the nineties, increasing numbers of squatters 'went under'

*One of the reasons for disallowing certain selections, as the Conditional Purchase Registers indicate, was that they were 'improved sufficiently to bar selection'. This exemption, which had stood since 1861, was repealed by the Act of 1889, after which the selector was required to pay the runholder or owner the capital value of the improvements.

to the banks and finance firms. Just as these financial problems were reaching a head, labour relations in the pastoral industry erupted in the 1890 shearing strike, when union leaders called out shearers in the middle of the shearing season.

During the eighties overseas visitors had noticed what they considered the effects of rising living standards amongst Australian workers:

> The working class are too well off for the occasional high-handed proceedings of the rich to affect them sensibly. For an agitation to be maintained there must be a real grievance at the bottom of it; and the only grievance that the Australian democrat can bring forward is, that having obtained the necessaries, he cannot without extra labour obtain also the luxuries of life.[61]

Others had noted an increasingly aggressive egalitarianism. Behind all these lay the old resentments provoked by the provisions and implications of the Masters and Servants Act and kindred legislation. But the sullen muttering was now replaced by militant unionism.

Relationships between Riverina squatters and selectors have already been discussed at some length, and although the reports of the select committees and Morris and Ranken highlighted the antagonisms, from 1884 to 1891 some reconciliation had taken place. Some squatters, even in 1891, were still obtaining land by selecting in their own names or by using dummies and Volunteer Land Orders.[62] But selectors had acquired land, and through selectors' associations were able to obtain concessions, had representatives in Parliament, and as the *Pastoral Times* noted, thereafter tended to turn conservative.[*63] The selector movement, considered radical in the seventies, now remained so only in its demands for protection, always a radical cry in a free-trade colony like New South Wales. One incident related to this *rapprochement* is worth recording. In 1890 T. M. Keogh, a lessee in the Lachlan district, died. Nineteen selectors signed a letter to his widow expressing regret, pointing out that during the last two droughts he had allowed them grass and water in a 'good-neighbourly' manner and that he 'always acted fairly and straight-forwardly with us and we could always depend on his word in business matters.'[64]

---

*The Broken Hill miners, in the strike of 1894, were sent to Deniliquin for trial, since this once notoriously pro-selector area was by then so conservative as to give short shrift to striking miners.

Between the permanent station hands and the squatter there was little cause for friction and even where managers replaced owners, relations seemed reasonable, though this may relate more to the fact that the Masters and Servants Act was still in force in 1891 than to any real difference. The increased number of unemployed and wandering men, however, coinciding with declining profits from squatting had reduced liberality to sundowners and swagmen. On stations as far apart as Echuca, Wagga and Hay, the 'sixpenny system' operated; on others, tools for digging the garden were supplied; on others again the 'Chinese treadwheel system' was used to irrigate gardens so cultivated. These were not aberrations of the self-help system but reflections of the changing socio-economic pattern. Men who regarded the customary donations of 'a panniken of flour, and meat expressly salted for [them]' as a right and not a privilege were also likely to believe, 'as an article of religion', that 'owners of land must be annoyed as much as possible', so that despite the efforts on some stations to make wayfaring men more comfortable, the men's huts were devastated, glass broken, sashes, bunks and flooring boards burnt and 'filthy doggerel written in conspicuous places'.[65]

In the late seventies, despite the sound and fury of selector-squatter struggles all around, the cut-out of shearing on Riverina stations was usually marked with general festivity. On Cobran station, west of Deniliquin, in 1876, 150 men and several neighbouring 'gentlemen and squatters' were entertained by the 'Cobran Brass Band'; two farces, *The Irish Tutor* and *Box and Cox*; and original songs—'The Boys of the Cobran Road' and 'Song of the Cobran Shearers'—sung in roaring style. The evening concluded with cheers for the performers, the manager of the shed, the proprietors of the station and the few ladies present.[66] After the 1890 strike such performances were rare. The traditional shearing races and festivities on Table Top station near Albury were only held in 1891 because the shed had used non-union shearers—'scabs' to the unionists.[67]

Between townsmen and squatters relations had also changed. The larger towns particularly were less dependent on the surrounding squatters. There had always been a tendency for station owners to deal direct with the capital cities and with increased absentee-ownership this had grown. 'Mr. Livingstone Learmonth of Groongal' could still give his £1,000 donation to the Hay hospital—'per Mr. Geo. Mair' his manager[68]—but even in this still basically pastoral district, a town of 2,700 had developed a life of its own. All over the Riverina, squatters were still Justices of the Peace and still held high positions in some town organizations, but eminent townsmen increasingly shared these honours. Smaller towns were more in need of assistance in 1891, and a town like The Rock, on the Albury-Wagga railway line, was grateful when squatter John King laid a turf wicket for the local cricket club (in which his sons played).[69] But the commercial interests of all towns, large and small, were well aware that they owed more of their prosperity to the increased selector population, whether grain-growers in the east or graziers in the west. At shearing time each year a minor boom occurred as large numbers of shearers and shed-hands congregated in towns like Wagga and Junee before moving off on the railway to stations further out. Amongst those who profited from this annual migration there was little sympathy with the leaders who called out the shearers in 1890, and general relief was felt amongst townsmen when shearing resumed.[70] In a more positive attempt to avoid trouble, townsmen of Narrandera, led by the mayor, sought to form a land-owning co-operative for working men.[71]

Although there is still scope for a detailed analytical study of the Australian Shearers' Union (A.S.U.) and its part in the industrial disputes of the nineties, the growth of unionism in the seventies and eighties has been outlined[72] and the major events in the 1890 strike have been described.[73] Contemporary pro-unionist accounts are also available.[74] Returns in the way of factual material to be derived from a study of Riverina newspapers are marginal, but have some importance for interpretation.

To the unionist spokesmen this was a struggle of Labour against Capital. As the ship-owners to the seamen and the mine-owners to the miners, so were the sheep-owners to the shearers. But although extreme speakers and journals on either side, as well as some later writers, paint a picture in unrelieved black and white, in an area like the Riverina there were a good many shades of grey. Union shearers, summoned at Hay under the Masters and Servants Act for breach of contract, were relieved at the ruling that levy by distress for payment of fines could only be inflicted on 'goods and chattels', not on their freeholds and selections.*[75]

The outback upheaval and metropolitan disturbances, indeed, produced only faint ripples in the Riverina. In Queensland and west and north-west New South Wales, where camps of over one

---

*Cf. the suggestion that the shearers were an aristocracy of labour who had attained their position to the detriment of the less skilled.

thousand union shearers were formed during the strike, effigies were burnt, armed men rode about, and violent incidents and threats abounded.[76] In Sydney, the 'Battle of Circular Quay' resulted when free labourers sought to load non-union wool for overseas shipping.[77] Although these occurrences and any number of alarming rumours were all reported in Riverina papers within forty-eight hours of their happening,[78] actual events in the Riverina were mild by comparison. At Tocumwal twenty union shearers who formed a camp spent most of their time trying to persuade non-union shearers crossing from Victoria to join them.[79] At a meeting of the Deniliquin branch of the A.S.U. it was decided not to form a camp there at all, only four members voting in favour of the motion.[80] Occasionally cases of assault and 'maliciously wounding' occurred as a result of taunts in hotel bars,[81] and at Junee railway station what could have developed into a brawl was quelled when thirty union and sixty non-union shearers were shepherded into the front and back carriages of the train by railway officials and police. As they were about to move off one shouted: 'Well, we'll have a good time at Narrandera anyhow. We stop there four hours remember, and if there is not murder I'm a Dutchman.' But action by authorities at Narrandera prevented violence.[82]

The mildness of events in the Riverina was largely the result of closer settlement. Just as many graziers and homestead lessees neglected to join the Pastoralists' Union (P.U.),*[83] so many selector-shearers and others failed to join the A.S.U.[84] R. A. Gollan cites the assertion of the *Shearers' Record* that 'only a small minority of shearers' remained outside the union,[85] but this is surely a matter of definition. Half the stations in the Riverina were committed to shear under the P.U. agreement[86] and all of them sent away wool in 1890 and 1891. The very threats of the A.S.U. to exclude members shearing under this agreement, and their attempts to block non-union wool, show how far they had over-estimated their strength and bargaining power. The *Wagga Wagga Advertiser*, generally fair to shearers, reported in August 1891 that the Kerarbury board was full and that plenty of non-

---

*Cf. 'A Jerilderie sheep-farmer': 'I have no intention of joining an association comprised of men who have always been antagonistic to my class, doing all that lay in their power to crush us out of existence and who now seek our aid to crush men of our class—workers like ourselves. Not Me. Though owner of a few thousand sheep now. I had to shear for a living at one time, and I know all about the gentle squatter.' ('W. W. Head Reports', *W.A.*, 23 July 1891.)

union shearers were offering: 'They all express disapproval of Unionism [it stated] and say the "call-out" last year was utterly unjustifiable as were also the late lawless proceedings in Queensland and on the Darling.'[87] At a P.U. meeting in Wagga, at which thirty-eight stations in the Murrumbidgee electorate were represented, W. Wilson said: 'It was stated by the Shearers' Union that they had more sheds this year than they had ever had before. Now he would state, that unless there was a thundering lot of traitors amongst the pastoralists, this was an infernal lie. (Hear Hear).'[88]

Technological advances had further weakened the position of the Shearers' Union. The shearing machine made it possible for novices to learn to shear in a few days,* and the development of telegraphs, railways, and coastal and inland shipping, which contributed so largely to the spread of federated unionism, also made it possible for 'scab' labour, troops and police to be sent rapidly to trouble spots.† With these technological advantages cancelling out, the greater capital resources of the pastoralists and growing unemployment which made for ample alternative labour[89] defeated the A.S.U. In the words of W. W. Head:

> By the help of a large heap of wealth filched from the workers in the past, with the aid of a Government willing to be used by those who were fighting the labourers, with the co-operation of the lying capitalist-ridden press and the assistance of black legs, the employers were enabled to win.[90]

It is difficult to escape the conclusion that the call-out of shearers in the middle of the 1890 shearing season was at least in part attributable to a desire by union leaders for a trial of strength. The growth of unionism, it has been suggested by Gollan, was due to the working class 'becoming conscious of itself as a class'.[91] It was not that the workers needed to be told their position on the social and economic scale. In Riverina society the reminders were continual, with the Masters and Servants Act to jog the memories of the forgetful.§ In 1890 the 'Brookong Rioters' had been in gaol

*See *P.T.*, 14 February 1891, where the Wolseley machine is recognized as a way to fight strikes.

†E.g., the shipping of Melbourne labour to Queensland; *W.A.*, 5 February 1891.

§The A.S.U. Shearing Agreement specifically sought to supersede the Masters and Servants Act (*P.T.*, 11 October 1890). For an example of the frequent references to the pastoralists' ability to dig up a 'reliable Geo. IV Act of some kind', see *W.A.*, 18 July 1891.

for two years and were still there.[92] What the workers needed was to be incited to action—to see life in terms of the class struggle. Hence the earnest searching for real or alleged abuses[93] and the decision to expel all members so un-class-conscious as to shear non-union.[94] Hence too the demands of the A.S.U. conference after the failure of the strike, 'that capable representatives be appointed to travel to distant centres during the off season for the purpose of holding public meetings with a view to neutralising the efforts now being made by the Pastoralists' Union to injure the A.S.U.'*

There was need for this doctrinaire stand. Anti-squatter outbursts in the late eighties and early nineties were as good an example of Galbraith's 'conventional wisdom' and 'social nostalgia'[95] as one is likely to find in Australian history.† Except for 'Millionare Tyson',[96] whose rise was as Smilesian as could be desired, and a handful of others, represented in the Riverina by the Learmonths, McCaugheys and Wilsons, squatting, as indicated, was considerably less profitable than in previous decades.§ By the nineties Smilesian sentiments were outmoded, but the image of the successful wealthy squatter—the bloated capitalist—intensified as the reality faded. With the failure of the 1890 strike and the conviction of shearers and their leaders,[97] alternative tactics were sought. In the A.S.U. conference that followed, a number of points were resolved, including the adoption of a political platform. Freedom of contract—the right of a shearer to leave 'at his mere pleasure'[98]—was demanded; Chinese and Kanaka labour denounced, though Aborigines were to be allowed to join the union; the decision reached that if the P.U. opposed the A.S.U., shearers were to stay at home in 1891; and a conference sought with the P.U.[99]

Notwithstanding the pastoralists' assertion that they did not 'wish to cover their boards with Kanakas and Chinamen, but that they merely [wished] to assert their right to engage whom they please', there were stations, where, in the interests of economy,

*W.A., 29 January 1891. Hence references to the men as 'tools of professional agitators who live upon their hard earnings' (*H.S.*, 18 February 1891) and to the call-out as the work of ignorant leaders, likened to Jack Cade; *P.T.*, 20 September, 8 November 1890.

†Except, of course, for the attempts to reproduce the English yeoman class.

§Cf. The evidence of W. G. Spence before the Royal Commission on Strikes, cited in *W.A.*, 20 January 1891; 'despite the rabbit pest, drought and increased rent, the pastoralist is better off today than he was five years ago.'

Aborigines did the mustering and as many as seventy Chinese were engaged for shearing.[1] And although pastoralists 'had to thank Mr. Spence for bringing them together', they were prepared to 'resist the tyranny of the Shearers' Union'.[2]

> Are the pastoralists of New South Wales and Victoria [asked J. Dill of Toogimbie] . . . to be dictated to by a few agitators who are living on the fat of the land, and kept in their position by men who cannot see where they are being led . . . it is not a question of fighting the unionists or unions at all, it is simply a question of freedom. Are we, the employers of labour in this colony, about to make a struggle for freedom, or are we about to have a reign of terror. Are a few men to be allowed to excite and befool others of their fellows, so that freemen are afraid to accept work. Are sheds to be burned down, freemen dragged out of their beds and maltreated, women insulted, wool burnt on the waggons, the grass and fences burnt, and working bullocks shot because their owners were freemen? . . . There is only one answer, we must all combine and join the Pastoralists' Union.[3]

The union shearers, for their part, licked their wounds, stated that the strike had been the 'grandest educator ever the workers had' and decided to counter the alleged aims of the pastoralists to 'crush the unions' by resorting to the ballot box, where they hoped to 'overthrow for ever the whole system of capitalism, and, abolishing the wage system altogether, institute a state of society where those who at present live on the earnings of labour will have to either do their share of the world's work or starve.'[4] At the desired conference of the P.U. and A.S.U. in August 1891 the words 'faithfully serve' were deleted from agreements and it was decided that 'employers shall be free to employ and shearers shall be free to accept employment whether belonging to the Shearers' or other Union or not without favour, molestation or intimidation on either side.'[5] Yet only one month later, on McPherson's Paika station near Balranald, three shearers were summonsed for leaving their hired service. They had complained that the sheep were 'daggy', but 'daggy' sheep were not mentioned in the agreement. A telegram from union headquarters at Creswick warned them that it was 'unwise to strike now', pointing out that if they left employment they were liable to imprisonment or forfeiture of earnings. In the Balranald court a squatter J.P. found them guilty under the Masters and Servants Act and fined them £5 each.[6]

In 1861-91 then, considerable increase had occurred in the

capital requirements of the pastoral industry, due both to the struggle for ownership of the land and the ensuing need, for both small man and big, to increase yields. As a result, Riverina sheep numbers had increased from less than one million to over thirteen million. Thousands of acres had been purchased at £1 per acre, a price which, for much of the area, was far beyond its real worth even decades later. To finance these purchases, pastoralists were increasingly committed to mortgage with finance firms and banks. Investment in fencing, water conservation, small-scale irrigation and pasture improvement, ringbarking and rabbit control further added to the burden, while wool prices failed to regain their buoyancy of the early seventies. For the pastoralist, economic opportunities were declining. At the same time, and in part related to declining profits, labour relations had steadily deteriorated.

While some reconciliation had occurred between selectors and squatters as the more successful amongst the former attained independence on the land, many of the disgruntled remainder, together with unionist shearers and labourers, welcomed the proposed trial of strength with the squatters. But the 1890 strike failed; partly because the very technological improvements in transport and communication which had made it possible to unite scattered rural workers into a union also provided pastoralists and governments with a weapon for strike-breaking. In part too the strike had less effect in the Riverina because the gap between Master and Servant had to some extent been filled. In the social and economic strata in the Riverina there were too many overlaps for the extreme version of the class struggle to be valid. In the seventies the graziers of the west and the farmers of the east may have looked radical to the squatters, but the rise of each successive wave on the left automatically moved former 'radicals' further to the right. The possession of private property had emasculated the Marxian dialectic; both horizontally and vertically the picture had been filled in.

The levelling effect of the pastoral or mining frontier, if it ever existed, had gone. So too, despite the sighs of social nostalgia from unobservant English visitors,[7] had much economic opportunity and social mobility. For Utopians it was better to leave Australia and seek a brave new world elsewhere. Those who remained sought redress in politics.

MASTERS AND SERVANTS NO MORE?

In the Riverina elections of 1860, despite the agitation for 'free selection', the squatters had emerged triumphant. During the following decade there was no serious challenge to their political domination of the Riverina. In the seventies, however, extensive land alienation was followed by an overall increase in both the rural and urban voting population, while the formation of free selectors' associations led to the election of selectors' representatives in the Assembly. But free-trade continued an 'essential element of the colony's dominant "liberal" orthodoxy.'[1] In the sixties Martin's tariff proposals had been defeated. Rising land sales in the seventies enabled the Parkes government to remove a number of the few existing tariff duties imposed earlier to meet budget difficulties and to withstand all protectionist pleas. Demands for protection increased in the late seventies and early eighties and were incorporated in the platforms of several workingmen's, industrial, and selector organizations. By 1881 there was a recognized 'Hay and Corn' party in Parliament.[2]

Drought in the eighties and the temporary inability of farmers to secure differential rates to enable them to compete in the Sydney market with wheat-growers from other colonies, who enjoyed cheaper sea transport, drove more farmers into the protectionist camp. In 1885 a 'Political Conference' was arranged in Sydney by the 'Land and Industrial Alliance', when some selectors' associations and farmers' unions united their requests for agricultural protection with the more extreme demands of manufacturers', miners' and industrial unions. Depressed economic conditions in 1886 saw a further 'grand wedding . . . of capital and labour' in Sydney in the 'Protection Union of New South Wales' which combined protectionist M.L.A.s, manufacturers, and representatives of farmers' and trade unions. In the meantime, in opposition, free-traders worked through the 'Freetrade Association'. By mid-1889 the faction system which had dominated the New South Wales Assembly had given way to 'two well organized and consolidated party machines'.[3]

Industrial Hall, Narrandera showgrounds: 'On a population basis, the most highly industrialized town in the Riverina in 1891 . . . boasting six saw-mills.'

Lutheran bush church of rough dressed pine, west of Henty

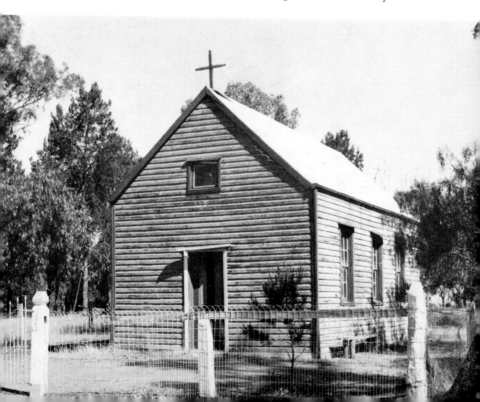

Ringbarking

But while in Sydney, at least until 1889, there may have been clear demarcation between free-traders and protectionists, attempts to shape the contest in all constituencies along these lines 'encountered everywhere a variable complex of local power-groups and issues with which they had to come to terms.'[4] By 1891 the question of federation of the Australian colonies had added a further twist to these complexities. Because Victoria was protectionist and New South Wales free-trade, the need for some sort of compromise was obvious if intercolonial federation was to become a reality. It was found in the formulation of a new catch-cry: 'intercolonial freetrade and protection against the rest of the outside world'. Unsatisfactory though this may still have been to residents of a border district hundreds of miles from their markets, it was the best offering and was adopted by most Riverina candidates. In addition to the free-trade-protection struggle and the varying loyalties of squatter, selector and urban groups, the failure of the 1890 strike led to swift organization of Labor Electoral Leagues. Evidence of any earlier existence of these in the Riverina awaits further research. In fact they seem to spring up between the 1890 strike and the 1891 elections and to depend largely on the presence of professional radical agitators like Arthur Rae who travelled widely in the Riverina seeking labour support in 1890-1. He gained little in the areas surrounding Deniliquin and Albury, but the Shearers' Union in Wagga and the Carriers' Union in Hay both formed excellent nuclei for political Labor activities and both nominated Labor candidates in 1891.

Under the New South Wales Electoral Act of 1880, the number of electorates and members had been increased and provision made for further expansion.[5] By 1891 there were five electorates in the Riverina, Albury municipality (pop. 5,447), with slight additions, having become a small separate single-member electorate.* The four major 1860 electorates remained with minor boundary changes but increased representation (see Figure 11). The Hume electorate, returning two members, was unchanged apart from the loss of Albury and contained the town of Corowa (1,171) and some half-dozen rural service centres. The Murray electorate, also returning two members, was unaltered with Deniliquin (2,273) still the main town. In the Balranald electorate which returned two members and from which the western portion

---

*Two years later, following the Parliamentary Electorates and Elections Act of 1893, 125 single-member electorates were formed. These included separate electorates for Wagga, Hay and Deniliquin.

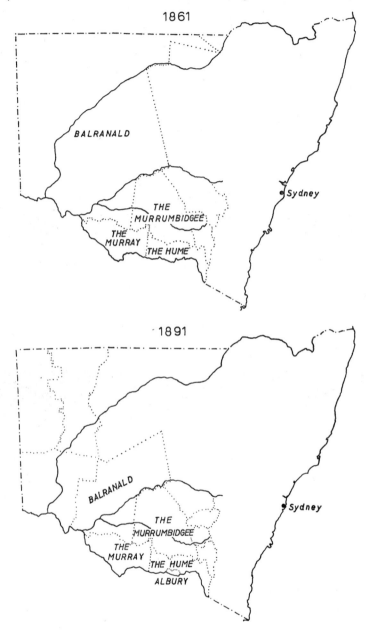

11   Riverina electorates 1861 and 1891
Source: T. A. Coghlan, *Wealth and Progress of New South Wales, 1892*

or Darling districts had been removed, Hay (2,741) was still the only town of any size. The Murrumbidgee electorate, returning three members, had lost the small Gundagai electoral district. Wagga (4,596) remained the largest town, while others included Narrandera (1,815), Junee (1,682) and a scatter of lesser farming centres.[6] While the total population of the area had increased from less than ten thousand to over sixty thousand[7] the number of members had grown from four to ten. In contrast with the four squatter members of 1860, those returned in 1891 comprised a merchant, a solicitor, a flour-miller, four selectors' representatives, one ex-pastoralist turned stock and station agent, and two Labor Electoral League (L.E.L.) candidates, one from the Wagga Shearers' Union and the other from the Carriers' Union at Hay. The unsuccessful nominees were equally heterogeneous.

Opinions varied as to the issues behind the dissolution of June 1891, but generally they were agreed to be the future fiscal policy of New South Wales, federation, the Labor vote, and attitude to the Parkes government.[8] This too was the first election under the 'payment of members system', which principle it was stated might be relied on to produce 'a swarm of politicians ready to sacrifice themselves on the altar of their country for the modest stipend of £300 per annum.'[9] To indicate their leanings, candidates were designated 'free-trade', 'protectionist' and 'federationist'. Allegiance or antipathy to Parkes prompted the labels 'ministerialist' or 'opposition', while other affiliations were covered by the terms 'Labor candidate' or 'farmers' representative'.*[10] A real difficulty of definition lay in the fact that at intercolonial conferences the ideal was stated to be 'Australian Federation, and Protection against the rest of the outside world.' Protection for New South Wales could thus he construed as anti-federationist.

The free-traders had published a platform; the protectionists had not, but in a 'bid for the labour vote', had accepted that of the L.E.L.; while the Amalgamated Farmers' Union of New South Wales had adopted a manifesto of its own concocting. On a number of points free-traders and the L.E.L. were agreed.[11] Both sought electoral reform to provide for the abolition of plural voting—'One Man One Vote' was the rallying cry—and stressed the need for a system of registration of voters to allow seamen,

---

*Of over 400 nominees for the whole of New South Wales, 200 were free-traders, 170-80 protectionists and 40-50 Labor candidates. Amongst the latter 'a proportion' were said to be free-traders and 'two or three protectionists', the rest running on a 'purely Labor line'.

shearers and other peripatetic workers to vote in any electorate; and the need for single-member electorates. In addition the L.E.L. sought to provide for the abolition of money deposits in elections and the six months' residence qualification; sought extension of the franchise to policemen and soldiers, and required all parliamentary elections to be held on one day, that day to be a public holiday, and all public houses to be closed during the hours of polling. Free-trade variations of this platform were an elective Upper House and the abolition of public hustings nomination.

On other questions both platforms sought to provide for the prohibition of the sweating system; the supervision and inspection of land boilers and machinery; amendments to the Mining Act to give greater protection and opportunity to miners; the extension of technical education—free-traders here required schools of mines, agricultural schools and model farms; extension to seamen of the provisions of the Employers Liability Act; a comprehensive national system of water conservation and irrigation; amendment of the Trades Union Act; and federation of the colonies on a national basis. Henry George's influence could be seen in the common plank demanding a tax on the unearned increment on land.

The L.E.L. also sought a number of other reforms, including an eight-hour working day; a Department of Labour and a National Bank; election of magistrates and reorganization of the military forces on a volunteer basis. Where the L.E.L. platform wanted simply 'the execution of all Government contracts in the colony',* the protectionists required 'control by the state or local governing body of such works or undertakings as railways, tramways, water supply, public lighting or other necessary works for the general good of the community, which, if vested in private owners, might create a monopoly prejudicial to the best interests of the people.' But where the free-traders required the amendment of the Trade Mark Act 'providing for the stamping and marking of all manufactures to show where they are made', the L.E.L. showed the real nature of their grievance by stating unequivocally

---

*In 1892 this was expanded to:
(a) All Government contracts to be executed in the Colony.
(b) Prohibition of the sub-letting of Government contracts.
(c) Standard Union wages to be paid in all Government and Municipal contracts;
Clause 14, Platform of the L.E.L., January 1892, in R. N. Ebbels, *The Australian Labor Movement*, p. 215.

that what they required was the stamping of all Chinese-made furniture. The general 'amendment of the Trades Union Act' sought by the free-traders was likewise stated more explicitly by the L.E.L. to involve the repeal of the Masters and Servants Act, the Agreements Validating Act (these first two to legalize the Shearers' Agreement), the Masters and Apprentices Act and the Trades Union Act.

Although the failure of the 1890 strike had diverted labour interest almost unanimously to Parliament, both within and without the fold there were critics. The moderately pro-Labor *Hay Standard* objected to the idea that the 'third or labour party' might achieve its aims by 'intimidation' and considered that the usefulness of its candidates would be 'greatly curtailed by the fact that they will not be free agents but the delegates of an outside organisation whose commands they will have to obey or forfeit their position.'*[12] A writer described by the *Wagga Wagga Advertiser* editor as 'an excellent specimen of the "fine old crusted Tory"' and on whose behalf the lack of a Primrose League in Wagga was regretted, wrote that he expected to see 'the various loud mouthed Union leaders attempting to run labour candidates (so called) into Parliament. Why labour and mere muscle should be represented any more than capital and brains, [he] for one [failed] to perceive.'[13] Internal critics asserted that true unionism should aim at the elevation of *all* workers and considered the Shearers' Union 'an aristocracy of labour consisting of five or six thousand workers whose better wages have been chiefly obtained at the expense of the unskilled and uncombined toilers.'[14]

Unsuccessful attempts had been made to ally the farmers with Labor.† W. W. Head, secretary of the Wagga branch of the A.S.U. had sent circulars to all farmers' unions urging farmers to co-operate with wage-earners, and pointing out that the United States Farmers' Alliance had joined with the Knights of Labor. Reforms sought by Labor, he said, were of as much interest to farmers as to wage-earners since all aimed at the abolition of monopoly.[15] Whatever the case may have been nearer to Sydney, Riverina farmers' unions were not interested. 'What earthly

---

*It was admitted however that 'roads and bridges members' were little better in this regard. Cf. also the Wagga reaction to Rae's abstinence from the Duke of Clarence vote and Labor members' acceptance of McMillan and Smith; see p. 282.

†It is probable that farmers who worked at shearing in their off-season were not members of the A.S.U.; providing a useful source of 'scab' labour in the wheat-sheep belt.

connection could there be seen between a Trades Union and societies formed to spread more enlightened views regarding agricultural matters?',[16] asked one writer, while at a combined general meeting in Wagga it was stated that, 'Farmers' Unions, when combined or otherwise, did not enter into politics'.[17] Besides, ill feeling still rankled over the conduct of the 1890 shearers' strike. Union shearers working for selectors 'knocked off work' on receiving the order to come out. Many selectors were under the impression that holders of less than five thousand sheep were exempt from the union ban. They were soon disillusioned and now opposed any move to unite farmers' unions with the L.E.L.[18] In short, the platforms of Riverina farmers' unions, as already indicated,* were strictly practical. Beyond the desire for protection, there was little that was doctrinaire in their policies. Within the wide range of these different platforms—free-trade, protectionist, farmers' union and L.E.L.—there was room for a variety of local and personal idiosyncrasy.

In the Murray electorate, centred on Deniliquin, there were three candidates, a petition to David McCaughey of Coree station, representative of a famous squatter family, having produced no result.[19] J. M. Chanter and R. Barbour, the sitting members, were selectors' representatives; protectionists of the 'intercolonial free-trade and protection against the outside world' type, while G. Chandler was a free-trader. All three, as might be expected of border representatives plagued with tariff questions, favoured federation.[20] Robert Barbour, sawmiller and selector of Moama, had first been returned in 1877, following a wave of free selection in the Deniliquin district. Since then he had maintained a continuous fight against squatterdom, his particular target being the squatter on whose run he had first selected, Henry Ricketson of Barratta. Ricketson *v.* Barbour cases had been so frequent over the intervening fifteen years as to become commonplace. It was almost an article of faith and certainly part of successive election campaigns that another such dispute should run concurrently.†[21] John Chanter was also a selectors' man. Educated in Adelaide and Melbourne, he had learnt farming in Victoria where he

---

*See pp. 208-9.
†The 1891 case involved an offer by Barbour to Ricketson of 3,000 acres of selected land on Ricketson's run for £9,000. Ricketson sought to dispute the validity of the selections on the ground that Fanny Barbour was a 'dummy' for her father. Earlier a select committee had been appointed at Barbour's instigation to investigate Ricketson's land transactions; *P.T.*, 17 October 1891.

founded a farmers' union. Crossing into New South Wales he settled at Moama as a free selector and champion of his fellows. His zeal in petitioning against anti-selector practices, and his representation of the selectors' association in attending conferences and interviewing Ministers, together with his formation of an agricultural and pastoral association, led to his nomination in 1882. To avoid splitting the selector vote he withdrew until 1885 when he was placed highest on the poll. In 1889 he was Minister for Agriculture and Mines. Both as Minister and M.P. he was notorious for smelling out scandal and abuse in land administration.[22]

In their combined election campaign, Chanter led with arguments for an elective Upper House and against plural voting, while Barbour discussed railways for the district and federation conventions. Both added personal advocacy of protection. Barbour had nine children who wanted work. There was none in Deniliquin. In Melbourne they would become 'barmaids and governesses'. Protection would bring industry to Deniliquin. Chanter also believed in protection because it would 'provide work for their children'; he had two who had learned trades and then had to do something else because there were no workshops and manufactories in Deniliquin.[23] The third candidate, Chandler, admitted that he did not differ much from the other candidates except with regard to free-trade and protection and he did not consider this a prominent question in the election.[24] Matters proceeded quietly until the free-trader Premier, Sir Henry Parkes, arrived in Deniliquin, ostensibly to open the new School of Arts. Both in that building and at a public meeting in the Town Hall, as became the long-standing champion of free-trade in Australia and the recipient of a gold medal from the Cobden Club,[25] he boosted free-trade and denigrated the two local protectionist members. Many members of his audience were former Victorians who favoured the protectionist policies of that colony. The result was a meeting of a kind rarely seen in that quiet town. Following excited attempts by Chanter to interrupt and refute, the meeting degenerated into uproar, dissent, boohoos, groans and ironical cheers. 'The larrikin element at the back of the hall seemed to be in a blaze of delight.' Finally the lights were turned down and amidst yelling and disorder the crowd dispersed. To avoid the surging mob waiting outside, Parkes delayed his departure and later left in a cab for his hotel.[26] A few days later the poll was declared. Chanter and Barbour had been re-elected

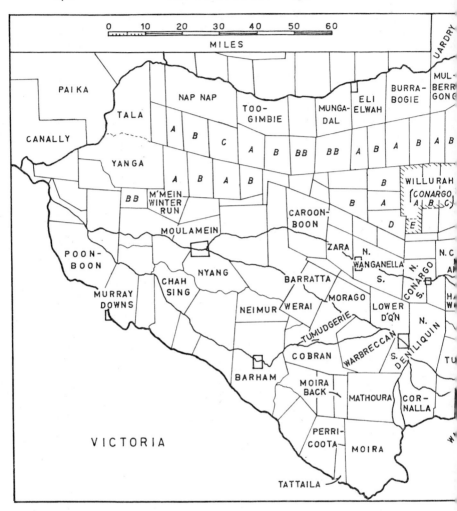

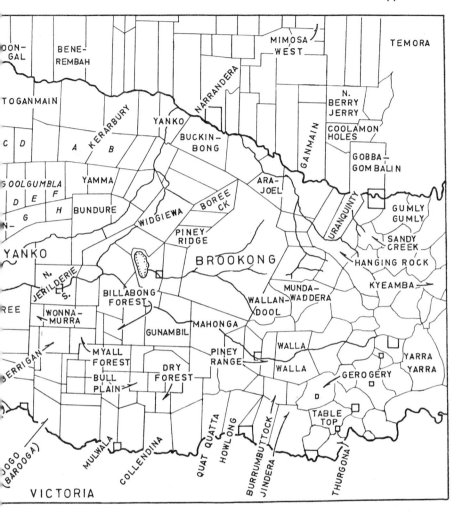

12   Riverina pastoral holdings

Because of boundary changes, names indicate location rather than
size at any specified time. Willurah was formed from parts of
Conargo backblocks A, B, C and E; Steam Plains from Yanko
backblocks A and B. Backblocks are indicated by 'BB' or 'A', 'B',
'C', 'D', etc.

Sources: *N.S.W. Government Gazette*; N.S.W. Lands Dept records and
maps; Willurah station records

with 956 and 918 votes respectively, while Chandler polled 573. In Deniliquin itself the voting had been Chanter 264, Barbour 274, and Chandler 208; Chandler's votes being ascribed to plumping by free-traders.[27] Elsewhere Chandler polled poorly. It had, throughout the district, been a day of heavy showers. At Berrigan 'the roads being in a frightful state', two-thirds of the voters had not polled,[28] but the result would have been little different if farmers had been able to travel.* In the district in which the Morris and Ranken report had alleged the greatest failure of selection, the selectors' representatives continued their almost unbroken fifteen-year run.[29]

By contrast, the campaigns in the Albury and Hume electorates caused little excitement. Although they had campaigned, neither the L.E.L. nor the farmers' unions had advanced candidates.[30] The sitting member for Albury, John Wilkinson, was a solicitor with Melbourne and Sydney connections, who described himself as a protectionist. Of his two original opponents one retired before nomination day;[31] the other, Luke Gulson, who 'held strong land views', was a free-trader.[32] For years annoyance at the pinpricks of the border customs house had stirred the Albury-ites and the more serious economic restrictions had prompted agitation for intercolonial free-trade or New South Wales protection. Now that there was some prospect of a change at last, and farmers in a retaliatory mood were already stipulating a New South Wales tariff on Victorian wheat and oats,[33] storekeepers in Albury began to have doubts. Protection in New South Wales could 'kill the Victorian drawbacks', and it was on these that Albury commercial interests had flourished. Furthermore, if protection existed on both sides of the Murray, the strangled trade of Wodonga would assert itself.[34] Wilkinson's protection, therefore, wisely followed the familiar formula of 'intercolonial freetrade and protection against the outside world'. At meetings in the district he identified himself with the farmers.[35] In reply to critics who stated that he had only attended Parliament nineteen times (as compared with Mr Brunker's two hundred attendances) he stated that, 'If they wanted men to be constantly in Sydney, they did not want a member to reside amongst them.' In favour of federation, he saw two possible results from it. The first was intercolonial free-trade, which would allow districts to deal with their natural markets—in Albury's case, Melbourne. The second was the

*The Berrigan results were: Barbour 43, Chanter 43, Chandler 9, Informal 1.

possibility of Albury being chosen as the federal city. To further critics he explained his disadvantage in that there had been no railway station or other public building to erect.[36] On election day, Luke Gulson, as ex-mayor, polled well in Albury, 360 of his 392 votes coming from the town. In the surrounding farming area however he was hopelessly outvoted, and Wilkinson, who polled 516 votes in Albury, received a total of 670.[37]

The interests of the surrounding district were identical with those of Albury. The five nominees for the Hume electorate included two protectionist-federationists, W. J. Lyne, grazier and selectors' representative* and James Hayes, Irish-born flour-miller; two free-trader federationists, W. A. Harper—'a stranger in your midst on a good mission . . . the measure rather than the man'[38]—and his shadow J. Lindeman; and John O'Brien, secretary of the Corowa Farmers' Union. Of these five the two protectionists were returned. The first, W. J. Lyne, Tasmanian born and educated, had settled in Queensland but returned to Tasmania as a council clerk. In 1876 he rented land near Albury.[39] From 1880 he had represented the interests of farmers and graziers. In his campaign he attacked the government for keeping local government and electoral reform dangling, and for its administration of the Land Act, especially in declaring reserves and Special Areas, which 'gave large landholders greater opportunity than selectors.' Although claiming to be a federationist he objected to a number of federationist resolutions and their proposed Constitution.[40] Hayes the flour-miller also opposed the government, favouring local farming interests.[41] Between them these two polled 71 per cent of the votes,† the same proportion as they had six years earlier,[42] indicating, as in the Murray electorate, the success of attempts to put the smaller man on the land.

The Murrumbidgee electorate was the most populous in the Riverina. Wagga itself seems to have attracted organization promoters; and shearers' unions, farmers' unions, clubs and societies proliferated. In 1891 six candidates—four protectionists, one free-trader and one L.E.L. member—struggled for the three seats. The most popular candidate was the sitting 'roads and bridges' member, Irish-Catholic protectionist James Gormly. Gormly had arrived in Sydney from Ireland in 1840 at the age of

---

*Although Lyne is classified by A. W. Martin and P. Wardle, *Members of the Legislative Assembly of New South Wales, 1856-1901*, as 'pastoralist' he was never a pastoral lessee. His speeches are pro-selector and anti-squatter.

†The final returns were: Lyne 1240, Hayes 1176, Harper 411, O'Brien 429, Lindeman 99.

four. His parents had settled at Gundagai until 1852 when, in the disastrous flood of that year, the town was swept away and they and most of their children drowned. James Gormly and one brother escaped by climbing a tree. A year later the seventeen-year-old was droving horses to the Victorian gold diggings. For forty years Gormly had traversed the district as horse dealer, coach and mail service proprietor, champion race rider, Lachlan station speculator, selector, patron of the turf and a variety of other occupations. Twice he was mayor of Wagga. In 1875 he founded and was president of the Wagga Free Selectors' Association and in 1877 attended the first general conference of free selectors in Sydney. Since 1877 he had represented the Murrumbidgee.[43] Up and down the railway, and cross-country by coach and buggy, his election campaign covered the whole district, while his speeches showed his familiarity with every aspect of life and every sectional interest in the constituency.[44] He condemned Special Áreas, the smallness of the 160-acre lots and the high prices; advocated the opening of reserves; opposed the extension of pastoral leases and the formation of large estates with a few boundary riders on them; and considered that dummyism should be prosecuted to the utmost.* At Coolamon he spoke on local self-government, electoral reform, how the Rabbit Bill was rushed through, how the estimates were passed, water conservation and irrigation, and federation.[45] Wherever he went he was loudly cheered and small towns came alive for his visits.[46] When the returns from the twenty largest centres had arrived, Gormly had topped the poll in fifteen.† In the final results he held 29 per cent of the votes.[47]

The second sitting member, Australian-born ex-bankrupt merchant George Dibbs,§ one-time free-trader but later protectionist, had represented various electorates before settling for the Murrumbidgee in 1885. A former Premier, and in 1891 leader of the opposition against Parkes, he began an election campaign in Wagga, but retired in June to contest South Sydney. With five other protectionists in the field the shared vote was inadequate

---

*Gormly is also classified by A. W. Martin and P. Wardle as a pastoralist. (Cf. note on W. J. Lyne, p. 279).

†By 1891 the number of polling places in the Murrumbidgee electorate alone had been increased to 34; W.A., 16 June 1891.

§Bankrupt 1867, paid creditors in full by 1875. (A. W. Martin and P. Wardle, op. cit., p. 60). Colonial Treasurer 1883-5; Premier and Colonial Treasurer and Secretary, October-December 1885; Colonial Secretary February 1886-January 1887; Premier and Colonial Secretary January-March 1889; *Parliamentary Handbook* (Sydney, 1920).

to return him, and within ten days of his retirement he resumed campaigning in Wagga, addressing electors on federation and 'other burning questions of the hour'. Despite the fierce opposition of the *Wagga Express* and the presence of two other protectionists, Dibbs snared 20 per cent of the votes to capture the third seat for Murrumbidgee.[48] From 1891 to 1894 he was again Premier. The third sitting member, David Copeland, a Wagga storekeeper and protectionist, after only one term in Parliament from 1889 failed to regain his seat.[49] A fourth protectionist, Patrick Heffernan, pastoralist of Clear Hills and substitute for the absent Dibbs, 'well known as a man of the most honourable and upright principles, strongly devoted to the interest of the agriculturalists',[50] was also unsuccessful. The sole free-trader candidate in 1891 was J. J. Peadon, Wagga storekeeper and 1890 President of the Wagga-based Amalgamated Farmers' Union of New South Wales. At a meeting in Wagga he sought to expound his hodge-podge platform which, as befitted a free-trade grocer, included the abolition of duties on fencing wire, galvanized iron, timber, sugar and tobacco. The meeting was the largest and liveliest held, those attending being evidently 'bent more upon obtaining amusement than political instruction.' The appearance of such a weak candidate was evidence to the *Wagga Wagga Advertiser* of the 'low ebb to which the free trade party [had] sunk in this constituency'. Following the meeting, the Wagga Free Trade Association published a large advertisement stating that they utterly repudiated Mr Peadon's candidature as damaging to the free-trade cause. Hence, despite Sir Henry Parkes' visit to Wagga, Peadon was defeated.[51]

It was the Labor Electoral League's representative, energetic 31-year-old* Arthur Rae, who took the second seat with 25 per cent of the votes. 'Firebrand Rae', 'Revolutionary Rae', 'never happy unless he is stirring up strife', was notorious for his role as an organizer of the Shearers' Union and the General Labourers' Union in the 1890 strike. Brought up on a charge under the Masters and Servants Act of inciting shearers against pastoralists, Rae had told the bench at Hay that he would 'just as soon go to hell to look for ice as come into that court and look for justice.'[52] Like his leader W. G. Spence—'King of the Shearers'—who, under the provisions of the same Act, had rendered himself liable

*The ages of other Riverina members in 1891 were: J. Wilkinson 39, Newton 41, Chanter 46, Lyne 47, R. B. Wilkinson 53, Gormly 55, Dibbs 57, Hayes 60, Barbour 65 (average 51).

to a fine of £165,000 with costs or imprisonment for 634 years and forty-eight weeks,[53] Rae also received cumulative sentences. Having served only one month he was released and in 1891, after attending meetings and conferences over a wide area of Australia, was nominated, in a contested ballot, as the Wagga L.E.L. candidate.[54] Many of Rae's votes came from that 'turbulent organization' the Shearers' Union, the prosperous Wagga branch of which had receipts of over £7,000 in 1890, of which £2,360 was sent to Sydney for strike purposes.[55] Following Rae's extensive tour of Riverina electorates, the Labor adherents, easily identified by their blue and white ribbons and rosettes, plumped for their man and Rae was returned, second only to Gormly, with 25 per cent of the votes; five hundred more, as the Labor followers could not have helped noticing, than Dibbs, the new Premier of New South Wales.[56]

Despite the cheering and 'musical honours', Rae's first year in Parliament did not satisfy all. Labor members had expressly agreed not to vote for a ministry containing strike-breakers like 'McMillan, the treasurer, and shoot-'em-down-Smith, the Minister for Works.' When Rae, like others, did, he was branded as a traitor.[57] Called to order on another occasion for lecturing Members in the House, he endured a blistering harangue on his ignorance and shortcomings.[58] And when, in keeping with his widely proclaimed republican intentions, he stood out alone against the vote of condolence moved in the Assembly on the death of the Duke of Clarence, he was castigated at a public meeting in Wagga. His explanation was booed and hooted and a vote of confidence motion by a few republican sympathizers amended. His action it was stated 'was an insult to the electors of the Murrumbidgee and a degradation to the electorate, which deeply regretted that one of its members should have so grossly misrepresented public feeling.' The amendment, to be carried to the government, was passed by an overwhelming majority, and with the singing of the National Anthem.[59]

Polling day in Wagga was marked by heavy flooding. In the worst inundation since 1870, buggies, horses and returning officers were swept away, rabbits climbed trees, seventy Chinamen were rescued in boats, two hundred people took refuge in the school, and the streets were crowded with 'people watching the advance of the water, the spectators being every now and then driven to higher levels.' At 11 p.m. on the night before polling, the gasworks were submerged and the town plunged into darkness. On polling day 'the town presented the appearance of being intersected with swiftly running rivers, the only dry land visible being a ridge running from the hospital to the public school. Throughout the day boats and vehicles were plying in every direction and men on horseback rode about from house to house.'[60] The building where the elections were to take place was flooded several feet deep. In anticipation of this, Wagga's returning officer, lawyer H. B. Fitzhardinge, had arranged for polling at the Australian Hotel, with its balcony overlooking the main street, and where a large downstairs dining-room and two bedrooms had been prepared as polling booths. Despite the inconveniences there were twenty more votes recorded than in the previous election.[61] As Arthur Rae commented at the moment of his success: 'That old English poet Shakespeare said there was a tide in the affairs of men which taken at the flood leads on to fortune. They must admit that at all events he had taken it at the flood. (laughter and cheers)'.[62]

The town of Hay, centre of the Balranald electorate, was further downstream and the flood had not reached it by election day. Despite lopping, the Balranald electorate was still enormous, extending from Booroorban on the Old Man Plain between Hay and Deniliquin to Nymagee over two hundred miles to the north; and from Carrathool on the Murrumbidgee, over 120 miles west to Euston on the Murray. This immense tract of unvarying flatness, its sole eminences the mountains of 'empties' outside the crossroads pubs, was the haunt of wrinkled squatters and Joseph Furphy's *Such is Life* teamsters. Its centre was Hay, a dusty railhead scarring the saltbush plain, where to the crack of the bullocky's whip and the lash of his profanity the creaking teams pulled in and out from stations hundreds of miles distant. By nomination time there were four candidates left; one protectionist and one free-trader having withdrawn.* Those remaining included A. L. P. Cameron,[63] bona fide homestead lessee, 'intercolonial freetrade and commonwealth protection' federationist, and Allan Lakeman,[64] a sitting pastoralist Member; both of whom were defeated. The successful candidates were Robert B. Wilkinson, free-trader, stock and station agent and ex-pastoralist; and James Newton, the Labor representative. Wilkinson had arrived in Victoria in 1852 as a fourteen-year-old, having been educated at

---

*Samuel Alexander Hamilton, free-trader (*H.S.*, 10 June 1891); J. Laynton Le B. Shropshire, protectionist, Labor and selectors' candidate, *H.S.*, 17 June 1891.

Hanwell college, and after working in country banks, joined in running a station near Wagga. In 1870 he founded the firm of Wilkinson and Lavender, stock and station agents of Sydney, Hay and Bourke. He represented Balranald continuously from 1880 to 1891.[65] His policy speech which largely favoured the squatters, indicated his preference for intercolonial free-trade, federation, local self-government, local control of land matters, extension of railways, government assistance against rabbits, greater power for country electorates and a quiet settlement of industrial disputes. This brought him 26 per cent of the votes and the second seat for Balranald.[66]

In view of its transport functions at the railhead it was appropriate that at one stage the mayor of Hay was a saddler and leather merchant. Equally appropriate was the fact that the saddler should be secretary of the Carriers' Union and Labor representative for Balranald. Lancashire-born James Newton had arrived in Victoria in 1857 as a child and was later apprenticed to a saddler. He moved to Hay at the beginning of the boom years in 1870. In addition to holding numerous local offices he was very active in both Masonic and Oddfellows Lodges and received honours rarely granted country members. His saddlery business brought him into close contact with teamsters and his endeavours resuscitated the Riverina Carriers' Union, by whose members he was nominated for Parliament.[67] His success was greeted enthusiastically in Hay. A special meeting of the Carriers' Union proudly arranged to welcome 'Mr. James Newton M.P.' At the railway station a large wagon drawn by ten grey horses was decked with flags. The mayor and town officials rose as the band struck up 'See the Conquering Hero Comes', while the Labor supporters burst into hearty and continued cheers. Newton, 'visibly affected by the warmth of the welcome', listened to the address 'on behalf of the members of the Carriers' Union and the labour bodies generally', then the whole procession and a crowd of spectators moved off down the main street.[68]

The extensive economic and social changes which had taken place within thirty years were thus far reflected in politics. Some of the differences observable in the two generations of electors were not exclusive to the Riverina, but rather the result of Australia-wide or world-wide trends. The rise of unionism and organized labour foreshadowed the eventual substitution of an employer-employee relationship for the old Master and Servant complex. In the 1890 strike, Jack may not have proved as good as

South from Mahonga on the Billabong: 'It was into such a forest that Ned Kelly rode'.

The pub on the One Tree Plain

Hay railway station

'See the Conquering Hero Comes'

his master or, at least, as strong, but by 1891 for a number of reasons the political power of squatters in the Riverina had been broken, as the presence of only one pastoralist sympathizer amongst ten Members shows.* Between the two extremes of pastoral worker and squatter of 1861, there had developed, partly through closer settlement and partly through related urbanization, a widely diverse range of occupations and interests, based on a redistribution of wealth and land. The gap in the society of 1861 had, at least to some extent, been filled.

In conclusion then, the greater diversification of Riverina economic and social life in 1891 seems in part to have resulted from the working out of the much-maligned free selection legislation; and even in their provocation of the selector-squatter struggle the Acts were important determinants in the course of economic development and population growth in the Riverina. Recently N. G. Butlin has suggested that the selector-squatter struggle has been over-emphasized by historians,[69] but an adequate knowledge of this struggle is necessary for any real understanding of the course of pastoral investment in New South Wales and the development of Australian rural society and its politics.

It could be argued that the influx of population during the gold-rush years would, as a result of natural increase, have generated pressure on existing resources, including land, and that this must have inevitably led to a struggle for redistribution of wealth. But disappointment with the results of the gold rushes had led men to agitate for economic independence on the land, and the existence of the land legislation which resulted makes

---

*It is possible that the power of the squatting interest in the Assembly in 1889 was somewhat less than A. W. Martin suggests in A. Barnard (ed.), *The Simple Fleece* (pp. 577-91). As Martin indicates (p. 589) there is some difficulty in distinguishing between the interests of selectors and squatters, particularly after the advent of the Homestead Lease in 1884. There is less difficulty, however, in determining the mode of tenure under which individuals held land and the sizes of their flocks. Martin's definition of a pastoralist as 'any man who appears to have had as his major occupation the grazing of sheep or cattle' (p. 578), he states himself, 'is admittedly a loose definition, but the available sources do not permit further refinement.' As has already been shown, two of the three Riverina members classified as 'pastoralists' in A. W. Martin and P. Wardle, op. cit., viz. Gormly and Lyne (see pp. 279 and 280 of this book) were actually selectors' representatives and anti-squatter. Further work on election campaigns in other electorates, and on parliamentary debates could possibly reveal others, and would certainly alter the trend of Martin's table after 1877. As he points out (p. 581), 'adequate explanation of the trends in pastoral membership of the Assembly would require a close examination of the changing structure of individual electorates, of the movements of political feeling, and of economic developments in the countryside.'

speculation on alternative possibilities unnecessary. Bad legislation it may have been, and in part undoubtedly was, bearing all
the marks of a measure passed in answer to political pressure-
group tactics and so-called popular agitation. In the sixties it had
little effect in the Riverina. The runs were locked up until the
leases expired in 1866, and drought years marked the middle of
what was generally, in an economic sense, a depressed decade.
The seventies, by contrast, opened with good seasons and high
wool prices, encouraging men to seek a stake in the land once
more. But the hastily contrived legislation of 1861 made no
provision for administration, and the long-standing deficiencies of
the N.S.W. Lands Department, most of which favoured the
squatters, became increasingly scandalous in the seventies as
erstwhile gold-rush migrants sought economic opportunity for
their sons.

Population pressure may have developed more steadily under
more normal conditions of demographic growth, but in Victoria
the fifties had been marked by unusually high mass migration,
and by the seventies the children of this vigorous new population
were approaching young manhood and womanhood. It was no
accident that the radical cries of the gold-rush population were
repeated in the land struggles of the seventies, nor even that a
further twenty years later, in the nineties, the blue flag of Eureka
flew again over the camps of men dissatisfied with their share of
the country's economic wealth. The migration of the fifties had,
by the seventies, produced masses of young adults whose marriages led to further population pressure in the nineties. In the
seventies the impact was greater but economic buoyancy and the
availability of land cushioned the blow as surplus population
spilled into the Riverina from Victoria and to a lesser extent from
the older settled districts of New South Wales. By the nineties
the effect of the third generation merges with the general increase
in population and it becomes difficult to trace direct demographic
causal relationships with the gold rushes. By the nineties too,
wool prices were down and economic conditions were generally
depressed, good land was harder to get and the laws had been
tightened. It was in the seventies that Robertson's Acts had their
most decisive influence.

High wool prices may have lured men on to the Riverina,
population pressure may have pushed them from behind, but free
selection enabled them to stay. Despite enormous difficulties and
all the misuses to which Robertson's Acts were put, large numbers

of selectors were successful in obtaining land which they used in a manner dictated by environment and markets, either for grazing in the west or, with the extension of railways, for ever-increasing wheat-growing in the east. Despite the statements of Morris and Ranken in 1883, there was in the Riverina no evidence of rural depopulation, either in the sense of a general movement of population from rural to metropolitan areas or from countryside to country town. Until 1891 at least, the movement was in the opposite direction. Both countryside and country towns were peopled by migrants moving out from the older settled districts, including urban areas. In fact the only observable depopulation at all is that which occurred locally in the southern and eastern Riverina when rationalization of holdings and selling-out took place as some of the original selectors moved on. And if the population appears remarkably mobile this is not so surprising. Men who had travelled half-way round the world seeking their fortunes in the fifties were not to be balked by trips of a few hundred more miles twenty years later when the time came to seek further opportunities for themselves and their families.

As a result of selector migration and closer settlement, both urban and rural populations in the Riverina grew side by side. Indeed a town's population growth depended largely on the prosperity of its agricultural or pastoral hinterland and rose and fell with the movements and prosperity of the selector population. A typical pattern saw rapid increase in town population in the seventies, relative decline with waning opportunities in the eighties as the selector frontier moved further north-west, and some recovery in the nineties. Despite a general slowing down of economic activity in the eighties, the migrations of the seventies had resulted, with natural increase, in a six-fold growth of Riverina population in thirty years, much of the increase being in the numbers of women and children. The growth of more respectable urban and farming communities and the vastly increased numbers of schools and churches took much of the rawness from the pastoral society typical of the fifties. The hundreds of schools in the Riverina in 1891—compared with six or so in 1861—reflects in part the growing concern of the state with education. But the existence of a youthful population to fill these schools, while related to living standards and chances of survival, may also be traced to the effects of free selection, even if only to that defective parliamentary draughtsmanship which for a time permitted selection by minors.

There was in fact no significant section of Riverina population whose fortunes were not tied up in some way with the selection legislation. Victorians and their families were drawn on (or pushed from behind); German farmers came from South Australia and Victoria because they could obtain land; and even the continued employment of the Chinese was related to the need to exploit to the full pastoral properties which had become so heavily mortgaged in combating the selector threat. And however much members of that aristocracy of labour, the Shearers' Union (and to a lesser extent the Carriers' Union), might fulminate against farmers providing scab labour during the 1890 strike, the purity of their own ideals was somewhat sullied by their ownership of land acquired by free selection.

Within the Riverina itself, different combinations of social, economic and geographical determinants produced differing attitudes and different climates of opinion amongst the voting population. In the Deniliquin district the typical successful selector was the small grazier, probably of Victorian origin, who, having acquired land, tended to turn conservative. No Labor Electoral League was formed in Deniliquin; nor even a camp of the Shearers' Union. Not that there was any real reconciliation between selector and squatter. The outrages of the seventies were still too fresh in the minds of men who had witnessed or participated in struggles like that of Joachim *v.* O'Shanassy. Nor had the town prospered. Deniliquin's economic throat had been very effectively cut in the internecine railway and tariff war between Victoria and New South Wales. The district's only effective outlet was through the Victorian tariff wall. Precariously perched out on their economic limb the voters of the Murray electorate favoured either New South Wales protection or a federation which would abolish Victorian protection. Consistently they returned to Parliament two protectionist selectors, Chanter and Barbour—both migrants from Victoria—and woe betide any New South Wales free-trading Premier who dared peddle his wares in that town.

In the drier area around Hay it was more difficult for the small man to establish himself, and those selectors who had acquired the larger holdings necessary to survive had more in common with the squatters. Indeed in two respects the Balranald electorate was unique. It was the only Riverina electorate to return anything like a squatter-sympathizer in 1891 and, as this indicates, stood alone in bearing much resemblance to the pastoral scene of thirty years earlier. Here a middle class between Master and Servant was slowest to develop and only a few smaller landholders and townsmen filled the gap. Transport workers dominated the 'lower orders'. But instead of humble obedient servants the Hay carriers were rampant radicals and fiery unionists, typical of many of the nomadic bush-workers portrayed in Furphy's *Such is Life* and *Rigby's Romance*. In 1891 the carriers returned their own union secretary to the N.S.W. Legislative Assembly.

Near Albury, by contrast, the small men were thickest. So prosperous had the town grown with intercolonial traffic, railway activity and the closer settlement of the fertile and well-watered surrounding country that it had become a separate electorate. Hundreds of small farms and dozens of little towns clustered in the Hume electorate beyond the main urban area. As in the Deniliquin district there was little that was radical here, and Arthur Rae had scant success in forming political Labor groups. Whether German or Australian-born, farmers had settled thickly on small holdings that were, in an area with certain rainfall and access to markets, economically viable. For the most part they were reasonably content.

The most complex of all Riverina electorates was that centred on Wagga. Here Victorian influence was least, but a significant number of families of Irish Catholic descent gave the area special characteristics and probably contributed both to the regular election of James Gormly and the ready hearing given to radical and even republican ideals in that town. For New South Welshmen, Wagga was something of a gateway to the Riverina. Here the shearing gangs congregated before moving out to the big sheds, and it was from Wagga that Arthur Rae, as secretary of the Shearers' Union, was sent into Parliament. It was Wagga, too, that gave birth a year later to that most fearsome mouthpiece of radicalism in the nineties, the *Hummer*. Yet the Murrumbidgee electorate also had its squatters, its farmers and its townsmen; and amongst these, on large stations and small farms and in tiny country towns, conservatives were just as common as radicals.

Indeed the usefulness of any such labels in describing the allegiances of the Riverina's population in 1891 is limited. The propagation of a completely new species was difficult in the existing climate of imperialism, and hybrids were more common. Bodily transplanted Britons had given way to a predominantly Australian-born population—70 per cent by 1891—but even amongst these Marxism was already at work producing new mutations. It would be misleading to compare the ex-convict

publican John Taylor of the Royal and that rabble-rousing republican Arthur Rae as typical men of 1861 and 1891. More meaning-
ful would be a contrast between that society which set Taylor
and the squatting nephews of Lord Brougham poles apart, and
that in which John Chanter, James Gormly and Arthur Rae were,
in their different ways, typical parliamentary representatives. Here
the differences are not so much of birth as of belief; here nationalism and internationalism struggle together uneasily in the womb,
nurtured indifferently by increasing literacy and the growth of
secular education.

But so long as National school history books dealt with the
claims of the Mother Country, and geographies dealt first with
the British Isles; so long as the National Anthem and saluting
the flag were standard rituals for all, including uniformed school
cadets armed with wooden rifles; so long would solitary dissident
republican voices fall on deaf or outraged ears. The effects of
thirty years of 'British' nationalist indoctrination are not thus
easily shrugged off. Twenty-five years later the entry of Australia
into an 'Imperialist' war was to spark off the conscription controversy—the reflection on a national scale of the complex system
of values already evident in the Riverina microcosm of 1891.

But whatever their national origins and allegiances, the men of
the Riverina in 1891 still attached vast importance to the ownership of 'a bit of land'. Indeed this was for many the ultimate
economic security. Their insistent search for it, within the framework of the selection legislation, and the changing relationship
between land and people, is too central a theme in Australian
history for it ever to be over-emphasized.

APPENDIX A (i)

Occupation Groups in Riverina Towns, c. 1861
(Selected from census lists on the basis of newspaper and other local evidence)

GOVERNMENT AND PROFESSIONAL
Government Service. Civil: officers and clerks (Crown Land Agents and Customs officials).
Police: Police Magistrates, Clerks of Petty Sessions, constables, etc.
Learned Professions. Legal: attorneys, solicitors.
Medical: physicians, surgeons, accoucheurs, dispensing chemists, apothecaries.
Clerical: denominational ministers.
Teachers: schoolmasters and mistresses, governesses.
Other Educated Professions. Architects, artists, editors, engineers, land surveyors, reporters.

TRADING AND COMMERCE
Accountants, agents, assurance officers, bankers, booksellers, chinaware dealers, commercial clerks, clothiers, corn-dealers, dealers, drapers, druggists, haberdashers, hay-dealers, hawkers, ironmongers, land agents, merchants, music sellers, stationers, timber-dealers, tobacconists.

PERSONS ENGAGED IN PROVIDING FOOD, DRINK AND ACCOMMODATION
Producers. Bakers, brewers, butchers, confectioners. cordial-makers, millers, maltsters, river fishermen, pastrycooks.
Distributors. Fruiterers, provision dealers, restaurateurs.
Distributors with Accommodation. Inn-keepers and hotel-keepers, boarding-house and lodging-house keepers, livery-stable keepers.

SKILLED WORKMEN
Masters, principals, hired workmen or apprentices in:
Superior Arts. Pianoforte makers, printers, watch-and-clock makers.

Metal. Blacksmiths, farriers, plumbers, tin workers.

Wood. Boatbuilders, cabinetmakers, carpenters, coopers, wheelwrights.

Stone and Earth. Brickmakers, bricklayers, builders, masons, slaters.

Leather and Skins. Bootmakers and shoemakers, saddlers, tanners.

Other Skilled Trades. Barbers and hairdressers, coachbuilders and trimmers, hatters, painters, upholsterers.

UNSKILLED AND MISCELLANEOUS

Unskilled. Fencers, gravediggers, lathmakers, sawyers, shingle-splitters, shinglers, sextons, well-sinkers, woodcutters, labourers.

Domestic.

Miscellaneous. Carriers, coachmen, dressmakers, milliners, newspaper people, staymakers, undertakers.

OCCUPATIONS NOT STATED

Annuitants, coach proprietors, contractors, independent gentlemen, vagrants.

APPENDIX A (ii)

Stated Male Occupations 1891*

Counties	Male population	Professional incl. govt not elsewhere classed	Domestic	Commercial		Industrial			Primary Producers			
				Mercantile	Transport and communications	Manufacturing	Building and construction	Indefinite	Agricultural	Pastoral	Mining	Other Primary Producers
Bourke	2,126	52	69	34	50	117	35	109	706	265	11	25
Boyd	630	8	23	11	13	43	22	17	89	239	1	39
Cadell	1,000	30	31	58	50	64	21	59	240	95	8	0
Caira	798	24	65	46	37	63	25	52	66	177	1	49
Clarendon	3,633	82	116	195	236	188	104	250	800	165	91	8
Cooper	2,165	58	131	201	106	254	97	147	302	225	0	48
Denison	1,186	20	55	50	8	41	58	56	415	145	0	9
Goulburn	4,912	176	194	405	182	417	279	245	677	424	73	13
Hume	2,989	66	108	121	73	195	256	249	753	207	7	22
Mitchell	1,533	22	74	24	56	50	67	72	446	241	11	34
Sturt	533	4	42	26	26	45	11	19	48	116	1	82
Townsend	2,194	75	158	147	85	169	72	127	258	357	0	39
Urana	1,956	29	110	74	54	109	70	95	369	508	0	53
Wakool	675	6	44	22	14	30	22	39	110	219	0	41
Waradgery	2,498	86	161	221	80	217	104	192	198	336	4	93
Wynyard	6,738	235	268	507	175	403	279	318	1,125	431	376	30

* Excluding 'indefinite occupations', 'dependants', and 'not stated'.
Source: *N.S.W. Census*, 1891.

APPENDIX B

Life Tables for Males and Females in New South Wales
1861-1875

Some demographic aspects of this study are impressionistic, others were amenable to quantification. The life tables below are based on data given by M. B. Pell, on the ages of people at death in New South Wales throughout the period 1860-75, in 'On the Rates of Mortality in New South Wales', *Journal of the Institute of Actuaries and Assurance Magazine,* vol. 21 (London, 1879), p. 260. The tables confirm impressions from newspaper and other sources regarding life expectancy, but the application to the census populations of 1861 and 1871 proved less useful. Net migration figures for the area under study were obtained, but these only indicate that there were, say, 1,000 more people of certain ages than were expected to survive under mortality conditions of the period. They give no indication of the number of transients (i.e., whether 3,000 came and 2,000 left). In an area and period where the population was particularly mobile it was necessary to supplement this with information of a more qualitative nature from other sources.

Life Table for Males in New South Wales 1861-1875

	qx	px	lx	dx	Lx	Tx	e°x
0- 1	0.110770	0.889230	100,000	11,077	93,353	4,675,116	46.75
1- 2	0.045178	0.954822	88,923	4,017	86,464	4,581,763	51.53
2- 3	0.018640	0.981360	84,906	1,582	84,115	4,495,299	52.94
3- 4	0.011807	0.988193	83,324	983	82,832	4,411,184	52.94
4- 5	0.008702	0.991298	82,341	716	81,983	4,328,352	52.57
5- 9	0.02489	0.97511	81,625	2,031	402,896	4,246,369	52.02
10-14	0.01458	0.98542	79,594	1,160	394,826	3,843,473	48.29
15-19	0.02092	0.97908	78,434	1,640	387,706	3,448,647	43.97
20-24	0.02814	0.97186	76,794	2,160	378,349	3,060,941	39.86
25-29	0.03451	0.96549	74,634	2,575	366,600	2,682,592	35.94
30-34	0.04447	0.95553	72,059	3,204	352,204	2,315,992	32.14
35-39	0.05514	0.94486	68,855	3,796	334,685	1,963,788	28.52
40-44	0.06623	0.93377	65,059	4,308	314,429	1,629,103	25.04
45-49	0.08436	0.91564	60,751	5,124	290,855	1,314,674	21.64
50-54	0.09916	0.90084	55,627	5,515	264,292	1,023,819	18.41
55-59	0.13432	0.86568	50,112	6,731	233,715	759,527	15.16
60-64	0.17824	0.82176	43,381	7,732	197,562	525,812	12.12
65-69	0.26782	0.73218	35,649	9,547	154,362	328,250	9.21
70-74	0.32187	0.67813	26,102	8,401	109,500	173,888	6.66
75+	0.54490	0.45510	17,701	9,645	64,388	64,388	3.64

Note: Lo estimated by assuming that 70 per cent of deaths at ages less than 1 occurred before 6 months, and 30 per cent between ages 6 and 12 months.

$$Lx = \frac{lx + (lx + 1)}{2} \text{ for ages 1-4 years.}$$

$$5\,Lx = \frac{5dx}{5mx} \text{ (Greville's method) for ages 5-75 years.}$$

Life Table for Females in New South Wales 1861-1875

	qx	px	lx	dx	Lx	Tx	e°x
0- 1	0.096093	0.903907	100,000	9,609	94,234	5,063,925	50.64
1- 2	0.044231	0.955769	90,391	3,998	88,392	4,969,691	54.98
2- 3	0.018683	0.981317	86,393	1,614	85,586	4,881,299	56.50
3- 4	0.011866	0.988134	84,779	1,006	84,276	4,795,713	56.57
4- 5	0.007966	0.992034	83,773	668	83,439	4,711,437	56.24
5- 9	0.02344	0.97656	83,105	1,948	410,623	4,627,998	55.69
10-14	0.01266	0.98734	81,157	1,027	402,903	4,217,375	51.97
15-19	0.01835	0.98165	80,130	1,470	396,654	3,814,472	47.60
20-24	0.02560	0.97440	78,660	2,013	388,010	3,417,818	43.45
25-29	0.03155	0.96845	76,647	2,418	377,046	3,029,808	39.53
30-34	0.04243	0.95757	74,229	3,149	363,206	2,650,056	35.70
35-39	0.05005	0.94995	71,080	3,556	346,284	2,286,850	32.17
40-44	0.05818	0.94182	67,524	3,928	327,743	1,940,566	28.74
45-49	0.06864	0.93136	63,596	4,365	307,005	1,612,823	25.36
50-54	0.07846	0.92154	59,231	4,647	284,498	1,305,818	20.05
55-59	0.11225	0.88775	54,584	6,127	257,653	1,021,320	18.71
60-64	0.14954	0.85046	48,457	7,246	224,153	763,667	15.76
65-69	0.22431	0.77569	41,211	9,244	182,944	539,514	13.09
70-74	0.30762	0.69238	31,967	9,833	135,241	356,570	11.15
75+	0.54150	0.45850	22,134	11,985	221,329	221,329	10.00

Note: Lo estimated by assuming that 70 per cent of deaths at ages less than 1 occurred before 6 months, and 30 per cent between ages 6 and 12 months.

$$Lx = \frac{lx + (lx + 1)}{2} \text{ for ages 1-4 years.}$$

$$5 \, Lx = \frac{5dx}{5mx} \text{ (Greville's method) for ages 5-75 years.}$$

NOTES

INTRODUCTION

[1] *V. & P.* (L.A. N.S.W.), 1883, vol. 2, pp. 77, 110.
[2] *History of Australian Land Settlement*, p. 230 (see also pp. 222–32).
[3] R. Henty, *Australiana*, p. 155.

1 THE PASTORAL INDUSTRY, 1851-1861

[1] *Two Expeditions into the Interior of Southern Australia during the years 1828, 1829, 1830 and 1831* (2 vols, London, 1833), in K. Fitzpatrick, *Australian Explorers*, p. 95.
[2] R. B. Ronald, *The Riverina, People and Properties*, p. 15; *N.S.W. G.G.*, 1848-50.
[3] Sir T. L. Mitchell, *Three Expeditions into the Interior of Eastern Australia; with Descriptions of the Recently Explored Region of Australia Felix, and of the Present Colony of New South Wales* (2 vols, London, 1838). For extracts see K. Fitzpatrick, op. cit., pp. 127-54.
[4] *South Australian Gazette*, 1 September 1838.
[5] *N.S.W. G.G.*, 1839.
[6] J. Jervis, 'The Western Riverina', *J.R.A.H.S.*, vol. 38 (1952), p. 4.
[7] R. B. Ronald, op. cit., p. 17.
[8] J. Phillips, *Reminiscences*, p. 57.
[9] Ibid., pp. 63-4.
[10] M. K. Beveridge, 'Pioneering on the Lower Murray', *V.H.M.*, vol. 1 (1911), p. 27.
[11] For a summary of the regulations and bibliography relating to the struggle, see C. J. King, *An Outline of Closer Settlement in New South Wales*, pp. 45-60.
[12] Gipps to Stanley, 3 April 1844, *H.R.A.*, I. xxiii. 510-11.
[13] *N.S.W. G.G.*, 7 October 1847.

[14] Gipps to Stanley, 16 April 1844, *H.R.A.*, I xxiii. 545-8.
[15] J. Phillips, op. cit., pp. 139-40.
[16] E.g., Adult male population on Bendigo goldfields (the nearest to Deniliquin) in 1854: February 8,300, August 23,500, December 15,000. G. Serle, *The Golden Age*, p. 388, Appendix 4.
[17] B. Fitzpatrick, *The British Empire in Australia*, p. 87; J. Phillips, op. cit., p. 97. Details regarding Ben Boyd's Kanakas from J. H. Watson, 'Benjamin Boyd, Merchant', *J.R.A.H.S.*, vol. 2 (1906-9), p. 137; B. Tunnock, 'Short History of the Shire of Numurkah', *V.H.M.*, vol. 23 (1950-1), p. 82; C. S. Ross, 'Some of the Murray Pioneers and Their Services to the State', *V.H.M.*, vol. 3 (1913), pp. 78-9; R. B. Ronald, op. cit., p. 24; J. Phillips, op. cit., p. 95.
[18] *Land, Labour, and Gold*, p. 141. See also Hobler MS., vol. 5, 6 April 1847, 10 May 1848, quoted in C. M. H. Clark, *Select Documents in Australian History*, 1788-1850, p. 280.
[19] Quotations and details from letters handed in to the *Pastoral Times*, Deniliquin, by the recipients for publication. *P.T.*, 4 and 25 May 1860.
[20] J. Gormly, *Exploration and Settlement in Australia*, p. 197; J. J. Baylis, 'The Murrumbidgee and Wagga Wagga', *J.R.A.H.S.*, vol. 13 (1927), p. 301.
[21] N. Bartley. *Opals and Agates*, p. 66.
[22] J. Gormly, 'Exploration and Settlement on the Murray and Murrumbidgee', *J.R.A.H.S.*, vol. 2 (1906–9), p. 42.
[23] N. Bartley, op. cit., pp. 61-6.
[24] Detailed descriptions and records of early River Murray traffic are

available in River Navigation files [n.d.] in the Adelaide Archives. See also D. Pike, *Paradise of Dissent*, pp. 452-3.

[25] N. Bartley, op. cit., p. 66.

[26] Details from J. Phillips, op. cit., p. 125-9.

[27] R. B. Ronald, op. cit., pp. 41-2; J. Gormly, *Exploration and Settlement in Australia*, p. 50.

[28] *P.T.*, 22 November 1861.

[29] R. B. Ronald, op. cit., p. 25.

[30] *N.S.W. Statistical Register*, 1859-61.

[31] *Census of Victoria*, 1861.

[32] N. Bartley, op. cit., p. 61.

[33] J. Phillips, op. cit., p. 108—after four years' occupation of Warbreccan.

[34] *P.T.*, weekly stock market reports, January to June 1859-60-61.

[35] Ibid.

[36] The best outline of the various stock routes and seasonal conditions is that in *S.M.H.*, 29 November 1859. Further details are to be found in *W.E.*, 1 June 1860 and *P.T.*, 2 June, 4 August 1859, 7 September 1860.

[37] R. B. Ronald, op. cit., pp. 41-3.

[38] The full story of the well on the Old Man Plain can be gleaned from *P.T.*, 26 May, 30 June, 15 September, 27 October 1859, 13 and 20 January, 20 April, 9 November 1860.

[39] *B.P.*, 9 September 1857, 17 January 1859; J. Jervis, op. cit., pp. 17-19.

[40] *P.T.*, 27 June 1860.

[41] *P.T.*, 27 April 1860. Dealers like Anstis and Baker of Ballarat, and Sweeny, who had 'slaughter houses, yards, tanneries', etc., could 'make the most of their purchases [and] . . . give fair prices', promoting a 'feeling of confidence between buyers and our station holders'. The fact that several thousands of fat cattle were 'bespoken' from herds on the Edward and Murrumbidgee, etc., tended to 'disconcert the arrangements of parties who prefer taking a chance of the markets'. See also *B.P.*, 9 September 1857, 7 July, 28 September 1858, and *P.T.*, 2 and 30 June, 1 September 1859, 27 April, 18 and 25 May 1860.

[42] *P.T.*, 2 June 1859. Other details cited from *P.T.*, 26 May, 9 June, 11 and 18 August, 1 September, 27 October, 8 December 1859, 3 February, 18 May, 29 June, 14 and 21 September, 2 November 1860.

[43] Ibid.

[44] Ibid., See also *S.M.H.*, 22 May 1862.

[45] *N.S.W. Statistical Register*, rainfall figures, 1857-69.

[46] *P.T.*, 17 February, 18 May, 1 June 1860.

[47] *P.T.*, 3 August 1860. See also T. A. Coghlan, *Labour and Industry in Australia*, vol. 2, pp. 687-717.

[48] *Maitland Mercury*, quoted in *P.T.*, 5 October 1860. The remainder of the paragraph is based on *P.T.*, 12 and 19 October, 9 and 16 November 1860.

[49] *A.B.* editorial, 1 December 1860.

[50] *P.T.*, 18 January, 10 May, 5 June 1861.

[51] *P.T.*, 16 August 1861.

[52] *P.T.*, 22 September 1859.

[53] The spread of 'the pleuro' is described in the following: *P.T.*, 26 October 1860, 21 January, 5, 12 and 19 April, 24 August, 6 December 1861; *A.B.*, 20 March, 7 and 11 December 1861.

[54] *Ovens Tribune*, quoted in *P.T.*, 6 December 1861.

[55] Port Phillip average fleece (i.e. washed). 'Greasy' prices for the same decade rose from 10¼d to 14⅞d. A. Sauerbeck, *Production and Consumption of Wool*.

[56] W. H. Lamb, 'Short History of the Willurah flock, 1860-1960', *Deniliquin Historical Society Newsletter*, no. 5, May-June 1960.

[57] *P.T.*, 8 and 22 December 1859.

[58] South Australian Archives. Research note no. 243 [n.d.]. Statistics of vessels moving up and down stream (Murray River Shipping) 1859-1909.

[59] *P.T.*, 20 July 1860; *A.B.*, 1 August 1860.

[60] *P.T.*, 10 August 1860, 4 January, 22 March, 6 September 1861.

[61] *P.T.*, 17 May 1861. (Italics added)

[62] *P.T.*, 8 February 1861.

[63] Peppin Diary.

[64] J. J. Westwood, *Journal*, p. 396; Peppin Diary.

[65] Abstract of runs appraised. V. & P. (L.A. N.S.W.) 1871-2, vol. 2.

[66] Deniliquin runs, *P.T.*, 22 November 1861; Widgiewa, *P.T.*, 13 January, 25 May 1860.

[67] Moira, *P.T.*, 10 August 1860, 13 September 1861; Perricoota and Tattaila, *P.T.*, 22 November 1861; Conargo, *P.T.*, 8 February, 17 May 1861; Tumudgerie, *P.T.*, 28 December 1860.

[68] N.S.W. Lands Dept Maps (N.S.W. State Archives), B.1531, B.1795 (1) A2, C.1722A, C.1633, C.1692 (1), C.2258, etc., and *S.M.H.*, 30 April 1856.

[69] Peppin Diary, 28 January to 8 April.

[70] Ibid., 2 February 1859.

[71] S. Mossman and T. Banister, *Australia Visited and Revisited*, p. 146.

[72] *P.T.*, 2 June, 18 August and 8 December 1859.

[73] *Parl. Deb.* (L.A. N.S.W.), 22 November 1861, in *A.B.*, 30 November 1861.

[74] *Journal*, pp. 302, 312, 354.

[75] *P.T.*, 20 October 1859.

[76] *B.P.*, 17 January 1857.

[77] Ibid.

[78] *P.T.*, 17 November 1859.

[79] A typical case occurred on the Barratta run. *P.T.*, 5 October 1860.

[80] E.g., *P.T.*, 16 March 1860, 'Splitters and Fencers wanted, . . .'.

[81] *A.B.*, 3 October 1860.

[82] *P.T.*, 9 June 1859.

[83] 28 July 1859.

[84] Ibid.

[85] *Maitland Mercury*, 17 December 1857; in J. Jervis, op. cit.

[86] Oppenheimer & Co., *P.T.*, 10 February 1860.

[87] *P.T.*, 20 July 1860.

[88] Kidd & Brickell's Stores. *A.B.*, 5 June 1861. Powell & Wigmore's Billabong Store, Jerilderie, had four tons for sale. *P.T.*, 10 May 1861.

[89] *P.T.*, 25 August 1859.

[90] *P.T.*, 13 July 1860.

[91] An *Armidale Express* article is quoted and questioned in *P.T.*, 6 December 1861—the claim was for an increase in weight from 50 lb. to 80 lb. and wool yield increase from 3 lb. to 6 lb. per sheep. See

also J. Jervis, op. cit., citing an article from the *Maitland Mercury*.

[92] See article on mustering in *B.P.*, 20 December 1856.

[93] *P.T.*, 20 October 1859.

[94] J. Phillips, op. cit., pp. 109-20. For a similar dispute near Albury, see A. Andrews, *First Settlement of the Upper Murray*, pp. 172-3.

[95] *P.T.*, 17 February 1860.

[96] 'Saltbush Bill' in *The Collected Verse of A. B. Paterson*, pp. 33-6.

[97] N.S.W. Lands Dept Map M.1665 b (N.S.W. State Archives).

[98] *P.T.*, 1 June 1860.

[99] *P.T.*, 7 September 1860.

[1] *P.T.*, 28 June 1861.

[2] 'Tom Collins', *Such is Life*, though for a later period, abounds in such incidents.

[3] *P.T.*, 8 September 1859; for a similar incident see 'Battle in the Bush', *S.M.H.*, 17 August 1868.

[4] A. B. Paterson, op. cit., pp. 33-6.

[5] *P.T.*, 24 February 1860.

[6] *P.T.*, 2 June, 18 August 1859.

[7] *P.T.*, 22 November 1861.

[8] William Cullen, Bull Plain. *A.B.*, 20 November 1861.

[9] *P.T.*, 12 October 1860; *A.B.*, 13 October 1860.

[10] *P.T.*, 20 October 1860.

[11] *P.T.*, 8 December 1859.

[12] *P.T.*, 1 March 1861.

[13] *Investment in Australian Economic Development*, p. 71.

[14] J. J. Baylis, 'The Murrumbidgee and Wagga Wagga', *J.R.A.H.S.*, vol. 13, pp. 255-6; A. Andrews, op. cit., p. 89.

[15] *B.P.*, 4 October, 20 December 1856; *P.T.*, 17 February 1860, 18 January 1861; J. Jervis, op. cit., p. 13.

[16] *P.T.*, 26 May, 25 August 1859, 7 December 1860; *S.M.H.*, 4 July 1867. In 1879 it was stated that the Yanko Cutting 'was now finished'. *Town and Country Journal*, 28 June 1879.

[17] *B.P.*, 24 November 1858; *S.M.H.*, 4 December 1858; *P.T.*, 26 May, 25 August 1859, 7 December 1860.

[18] Reprinted in full in *P.T.*, 26 May 1859, from which all references are taken. See also J. Jervis, op. cit.

[19] *P.T.*, 7, 21, 28 July 1859.

[20] *P.T.*, 23 March 1860.

21 *P.T.*, 6 January 1866. See also 15 September 1866.

22 J. Jervis, op. cit. See also Peppin Diary, where carting of water and supplies to shepherds was a never-ending task.

23 E.g., Desailly's summer run. A. Andrews, op. cit., p. 166. See also Snowvale summer station, *W.E.*, 31 October 1862; Long Plains summer run, *P.T.*, 1 January 1876; also *W.A.*, 5 January, 1878.

24 J. J. Baylis, 'The Murrumbidgee and Wagga Wagga', *J.R.A.H.S.*, vol. 13 (1927), p. 255.

25 *S.M.H.*, 26 October 1856.

26 McKay, Dods & Co., *P.T.*, 6 April, 8 June 1860; B. H. Dods, *P.T.*, 6 September 1861.

27 Perhaps inspired by one settler's offer of £1,000 for the first *artesian* well near the Billabong (*P.T.*, 1 September 1859), J. T. Neilson applied for a 160-acre free grant as compensation for a well sunk at his own expense on the road between Wanganella and Hay (J. Jervis, op. cit., p. 25).

28 *P.T.*, 21 July, 10 November 1859.

29 *P.T.*, 24 November 1859.

30 *P.T.*, 23 June 1859; J. Jervis, op. cit., p. 25; J. Phillips, op. cit., p. 142.

31 *P.T.*, 2 June 1859.

32 *P.T.*, 14 September, 1860.

33 *P.T.*, 24 November 1859.

34 *P.T.*, 5 October, 21 December 1860, 22 November 1861.

35 E.g., Watson and Hewitt on Tuppal, *P.T.*, 26 October 1860.

36 *P.T.*, 20 October 1859, 20 January, 14 and 21 September, 19 October 1860, 6 September 1861 and *N.S.W. G.G.*, 1859 and 1860.

37 See also *P.T.*, 2 June, 29 September 1859.

38 Peppin Diary, 20 April.

39 Ibid., 13 April 1859.

40 *Investment in Australian Economic Development*, pp. 60-84.

41 *P.T.*, 22 November 1861.

42 *P.T.*, 10 August 1860.

2 THE GROWTH AND FUNCTIONS OF TOWNS

1 J. Jervis, 'The Western Riverina', part II, 'Establishment of Denili-quin Township', *J.R.A.H.S.*, vol. 38 (1952), pp. 78-9.

2 See J. H. Shaw, *Urban Evolution of Wagga Wagga*.

3 *A.B.*, 14 July 1860.

4 For early growth of towns, use has been made of a number of reliable secondary sources—if works fifty years old may be included in this category—notably A. Andrews, *First Settlement of the Upper Murray* and J. Jervis, op. cit., particularly where these have made use of source material no longer available. The lack of such sources, and the loss of early Wagga newspapers has rendered treatment of that town somewhat scant. For further details on Albury before 1845, see A. Andrews, op. cit., and for later period, W. A. Bayley, *Border City*.

5 *A.B.*, 29 August 1860, recollections of C. G. N. Lockhart.

6 See A. Andrews, op. cit., pp. 75-7, 82.

7 From the journal of Lady Franklin, wife of the Governor of Tasmania, who travelled the overland route in 1839; quoted in various newspapers and W. A. Bayley, op. cit., pp. 23-4.

8 Ibid., see also A. Andrews, op. cit., p. 76.

9 A. Andrews, op. cit., pp. 94-7.

10 See K. Fitzpatrick, *Australian Explorers*, pp. 237-8; W. A. Bayley, op. cit., pp. 46-8; also J. H. Heaton, *Australian Dictionary of Dates and Men of the Time*, p. 176.

11 Details of Albury in 1851 from W. A. Bayley, op. cit., pp. 26-39.

12 J. Jervis, op. cit., pp. 78-9.

13 J. J. Baylis, 'The Murrumbidgee and Wagga Wagga', *J.R.A.H.S.*, vol. 13 (1927), p. 254.

14 J. Jervis, op. cit., pp. 80-1.

15 Ibid., and newspaper accounts of sales and purchasers on various land sale dates, compared with lists of residents and occupations compiled from all available sources.

16 *W.E.*, 28 May 1859, Letter to the Editor. See also *B.P.*, 4 October 1856.

17 *Land, Labour, and Gold*, quoted in 'Some Account of Albury', *B.P.*, 4 October 1856.

[18] S. Mossman and T. Banister, *Australia Visited and Revisited*, p. 139, 'the traffic has of course made the place what it is'.

[19] W. A. Bayley, op. cit., p. 30; *B.P.*, 4 October 1856.

[20] *B.P.*, 4 October 1856, 8 November 1856.

[21] *B.P.*, 8 November 1856.

[22] *Proceedings of the Royal Geographical Society of Australasia (South Australian Branch)*, vol. 18 (1856), pp. 49-55 (McDonnell) and *B.P.*, 8 November 1856 (Young).

[23] *B.P.*, 11 October 1856, 6 December 1856. See also 'Imports via Goolwa' in *N.S.W. Statistical Register*.

[24] *B.P.*, 24 January 1857.

[25] *A.B.*, 22 August 1860.

[26] A series of their letters appears in W. Kirchner, *Australien und seine Vortheile für Auswanderung*, pp. 59-159 (that quoted is from pp. 154-5). See also *B.P.*, 4 October 1856; *Corowa Free Press*, 22 November 1895, 'Reminiscences of G. H. Mott' and G. Nadel, 'Letters from German Immigrants in New South Wales', *J.R.A.H.S.*, vol. 39 (1953-4), pp. 253-66.

[27] Petition listing German families in *B.P.*, 9 May 1857.

[28] *N.S.W. Census*, 1861.

[29] *A.B.*, 28 February, 29 August, 21 and 24 November 1860, 9 February, 7 and 14 September, 23 October 1861.

[30] Cf. *P.T.*, 3 August 1860, 'We depend on two sources for our existence—the district squatters and the overland traffic in cattle and sheep.'

[31] *P.T.*, 25 May, 12 October 1860. There are several versions of the 'turpentine man' incident, one of which lays the blame on visiting bushrangers.

[32] *P.T.*, 12 October 1860.

[33] *S.M.H.*, 9 February 1857.

[34] *P.T.*, 15 September 1859. E.g., Edward Herbert, North Deniliquin, who lived in a single room adjoining his shop. His 'fortune' was estimated locally at £8,000.

[35] J. Jervis, op. cit., p. 146; *S.M.H.*, 10 December 1856; *B.P.*, 20 December 1856.

[36] *P.T.*, 30 June 1859.

[37] *S.M.H.*, 23 May, 9 December 1858.

[38] List of purchasers at Hay land sales, *P.T.*, 20 October 1859. Occupations from newspapers and other local sources.

[39] Population data in this and the two following paragraphs compiled from *N.S.W. Census*, 1861.

[40] *P.T.*, January-December 1861.

[41] Details of these local industries are scattered through the local newspapers already cited, throughout the period.

[42] *B.P.*, 8 November 1856.

[43] 1 November 1856.

[44] Series of Pritchard's advertisements, 1856-61.

[45] *B.P.*, 28 February 1857.

[46] *N.S.W. Census*, 1861.

[47] *P.T.*, 10 February 1860.

[48] *S.M.H.*, 30 November 1858; *P.T.*, 27 September 1861.

[49] *P.T.*, 9 June 1859. Cf. Henry Hopwood in S. Priestly, *Echuca, A Centenary History*, pp. 39-62 'Hopwood's Township'; also J. Jervis, op. cit., pp. 28-9.

[50] Ibid., J. Jervis, op. cit., pp. 28-9; see also *P.T.*, 26 May 1859.

[51] E.g., J. J. Westwood, *Journal*, pp. 309, 342.

[52] *P.T.*, 8 September, 29 December 1859.

[53] *P.T.*, 17 November 1859, 12 October 1860, 7 June, 20 September 1861.

[54] *A.B.*, 20 February 1861.

[55] *B.P.*, 16 May 1857; *A.B.*, 31 October 1860, 13 February 1861.

[56] *A.B.*, 19 September 1860.

[57] E.g., *A.B.*, October 1860 issues. On 15 October those present at council were Alderman Jones and the Town Clerk. Absentees were the Mayor (in Sydney), Aldermen Dornan, Everett, Roper, Kidd, Horsley (at Lob's Hole), McLaurin (at Tumut) and Wise (at Kiandra).

[58] *A.B.*, June-July 1860.

[59] *A.B.*, 5 September, 3 October, 3, 14 November 1860, 26 January, 27 March 1861, and May-August 1861.

[60] *B.P.*, 20 December 1856. See also Prospectus, *Albury Banner*, 4 July 1860.

[61] N. Bartley, *Australian Pioneers and Reminiscences*, p. 23.

[62] *P.T.*, 26 May 1859.

[63] E.g., W. Hayes's advertisement in *P.T.*, 17 November 1859.

[64] E.g., 'John Murphy, Manufacturer of Cabbage Tree and all kinds of hats', South Deniliquin. *P.T.*, 14 July 1859. Marshall & Waring's Deniliquin store, 'Boots and shoes from the first houses in England and Scotland'. *P.T.*, 16 June 1859. Daniel Henderson, Manchester House and W. J. Hobbs' Albury Emporium, *A.B.*, 22 August 1860.

[65] *W.E.*, 31 October 1862; *A.B.*, 3 October 1860, 1 June 1861. See also Kennedy papers, MS., draft D, for girls' and women's work on homesteads.

[66] Advertisements in local newspapers, 1856-62.

[67] For discussion of the various contemporary systems: Lancasterian; Bell (or National Society for Promoting the Education of the Poor in the Principles of the Established Church throughout England and Wales); and the British and Foreign Schools Society, see G. Nadel, *Australia's Colonial Culture*, pp. 189-92 and M. W. Thomas, *Young People in Industry 1750-1945*. For the Australian solution see G. Nadel, op. cit., pp. 202-13, 233-7, 261.

[68] *P.T.*, 8 December 1859.

[69] *W.E.*, 6 November 1858. A tannery was established in Albury in 1856. B.P., 20 December 1856.

[70] J. J. Westwood, *Journal*, pp. 401-3; *S.M.H.*, 4 August 1862; *B.P.*, 3 January 1857.

[71] *A.B.*, 1 December 1860.

[72] E.g., Peppin Diary. Geo. Peppin Jr regularly recruited casual labour from Deniliquin for all operations on Wanganella.

[73] E.g., *P.T.*, 26 October 1860. A 'Labour Market' existed at Sandhurst (Bendigo) and a registration office in Deniliquin.

[74] *P.T.*, 6 December 1861.

[75] *P.T.*, 10 November 1859.

[76] *P.T.*, 10 November, 26 May 1859.

[77] *B.P.*, 3 January, 21 March, 1857.

[78] *W.E.*, 19 March 1859.

[79] 14 July 1859.

[80] Police court reports in local Press 1856-60, E.g., *W.E.*, 9 April 1859.

Reward offered for capture of Incendiarist, with subscription list.

[81] *P.T.*, 10 November 1859.

[82] *P.T.*, 20 October, 10 November 1859.

[83] *P.T.*, 27 April 1860.

[84] *A.B.*, 28 August 1861.

[85] *P.T.*, 18 January 1861.

[86] *P.T.*, 3 November, 1 December 1859; *A.B.*, 5 and 22 September, 24 November, 8 December 1860; *B.P.*, 4, 25 October 1856, 17 April 1858; *S.M.H.*, 7 January, 9 July 1856.

[87] See ch. 3. Claims of Morris Asher, pp. 121-2.

[88] *A.B.*, 28 July, 3 September 1860, 24 August 1861.

[89] Weekly newspaper reports on court hearings in Wagga, Deniliquin and Albury.

[90] *P.T.*, 1 December 1859.

[91] *B.P.*, 28 March, 25 April 1857.

[92] 20 January 1860.

[93] *A.B.*, 24 October 1860.

[94] Peppin Diary, 7 July.

[95] *Opals and Agates*, p. 59.

[96] *Journal*, pp. 346-7, 390-1.

[97] C. Rolleston, Auditor-General N.S.W., in *Transactions of the Royal Society of New South Wales*, 1870, p. 50. See also 'Criminal Statistics of N.S.W., 1860-73', ibid., 1874, pp. 19-28.

[98] *A.B.*, 17 October 1860.

[99] *B.P.*, 21 March 1857.

[1] Ibid.

[2] *P.T.*, 8 June 1860; *A.B.*, 9 November 1860.

[3] E.g., *P.T.*, 25 August 1859, 20 April 1860, 26 July 1861.

[4] *P.T.*, and *A.B.*, 1859-61, various issues.

[5] *A.B.*, 30 January 1861.

[6] 28 July 1860.

[7] Kennedy papers, MS., draft C, p. 16.

[8] *P.T.*, 27 July 1860. Brief reference to the Melbourne side of this story occurs in K. S. Inglis, *Hospital and Community*, pp. 21, 153-4.

[9] Sources for South Deniliquin hospital details: *P.T.*, 15, 22 September, 6 and 20 October 1859, 25 May, 27 July, 21 September. 1860.

[10] Sources for Deniliquin Working Men's Hospital: *P.T.*, 1 January, 26 February, 26 May, 14 July, 24

November, 1 December 1859, 13 January, 15 June, 21 September 1860, 22 March 1861.
[11] *E.g., P.T.,* 25 May 1860.
[12] *P.T.,* 27 April, 15 and 25 May 1860.
[13] *P.T.,* 25 August 1859.
[14] *E.g., P.T.,* 22 September 1859; *W.E.,* 31 October 1862.
[15] *P.T.,* 9 June, 25 August 1859; Kennedy papers, MS., draft C, p. 44; N. Bartley, op. cit., p. 60 and other contemporary sources.
[16] E.g., letter in *P.T.,* 21 July 1859.
[17] *P.T.,* 8 February 1861.
[18] Letter to the Editor, *P.T.,* 21 July 1859.
[19] *W.E.,* 30 October 1858; *A.B.,* 11 August 1860. Indecent assault and rape charges were relatively rare. *A.B.,* 17 October 1860. One 'kept woman' seeking to double her security, was faced by 'two lords of creation' on one day. *A.B.,* 11 August 1860. Only once in several years reporting was an abduction case recorded, that of a fifteen-year-old girl—a common enough age for marriage. *W.E.,* 19 February 1859.
[20] *P.T.,* 27 April 1860.
[21] *P.T.,* 27 January 1860.
[22] *P.T.,* 20 January 1860, 1 February 1861.
[23] 5 January 1861.
[24] 22 September 1860.
[25] *A.B.,* 27 January 1860, 24 August 1861; *W.E.,* 26 February 1859; *P.T.,* 30 March 1860. Kennedy papers, MS., draft C, p. 20a.
[26] *A.B.,* 25 October 1856.
[27] W. A. Bayley, op. cit., p. 61. This number included many German children.
[28] *A.B.,* 22 August 1860.
[29] *W.E.,* 4 December 1858, 5 March 1859.
[30] Rusden diary, quoted in A. G. Austin, *Australian Education 1788-1900,* p. 52. The first inspectorial report was republished in *W.E.,* 31 October 1862.
[31] See A. G. Austin, op. cit., pp. 47-63.
[32] *A.B.,* 11 and 15 May 1861.
[33] *P.T.,* 30 March, 1 June, 6 and 27 July, 14 September 1860. Key became manager of the Royal for

Taylor and presently committed suicide.
[34] *P.T.,* 25 January 1861.
[35] *B.P.,* 19 December 1857. tricts you can go fifty miles in any direction without meeting anything in the shape of a school house. In Victoria this is not the case' (*A.B.,* 5 January 1861).
[36] J. Phillips, op. cit., pp. 80-2.
[37] Biographical details, letters, etc. are available in E. Strickland, *The Australian Pastor: A Record of the Remarkable Changes in Mind and Outward Estate of H. Elliott* and *B.P.,* 17 April 1858.
[38] *B.P.,* 19 December 1857.
[39] E. Strickland, op. cit., p. 70.
[40] *Journal,* pp. 292-3, 370, 379, 385.
[41] Ibid., pp. 338, 342, 344, 406-7.
[42] Ibid., p. 406.
[43] Ibid., pp. 307, 311, 314-5.
[44] Ibid., p. 292.
[45] Ibid., pp. 307-9.
[46] Ibid., p. 310.
[47] Ibid., pp. 339, 345-8, 397.
[48] Ibid., pp. 355-7, 361, 354, 401-2.
[49] Ibid., p. 391. Westwood wrote an indignant letter about this to the *Pastoral Times,* 23 January 1864. It was published without comment.
[50] J. J. Westwood, *Journal,* pp. 312, 315, 337-8, 341, 350, 352, 357-8, 399, 401, 417-9.
[51] Ibid., pp. 359-60.
[52] Ibid., p. 336.
[53] J. Steele, 'Early Days of Picton', *J.R.A.H.S.,* vol. 1 (1901-6), p. 167.
[54] For dates of erection and costs, see J. Jervis, op. cit., pp. 86-90.
[55] *A.B.,* 21 July 1860. Letter from 'a true Catholic' replying to 'a Catholic'.
[56] *A.B.,* 28 July, 3 October, 30 November 1860; *W.E.,* 25 December 1858; A. Andrews, op. cit., p. 76. Cf. G. Nader, *Australia's Colonial Culture,* pp. 111-52. Though mainly concerned with the Sydney Mechanics' Institute, Nadel outlines the aims and history of that body in Australia, and includes an appendix on Mechanics' Institutes in Great Britain (pp. 285-7).
[57] *A.B.,* 21 July 1860.
[58] *A.B.,* 11 May 1861; *B.P.,* May 1857; *W.E.,* 19 February, 2 and

23 July 1859. Further support might be gained, it was thought, and others attracted to the benefits of the 'very rudiments of education' if the title were changed to the 'Young men's improvement society. *A.B.*, 16 January 1861.
[59] 2 July 1859.
[60] *A.B.*, 21 and 28 July 1860; *W.E.*, 8 October 1938. Dates of formation of Mechanics' Institutes: Albury, 1858 (*A.B.*, 16 January 1861); Wagga, 1859 (*W.E.*, 2 July 1859); Deniliquin, attempts 1859, 1860 (*P.T.*, 24 November 1859, 6 March 1861) finally successful 1864 (J. Jervis, op. cit., p. 128).
[61] *A.B.*, 28 July 1860.
[62] *A.B.*, 30 March, 3 July 1861.
[63] E.g., *B.P.*, 4 October 1856, 21 July, 29 August 1860; *W.E.*, 31 October 1862; *A.B.*, 4 September 1861. Details of Lodges: *A.B.*, 28 July, 15 August 1860; *P.T.*, 16 June, 21 July 1859; *W.E.*, 25 December 1858, 31 October 1862.
[64] *W.E.*, 8 January 1859; *P.T.*, 29 December 1859.
[65] *W.E.*, 15 January 1859.
[66] *A.B.*, 2 January, 18 December 1861; *W.E.*, 5 March 1859.
[67] *W.E.*, 19 and 26 February 1859.
[68] *W.E.*, 5 March, 9 July 1859, 31 October 1862; *P.T.*, 25 August 1859.
[69] A. Andrews, op. cit., p. 95.
[70] *A.B.*, 9 February 1861. See also *A.B.*, 1 and 15 August 1860, 16 January, 13 and 16 February 1861, and *B.P.*, 4 October 1856, a man with £70 on his person 'taken while tossing in the street.'
[71] *P.T.*, 29 September 1859.
[72] Peppin Diary. See also J. J. Westwood's *Journal* for references to 'Chestnut' and 'Browny'.
[73] 28 September 1860.
[74] Various references, *A.B.*, *W.E.*, *P.T.*, 1859-61.
[75] *A.B.*, 5 and 9 January 1861.
[76] Ibid.; *P.T.*, 30 March 1860.
[77] *B.P.*, 21 March 1857.
[78] *B.P.*, 21 and 28 February, 1857.
[79] *P.T.*, 30 June 1859.
[80] *B.P.*, 28 February 1857.
[81] *P.T.*, 22 December 1859, 4 May 1860; *A.B.*, 4 May, 4 July, 26

December 1860, 17 August, 28 December 1861.
[82] 21 September, 26 October, 2 and 16 November 1860.

3 MASTERS AND SERVANTS

[1] *V. & P.* (L.A. N.S.W.), 1865-6, vol. 1, pp. 666-7.
[2] *P.T.*, 4 August 1859.
[3] *P.T.*, 14 July 1859.
[4] Kennedy papers, MS., draft C, pp. 1-69.
[5] Ibid.
[6] Miscellaneous references including, for Albury families, A. Andrews, *The First Settlement of the Upper Murray.*
[7] *P.T.*, 28 December 1860, 8 August 1890.
[8] Tombstone inscriptions in Deniliquin cemetery.
[9] *H.S.*, 3 October 1891.
[10] S. Mossman and T. Banister, *Australia Visited and Revisited*, p. 70; N. Bartley, *Opals and Agates; B.P.*, 28 February 1857; *H.S.*, 3 October 1891; C. S. Ross, 'Some of the Murray Pioneers and Their Services to the State', *V.H.M.*, vol. 3, p. 81; R. B. Ronald, *The Riverina, People and Properties;* A. Andrews, op. cit., p. 68 and miscellaneous newspaper references.
[11] *N.S.W. G.G.*, run lists; A. Andrews, op. cit., pp. 149-81 and newspaper references.
[12] A. Andrews, op. cit., pp. 149-81; notes great difficulty in tracing changes in ownership of runs around Albury, even with family records available.
[13] Willurah station records.
[14] *N.S.W. G.G.*, and newspaper sources.
[15] Kennedy papers, MS., draft C, p. 60.
[16] R. B. Ronald, op. cit., pp. 18-19, cites the Hobler, Crisp, Tyson and Darchy families as examples.
[17] C. K. Chapman, 'Swan Hill—Past and Present', *V.H.M.*, vol. 23, no. 1 (1950-1), p. 5.
[18] C. S. Ross, op. cit., p. 75.
[19] See pp. 52-3.
[20] C. M. Lloyd of Yamma station

often had visitors while still living in a one-roomed hut with his wife in the early sixties. 'After tea they would sit around the fire yarning until bed time, when he would show them the front door saying, "Gentlemen, there is your bedroom".' The visitors would camp out under a tree. J. J. Baylis, 'The Murrumbidgee and Wagga Wagga', J.R.A.H.S., vol. 13 (1927), p. 302.
[21] R. Henty, *Australiana or My Early Life*, pp. 162-8.
[22] Ibid., p. 167.
[23] *P.T.*, 22 December 1859.
[24] Kennedy papers, MS., draft C, p. 23.
[25] Ibid., pp. 46-7.
[26] Ibid., pp. 56-7.
[27] Ibid., draft D, p. 91. Cf. Amy Cruse, *The Victorians and Their Books*. See also N. Bartley, *Opals and Agates*, p. 59.
[28] See for example, R. Henty, op. cit., p. 155.
[29] *P.T.*, 8 February 1861; R. B. Ronald, op. cit., p. 26; J. Phillips, Reminiscences, pp. 143-6 (with illustration of a 'kangaroo drive'); Peppin Diary, 17 August.
[30] Kennedy papers, MS., draft C, p. 52. Cf. the case of one Pyman *A.B.*, 23 January 1861, on two charges of sly-grog selling and hawking, described as 'one of those men, the pest of the stations, going from one to another on the pretext of selling useful articles but in reality supplying the men with grog.'
[31] Various newspaper references 1859-61.
[32] *P.T.*, 25 May, 1 June 1860.
[33] The 'Victorian invasion', in its 'sinister' connotation, was a product of later decades. See chapters 5 and 7.
[34] R. Henty, op. cit., p. 155.
[35] *P.T.*, 27 October 1859.
[36] The expression occurs frequently in the local press. An Albury photographer advertised a 'View of Albury' to 'send to friends at home' (*A.B.*, 22 September 1860), while occasions like Christmas provoked a spate of activities and writing nostalgic with reminiscences of 'home'. E.g., see *A.B.*, 26 December 1860, 24 December 1861.
[37] *P.T.*, 1859-61.
[38] E. Strickland, *The Australian Pastor*, p. 63.
[39] N. Bartley, op. cit., p. 61.
[40] Mossman and Banister, op. cit., p. 84.
[41] E.g., *P.T.*, 16 August 1861; 28 July 1859.
[42] *P.T.*, 30 August 1861. Samuel Smiles's *Self Help* was published in 1859. Newspaper editorials frequently echo its sentiments.
[43] 25 August 1859, 26 March 1864 and numerous other references.
[44] 27 February 1869. Taylor sued D. G. Jones, the editor, for libel, but lost.
[45] S. Mossman and T. Banister, op. cit., p. 79. Cf. N. Bartley, op. cit., p. 73 and *P.T.*, 10 November 1859, visit of Augustus Morris to the Deniliquin Working Men's Hospital.
[46] Ibid.
[47] *P.T.*, 7 July, 15 September 1859, 24 November 1860.
[48] *W.E.*, 31 October 1862.
[49] Ibid.
[50] *P.T.*, 9 January 1864.
[51] A. Andrews, op. cit., p. 72. The reference is to Commissioner of Crown Lands Henry Bingham.
[52] *W.E.*, 31 October 1862.
[53] *B.P.*, 15 November 1856.
[54] 8 October 1938.
[55] *Journal*, p. 418.
[56] *A.B.*, 9 February 1861.
[57] *W.E.*, 19 February, 9 April 1859.
[58] Steve Jicknis, 'the Swede', killed by falling timber while insisting on returning for further goods.
[59] *P.T.*, 26 May 1859.
[60] For a discussion in detail see P. Loveday and A. W. Martin, *Parliament, Factions and Parties*, chapters 1 and 2.
[61] A. W. Martin and P. Wardle, *Members of the Legislative Assembly of New South Wales 1856-1901*, p. 142.
[62] *W.E.*, 28 May 1859.
[63] *P.T.*, 9 June 1859.
[64] Ibid.
[65] *W.E.*, 13 August 1859; *P.T.*, 26 May, 14 July 1859.
[66] Martin and Wardle, op. cit., p. 155.

[67] All details in the paragraph concerning Hay's 1859 election are from *P.T.*, 16 June 1859.
[68] *P.T.*, 23 June 1859.
[69] Ibid.
[70] *P.T.*, 7 December 1860.
[71] Willoughby's business was later extended to include well sinking and contracting.
[72] *P.T.*, 7 December 1860.
[73] 16 June 1859.
[74] Martin and Wardle, op. cit., p. 6.
[75] 'The Coming Men', by Hugh K. Walker. *W.E.*, 18 June 1859.
[76] *P.T.*, 30 June 1859.
[77] Ibid.
[78] *P.T.*, 30 June 1859.
[79] *P.T.*, 14 July 1859.
[80] Hugh K. Walker, 'A Radical Paean'; *W.E.*, 9 July 1859.
[81] For details see P. Loveday and A. W. Martin, op. cit.
[82] 14 July 1860.
[83] *A.B.*, 5 December 1860.
[84] *A.B.*, 12 December 1860.
[85] *A.B.*, 28 November 1860.
[86] *A.B.*, 5 December 1860.
[87] 15 December 1860.
[88] 12 January 1861.
[89] An Act to Amend the Electoral Law, 22 Vic., no. 20, 24 November 1858.
[90] *N.S.W. Statistical Register*, 1859-62; *N.S.W. Census*, 1861.

4 UNLOCK THE LANDS

[1] Except where particular references are given, the arguments here cited are summarized from a large number of editorials, articles and letters in the *Pastoral Times*, Deniliquin; *The Albury Banner* and *The Border Post*, Albury; and the *Wagga Express*. E.g., *A.B.*, 1, 29 September 1860, 16 January, 9 February, 9 October 1861; *B.P.*, 1 November 1856; *P.T.*, 4 and 25 August 1859, 11 May, 26 October 1860; *W.E.*, 20 November 1858, 23 and 30 April, 7 and 21 May 1859.
[2] *P.T.*, 4 August 1859 cites Caroline Chisholm and her views.
[3] *A.B.*, 29 September 1860.
[4] *P.T.*, 4 August 1859.
[5] 23 April 1859. One of a series of articles entitled 'The Land Clamour'.
[6] Ibid.
[7] Ibid.
[8] *P.T.*, 4 August 1859.
[9] *W.E.*, 30 April 1859. 'The Land Clamour', II.
[10] *W.E.*, 7 May 1859.
[11] 23 April 1859. 'The Land Clamour', I.
[12] *W.E.*, 21 May 1859.
[13] 26 October 1860.
[14] Gipps to Stanley, 3 April 1844, in *H.R.A.*, I, xxiii, 510.
[15] J. Phillips, *Reminiscences*, pp. 60-1.
[16] Imperial Act of 1846 (9 & 10 Vic. c. 104) Orders-in-Council, 9 May 1847, II, 1. For details and discussion see C. J. King, *An Outline of Closer Settlement in New South Wales*, pp. 45-60; K. Buckley's two articles 'Gipps and the Graziers of New South Wales', in J. J. Eastwood and F. B. Smith (eds), *Historical Studies: Selected Articles. First Series*.
[17] *W.E.*, 8 October 1938, p. 13; J. J. Baylis, 'The Murrumbidgee and Wagga Wagga', *J.R.A.H.S.*, vol. 13 (1927), p. 303. See also *W.E.*, 20 November 1858.
[18] N. Bartley, *Opals and Agates*, p. 62.
[19] 18 and 30 January.
[20] Mossman and Banister, *Australia Visited and Revisited*, p. 76.
[21] *S.M.H.*, 30 November 1858.
[22] Lands Department plans and maps transferred to N.S.W. Archives.
[23] *B.P.*, 20 November 1856. 'Statistics of districts bordering on the Murray', and *South Australian Register*'s report of Governor McDonnell's visit.
[24] A. Andrews, 'The First Settlement of the North-East of Victoria', *V.H.M.*, vol. 5, p. 31; J. J. Baylis, op. cit., p. 255.
[25] *P.T.*, 18 January 1861. Farewell speech of H. S. Lewes of Moira on leaving Deniliquin for England.
[26] Peppin Diary, January-June, December.
[27] *A.B.*, 17 August 1861. See also *A.B.*, 2 February 1861. Albury £8 10s and £12, Deniliquin £8 and £12.
[28] Details from *P.T.*, 14 July, 8 December 1859, 18 May, 6 and 27 July 1860.
[29] *A.B.*, 22 June 1861.

[30] *P.T.*, 30 June 1859, 17 February 1860; *A.B.*, 22 August 1860; *P.T.*, 5 October 1860, 8 February, 28 June 1861; *A.B.*, 8 February, 1 June 1861.

[31] *P.T.*, 30 June 1859.

[32] Ibid. The claim that there was something 'radically wrong' in the Survey Department was also supported in Albury; see *A.B.*, 18 July 1860.

[33] *P.T.*, 23 June 1859.

[34] *P.T.*, 20 October 1859.

[35] E.g., *P.T.*, 11 May 1860.

[36] W. Howitt, *Land, Labour, and Gold*, vol. 2, pp. 245-8; *P.T.*, 25 August 1859.

[37] *P.T.*, 21 July 1859, citing *N.S.W. G.G.*

[38] *P.T.*, 23 June 1859.

[39] Details of Carter's case from *P.T.*, 8 December 1859, 18 May, 6, 27 July 1860.

[40] *P.T.*, 23 June 1859.

[41] 13 February 1861.

[42] *B.P.*, 4 October 1856, 17 January 1857. For villages see also parish maps and *P.T.*, 25 August 1859.

[43] *A.B.*, 12 September, 31 October 1860. See also 23 January, 6 February, 1, 22, 29 June 1861, and parish maps.

[44] Property owners appealed unanimously against early assessments of rates, which varied from 2s 6d per acre for unimproved country land to 35s. See *A.B.*, 6 April 1861; further information on acreages cropped is taken from scores of advertisements of farms for sale or to let in *A.B.*, *B.P.*, *W.E.*, 1856-61.

[45] *P.T.*, 25 August 1859.

[46] *P.T.*, 24 May 1861.

[47] C.S. Ross, 'Some of the Murray Pioneers and their services to the state', *V.H.M.*, vol. 3 (1913), p. 70; opinion of E. P. S. Sturt, Crown Lands Commissioner (and brother of explorer Charles Sturt). For surveyors' opinions see J. Jervis, op. cit., p. 7, and squatters' opinions, *P.T.*, 20 September 1861.

[48] Cf. *P.T.*, 24 February 1860.

[49] *B.P.*, 13 December 1856; *P.T.*, 24 November 1859, 3 February 1860. For advantages, experiments and success with *Sorghum saccharatum* see *W.E.*, 6 November 1858; *P.T.*,

7 July 1859, 20 and 27 January, 16 March 1860. For Cape barley see *P.T.*, 4 August 1859.

[50] See reports of Albury land sales in *B.P.* and *A.B.*, 1859-61.

[51] Ibid.

[52] Peppin Diary; newspaper advertisements 1856-61.

[53] Details of the activities of these 'capitalist farmers' may be gleaned from advertisements and other references in the Albury and Wagga newspapers for the period.

[54] *B.P.*, 3 January, 7 February 1857.

[55] Denison, *B.P.*, 14 March 1857; Daniels, *B.P.*, 7 December 1861.

[56] *A.B.*, 3 October 1860; *W.E.*, 15 January 1859; *P.T.*, 9 June 1859, 13 November 1860.

[57] 13 August 1859.

[58] *P.T.*, 25 August 1859.

[59] Ibid.

[60] *W.E.*, 13 August 1859.

[61] *A.B.*, 29 May 1861; J. J. Baylis, op. cit., p. 255.

[62] *A.B.*, 16 March, 15 and 25 May 1861.

[63] *P.T.*, 29 June 1860.

[64] Mossman and Banister, op. cit., p. 87.

[65] W. Howitt, op. cit., cited in *B.P.*, 4 October 1856.

[66] *B.P.*, 20 December 1856.

[67] *A.B.*, 7 December 1861.

[68] *B.P.*, 11 October 1856. See also E. Dunsdorfs, *The Australian Wheat Growing Industry*, table, p. 150.

[69] *B.P.*, 24 January 1857.

[70] See various newspaper articles and advertisements 1856-61.

[71] *P.T.*, 19 October 1860.

[72] *W.E.*, 30 October, 11 December 1858, 5 March 1859. Although there is no evidence that it was used, 'T. C. Riddle's Superphosphate of Lime,' manufactured by him at Geelong'— and produced by the action of sulphuric acid on bones—was also advertised in Wagga. *W.E.*, 5 February 1859.

[73] *B.P.*, 21 March 1857; *W.E.*, 5 March 1859; *A.B.*, 23 February 1861.

[74] J. Chandler, *Forty Years in the Wilderness*, cited by A. J. Hopton in 'John Chandler, Goldfields Carrier', *V.H.M.*, vol. 24 (1952), p. 92.

[75] 15 November 1856.

[76] *A.B.*, 8 September 1860. Payne *v.* Kelly.

[77] *A.B.*, 16, 23 November 1861; J. Jervis, op. cit., p. 20.

[78] *B.P.*, 15, 22 November 1856, 7 March 1857; *P.T.*, 11 October 1861; *A.B.*, 7 December 1861.

[79] *A.B.*, 21 December 1861.

[80] *A.B.*, 11 August, 12 September 1860. Insolvencies occurred at Piney Range, on the Billabong, over thirty miles from Albury.

[81] *A.B.*, 11 December 1861.

[82] Full details of Members' statements, Legislative Assembly Debates, Robertson's speeches, and the text of the Bills and Acts, together with local comment, appeared in the local press throughout the period. E.g., *A.B.*, 17 October 1860, 9 February, 30 October 1861; *P.T.*, 16 June, 13 October, 3 November 1859, 18 May, 13 July 1860, 6, 15 February 1861.

[83] For a brief summary of the passing of the Acts see P. Loveday and A. W. Martin, *Parliament, Factions and Parties*, pp. 32-3. See also D. W. A. Baker, 'The Origins of Robertson's Land Acts', in J. J. Eastwood and F. B. Smith (eds), *Historical Studies: Selected Articles. First Series.*

[84] Progress report, Select Committee on Reserves. *V. & P.* (L.A. N.S.W.), 1865-6, vol. 3, p. 77. See also *P.T.*, 6 January 1866 for discussion of the use made of reserves.

[85] *V. & P.* (L.A. N.S.W.), 1865-6, vol. 3, p. 100.

[86] *V. & P.* (L.A. N.S.W.), 1865-6, vol. 3, pp. 89-100, 169, Appendix C and maps.

[87] 6 January 1866.

[88] *V. & P.* (L.A. N.S.W.), 1872, p. 154.

[89] Ibid, 1865-6, vol. 3, p. 143; *P.T.*, 5 March 1864.

[90] *S.M.H.*, 12, 14 May 1858; *P.T.*, 29 December 1859, 16 September 1865; *V. & P.* (L.A. N.S.W.), 1858, vol. 1, p. 1021. Petition: *V. & P.* (L.A. N.S.W.), 1863-4, p. 669.

[91] *P.T.*, 15 November, 6 December, 1862, 26 December 1863; Melbourne *Argus*, 7 January 1864. The Separation Fund amounted to £10,000, of which one squatter

contributed £2,000. *P.T.*, 27 September 1861, 7 May 1864.

[92] *V. & P.*, (L.A. N.S.W.), 1865-6, vol. 3, p. 642; *P.T.*, 17 January 1863.

[93] *P.T.*, 5 September 1865, 22 December 1866. The delegates, four in number, apart from 'Mr Corbett as secretary' (added as an afterthought), included squatters F. A. Gwynne, W. A. Brodribb and Patrick Brougham. For the Colonial Secretary's reply to the petition see *V.& P.* (L.A. N.S.W.), 1863-4, vol. 2, p. 690. Fuller treatment of the separation movement during this period is given in J. Craig, 'The Riverina Separation Movement, 1858-1867' (unpublished B.A. thesis, University of Adelaide, 1963).

[94] Conditional Purchase Registers, Wagga and Albury 1862-6. E.g., T. H. Mate selected on his Tarcutta run, Devlin on Ganmain run, etc.

[95] *P.T.*, 6 January 1866, noted that despite the absence of trees and stones in the Riverina, many preferred Victoria's 2s per acre per annum 'rent' to the New South Wales system of 5s per acre deposit.

[96] *N.S.W. Statistical Register.*

[97] *P.T.*, 6 January 1866.

5 SMASH THE CROOK AND SPEED THE PLOUGH

[1] *History of Australian Land Settlement 1788-1920*, pp. 222-32.

[2] Ibid., p. 230.

[3] See for example, E. Shann, *An Economic History of Australia*, pp. 199-211 (first published 1930); C. M. H. Clark, *Select Documents in Australian History 1851-1900*, pp. 126-34; R. A. Gollan, *Radical and Working Class Politics*, pp. 44-7; and more recently Manning Clark, *A Short History of Australia*, p. 135.

[4] E.g., Select Committee on Reserves, *V. & P.* (L.A. N.S.W.), 1865-6, vol. 3, p. 77; Select Committee on the Administration of the Land Laws, *V. & P.* (L.A. N.S.W.), 1872, vol. 2, pp. 147-97.

[5] Ibid., 1865-6, vol. 3, p. 77.

6 Ibid., 1872, vol. 2, pp. 190-1.
7 Ibid.
8 Ibid.
9 Ibid., p. 158, Q. 182-3.
10 Ibid., p. 903.
11 Ibid., p. 940, Q. 787.
12 Ibid., 1873-4, vol. 3, p. 940, Q. 787-90 and 1872, vol. 2, p. 153, Q. 38.
13 *V. & P.* (L.A. N.S.W.), 1873-4, vol. 3, p. 950; 1872, vol. 2, pp. 155, 161.
14 *V. & P.* (L.A. N.S.W.), 1872, vol. 2, pp. 913-14.
15 Ibid., pp. 981-4.
16 Ibid., pp. 923, 925, 926, 943-4, 951. Neither Landale nor Broughton, the land agent, both of whom appeared before the committee, made a convincing defence of this action.
17 Ibid., p. 947. In explanation of this the *Pastoral Times* stated that the application was accompanied by samples of anti-squatter pamphlets, published in Deniliquin, which ridiculed 'straight Robert' and generally indicated the difficulties pastoralists near Deniliquin were having in protecting their runs.
18 Ibid., pp. 925, 927, 930-1.
19 Ibid., pp. 930-1, 937, 951, 959.
20 Ibid., p. 914.
21 Ibid., p. 943.
22 Ibid., p. 973.
23 Ibid., p. 930. See also petition of the Murray District Free Selectors' Association to Premier Parkes in *S.M.H.*, 4 September 1874, reprinted in *P.T.*, 19 September 1874.
24 *V. & P.* (L.A. N.S.W.), 1873-4, vol. 3, pp. 904, 933, 938.
25 Conditional Purchase Register, Albury, 1874. George and Frederick Peppin similarly took six orders each in 1873. *V. & P.* (L.A. N.S.W.), 1873-4, vol. 3, p. 927.
26 Ibid., 1883, vol. 2, p. 95.
27 Ibid., 1873-4, vol. 3, pp. 891-1002, Third progress report. The committee originally included John Robertson, author of the Acts.
28 *V. & P.* (L.A. Vic.), 1862-3, vol. 2, pp. 1091-152.
29 A detailed history of this railway appears in *P.T.*, 5 July 1876.

30 E.g., C. Robinson, *New South Wales, the Oldest and Richest of the Australian Colonies.*
31 *V. & P.* (L.A. N.S.W.), 1873-4, vol. 3, pp. 939, 958, 983. E.g., p. 983, Q. 1611, 'so that not only did we not sell our land but we also lost a valuable class of settlers to increase our population'.
32 Ibid., p. 942.
33 Ibid., 1873-4, vol. 3, pp. 894-9.
34 Ibid., pp. 902, 930-3, 941, 961, 971.
35 Ibid., p. 974.
36 Ibid., pp. 915, 959.
37 Ibid., p. 958.
38 Ibid., pp. 978, 962.
39 Ibid., pp. 940, 973.
40 Ibid., p. 984, Q. 1640. 'You do not mean to say that the Crown lessee encloses these reserves?'
41 Ibid., p. 927.
42 Ibid., pp. 927, 943, 946.
43 Ibid., pp. 948-9.
44 Ibid., p. 955.
45 Ibid., p. 929.
46 Ibid., p. 945.
47 Ibid., p. 979.
48 Ibid., p. 972.
49 Ibid., pp. 902, 934, 956, 972, 986-7.
50 *R.G.*, 19 November 1873. *V. & P.* (L.A. N.S.W.), 1873-4, vol. 3, p. 986.
51 Mate *v.* Nugent, 8 N.S.W. Supreme Court Reports, p. 246, and Chisholm *v.* Macauley, 7 ibid., pp. 314, 343; *V. & P.* (L.A. N.S.W.), 1875, vol. 3, pp. 367-78.
52 *P.T.*, 14 October 1876.
53 Except where a specific reference is given, details in Joachim *v.* O'Shanassy are taken from the correspondence on the case in *V. & P.* (L.A. N.S.W.), 1873-4, vol. 3, pp. 847-68; the reports and comments in *P.T.*, 16 August, 4 October 1873, 22 January, 8 April, 13 May, 14 October 1876; and the compilation from the *Riverine Herald* (Echuca) and other sources in A. Morris, *Rich River.*
54 See for example, the comments of William Hay, M.L.A. for Murray, in *V. & P.* (L.A. N.S.W.), 1873-4, vol. 3, pp. 901-5.
55 Ibid., pp. 942, 954, 961.

[56] *P.T.*, 16 August, 4 October 1873; *V. & P.* (L.A. N.S.W.), 1873-4, vol. 3, p. 942.

[57] *V. & P.* (L.A. N.S.W.), 1873-4, vol. 3, p. 852.

[58] A. Morris, op. cit., p. 88.

[59] *V. & P.* (L.A. N.S.W.), 1873-4, vol. 3, p. 983.

[60] *R.G.*, 28 January 1874. The *Age* article is reprinted in the same issue.

[61] *R.G.*, 28 February 1874 quoting the *Riverine Herald*. The fine amounted to 10s with 3s 6d costs.

[62] *R.G.*, 29 April 1874.

[63] *V. & P.* (L.A. N.S.W.), 1875, vol. 3, pp. 367-78. The appeal to the Privy Council took place despite serious doubts of the Attorney-General as to the ability of Her Majesty's Most Honorable Privy Councillors to treat matters of Colonial Law (p. 372).

[64] See, for example, *R.G.*, 11 March 1874.

[65] Data used here and in the following paragraph has been compiled from Conditional Purchase Registers in the land offices or court-houses in Wagga, Albury and Deniliquin.

[66] E.g., Petition of selectors favouring family selection, from the Albury and Bowna district. *V. & P.* (L.A. N.S.W.), 1875, vol. 3, pp. 347-8. Cf. Petition of squatters asking that selection by minors be disallowed. *V. & P.* (L.A. N.S.W.), 1873-4, vol. 3, p. 1,000.

[67] *P.T.*, 8 April 1876, 13 May 1876.

[68] See petition against this practice to Governor Sir Hercules Robinson, on his visit to Deniliquin, from the Murray District Selectors' Association. *P.T.*, 2 December 1876.

[69] *W.A.*, 26 June 1878. Population of Urana: 1871, 113; 1881, 398; 1891, 397; 1901, 301. *N.S.W. Censuses.*

[70] *P.T.*, 7 October 1876. Jindera remained too small to be recorded separately until 1891 when its population was given as 371. *N.S.W. Census.*

[71] *S.M.H.*, reprinted in *P.T.*, 28 August 1877; *V. & P.* (L.A. N.S.W.), 1883, vol. 2, p. 153.

[72] *P.T.*, 12 August 1876. The Deniliquin association had formed in November 1873. See *V. & P.* (L.A. N.S.W.), 1873-4, vol. 3, p. 941.

[73] *P.T.*, 22 July 1876. *V. & P.* (L.A. N.S.W.), 1876-7, vol. 3, p. 1287.

[74] *V. & P.* (L.A. N.S.W.), 1875-6, vol. 3, pp. 510, 514. Alienated land on the Yanko reserve, 1858-76: auction, 7,286 acres; pre-emption, 4,338; improved, 4,142; conditional purchase, 677; total, 16,444 acres. Ibid., p. 1285.

[75] Ibid., p. 1283.

[76] *P.T.*, 22 July 1876.

[77] Ibid.

[78] See their petition in *V. & P.* (L.A. N.S.W.), 1875-6, vol. 3, pp. 559-60.

[79] *P.T.*, 16 September, 14 and 21 October 1876. Farnell had the soil analysed for the government. It was stated not to have the necessary ingredients for grain-growing and that if it had, the rainfall would have been inadequate. Others pointed out that it was 'no better than the general run of saltbush soils.' Correspondence relating to the Yanko reserve is in *V. & P.* (L.A. N.S.W.), 1875-6, vol. 3, pp. 489-568.

[80] Ibid.

[81] Ibid., p. 565.

[82] Ibid.

[83] Ibid., p. 566.

[84] Ibid.

[85] See *P.T.*, 4 November, 2 December 1876, etc., for weekly receipts from land offices at Urana, Hay and other towns.

[86] *P.T.*, 8 and 15 January, 12 February 1876, gives reports of enquiries in the Deniliquin Land Enquiry Court.

[87] *P.T.*, 12 August 1876.

[88] *S.M.H.*, 30 October 1877; *W.A.*, 8 June, 1878; *P.T.*, 17 February and 7 April 1883, 17 October 1891.

[89] *P.T.*, 21 April 1883.

[90] *W.A.*, 9 February, 26 June 1878.

[91] See *W.A.*, 2 February, 25 May, 26 June 1878. For an outline of the political situation which led to Farnell's Bill and its defeat, and the impact of selector groups on the faction system, see P. Loveday and A. W. Martin, *Parliament, Factions and Parties*, pp. 101-3.

[92] *Annual Report of the Department of Lands*, 1880, 1881.

[93] A brief though fairly adequate summary of related Bills and legislation may be found in C. J. King, *An Outline of Closer Settlement in New South Wales*. He subscribes to the belief that the Morris and Ranken report was 'an able analysis'.

[94] 20 January, 1883.

[95] *V. & P.* (L.A. N.S.W.), 1883, vol. 2, pp. 77-248, Report of Inquiry into the State of the Public Lands and the Operation of the Land Laws.

[96] Ibid., p. 109.

[97] Ibid., p. 91.

[98] Ibid., pp. 83, 90-2, 95, 121.

[99] Ibid., p. 89.

[1] Ibid., p. 118.

[2] Ibid., p. 95.

[3] Ibid., p. 83.

[4] Ibid., p. 91.

[5] Ibid., pp. 78, 105, 107, 118.

[6] *V. & P.* (L.A. N.S.W.), 1883, vol. 2, p. 78.

[7] Ibid., p. 93.

[8] *V. & P.* (L.A. N.S.W.), 1883, vol. 2, p. 78.

[9] Ibid., pp. 93, 122-3.

[10] Ibid., p. 108.

[11] Annual Stock Returns, reprinted in *P.T.*, 10 February 1883; see also *Parl. Deb.* (L.A. N.S.W.), 1883, vol. 8, p. 507.

[12] *V. & P.* (L.A. N.S.W.), 1883, vol. 2, p. 95.

[13] *P.T.*, 30 June 1866, 28 September 1867, 12 February 1876; *V. & P.* (L.A. N.S.W.) 1873-4, vol. 3, p. 972.

[14] *R.G.*, 12 November 1873; *V. & P.* (L.A. N.S.W.), 1883, vol. 2, p. 122.

[15] *Wealth and Progress of New South Wales 1888-1889*, p. 242.

[16] A summary of the process is given in *P.T.*, 13 January, 12, 19, 26 May, 20 October and 3 November 1883. See also C. J. King, op. cit., pp. 91-9.

[17] Some discussion of this is included in the chapters which follow.

[18] For summaries of the provisions of the 1884 Act (48 Vic., no. 18), see C. J. King, op. cit., pp. 97-105 and T. A. Coghlan, op. cit., pp. 216-19.

[19] 17 June 1887.

[20] *P.T.*, 27 January 1883.

[21] For Copeland's reply to such charges see *Parl. Deb.* (L.A.

N.S.W.), 1887, vol. 25, pp. 162-5, 521-33.

[22] For summary see C. J. King, op. cit., pp. 97-105, and T. A. Coghlan, op. cit., pp. 216-19.

6   THE YEOMAN FARMER

[1] See chapter 7, Figure 8 and Tables 14-16.

[2] E. Dunsdorfs, *The Australian Wheat Growing Industry*, p. 165.

[3] See soil map, Figure 4.

[4] For further details see Railway Differential Rates (Return to an Order) in *V. & P.* (L.A. N.S.W.), 1888-9, vol. 2, p. 805-90.

[5] The economic changes for the industry as a whole are covered in E. Dunsdorfs, op. cit., pp. 114-86.

[6] For examples see *P.T.*, 7 July 1883, 10 March 1883; *W.A.*, 2 April, 10 December 1891.

[7] *W.A.*, 24 February 1891.

[8] See advertisements and descriptions in *W.A.*, 1891. E.g., Thurroma Park near Jerilderie, *W.A.*, 31 January 1891.

[9] See for example the case Ah Foo *v.* Geo. Lindon, *W.A.*, 31 January 1891.

[10] Details from *W.A.*, 15 November 1890, 3 March 1891.

[11] *W.A.*, 15 November 1890.

[12] Typescripts [n.d.] entitled 'Walla Walla: Early History of Prosperous Farming Settlement' in Walla Walla Church papers.

[13] *B.P.*, 9 January 1891. Examples of these, specially made of 'shiny metal' were exhibited at the Wagga show.

[14] *W.A.*, 18 and 28 October 1890.

[15] *W.A.*, 10 July 1890, 3 January 1891.

[16] *W.A.*, 25 December 1890.

[17] *W.A.*, 19 May 1891.

[18] Newspaper references 1890-1—see also *V. & P.* (L.A. N.S.W.), 1891-2, vol. 8, p. 87. Report of Conference on Rust in Wheat.

[19] See *W.A.*, 9 January 1878; *P.T.*, 22 December 1883; *B.P.*, 16 January, *W.A.*, 1, 3, 6 January 1891.

[20] See E. Dunsdorfs, op. cit., pp. 165-6.

[21] *W.A.*, 1 July 1890, 3 March, 8 August, 22 December 1891.

22 *B.P.*, 15 January 1892.
23 *B.P.*, 5, 15 January 1892.
24 *W.A.*, 1, 13 January, 3 February, 24 December 1891. See also soil map, Figure 4.
25 *W.A.*, 21 October, 22 November 1890, 14 April 1891.
26 The more readily available secondary sources include: A. Lodewyckx, *Die Deutschen in Australien;* Th. Hebart, *Die Vereinigte Evangelisch–Lutherische Kirche in Australien;* an abridged English version of the same (ed. E. Stolz) entitled *The United Evangelical Lutheran Church in Australia;* and A. Brauer, *Under the Southern Cross;* the last three being more concerned with church history. As well there are a number of locally published or typescript church jubilee pamphlets. To supplement these sources, a series of interviews with 'Germans over eighty' (those who were children on farms in 1891), was undertaken in November 1964 in the Henty-Walla Walla area. Assistance in arranging interviews was given by Dr Lohe, President-General of the U.E.L.C.A., Adelaide, and Pastor M. Stolz, N.S.W. President U.E.L.C.A., Henty.
27 Walla Walla and Alma Park Parish Registers.
28 See G. L. Buxton, *South Australian Land Acts, 1869-1885.*
29 Walla Walla Church papers; E. Grosse, *Back to Walla Walla,* 1959; G. J. Kotzur, *History of the Pioneers and Wallandool-Alma Park Salem Congregation;* J. P. T. Stolz, *History of the Zion Evangelical Lutheran Congregation and its Organizations, Walla Walla, N.S.W.*
30 Conditional Purchase Registers, Albury.
31 For details of this gradual northward spread, see Th. Hebart, op. cit.; J. T. P. Stolz, op. cit.; A. Brauer, op. cit.
32 *N.S.W. Census,* 1891.
33 Walla Walla Church papers.
34 Ibid.
35 Ibid.
36 Conditional Purchase Register, Albury.

37 Interview with Mrs Emilie Krause (*née* Klemke), b. 1881 (November 1964).
38 Interview with Gottfried Klemke, b. 1882 (November 1964).
39 Krause interview.
40 Krause and Klemke interviews; also interviews with Gotthilf Johannes Kotzur and Theodor Benjamin Wenke (November 1964). The details of farm life which follow are based on these interviews, checked where necessary from written sources, including those already listed, and government publications.
41 Krause interview.
42 Klemke interview.
43 Interviews cited and E. Grosse, op. cit.; C. J. Kotzur, op. cit.; J. T. P. Stolz, op. cit.
44 See *W.A.*, 13 January 1891.
45 For a list of varieties grown in South Australia in 1868, see *South Australian Parliamentary Papers,* 1868-9, vol. 2, 'Report of Commission. Diseases in Cereals'.
46 See *W.A.*, 31 January, 20 August 1891; *B.P.*, 2 June 1891.
47 See A. G. Austin, *Australian Education 1788-1900,* chs 6-7, 'Defining the Constitutional Code of Public Education' and 'Interpreting the Constitutional Code of Public Education'.
48 *W.A.*, 2 May 1891.
49 43 Vic., no. 23. Attendance was compulsory, and local residents were no longer required to subscribe one-third of the building costs. For a discussion of the 'secular' and 'compromise' solution see A. G. Austin, op. cit., pp. 168-70; and for the Parkes-Vaughan debate, ibid., pp. 208-12.
50 Report of the Minister of Public Instruction, 1882, pp. 212, 214.
51 Ibid.
52 Ibid.
53 Ibid., 1890.
54 R. Goode, 'The Rock', contains extracts from school journals and correspondence, with some early town history.
55 *P.T.*, 17 February 1883.
56 *W.A.*, 3 February 1891.
57 E.g., *W.A.*, 3 February 1891.
58 *W.A.*, 5 March 1891.

[59] *W.A.*, 31 January 1891.
[60] *W.A.*, 26 March, 7 April, 19 December 1891.
[61] *W.A.*, 15 September 1891.
[62] *H.S.*, 2 September 1891.
[63] Newspaper notices, 1891.
[64] R. Goode, op. cit.
[65] Formed to encourage the government to provide railway facilities and to promote certain lines. See *W.A.*, 10 July, 3 August 1890, 19 March, 20 August, 13 October 1891.
[66] *W.A.*, 31 January 1891.
[67] *W.A.*, 10 and 19 July 1890, 19 February, 14 April, 9 May 1891.
[68] *W.A.*, 20 August 1891.
[69] See 'The O'Connell Case'; *W.A.*, 18 December 1890, 1, 22, 31 January, 19 February, 26 March 1891; *B.P.*, 16 January 1891.
[70] *W.A.*, 5 and 12 March, 4 April 1891.
[71] *W.A.*, 19 February, 4 and 7 April, 28 July 1891.
[72] Green's Gunyah meeting, *W.A.*, 14 May 1891; Urangeline Creek meeting, *W.A.*, 21 May 1891.
[73] *B.P.*, 2 June 1891.
[74] *W.A.*, 4 October 1890.
[75] 'On Our Selection' and 'Our New Selection', appeared in the *Bulletin* in the nineties and have been reprinted many times. The setting is the Darling Downs, Queensland.

7 TOWN GROWTH AND TOWN LIFE, 1891

[1] *P.T.* and *D.C.* See also C. Lyne, *The Industries of New South Wales*, pp. 248-53.
[2] *R.G.*, 31 December 1873, 5 January 1891, 5 October 1891; other details from *H.S.* See also C. Lyne, op. cit.
[3] *C.F.P.* and *N.A.* A special issue, *N.A.*, 20 April 1935, contains extracts from newspapers before 1890, which were later destroyed by fire. A further printing of these extracts appears in a centenary issue dated April 1963. Narrandera became a municipality (borough) in 1884.
[4] *V. & P.* (L.A. N.S.W.), 1883-4, vol. 11, pp. 659-66.

[5] See S. Priestly, *Echuca*.
[6] *V. & P.* (L.A. N.S.W.), 1883-4, vol. 11, p. 660.
[7] *B.P.*, 8 January 1892.
[8] Ibid., G. R. Dibbs, addressing a meeting at Wagga.
[9] Ibid.
[10] Ibid., the figures for imports in 1889 and 1890 are similar; *B.P.*, 23 January 1891, 22 January 1892.
[11] *B.P.*, 23 January 1891.
[12] This general summary is based on council balance sheets published in local newspapers. See for example, *H.S.*, 8 April 1891, 2 September 1891, where receipts and expenditure of over £4,000 for each half-year are listed and overdraft varies from £1,000 to £2,500.
[13] *P.T.*, 17 February 1883.
[14] *W.A.*, 30 April 1891.
[15] *W.A.*, 14 March 1891.
[16] *P.T.*, 17 February 1883.
[17] *W.A.*, 1 January 1891.
[18] *R.G.*, 15 April 1874.
[19] 3 March 1891.
[20] *V. & P.* (L.A. N.S.W.), 1883-4, vol. 11, p. 660.
[21] 25 August 1883.
[22] *B.P.*, 16 January 1891; *W.A.*, 17 January 1891; *B.P.*, 20 February 1891; *H.S.*, 24 January 1891.
[23] See the case of two half-caste Aborigines who assaulted and robbed Mir Hira, in *W.A.*, 10 July 1890.
[24] See *W.A.*, 31 January 1891. The case cited is from *P.T.*, 13 January 1883.
[25] *P.T.*, 9 June, 28 July 1883; *W.A.*, 10 March 1891; *H.S.*, 29 August 1891.
[26] 45 Vic., no. 11.
[27] See Report upon Chinese Camps compiled by Sydney Chinese merchant Quong Tart and Police Sub-Inspector Brennan; with statistics in *V. & P.* (L.A. N.S.W.), 1883-4, vol. 11, pp. 659-66. Newspaper research corroborates their findings.
[28] Ibid., p. 662.
[29] Ibid., p. 663.
[30] *P.T.*, 9 September 1876.
[31] 12 January 1881.
[32] Quong Tart, in *V. & P.* (L.A. N.S.W.) 1883-4, vol. 11, p. 665.
[33] Newspaper reports of court cases.

34 *W.A.*, 17 December 1891.

35 *V. & P.* (L.A. N.S.W.), 1883-4, vol. 11, p. 662.

36 *W.A.*, 17, 29 January 1891; *H.S.*, 14, 31 January, 11 February 1891; *B.P.*, 5 February 1891.

37 *P.T.*, 18 January 1890.

38 Ibid.

39 *P.T.*, 18 January 1890.

40 *H.S.*, 31 January 1891.

41 Ibid.

42 *W.A.*, 5 May 1891.

43 See *W.A.*, 29 January, 21 July 1891; *P.T.*, 3 and 24 January 1891.

44 *W.A.*, 10 January 1891.

45 *P.T.*, 5 and 12 July 1890; *W.A.*, 21 July 1891; *H.S.*, 22 July 1891. Treatment of leprosy in 1891 had hardly even reached the 'chaulmoogra oil' stage.

46 *W.A.*, 23 July 1891.

47 Ibid.

48 *W.A.*, 27 March 1878. Other church schools included St Joseph's (Catholic), *W.A.*, 19 December 1891 and St John's (Anglican), *W.A.*, 15 January 1891.

49 *P.T.*, 3 March 1883.

50 *P.T.*, 24 May 1890.

51 See for example the advertisement of one fruit-grower which concludes 'no business transacted on Sunday', in *W.A.*, 26 February 1891.

52 *P.T.*, 21 April 1883, 12 April 1890; *W.A.*, 8 July 1890, 12 February, 26 March, 11 April 1891.

53 *H.S.*, 31 October 1891; *W.A.*, 13 October 1891; *B.P.*, 23 January 1891.

54 *R.G.*, 4 March 1874; *H.S.*, 29 August 1891; *W.A.*, 6 January 1891, 4 June 1891.

55 *W.A.*, 13 January 1891.

56 Where not otherwise indicated, details regarding Wagga schools are taken from an anonymous typescript [n.d.], entitled 'Wagga Wagga Public School'. Some of the material subsequently appeared in a school centenary pamphlet (Wagga, 1961).

57 Ibid.

58 *W.A.*, 19 December 1891; B.P., 10 July 1891.

59 *W.A.*, 19 December 1891.

60 *W.A.*, 9 May 1891; *H.S.*, 9 September 1891.

61 Newspaper reports and advertisements.

62 *W.A.*, 7 October 1890, 18 February, 16 April, 12 December 1891.

63 *W.A.*, 3 February, 3 March 1891; *B.P.*, 5 January 1891.

64 *P.T.*, 8 February, 7 June 1890; *H.S.*, 1 April 1891; *W.A.*, 10 March, 1 October 1891.

65 *W.A.*, 2 April 1891; *P.T.*, 8 March 1890.

66 See *W.A.*, 14, 28 October 1890, 1, 8 January, 19 May 1891.

67 Newspaper advertisements 1890-1.

68 *H.S.*, 27 May 1891.

69 *H.S.*, 16 December 1891.

70 *P.T.*, 10 February 1883.

71 *W.A.*, 24 January 1891.

72 *W.A.*, 10 July 1890.

73 *W.A.*, 1 January 1891. Cf. *P.T.*, 15 March 1890, when it was proposed to invite Henry George himself to lecture at Deniliquin.

74 *P.T.*, 15 February, 5, 12 April 1890.

75 Newspaper sources 1890-1; *New South Wales in 1881*, compiled and edited by T. Richards, pp. 100-1.

8 THE CHANGING PASTORAL SCENE

1 E.g., *P.T.*, 18 November 1876.

2 E.g., Willeroo, *P.T.*, 11 January 1890.

3 G. E. Ashcroft, on Corrong run on the Lachlan, probably in imitation of Tyson, lessee of the run. *P.T.*, 14 January 1890.

4 See *V.& P.* (L.A. N.S.W.), 1883, vol. 2, pp. 119-20.

5 *P.T.*, 14 June 1890.

6 *P.T.*, 15 November 1890. In the late forties this station had changed hands for a 'sow and litter'.

7 *V. & P.* (L.A. N.S.W.), 1885-6, vol. 6, pp. 387-981, 1st and 2nd reports; 1887, vol. 5, p. 515 and supplementary volume, 3rd report.

8 *P.T.*, 18 January, 15 February, 1 March 1890, 17 January 1891.

9 For a discussion on vegetation changes up to 1870 see O. B. Williams, 'The Riverina and its Pastoral Industry', in A. Barnard (ed.), *The Simple Fleece*, pp. 411-34.

[10] *P.T.*, 10 June 1876; *W.A.*, 11 November, 23 August 1890; *P.T.*, 21 February 1891.

[11] W. B. Clarke, 'Effects of Forest Vegetation on Climate', *Transactions of the Royal Society of N.S.W.*, 1876, p. 213.

[12] *S.M.H.*, reprinted in *R.G.*, 11 June 1881. For the belief that forests influenced rainfall—and its South Australian extension, 'rain follows the plough', see G. L. Buxton, *South Australian Land Acts, 1869-1885*, pp. 50, 62. For the protest of the Murray District Selectors' Association against ringbarking on this account see *R.G.*, 11 June 1881.

[13] *V. & P.* (L.A. N.S.W.), 1885-6, vol. 6, p. 69. He stated further that in the central Murray District nearly all the mature pine had been cut out.

[14] See 'The Kelly Raid on Jerilderie' by 'One Who Was There', in H. C. Lundy, *Jerilderie, 100 years (1858-1958)*.

[15] See the report on Chinese camps in Riverina, in ...*V. & P.* (L.A. N.S.W.), 1883-4, vol. 11, pp. 659-66.

[16] *P.T.*, 17 March 1883.

[17] *W.A.*, 10 July 1890.

[18] *Town and Country Journal*, reprinted in *R.G.*, 17 August 1881.

[19] *R.G.*, 17 August 1881.

[20] For a brief study, see B. V. Fennessy, 'Competitors with Sheep', in A. Barnard (ed.), *The Simple Fleece*, pp. 227-33.

[21] *H.S.*, 4 April 1891.

[22] *W.A.*, 28 November 1891; *B.P.*, 24 April 1891; *H.S.*, 21 January, 16 December 1891.

[23] *H.S.*, 8 July 1891.

[24] *W.A.*, 24 February, 7 April 1891; *B.P.*, 8 January 1892, p. 16.

[25] *P.T.*, 12 May 1883; *W.A.*, 2 October 1890, 10 January 1891.

[26] Various newspaper references.

[27] On Benduck run twenty-five miles were erected early in 1891. (*H.S.*, 31 January 1891.) *B.P.*, 24 April 1891, stated '600 miles of wire netting fences are being erected in the district, irrespective of the provisions of the Rabbit Act'.

[28] On Tyson's Tupra station 920,000 were killed in 1890 (*H.S.*, 23 December 1891); see also *P.T.*, 1, 22 February, 1 March, 4 October, 6 December 1890.

[29] See for example, the case of Uardry run on the Hay line in *Official Report of the National Australasian Convention Debates*, First Session, pp. 1118-9.

[30] For an outline of this change see N. G. Butlin, *Investment in Australian Economic Development*, pp. 299-333. Fuller treatment is given in R. H. T. Smith, 'Transport and Commodity Movement in Southern New South Wales', Ph.D. thesis, A.N.U.

[31] A similar blockage occurred at Deniliquin, *P.T.*, 4 October 1890.

[32] *W.A.*, 12 January 1878.

[33] *B.P.*, 22 January 1892.

[34] *W.A.*, 7 February, 8 December 1891; *B.P.*, 6 February 1891, 5 February 1892; H. E. Peck, *Memoirs of a Stockman*, p. 268.

[35] Percy Clarke, *The 'New Chum' in Australia*, p. 158; A. P. Wood, *Transactions of the Royal Society of N.S.W.*, vol. 17, 1883, p. 149; *P.T.*, 28 April, 2 June 1883. See also Annual Reports of the Chief Inspector of Stock, in *V. & P.* (L.A. N.S.W.).

[36] *W.A.*, 16 January 1878. It was frequently stated that railing stock deteriorated their condition more than droving them would have done.

[37] See trespass and impounding notices in newspapers, and particular cases in *P.T.*, 1 February 1890; *B.P.*, 15 January 1892; *W.A.*, 10 October 1891.

[38] *P.T.*, 15 February, 8 March, 26 July 1890; *H.S.*, 10 June 1891.

[39] *H.S.*, 19 September 1891; *W.A.*, 29 December 1891.

[40] *R.G.*, 10 and 31 December 1873, 26 March 1881; *W.A.*, 4 September 1890. On Coree station in 1890, engines and centrifugal pumps supplied water for wool-washing from the Billabong, but this was unusual in the Riverina. *P.T.*, 15 November 1890.

[41] *P.T.*, 16 and 23 August, 8 and 15 November 1890.

[42] See Annual Reports of the Chief Inspector of Stock in *V. & P.* (L.A. N.S.W.).

[43] *B.P.*, 15 January 1890, 5 January 1892; *H.S.*, 2 December 1891; *W.A.*, 8 January, 10 March 1891.

[44] 'The Broken Down Squatter', *B.P.*, 3 July 1891.

[45] J. Phillips, *Reminiscences*, pp. 15-70. Warbreccan was purchased in 1886 by the Hon. William McCulloch for £150,000. The price included 64,000 acres and 50,000 sheep and lambs; R. Wallace, *The Rural Economy and Agriculture of Australia and New Zealand.*

[46] All details regarding Willurah, unless otherwise stated, are taken from Willurah station records, journals, correspondence, etc., in the possession of the John Lamb Pastoral Co., Willurah, hereafter referred to as Willurah station papers.

[47] Biographical details regarding Ross are scanty. He appears as a citizen of Germanton (now Holbrook) in 1891 where he is chairman of a School of Arts meeting and of the Pastoral, Agricultural, and Horticultural Society; *B.P.*, 6 March 1891.

[48] In another letter Best, who was leaving Hay after five years, was pleased to note that the squatters of the district were preparing to give him 'substantial proof of the goodwill entertained towards [him]'.

[49] *V. & P.* (L.A. N.S.W.), 1883, vol. 2, p. 91.

[50] Details of the leasehold and resumed areas on all pastoral holdings in New South Wales from 1884 are given in W. Hanson, *The Pastoral Possessions of New South Wales.*

[51] *P.T.*, 10 June 1876.

[52] *V. & P.* (L.A. N.S.W.), 1883, vol. 2, p. 121.

[53] b. 1827, d. 8 November 1919 at Narringa, Gunbar, N.S.W.

[54] Much of this country had been abandoned during the 1864-6 drought. Cf. W. H. Tietkens (explorer) who travelled the area in 1865 noting abandoned homesteads. 'Experiences in the Life of an Australian Explorer,' *J.R.A.H.S.*, vol. 5 (1919), pp. 47-8.

[55] *Investment in Australian Economic Development*, p. 89. Butlin cites Shann, Fitzpatrick and Roberts.

[56] See chapter 1. In the 1870-1 appraisals, half the improvements on pastoral leases in New South Wales were in the Murrumbidgee district—mostly in the area under study.

[57] Op. cit., p. 89. Cf. p. 379, where he states, 'land sales may have been spontaneous during the years 1871-73 . . . considerable pressures on pastoralists to buy, or at any rate "peacock" land . . . strenuous struggle between pastoralists and selectors in which pastoralists acquired title to very considerable areas of pastoral lands'.

[58] Ibid., p. 379.

[59] See C. J. King, *An Outline of Closer Settlement in New South Wales*, p. 107.

[60] Op. cit., pp. 168-9; see also the sections 'The Growth of Mortgage Finance', pp. 125-47 and 'The Growth of Debts and Excess Capacity', pp. 166-80.

[61] R.E.N. Twopeny, *Town Life in Australia.*

[62] See for example, *W.A.*, 31 January 1891; *H.S.*, 14 and 29 April 1891.

[63] 6 August 1881.

[64] *P.T.*, 14 June 1890.

[65] *P.T.*, 7 March 1891.

[66] *P.T.*, 21 October, 1876.

[67] *W.A.*, 12 November 1891.

[68] *H.S.*, 31 January 1891.

[69] *W.A.*, 6 January 1891.

[70] *W.A.*, 2, 11 October 1890, 18 July, 13 August 1891.

[71] *W.A.*, 22 November 1890.

[72] See R. A. Gollan, *Radical and Working Class Politics*, chs 5-8.

[73] The following note, from L. F. Fitzhardinge, *William Morris Hughes*, vol. 1 (Sydney, 1964), covers the sources and their relevance: 'The fullest and most objective narrative is still that of Coghlan. Some recent re-examinations are: R. Gollan, *Radical and Working Class Politics* (Melbourne, 1960), 129-35, who reflects in the main the or-

thodox view; Jean E. O'Connor, '1890—A Turning Point in Labour History', *Hist. Stud.*, No. 16 (May 1951), who draws attention to the importance of the 'new unionism'; and N. B. Nairn, 'The 1890 Maritime Strike in New South Wales', *Hist. Stud.*, No. 37 (November 1961), 1-8, who calls in question many of the generally received ideas.'

Events in the shearing dispute in the Riverina tend rather to support Nairn's thesis.

[74] E.g., W. G. Spence, *Australia's Awakening; History of the A.W.U.* (Sydney, 1911).

[75] *W.A.*, 2 October 1890.

[76] See, for example, my short note 'An Incident at Barcaldine' in *Labour History* (November 1964), p. 22; *W.A.*, 1890-1.

[77] See V. Palmer, *The Legend of the Nineties*, p. 138; *W.A.*, 20 September 1890.

[78] See, for example, 'Flogging at Whitton', *H.S.*, 1 August 1891.

[79] *W.A.*, 11, 23 July 1891.

[80] *P.T.*, 11 July 1891.

[81] E.g., *W.A.*, 21 January 1891.

[82] *W.A.*, 13 August 1891.

[83] *W.A.*, 25 July 1891.

[84] *W.A.*, 1 August 1891.

[85] R. A. Gollan, op. cit., p. 103.

[86] *W.A.*, 23 July 1891; *P.T.*, 19 August, 13 September 1890, 1 August 1891.

[87] *W.A.*, 1 August 1891.

[88] *W.A.*, 21 May 1891.

[89] For discussion see editorial in *W.A.*, 11 August 1891.

[90] *P.T.*, 21 February 1891.

[91] R. A. Gollan, op. cit., p. 104.

[92] *P.T.*, 15 March 1890.

[93] For a lengthy discussion, see J. R. Canning, Letter to the Editor, in *W.A.*, 28 July 1891.

[94] *W.A.*, 2 September 1890.

[95] J. K. Galbraith, *The Affluent Society*, ch. 2; and *The Liberal Hour*, ch. 8.

[96] *W.A.*, 8 November 1890 credits him with £6 million.

[97] *P.T.*, 27 December 1890; *W.A.*, 2, 4 October 1890, 24 February 1891.

[98] *W.A.*, 2 October 1890.

[99] *W.A.*, 29 January, 7, 25 July 1891.

[1] *W.A.*, 28 March, 4 July 1891. Squatters engaging in such practices were excluded from the Pastoralists' Union in 1891.

[2] *H.S.*, 2 May 1891.

[3] Ibid.

[4] *P.T.*, 21 February 1891.

[5] *W.A.*, 8 August 1891.

[6] *H.S.*, 9 September 1891; *W.A.*, 12 September 1891.

[7] R.E.N. Twopeny, 'Social Relations', op. cit., p. 111:
'Struggling men are less ashamed of struggling and are not made to feel the defects of their conditions so keenly. In a society the position of whose members is constantly changing, the style of life is of less importance. The millionaire of to-day hadn't a sixpence yesterday, and may not have one again to-morrow . . . Constant intercommunication is thus kept up between class and class, rich and poor; they learn better to understand each other's position, and a clearer understanding generally leads to mutual respect.'

9   MASTERS AND SERVANTS NO MORE?

[1] P. Loveday and A. W. Martin, *Parliament, Factions and Parties*, p. 122.

[2] Ibid., p. 126.

[3] Ibid., pp. 126-35.

[4] Ibid., p. 139.

[5] *N.S.W. Parliamentary Record* (Sydney, 1920), p. 6.

[6] All population figures from *N.S.W. Census*, 1891.

[7] *N.S.W. Census*, 1861, 1891. Boundary changes make precise comparison impossible.

[8] *B.P.*, 5 June 1891; *W.A.*, 4, 6, 13 June 1891.

[9] *W.A.*, 6 June 1891.

[10] *W.A.*, 13 June 1891.

[11] Free-trade platform. *B.P.*, 5 June 1891. L.E.L. platform in R. N. Ebbels, *The Australian Labor Movement 1850-1907*, pp. 211-2.

[12] *H.S.*, 8 July 1891.

[13] *W.A.*, 6 June 1891.

[14] *W.A.*, 8 September 1891.
[15] *W.A.*, 5 May 1891.
[16] *W.A.*, 27 September 1890.
[17] *W.A.*, 28 August 1890.
[18] *W.A.*, 4 October 1890.
[19] *W.A.*, 4 June 1891.
[20] *B.P.*, 19 May 1891.
[21] *S.M.H.*, 30 October 1877; *W.A.*, 5 January, 8 June 1878. 'The Great Trespass Action'; *P.T.*, 17 February 1883, 17 October 1891; A. W. Martin and P. Wardle, *Members of the Legislative Assembly of New South Wales 1856-1901*, pp. 9-10.
[22] A. W. Martin and P. Wardle, op. cit., p. 33; also unpublished notes [n.d.] communicated by B. Graham, Department of Political Science, Australian National University, who comments 'almost certainly written for the federal election campaign of April-May 1917'.
[23] *P.T.*, 16, 30 May, 27 June 1891.
[24] *P.T.*, 27 June 1891.
[25] See P. Loveday and A. W. Martin, op. cit., p. 122.
[26] *P.T.*, 27 June, 4 July 1891.
[27] *P.T.*, 4 July 1891.
[28] *B.P.*, 4 July 1891.
[29] See A. W. Martin in A. Barnard (ed.), *The Simple Fleece*, pp. 580-1, for a discussion of the two-year resurgence of squatter power in 1880-2.
[30] *H.S.*, 15 April 1891; *W.A.*, 25 July 1891.
[31] Wm Affleck of Gundaroo; pastoralist, newspaper proprietor and uncompromising free-trader. *B.P.*, 2 June 1891; *W.A.*, 4 June 1891.
[32] *B.P.*, 9 June 1891.
[33] 9d per bushel on wheat, 6d per bushel on oats; *P.T.*, 21 November 1891.
[34] *W.A.*, 28 August 1891.
[35] *W.A.*, 28 August 1890.
[36] *B.P.*, 19 May 1891.
[37] *B.P.*, 23 June 1891.
[38] *B.P.*, 12 June 1891.

[39] A. W. Martin and P. Wardle, op. cit., p. 133.
[40] By 1900, in his astonishment at Lyne being offered the Premiership of the new Commonwealth, Deakin referred to him as 'the anti-federalist of New South Wales'; see J. A. La Nauze, *The Hopetoun Blunder*.
[41] *B.P.*, 12 May 1891.
[42] *B.P.*, 3 July 1891.
[43] J. Gormly, *Exploration and Settlement in Australia*; A. W. Martin and P. Wardle, op. cit., p. 87; W. A. Bayley, *History of the Farmers and Settlers' Association of N.S.W.*, and various issues of the *Wagga Express* and *Wagga Advertiser*.
[44] *W.A.*, January-July 1891.
[45] *W.A.*, 21 April 1891.
[46] *B.P.*, 3 July 1891.
[47] *W.A.*, 2 July 1891.
[48] *W.A.*, 4, 6, 20, 25 and 27 June 1891.
[49] *W.A.*, 6 June 1891.
[50] *W.A.*, 11 June 1891.
[51] *W.A.*, 4, 6, 11, 18 and 20 June 1891; W. A. Bayley, op. cit., p. 34.
[52] *H.S.*, 3 January, 19 September, 4 November 1891.
[53] *H.S.*, 7 January 1891.
[54] *W.A.*, 7 May, 4, 11 June 1891.
[55] *H.S.*, 31 January 1891.
[56] *W.A.*, 2 July 1891.
[57] *W.A.*, 23 July 1891.
[58] *P.T.*, 12 September 1891.
[59] *B.P.*, 29 January 1892.
[60] *W.A.*, 27 June, 2 July 1891.
[61] Ibid.
[62] Ibid.
[63] *H.S.*, 10 June 1891.
[64] *H.S.*, 17 June 1891; A. W. Martin and P. Wardle, op. cit., p. 123.
[65] A. W. Martin and P. Wardle, op. cit., pp. 225-6.
[66] *H.S.*, 17 June, 4 July 1891.
[67] *H.S.*, 4 July 1891; A. W. Martin and P. Wardle, op. cit., p. 160.
[68] *H.S.*, 4 July 1891.
[69] *Investment in Australian Economic Development*, p. 89.

SELECT BIBLIOGRAPHY

I *Official Contemporary Sources*

A. MANUSCRIPT

Conditional Purchase Registers (Crown lands offices, Albury, Deniliquin, Corowa, Hay, Moama, Narrandera, Urana, Wagga Wagga).

New South Wales Lands Department maps and plans (State Archives).

B. PRINTED

Annual Report of the N.S.W. Department of Lands. Sydney, 1880-1.

Annual Report of the N.S.W. Minister of Public Instruction. Sydney, 1880-1890.

Coghlan, T. A., *Wealth and Progress of New South Wales 1888-1889.* Sydney, 1889.

Historical Records of Australia, series I, vol. xxiii, 1925.

New South Wales Censuses, 1851, 1856, 1861, 1871, 1881, 1891, 1901.

New South Wales Census 1891, Statistician's Report.

New South Wales Government Gazette, 1839-91.

New South Wales Legislative Assembly Parliamentary Debates, 1879-87.

New South Wales. Votes and Proceedings of the Legislative Assembly, 1858-92.

New South Wales Parliamentary Record. Sydney, 1920.

Official Report of the National Australasian Convention Debates, First Session. Adelaide, 1897.

South Australian Gazette, 1838.

South Australian Parliamentary Papers, 1857-86.

Statistical Register of New South Wales, 1847-92.

Statistical Register of Victoria, 1851-73.

Victorian Censuses, 1851, 1854, 1857, 1861.

Victoria. Votes and Proceedings of the Legislative Assembly, 1856-69.

Victoria. Votes and Proceedings of the Legislative Council, 1853-5.

II   *Other Contemporary Sources*

A.   MANUSCRIPT

Gibson family papers, 'Keringal', Hay.

Kennedy, Mary, Reminiscences, drafts C and D (part typescript), Mitchell Library.

Peppin, George Jr, Diary, 1859, Mitchell Library (referred to in Notes as Peppin Diary).

Walla Walla and Alma Park Parish Registers, United Evangelical Lutheran Church of Australia, Walla Walla (referred to in Notes as Walla Walla Church papers).

Willurah station records, John Lamb Pastoral Company, Willurah.

B.   NEWSPAPERS

Argus, Melbourne
Albury Banner and Wodonga Express
Australischer Christenbote, Adelaide
Border Post, Albury
Corowa Free Press
Deniliquin Chronicle
Hay Standard
Narrandera Argus
Pastoral Times, Deniliquin
Riverine Grazier, Hay
South Australian Register, Adelaide
Sydney Morning Herald
Town and Country Journal, Sydney
Wagga Wagga Advertiser
Wagga Wagga Express and Murrumbidgee District Advertiser (referred to in text as *Wagga Express*)

C.   BOOKS

Andrews, A., *Fifty Years of the Albury and Border Pastoral, Agricultural and Horticultural Society.* Albury, 1907.

——, *Incidents in the History of Albury Municipality.* Albury, 1909.

Bartley, N., *Opals and Agates.* Brisbane, 1892.

——, *Australian Pioneers and Reminiscences.* Brisbane [1896].

Bonwick, J., *Romance of the Wool Trade.* London, 1887.

Bride, T. F. (ed.), *Letters from Victorian Pioneers*. Melbourne, 1898.

Brodribb, W. A., *Profits of a Small Sheep-walk on the Western Portion of New South Wales, Called the Salt-Bush Country*. London, 1862.

——, *Recollections of An Australian Squatter, or Leaves from My Journal Since 1835*. Sydney [1883].

——, *The Great Australian Colonies*. London, 1862.

Bruce, Alexander, *Scab in Sheep and Its Cure*. 3rd ed., Sydney, 1867.

——, *Report on Inoculation for Pleuro-Pneumonia in Cattle*. Sydney, 1869.

Clarke, Percy, *The 'New Chum' in Australia*. London, 1886.

Curr, E. M., *Recollections of Squatting in Victoria Then Called the Port Phillip District (from 1841 to 1851)*. Melbourne, 1883.

Finn, Rev. W. M., *Glimpses of North-Eastern Victoria, and Albury, New South Wales*. Melbourne, 1870.

Hanson, W., *The Pastoral Possessions of New South Wales*. Sydney, 1889.

Haygarth, Rev. H. W., *Recollections of Bush Life in Australia, During a Residence of Eight Years in the Interior*. London, 1861.

Heaton, J. H., *Australian Dictionary of Dates and Men of the Time*. Melbourne, 1879.

Henty, R., *Australiana or My Early Life*. London, 1886.

Howitt, William, *Land, Labour, and Gold*. 2 vols. London, 1855-8.

Kinloch, A., *The Murray River: Being a Journal of the Voyage of the 'Lady Augusta' Steamer from the Goolwa, in South Australia, to Gannewarra, above Swan Hill, Victoria*. Adelaide, 1853.

Kirchner, W., *Australien und seine Vortheile für Auswanderung*. 2nd ed., Frankfurt, 1850.

Lyne, C., *The Industries of New South Wales*. Sydney, 1882.

Mossman, S. and Banister, T., *Australia Visited and Revisited*. London, 1853.

[Phillips, J.], *Reminiscences of Australian Early Life by A Pioneer*. London, 1893 (referred to in Notes as J. Phillips, *Reminiscences*).

Reid, G. H., *An Essay on New South Wales, the Mother Colony of the Australias*. Sydney, 1876.

Richards, T. (ed.), *New South Wales in 1881*. Sydney, 1882.

Robinson, C., *New South Wales: The Oldest and Richest of the Australian Colonies*. Sydney, 1873.

'Rudd, Steele' [A. H. Davis], *On Our Selection*. Sydney, 1899.

Rusden, G. W., *History of Australia*. 3 vols. London, 1883.

Sauerbeck, A., *Production and Consumption of Wool*. London, 1878.

Smiles, S., *Self-Help*. London, 1886 (first published in 1859).

Strickland, E., *The Australian Pastor: A Record of the Remarkable Changes in Mind and Outward Estate of H. Elliott*. London, 1862.

Trollope, Anthony, *Australia and New Zealand*. Melbourne, 1876.

Twopeny, R. E. N., *Town Life in Australia*. London, 1883.

Wallace, R., *The Rural Economy and Agriculture of Australia and New Zealand*. London, 1891.

Westwood, J. J., *The Journal of J. J. Westwood (Evangelist); or, An Account of Eight Years' Itineracy to the Townships and Squatting Stations of Victoria, New South Wales, South Australia and Tasmania*. Melbourne, 1865 (referred to in notes as J. J. Westwood, *Journal*).

III   Later Works

A.   BOOKS

Alexander, F., *Moving Frontiers*. Melbourne, 1947.

Allen, H. C., *Bush and Backwoods: A Comparison of the Frontier in Australia and the United States*. Michigan, 1959.

Allin, C. D., *History of the Tariff Relations of the Australian Colonies*. Minneapolis, 1918.

Anderson, R. H., *The Trees of New South Wales*. Sydney, 1947.

Andrews, A., *The First Settlement of the Upper Murray 1835-1845*. Sydney, 1920.

Austin, A. G., *Australian Education, 1788-1900*. Melbourne, 1961.

Austin, H. B., *The Merino, Past, Present and Probable*. Sydney, 1947.

Barnard, A. *The Australian Wool Market, 1840-1900*. Melbourne, 1958.

——, (ed.), *The Simple Fleece*. Melbourne, 1962.

Bassett, M., *The Hentys: A Colonial Tapestry*. Melbourne, 1962.

Bate, Weston, *A History of Brighton*. Melbourne, 1962.

Bayley, W. A., *Border City*. Albury, 1954.

——, *History of the Farmers and Settlers' Association of N.S.W.* Sydney, 1957.

Bean, C. E. W., *The Dreadnought of the Darling*. London, 1911.

——, *On the Wool Track*. Sydney, 1945.

Billis, R. V. and Kenyon, A., *Pastures New*. Melbourne, 1930.

——, *Pastoral Pioneers of Port Phillip*. Melbourne, 1932.

Bolton, G. C., *A Thousand Miles Away: A history of North Queensland to 1920*. Brisbane, 1963.

Brauer, A., *Under the Southern Cross*. Adelaide, 1956.

Breakwell, E., *The Grasses and Fodder Plants of New South Wales*. Sydney, 1923.

Briggs, Asa, *Victorian People*. London, 1954.

Butlin, N. G., *Investment in Australian Economic Development, 1861-1900*. Cambridge, 1964.

Buxton, G. L., *South Australian Land Acts, 1869-1885*. Adelaide, 1966.

Cambage, R. H. and Maiden, J. H., 'The Western Plains' in British Association for the Advancement of Science, *Handbook for New South Wales*. Sydney, 1914.

Clark, C. M. H., *Select Documents in Australian History*. 2 vols. Sydney, 1958.

——, *A Short History of Australia*. Chicago, 1963.

Coghlan, T. A., *Labour and Industry in Australia*. 4 vols. London, 1918.

'Collins, Tom' [Joseph Furphy], *Rigby's Romance*. Sydney, 1946.

——, *Such is Life*. Sydney, 1962.

Cox, E. W., *The Evolution of the Australian Merino*. Sydney, 1936.

Crombie, Andrew, *After Sixty Years or Recollections of an Australian Bushman*. Brisbane, 1927.

Cruse, Amy, *The Victorians and Their Books*. London, 1935.

Dunsdorfs, E., *The Australian Wheat-Growing Industry 1788-1948*. Melbourne, 1956.

Eastman, H. M., *Memoirs of a Sheepman*. Deniliquin, 1963.

Ebbels, R. N., *The Australian Labor Movement, 1850-1907*. Sydney, 1960.

Fetherstonhaugh, Cuthbert, *After Many Days*. Melbourne, 1917.

Fitzpatrick, B., *The British Empire in Australia: An Economic History 1834-1939*. Melbourne, 1949.

Fitzpatrick, K., *Australian Explorers*. London, 1958.

Foley, J. C., *Droughts in Australia: A Review of Records from the Earliest Years of Settlement to 1955*. Commonwealth of Australia, Bureau of Meteorology, Bulletin 43. [Melbourne], 1957.

Galbraith, J. K., *The Affluent Society*. London, 1962.

——, *The Liberal Hour*. London, 1963.

Garland, W. J., *The History of Wagga Wagga*. Records of the Education Society, no. 17. Sydney, 1917.

Gollan, Robin, *Radical and Working Class Politics: A Study of Eastern Australia, 1850-1910*. Melbourne, 1960.

Gormly, J., *Exploration and Settlement in Australia*. Sydney, 1921.

Greenwood, Gordon (ed.), *Australia: A Social and Political History*. Sydney, 1955.

Hastie, W. J. H., *The Story of Moulamein (N.S.W.) 1851-1951*. Moulamein, 1951.

Hawdon, Joseph, *The Journal of a Journey from New South Wales to Adelaide Performed in 1838*. Melbourne, [1952].

Hebart, T., *Die Vereinigte Evangelisch-Lutherische Kirche in Australien*. Adelaide, 1938.

Henderson, Alexander (ed.), *Early Pioneer Families of Victoria and Riverina*. Melbourne, 1936.

——, *Australian Families*. Melbourne, 1941.

Holmes, J. McD., *The Murray Valley*. Sydney, 1948.

Inglis, K. S., *Churches and the Working Classes in Victorian England*. London, 1963.

——, *Hospital and Community: A History of the Royal Melbourne Hospital*. Melbourne, 1958.

Irvin, E., *Letters from the River: A Boat Trip down the Murray in 1875*. Wagga, 1950.

——, *Place of Many Crows*. Wagga, 1953.

——, *Early Inland Agriculture: Farming in the Southern Districts of New South Wales*. Wagga, 1962.

Joyce, Alfred (ed. G. F. James), *A Homestead History*. Melbourne, 1963.

Kiddle, Margaret, *Men of Yesterday: A Social History of the Western District of Victoria, 1834-1890*. Melbourne, 1961.

King, C. J., *An Outline of Closer Settlement in New South Wales*. Sydney, 1957.

Kotzur, G. J., *History of the Pioneers and Wallandool-Alma Park Salem Congregation*. Walla Walla, 1962.

La Nauze, J. A., *The Hopetoun Blunder*. Melbourne, 1957.

Lodewyckx, A., *Die Deutschen in Australien*. Stuttgart, 1932.

Loveday, P. and Martin, A. W., *Parliament, Factions and Parties*. Melbourne, 1966.

Lundy, H. C., *Jerilderie, 100 Years (1858-1958)*. Jerilderie, 1958.

Lynd, R. S. and H. M., *Middletown. A Study in American Culture*. New York, 1929.

McCaughey, Patricia, *Samuel McCaughey: A Biography*. Sydney, 1955.

McConnell, T. R., *The History of Barham*. Melbourne, 1951.

McIntyre, A. J. and J. J., *Country Towns of Victoria: A Social Survey*. Melbourne, 1944.

Martin, A. W. and Wardle, P., *Members of the Legislative Assembly of New South Wales, 1856-1901*. Canberra, 1959.

Martin, C. S., *Irrigation and Closer Settlement in the Shepparton District, 1836-1906*. Melbourne, 1955.

Morris, A., *Rich River*. Echuca, 1952.

Nadel, G. H., *Australia's Colonial Culture*. Harvard, 1957.

Palmer, V., *The Legend of the Nineties*. Melbourne, 1954.

Paterson, A. B., *The Collected Verse of A. B. Paterson*. Sydney, [1950] (first published in 1921).

Peck, H. E., *Memoirs of a Stockman*. Melbourne, 1942.

Perry, T. M., *Australia's First Frontier: The Spread of Settlement in New South Wales 1788-1829*. Melbourne, 1963.

Pike, D., *Paradise of Dissent*. Melbourne, 1957.

Priestly, S., *Echuca, A Centenary History*. Brisbane, 1965.

Roberts, S. H., *History of Australian Land Settlement 1788-1920*. Melbourne, 1924.

———, *The Squatting Age in Australia, 1835-1847*. Melbourne, 1935.

Robertson, J. E., *Progress of Wagga Wagga and District*. Wagga, 1914.

Ronald, R. B., *The Riverina: People and Properties*. Melbourne, 1960.

Serle, G., *The Golden Age*. Melbourne, 1963.

Shann, E. O. G., *An Economic History of Australia*. Cambridge, 1948.

Shaw, J. H., *Urban Evolution of Wagga Wagga*. Armidale, 1960.

Spence, W. G., *Australia's Awakening: Thirty Years in the Life of an Australian Agitator.* Sydney, 1909.

Stephens, C. G., *A Manual of Australian Soils.* Melbourne, 1953.

Stolz, E. (ed.), *The United Evangelical Lutheran Church in Australia.* Adelaide, 1938.

Stolz, J. P. T., *History of the Zion Evangelical Lutheran Congregation and its Organisations, Walla Walla, N.S.W.* Tanunda, 1944.

Thomas, M. W., *Young People in Industry 1750-1945.* London, 1945.

Wadham, S. M. and Wood, G. L., *Land Utilization in Australia.* Melbourne, 1939.

Ward, Russel, *The Australian Legend.* Melbourne, 1958.

Warner, W. Lloyd, *Structure of American Life.* Edinburgh, 1952.

Webb, W. P., *The Great Plains.* Boston, 1931.

Wellings, H. P., *Benjamin Boyd in Australia (1842-1849).* Sydney, [n.d.].

'West, James' [Carl Withers], *Plainville, U.S.A.* New York, 1945.

B. ARTICLES

Andrews, A., 'The First Settlement of the North-East of Victoria', *V.H.M.*, vol. 5, 1916.

Andrews, J., 'Pioneer Farming in the Western Riverina', *A.N.Z.A.A.S. Report,* vol. 21, 1932.

Baker, D. W. A., 'The Origins of Robertson's Land Acts', in J. J. Eastwood and F. B. Smith (eds), *Historical Studies: Selected Articles. First Series.* Melbourne, 1964 (an abridgment of his A.N.U. Ph.D. thesis).

Baylis, J. J., 'The Murrumbidgee and Wagga Wagga', *J.R.A.H.S.*, vol. 13, 1927.

Beveridge, M. K., 'Pioneering on the Lower Murray', *V.H.M.*, vol. 1, 1911.

Buckley, K., 'Gipps and the Graziers of New South Wales, 1841-1846', in J. J. Eastwood and F. B. Smith (eds), *Historical Studies: Selected Articles. First Series.* Melbourne, 1964.

Butlin, N. G., ' "Company Ownership" of N.S.W. pastoral stations, 1865-1900', *Historical Studies, Australia and New Zealand,* vol. 4, no. 14, May 1950.

Campbell, J. F., ' "Squatting" on Crown Lands in New South

Wales', *J.R.A.H.S.*, vol. 15, 1929; supplementary paper, vol. 17, 1932.

Chapman, Mrs C. K., 'Swan Hill—Past and Present', *V.H.M.*, vol. 23, 1950.

Clarke, W. B., 'Effects of Forest Vegetation on Climate', *Journal and Proceedings of the Royal Society of N.S.W.*, vol. 10, 1876.

Davis, C. M., 'Merino Sheep on the Australian Riverina', *Geographical Review*, vol. 44, 1954.

Dixon, S., 'The Effects of Settlement and Pastoral Occupation in Australia upon the Indigenous Vegetation', *Transactions and Proceedings of the Royal Society of South Australia*, vol. 15, 1891-2.

Gormly, J., 'Exploration and Settlement on the Murray and Murrumbidgee', *J.R.A.H.S.*, vol. 2, 1906.

Hamilton, A. G., 'On the Effect which Settlement in Australia has produced upon Indigenous Vegetation', *Journal and Proceedings of the Royal Society of N.S.W.*, vol. 26, 1892.

Hopton, A. J., 'John Chandler, Goldfields Carrier', *V.H.M.*, vol. 24, 1951.

Jervis, J., 'The Western Riverina', *J.R.A.H.S.*, vol. 38, 1952.

Kenyon, A. S., 'The Story of the Mallee', *V.H.M.*, vol. 4, 1914.

———, 'The Overlanders', *V.H.M.*, vol. 10, 1925.

Lamb, W. H., 'Short History of the Willurah flock, 1860-1960', *Deniliquin Historical Society Newsletter*, no. 5., May-June 1960.

Lewis, J., 'Some notes on the Early Navigation of the River Murray', *Proceedings of the Royal Geographical Society of Australasia (South Australian Branch)*, vol. 18, 1917.

McKeown, G. M., 'The Wagga Experimental Farm', *Agricultural Gazette of New South Wales*, vol. 12, 1901.

McKinney, H. G., 'Irrigation in its relation to the Pastoral Industry of New South Wales', *Journal and Proceedings of the Royal Society of N.S.W.*, vol. 23, 1889.

Nadel, G., 'Letters from German Immigrants in New South Wales', *J.R.A.H.S.*, vol. 39, 1953.

Nairn, N. B., 'The 1890 Maritime Strike in New South Wales', *Historical Studies, Australia and New Zealand*, vol. 10, no. 37, November 1961.

Parker, R. S., 'Australian Federation: The Influence of Economic Interests and Political Pressures', in J. J. Eastwood and F. B. Smith (eds), *Historical Studies: Selected Articles. First Series.* Melbourne, 1964.

Price, A. Grenfell, 'South Australian efforts to control the Murray', *Report of the Australian and New Zealand Association for the Advancement of Science,* vol. 18, 1926.

Price, C. A., 'German Settlers in South Australia, 1838-1900', *Historical Studies, Australia and New Zealand,* vol. 7, no. 28, May 1957.

Rolleston, C., 'On the results of Wheat Culture in New South Wales for the last ten years', *Transactions of the Royal Society of N.S.W.,* vol. 2, 1868.

———, 'On Post Office Savings Banks, Friendly Societies and Government Life Assurance', *Transactions of the Royal Society of N.S.W.,* vol. 4, 1870.

———, 'Criminal Statistics of New South Wales, 1860-1873', *Transactions of the Royal Society of N.S.W.,* vol. 8, 1874.

Ross, C. S., 'Some of the Murray Pioneers and Their Services to the State', *V.H.M.,* vol. 3, 1913.

Steele, J., 'Early Days of Picton', *J.R.A.H.S.,* vol. 1, 1901-6.

Tietkens, W. A., 'Experiences in the Life of an Australian Explorer', *J.R.A.H.S.,* vol. 5, 1919.

Tunnock, B., 'Short History of the Shire of Numurkah', *V.H.M.,* vol. 23, 1950.

Wade, L. A. B., 'A Review of Water Conservation in New South Wales', *Journal and Proceedings of the Royal Society of N.S.W.,* vol. 37, 1903.

Watson, J. H., 'Benjamin Boyd, Merchant', *J.R.A.H.S.,* vol. 2, 1907.

Wood, A. P., 'On Tanks and Wells of New South Wales, Water Supply and Irrigation', *Journal and Proceedings of the Royal Society of N.S.W.,* vol. 17, 1883.

C.   UNPUBLISHED THESES

Craig, J., 'The Riverina Separation Movement, 1858-1867', B.A., University of Adelaide, 1963.

Langford-Smith, T., 'Landforms, Land Settlement and Irrigation in the Murrumbidgee, N.S.W.', Ph.D., Australian National University, Canberra, 1958.

Parnaby, J. E., 'The Economic and Political Development of Victoria, 1877-1881', Ph.D., Melbourne, 1951.

Rutherford, J., 'Integration of Irrigated and Dryland Farming in the Southern Murray Basin', Ph.D., Australian National University, Canberra, 1960.

Smith, R. H. T., 'Transport and Commodity Movement in Southern New South Wales', Ph.D., Australian National University, Canberra, 1961.

Waterson, D. B., 'Town and Country: The development of society on the Darling Downs, 1859-1893', Ph.D., Australian National University, Canberra, 1964.

IV   *Miscellaneous*

Basch & Co., *Atlas of the Settled Counties of New South Wales.* Sydney, 1868-70.

Baillière, *New South Wales Gazetteer* and maps, various dates.

Division of Reconstruction and Development, Premier's Department, N.S.W. (all with maps):

The Central Murray Region. Sydney, 1947.
The Lachlan Region. Sydney, 1949.
The Murrumbidgee Region. Sydney, 1947.
The Upper Murray Region. Sydney, 1947.

Department of National Development, Canberra, *Report on the Resources and Development of the Murray Valley,* vol. 1, Report; vol. 2, Maps. Canberra, 1947.

Goode, R., 'The Rock', duplicated typescript, a compilation from early school and town records. Wagga, 1962.

Grosse, E., 'Back to Walla Walla', duplicated typescript. Walla Walla, 1959.

'Murray River Shipping 1859-1909', Research Note no. 243, [n.d.], South Australian Archives, Adelaide.

'River Navigation' files, South Australian Archives, Adelaide.

Sands' Country Directory, various dates.

W.E., Riverine Directory, various dates.

'Wagga Wagga Public School', anonymous typescript, [n.d.], a compilation from early school records (in private possession).

'Walla Walla: Early History of Prosperous Farming Settlement', anonymous typescript, [n.d.], in Zion Lutheran Church papers, Walla Walla (in private possession).

INDEX

Aborigines, 91; as selectors, 165; attacks on settlers, 56, 95n.; in towns, 69n., 94; labour, 86n., 265; native police, 76n.; syphilis, 86

Adams, P.F., 134, 135, 149, 154–6, 162

Age, 169

Agricultural Gazette, 196

Agriculture: area cultivated, 136–8, 189–91; capitalization, 138–42, 144, 194–5; Department, 196; difficulties, 138–46; effect (of gold rushes) 60–3, (of South Australian farming) 62; experiments, 196; export figures qualified, 226n.; extent (1861) 136–7, (1891) 189–91; labour, 144, 147, 195, 199; market gardens, 137; markets, 145–6, 195–200 *passim;* mechanization, 141, 143–4, 194–6, 198–200 *passim;* squatters, 131–2, 141n., 143n.; steam power, 194–5; success dependent on environment, 132, 138, 196–7; techniques, 143–4; transport, 3n., 145–6, 171n., 172n., 197–200 *passim,* 268; wheat consumption, 191; yield, 132, 138, 189–98 *passim; see also* Farmers; Free selection before survey; Horses; Land sales; Orders-in-Council (1847); Railways; Reserves; Selectors; Vinegrowing

Albury: Agricultural Society, 62, 97, 143, 144; agriculture, 40, 60, 61–3, 131–47 *passim,* 189, 196, 197–202, 289; building activity, 66, 69, 75; Chinese, 63–4, 225, 247; Chinese bones, 228; churches, 89, 92–3, 207, 234–5; civic pride, 69–70; customs, 226; description (1850s) 60; early settlement, 15, 16, 18; economic functions, 72–6, 214–20; effect of gold rushes, 60–3; free selection, 127, 130, 135–6, 151, 163, 170–86 *passim,* 258; gaol, 77n., 78–9; growth (1851) 57–8, (1856) 60, (1861) 72, (1861–91)

214–16; intercolonial traffic, 60, 61–2, 98; land sales, 8, 61, 110, 111, 136, 138, 146, 170, 224; municipality, 70, 110; newspapers, 66, 70, 71, 130; organizations, 94; pastoral industry, 37–41 *passim,* 247, 256, 261; pleuro-pneumonia, 32–3; politically conservative, 269; population (1851) 56n., 58, (1856) 56n., (1861) 56n., 65, 72; railways, 226, 250; selection by minors, 170–1; Selectors' Association, 173; Show, 202; stock traffic, 24–5, 45, 46; surveys, 134, 136, 154, 156; transport, 75, 132n., 145–6; water supply, 227; *see also* Crime; Elections; Electoral boundaries; Germans; Hospitals; Schools; Squatters; Vinegrowing

Albury Banner and Wodonga Express, 24, 41, 83, 101, 122, 127, 135, 146, 198; Anglo-Saxon virtues, 198; civic pride, 70; founded, 71; value of education, 86–7; watch on politics, 121, 130

Alcohol, 58, 98, 232–4; Band of Hope, 233–4; crime and drinking habits, 80–2, 109, 230; sly-grog sellers, 107; sobriety of farmers, 230–1; *see also* Diseases; Hospitals; Justice

Angel family, 131, 203

Asher, Morris, 97–8, 119–27 *passim*

Backblocks, 43, 49–51, 252, 253, 257

Badham, S.D., 98, 119–20, 121n.

Balranald, 59, 76, 117, 211–18 *passim,* 235, 249; *see also* Elections

Barber, Charles, 15, 40, 102

Barbour, Robert, 173, 176, 274–8, 281n., 288

Bartley, Nehemiah, 71, 80, 107n., 109

Beechworth, 25, 32, 61, 63, 66, 68, 88, 145, 146

Bendigo, 21, 22, 25, 61, 68, 75

Beveridge family, 17, 96n.

Booligal, 49, 213, 257